In Pursuit of Sanity

A MEMOIR OF MY LIFE'S SPIRITUAL JOURNEY

LAVINIA LYNN REYNOLDS

Edited and Typed by Vera A. McKinney

Order this book online at www.trafford.com
or email orders@trafford.com

Most Trafford titles are also available at major online book retailers.

Print information available on the last page.

ISBN: 978-1-4907-5626-4 (sc)
ISBN: 978-1-4907-5628-8 (hc)
ISBN: 978-1-4907-5627-1 (e)

Library of Congress Control Number: 2015903227

Trafford rev. 02/25/2015

 www.trafford.com

North America & international
toll-free: 1 888 232 4444 (USA & Canada)
fax: 812 355 4082

A love story about a serious generational curse, child mental abuse, abortions, drugs and alcohol abuse, rape, physical abuse, crime and mental illness

From my heart . . . for my precious daughter, my four beloved sons, my confidants and friends, my special daughter-in-law, all my darling grandchildren, my dear sister and brothers, and my closest relatives . . . in honor of Mama and Daddy, with all my love.

Contents

Acknowledgments

First and foremost, I thank God the Father, Jesus, and the Holy Spirit for saving my life, for delivering me, and for providing me the wisdom, memory, and knowledge to write and distribute this book he predestined me to write.

I begin with a list of people who have made a tremendous impact on my present life and this book. God has made my life over with the aid of so many people that I could never acknowledge everyone. I do want you to know that I am grateful for all you have given me.

To my family, I love you, and thank you for your support, understanding, and your love. I thank God for you and pray that he blesses you to feel his love.

I will now attempt to thank my new family in Christ:

Bishop Samuel L. Duncan, Jr.—I know, without any doubt, that God ordered my steps and led me to your church. I realize today that I didn't come to LCOGIC just to see my children as I thought. It was all in God's plan that you be shepherd over my soul. Ever since the first message I heard you preach, I was drawn to your church. There is a divine connection between us. Thank you for everything. I've always valued your wisdom. I've heard every word you've ever spoken to me.

Elect Lady Dorothy Duncan—You have said things that left me seeking God for understanding and answers. You are that godly mother I never had in my mother. I will honor you both as long as I live.

Evangelist Joyce Jackson—You have been a prayer warrior that's been praying for me over a decade. I remember saying to you one morning on our way to Morning Prayer after God had delivered me, "Sister Jackson, you thought all the years you prayed for me were in vain. God is completing his work." You said, "Yes, he is, and what a work he has done!" I love you dearly.

Sister Nora Henderson—You always looked like my first mother-in-law. You've always been so loving and kind. I love being part of the Sunday school class you co-teach. Thank you for your godly love.

Mother Julia Shane—You have opened up the church every Saturday morning to allow me to spend time alone with my Father. Thank you for always opening up God's doors.

LCOGIC Choir—Wow! When I was a child I loved to dance. I stopped dancing because I didn't want to blow my high when I got older. When God changed me, he blessed me to be a worshipper through dancing. I've been to other churches; I don't feel the anointing from no other church choir like I do ours. You are the best!

Mothers of LCOGIC Sunday School Class—My dad taught me that if I wanted wisdom, spend a lot of time with the elderly—one of the best things he taught me. I love being among you all.

LCOGIC Family Prayer—To all those who come: thanks for praying with me and allowing me to vent as I healed. You just don't know how you've helped me maintain my sanity through prayer!

Patricia Castro—I remember once I was in church and you said, "I like your style, sister." Then you tried to get me to be friendly. I am so sorry. I was so messy then, but today I value your friendship and your help with our clothing ministry. I like your business knowledge.

Nora Smith—Thank you for believing in me and praying with me every Tuesday and Thursday morning. You are a blessing in my life.

Elder Ray Taylor—Thank you for all you taught me about how to study the Bible on my own. I love my Strong's Concordance. I will always be grateful for the teaching you gave me. In basic training, I needed the knowledge.

Charlotte Hopkins—My sista, my friend, thank you for giving me the confirmation to write this book. God said it first. And then you said it second: "You need to write a book. What kind of life did you live? I ain't never heard nothing like this in my life!"

Rosie Cannon—My friend who has been there for me through the good and the bad, somebody that I could talk to any time of the day or night—God bless you!

To that beloved sista in Christ—The one that whispered in my ear and said to me, "What was needed was for me to take a good look at LaVinia." I love you, and I thank you. You helped me keep my cool. Thank you from my heart.

Pamela Dunavant—You proved to be a friend when I needed one most. I'll never forget you. Thanks for sticking by me when I had no one. Thanks for believing in me.

Joe Wood—Even though I disliked you for calling the police when I had my first nervous breakdown, I learned that you were one of the guardian angels God placed in my life to protect me from myself. You stopped my house from burning down when I left a pot on the stove. You've been more than a neighbor. I thank both you and your wife. Good looking out!

Patsy King—You are one of God's chosen women. You keep on blessing me with your presence. I thank you for allowing me to reach out to people with the clothes you've donated.

The Women's Center of Lansing—I thank you all for the kindness you showed me and also the growth you allowed me to make. The center became my home away from home at the time I needed it to be.

Action of Greater Lansing—Thank you for allowing me to be a part of Action. I feel empowered!

Gamaliel Fire of Faith—Thank you for helping me give birth to the leader in me. Your training was awesome!

Dr. John Parrish—You gave me so much when I came to The Cove for the spiritual retreat. Your mild mannerism was calming to my spirit. I pray I can come every year. Thank you for your prayers and support as I wrote this book. You've been a blessing in my life.

My Therapist—It's been a ride, but you have helped me in ways no other therapist ever did. When you told me you didn't believe in medication and that you believed if a person talked about their issues with truth and courage, they could be healed. You were right! God was the director. I thank you for your help.

Vera A. McKinney—Thank you for all your help.

Introduction

I am so grateful that you have chosen to read my memoir—my story of child abuse, drug addiction, abortions, rapes, domestic abuse, and mental illness. My prayer is that you will feel my pain and understand the generational curses, which I learned, through research, began back during slavery in my family. At a very young age, these curses manifested in me in more ways than one and has affected me and my family. I hope that you can relate to my story as it touches your life and that you will use my life's story to help you change whatever is in your life that is destroying you.

All of us have either done something wrong or had something wrong done to us. The Holy Spirit (if called upon) is an ever-ready help in time of need. Before you make a decision that you are alone in this cruel world, hear me out. This is my story. I keep it real, raw, and true. I expose myself in hopes that my memoir will help you deal with and be willing to be honest about your past so that you can be set free. I am here to let you know that you are not alone and that if God can change me, he can change anyone. Jesus is real!

Furthermore, I am so honored that God chose me as one he speaks to as I walk down the street at five thirty in the morning, something I do often because nobody is outside, except me and God. One time I asked the Lord, "Father, why did you save me? Everybody I hustled with is dead. Mama and Daddy are dead. Why am I alive?" God started speaking back to me. He told me that he had a purpose for my life. He told me that I was his trophy. I was his living witness that he is the same God today as he was over two thousand years ago.

People don't believe that miracles happen today. People don't even believe in Christ today. God told me that I am to write about the many testimonies in my life. I am to share with the world that he is real. This generation has been run off from God's house due to untruths taught. God is love, and he loves us no matter what we have done. He loves us so much that he gave his only Son. God wants us to come to him and give our lives to him. He wants us to realize that there is a place called hell, and if we don't repent, that's where we are headed.

This memoir is not written to entertain anyone. It is written to teach the Christians what God's purpose is, not just for my life but for all Christians' lives. We are to be servants of God. We are to serve, not be served. God wants people to know that he loves them and that the church is a hospital for the lost soul. It is a place where we turn our life over to God. It is his house. It is not any one person's house.

The many strongholds that Satan controls us with can only be lifted through prayer and being a part of God's house. Prayer is the answer, yet when we are knee-deep in sin, we turn further away from God, but that is the time that we need to get closer to him.

I wrote from my heart about issues that most people will never share with anyone, let alone the world. God has placed in me to do this because he wants people to know that they are not alone. I was that family member that God allowed to go through more than the average person, and there are so many more like me. This memoir is for them, yet it is also for those of us that have been in the church most of our lives and have formed a judgmental opinion of those that are lost in deep sin.

I was always looking for love in all the wrong places—men, sex, drug addiction, and clothes. I became a person that even I didn't recognize. I became an addict hopelessly lost to whatever sin made me feel temporarily better for the moment. I became very lonely, desperate, immoral, and hell-bent on self-destruction. I hated myself. I wanted to die at some point in my life, but God had another plan for me. He picked me up and brushed me off. He turned my midnight into daylight. He did for me that which only he could.

I tried so many times to change, only to make it last two or three years, and then I was right back at that which I was familiar with. But when God washed me clean through the blood of his Son, Jesus Christ, I knew I'd never turn back. When God said to me, "It's over," I cried, I praised him, and I worshiped him because I heard him. I heard him loud and clear. God, through his Son, Jesus, and the Holy Spirit, is really doing the same miracles he did over two thousand years ago. You will realize that as you read my memoir.

Chapter One

NOW I LAY ME DOWN TO SLEEP

It was Sunday morning. I woke up excited! I knew I would be wearing a pretty new dress and fancy shoes on that day, something that I did every Sunday throughout my childhood. I put on a beautiful red velvet dress with a laced bottom petite skirt and cancan slip underneath. My shoes were shiny patent leather. Mama washed, pressed, and curled my hair the day before—that was expected every other Saturday throughout my childhood.

I am Lavinia, pronounced "la-veen-ya." My sister and brothers couldn't pronounce my name when we were younger so they affectionately called me Beanie. I was told that it started off as Veanie by Mama and my aunt; but my sister, brothers, and cousins changed it to Beanie. Mama called me Bean for short.

I loved wearing new clothes, especially whenever we went to church. It made me feel very special. We went to church every Sunday when I was a small child. Mama told me that Daddy was a deacon in the church when I was four or five years old. As a family, we often studied the Bible at home. During the summer months, we attended vacation Bible school. That's where I first learned the song, "Jesus Loves Me." I didn't realize it at the time, but the words to that song would be my help throughout my life.

My youngest brother, Johnny, was quite funny during that time of my life. He would imitate the preacher when we returned home from a long boring day at church. If you've ever attended a black church in the 1960s, you can imagine the style of the preaching and how he mimicked the preacher. "Come . . . come to Jesus," he would say. We would laugh because he sounded just like the preacher at the time. Our granny called him Johnny Preacher.

Mama's birth name was Patty. She was the eldest of six children. Granny was Mama's grandmother on her mother's side. When Mama lost her mother unto death, she and three of her siblings were sent to live in Detroit to be raised by her grandmother on her father's side. The other two siblings were raised in Pontiac by Granny.

Mama felt that because she was the oldest, she was responsible for keeping them together as a family. She once told me that, for years, she hated her father. She felt it was his fault that her mother died. It's my understanding that she was diagnosed with tuberculosis after giving birth to six children before she reached the age of thirty.

I was also told that my granddaddy Frankie, as we called him, was a "rolling stone," living from house to house. I wonder what type of woman my grandma was. I do know that two of Mama's sisters were not Granddaddy Frankie's biological children, the two that Granny raised.

My daddy's name was Charles. Mama called him Charlie. My mama met him on one of her visits to Pontiac. Daddy was engaged to another woman while he was serving in the navy, but when his service ended and he returned home, he learned that his best friend had married her. Daddy was quite upset. It's my understanding that that's when my daddy started drinking. Daddy shared with me years later that when he was a baby, his mother, who was an alcoholic, left him on his aunt's porch and never returned. Auntie raised Daddy. He had two elder brothers that she also raised.

Mama told me that when she became pregnant by Daddy, my great-grandma made her give up her baby, whom they had named John, for adoption. Daddy didn't like that idea, and he told Mama,

"No son of mine will go through what I did!" Then he asked Mama to marry him. After they married, they were able to get their baby from the foster home he was in while waiting to be adopted. Mama told me that Daddy changed the baby's name to Charles, Jr. Family members told me that, right after they married, the fighting between the two of them began.

Mama and Daddy had issues when they met. However, they tried to do what every other American family did at that time: live the average American dream. Daddy went to work, and Mama stayed home to care for their baby. A year and a half later, another child was born. Her name was Vanessa, my sister. Eleven months later, another girl was born, which was yours truly. A year and a half later, my youngest brother, Johnny, was born into this world.

Mama shared with me some pictures and memories of those years. I don't remember a lot from that era, but I do remember a picture she showed me of myself when I was a baby. I had very big eyes and was bow-legged. The only hair I had was growing in the center of my head. Mama said she often placed a little rubber band around my inch of hair and a barrette. Whenever she told me that story, I thought about the little girl, who wore her hair the same way, on that cartoon show on television about a family who lived in the Stone Age. Mama shared that we lived on Jaden Street in a row of homes that she referred to as the projects. I remember them being made of brick with large concrete steps. I was sitting on the steps in the picture.

Daddy started working for the city as a garbageman. Family members told me that Daddy used to drink and fight with Mama during this time. I was also told that my eldest brother got a whooping every day because he wet the bed every night. They said that he had other issues as well. From the pictures I had seen, we looked like the average family. The pictures of Daddy showed how handsome he was. One picture that I remembered throughout the years was when he was in the navy. He had the most beautiful smile on his face, and his teeth were gorgeous! I remember Mama being very pretty. She was very shapely, with a small waste line. She had a figure that most women would kill to have!

The first memory I have from childhood was when I was almost five years old. We had moved from Jaden Street to Rail Street. Daddy had bought his first house. I have a lot of memories from that time, and what I didn't have knowledge of, Mama shared her version.

When we were little children, we were left home alone a lot. By this time, Mama also had to get a job because the mortgage was high and more money was needed. Mama worked cleaning houses for rich white people in Bloomfield and Birmingham. They would give her lots of appliances and furniture for our home and all kinds of toys and bikes for us. They liked her a lot.

School had begun that year for me. I was excited to go to kindergarten. All kindergarteners had to bring a rug to lie on during nap time. During nap time, all the kids would fall asleep, but I couldn't. I found myself asking God, "Help my mama make it through her day at work."

Daddy worked during the weekday and was home with us on Saturdays. At least, he was supposed to be home with us. But he would leave home soon after Mama left for work and go to the bar and be with other women—women of the streets—I later learned.

Mama was a good mother during this time of our lives. Whenever she wasn't working, she spent all her time with us. Mama loved being a homemaker. I remember as a small child having days that I worried about Mama and Daddy. Mama didn't drink or smoke at that time, but I do remember her going to Mr. Hill's house whenever Daddy wasn't home. She told me that Mr. Hill was an old man that loved helping us.

Daddy would come home on Saturdays so drunk that he would fall down and break things that Mama had placed in our home to make it a "good-looking home." We started off very young taking care of Daddy whenever he was drunk. Our house had a bedroom downstairs. We would remove his regular clothes and put him in his pajamas, after cleaning the blood from the cuts he would get from broken glass, either at home or at the bar, and put him to bed. We learned at a very young age the roles we would play our entire childhood.

Mama made sure that as small children we stayed well groomed and went to school very clean and neat. She kept mine and my sister's hair pressed and curled. Mama didn't believe in having her girls looking any other way than like pretty little dolls; and as small girls, she kept us looking beautiful. The "boys," as we called them, weren't fussed over as much as the girls were, but Mama still kept them clean and neat.

Mama was obsessed with appearance and trying to impress people. She always told me, "A first impression is a lasting impression." Daddy was a neat and clean man as well. He was a cook when he served in the navy. He believed in earning a living through hard work and honesty. Daddy always instilled in us the importance of keeping our word: "Your word is your bond. After all that's said and done, your word is all you have," he would say.

Once Daddy was in bed and asleep, my sister and I would start cleaning up the glass and blood so that when Mama returned from work, her house would be the same as she left it—clean. She would be so tired when she got home. We didn't want her to see how her house really looked. We knew she still had to cook dinner. Besides, she already knew that Daddy had not been home with us because she called several times during the day. Whenever she called, she always asked me what was happening and I always told her the truth. Daddy always managed to make it back home before Mama returned from work. She would come home, take a bath, and then make dinner.

Weekdays during this time of our lives were normal, at least what we thought was normal. However, every Friday evening and Saturday, the drama and chaos would take place, especially payday Fridays. Then Sunday morning, we got up, put on our best clothes, and went to church as a family. Mama always cooked dinner when she came home from work. Sometimes we would eat without Daddy. Once he sobered up from his nap, the arguing would begin. It never failed. Mama always felt she had to "check" him for leaving us alone and getting drunk. That's when all hell would break loose. The actual fighting didn't take place until we were in bed. I guess they thought we were asleep, but we heard it all.

I cried a lot when I was a child. I experienced emotions that no child should ever experience. The fear was overwhelming. But there were some moments on Rail Street that were normal, like in any other child's life, like the times I would help them tend to our garden. I enjoyed the time I spent with Mama whenever she washed, pressed, and curled my hair. She always fixed my sister's hair first because it was thick and always said she'd do the hardest job first.

Anyway, one day we were in the kitchen and Mama was pressing my hair. We heard a loud boom outside. It was summertime. The front door was open. Mama quickly laid the pressing comb down. I jumped up from the chair I was sitting on and ran to the door. I saw a car that had struck a huge tree head on directly across the street from our house. Mama had made it to the front door of the house by this time, and together, we noticed that a small child's head was hanging out of the window on the driver's side of the car. It was a little girl.

Neighbors came from their homes to see what was happening. My sister and brothers were playing in the backyard and also came running around to the front to see the accident. We watched a man who was bleeding from his head jump out of the car on the passenger side and take off running up the street. My brother, Charles, Jr., ran after him. "Charles, Jr.," my mother hollered, "you come back here!" Charles, Jr. kept running. Other neighbors also chased after the man.

Mama turned and went for the telephone. My sister Vanessa, my youngest brother Johnny, and I curiously looked at one another, thinking, *Where is Charles, Jr. running?* We were small kids, but we knew that his actions could be dangerous. Even the neighbors who were running after this man knew not to get too close. Charles, Jr. was right on him. The man was drunk and couldn't get away from him. The grown-ups on the street were awestruck at how Charles, Jr. stayed up on that man until the police caught him. Then Charles, Jr. turned around and ran all the way back home.

In the meantime, the ambulance had arrived in front of our house. We were all gathered around watching. The little girl was lifeless. After they pried the car door open, I saw them remove her little body from the car. I realized she was dead. That was the first time I ever saw such. I remember to this day the compassion I felt for her. I also remember solemnly saying, "God, please take her to heaven." In church, I learned that heaven is where you go when you die. I also asked Mama if the little girl would go to heaven. Mama said, "All kids go to heaven if they die." It was comforting to know that she would be going to heaven. Anyway, we went back inside the house. Mama finished pressing my hair. The next day we went to church.

Summer had come and we were out of school. Mama didn't want us alone all summer long, so Daddy said his nephew, Teddy, would babysit us. I later learned that Teddy was on drugs, which explains why he allowed us to get into so much trouble that summer. Teddy let us do whatever we wanted. Charles, Jr. would go outside to play, while we would stay and play inside.

One day Charles, Jr. came inside and talked Johnny into going outside with him. He told Johnny that he had snatched our neighbor's clothes from her clothes line and buried them in the yard next door to our house. He wanted Johnny to go with him that day and help him steal more clothes and bury them. Later that night, when they were discussing it, they asked me and Vanessa if we wanted to steal her clothes from the line the next day. Vanessa didn't want to, but I agreed to do it. The next morning, when we went outside to play, Vanessa stayed in the house with Teddy. My brother and I went outdoors into our neighbor's yard and yanked her clothes from the line and ran to the yard next door to our house.

We were digging a hole when the lady walked up to us and angrily said, "Gimme my clothes and dig up my other clothes! Is your mother home?"

I said, "No."

"Who's home with you?" she asked.

"Our cousin, Teddy," we said.

She stormed over to our house and knocked on the door. We quickly ran inside our house through the back door and told Teddy that the lady was at our front door. As he was opening the front door, he said to us, "What did y'all do?" She told Teddy what happened and that she wanted every piece of her clothing returned.

After she finished speaking with Teddy, he had the nerve to flirt with her: "You sho' is a pretty lady. Do you have a husband?" That's how Teddy was. He didn't care what we did. He just made sure when Mama and Daddy returned home, we were in the house, had done our chores, and everything looked like he had done his job. Teddy wasn't a babysitter; he just wanted to get paid! We thought he was cool!

On the other hand, he told Mama what we had done because the lady said that she would be back. We went outside and dug up her clothes from the ground. Once we were finished, Charles, Jr. took them back to her. When Mama came home and heard about it, the three of us got a whooping. My sister never got into trouble, and this would be the last time that I got a whooping as a child. It wasn't the last time I got into trouble, but it was the last time I was disciplined in that manner. My eldest brother continued to get whoopings for a while. My youngest brother didn't get whipped very much after that because Mama always said he wouldn't be in trouble if he wasn't following Charles, Jr. around and doing what he said and did. Charles, Jr. was our big brother, and we did whatever he said and did.

Other kids were always jealous of us. Charles, Jr. got into a fight when he was a little kid. He was attending school when another boy pushed him down the stairs. Charles, Jr. hit his head, so Mama had to leave work and take him to the hospital. I remember this so well because Mama always said that when Charles, Jr. fell and hit his head, the doctors said that if any damage was done, they were unable to tell at that point, but time would tell.

After school one day, I was walking home with my sister. We didn't go our usual route. We were walking along and talking when a dog started chasing after us. We cried and ran home as fast as we could! When we made it home, Mama was there and made us feel safe. She told us to never come home that way again and to go the way she told us to use every day. I was okay with that because that dog put the fear of dogs I've had all my life in me. Since then, I've never really liked dogs.

Mama's youngest sister, Aunt Penny, had moved into an apartment building down the street from us. She was a young mother that Mama felt she had to watch over. Aunt Penny was beautiful to me. Whenever I was around her, I was fascinated. When I was a little girl, I watched her behavior. I liked the fact that she kept good-looking men around her. Aunt Penny had a daughter named Angie, and her father was the finest-looking man I had ever seen! I thought Aunt Penny had it "going on!"

Mama, however, would share very upsetting things with me about Aunt Penny. Mama would get phone calls in the middle of the night and get out of her bed and go to Aunt Penny's apartment. She would always come back with my cousin, Angie. We loved Angie being with us. My sister and I felt we had to take care of her. Actually, everybody in the house felt they had to take care of Angie; even Daddy treated her like she was one of us. Mama would be so mad at her sister for leaving Angie, but she always tolerated her.

Mama didn't realize it but she had back then what we call codependency issues today. Angie liked being with me. She was only a year younger than me, but during that time, it just seemed like Johnny and Angie were so much younger than me, maybe because I had already taken on the role of a caretaker, yet I was only a child myself.

I remember playing outside one day. Mama's granddad in Detroit had left her his car when he died. Mama couldn't drive it right away so it was parked in our backyard. It was an antique, at least twenty years old. We were told not to play around the car, but when Mama wasn't home, my brother, Charles, Jr., never listened to what he was told. And whenever he did something, Johnny and I followed. The car was one of those big old cars, maybe a 1940s model or something.

Anyway, we were playing in and around it. I don't know how I did it, but I closed the front door, and my right thumb was shut in the door. All I could do was holler and cry! My brother, Charles, Jr., came to my rescue and opened up the door and freed my thumb. I still remember what that pain felt like. I think it hurt more once it was freed than when it was stuck! My thumb was swollen, bent, and I couldn't straighten it.

Mama came home and took me to the hospital. I don't remember much about my thumb after that because, as other little children would have, I didn't get much time to feel special. For not long after that happened, another tragedy would take place. Throughout the years, that scar always reminded me of the pain I felt on that day. I had no idea that worse was yet to come.

I remember the tension in our home. Mama and Daddy argued daily. Daddy was losing our home. I would be lying in bed and hear them. I always prayed, "God, please don't let them start fighting, please." Some nights they wouldn't, other nights they would. I would hear Mama say things like, "If you hadn't been hoe hopping and throwing your money away, we wouldn't have gotten behind in our house payments." In return, Daddy would snap back and say, "Why do you keep running to old man Hill's house?" Words like this carried on for weeks.

Then one day Mama told us we were moving. She was devastated. Mama was so proud of her home. Now she was being knocked down off this I'm-doing-so-well-in-life peg. Daddy never said much to us about family issues. He believed that it was grown folks' business. He felt making sure we weren't homeless was one of his primary responsibilities. Mama, however, shared everything with us, especially when Daddy wasn't home. I remember feeling very hurt and sad for Mama.

> Now I lay me down to sleep.
> I pray the Lord my soul to keep.
> If I should die before I wake,
> I pray the Lord my soul to take.

Dear God,

Please help our family. Stop Daddy and Mama from fighting. Help Mama to get through her week at work, Daddy too. Watch over my sister and my brothers, my cousins too. God, please keep us safe tonight. I love you, God. Amen.

Out of the mouth of babes and sucklings hast thou ordained strength because of thine enemies, that thou mightest still the enemy and the avenger.

—Psalm 8:2 (KJV)

Chapter Two

....

NEWBERRY STREET

....

The first memory I have of Newberry Street is Mama being sad. I was entering into the second grade when we moved. The house we moved into was very dirty. Actually, it was filthy! Mama told me that Daddy said the basement was once used for prostitution and the house was an after-hours joint. Moving here was the beginning of Mama treating me like I was her girlfriend, her partner. She talked with me about everything. Mama and I had secrets that no adult girlfriends should have, not to speak of a child and a grown woman!

Mama and Daddy continued working. All of us were enrolled in school by this time, so the only time Teddy babysat was on the weekends, occasionally. Most of the time, when we weren't in school, my eldest brother, Charles, Jr. babysat us. Mama applied for a job as a nurse's aide at the hospital. Thankfully, she was hired for the position. Every morning, she left home by six thirty because we only had one car, and Daddy had to take her to work before himself. My siblings and I got out of bed between 7:00 a.m. and 7:30 a.m. daily to get ready for school.

Roaches were everywhere when we first moved into this house. The house had a concrete block wall in front. It also had a closed-in front porch. Then after passing the second door, you entered the living room. Off from the living room to your left was our parents' bedroom. Straight ahead past the living room was the dining room.

Off to your left of the dining room was a door that led to the basement. It was closed at all times.

The walls and floors were full of holes. I could see down into the basement through a hole that was in the floor of my bedroom. Mama placed the head of the bed over the hole, but once I got into bed, if I looked down between the headboard and mattress, I could see the concrete basement floor. The basement was even worse than the house! It was an old house that had two back doors: one was the entrance to the kitchen and the other entrance led to the basement. There were a lot of old clothes and furniture in the basement.

When our parents were away from home, we would play a game, scary house, down in the basement called. One day, when Mama and Daddy were at work, Charles, Jr. ventured off into the basement. It was very intriguing to him. He went down there every chance he got. Then he started taking Johnny with him. They would use their imagination and come up with different games to play. After we did our chores, my sister and I played with our paper dolls, something we did almost every weekend and every day during the summer. The boys' games were a lot more fun than playing with paper dolls.

One Saturday Charles, Jr. told Johnny to ask us if we wanted to play scary house. We used the basement as our spooky house. Charles, Jr. made cars out of cardboard boxes for us to ride in. He would push us around in the boxes, and Johnny would jump out and scare us. To be honest, Johnny wasn't really needed because that basement was scary enough! It was divided into two sections like the upstairs. You could tell that, at one time, somebody lived down there. The furniture looked like saloon furniture from the 1920s and 1930s. The clothes that were left behind looked like the dresses prostitutes wore back then. Even the men's suits were like those of old. A couple of times, Charles, Jr. opened the basement door and we ventured up the stairs and outside. We didn't stay outside long because we weren't supposed to be down in the basement, not to mention outside.

Whenever Mama wasn't working, she would clean and paint the house. I remember Daddy bringing home some bright yellow paint that he got from his job to paint the kitchen. By this time, he had been promoted from garbageman to working in the paint and sign shop. The yellow paint used to line the streets was the same color as our kitchen. Mama was on a mission to make her home as livable as she could. More chaos started at this point.

Daddy was working weekdays and, as Mama put it, "hoe hopping" on the weekends. He got clipped every other payday. Mama said, "His hoes took his money"; that meant my parents were always short on bill and food money. Mama was working daily, but she wanted more than their money could buy. She wanted to "impress the Joneses," as people often phrased. I can honestly say that I believe that's why the stealing started.

One time Mama, Vanessa, and I were in the grocery store. Vanessa and I were so excited. We ran off to the toy section. Mama continued looking for the food she needed. That day we saw a toy necklace and bracelet set. It was so beautiful! We ran back to Mama. With excitement in our voices, we asked, "Mama, can we have this? Please, please!" Mama took the packages with the toy jewelry inside them and proceeded to open them. She took out the necklaces first and put them around each of our necks. Then she removed the bracelets and placed them around both of our wrists. Then she said, "There. It's yours." Vanessa took off hers and said, "No, I am not doing that!" But me—I wasn't about to take off mine—I was happy! I kept staring at my bracelet and thought, *Wow, this is so pretty!*

Mama made her way to the checkout lane as Vanessa and I followed. Mama placed the food on to the checkout counter. After paying for the food, we walked out of the door. I stared at my bracelet all the way out of the door. Vanessa didn't say anything to Mama, but when we got home, we went into our bedroom, and she said to me, "Beanie, you and Mama go' get in trouble." I paid her no attention. I just kept smiling and looking at my new pretty bracelet.

Later, when we went to church, I learned about the Ten Commandments from the Bible, particularly the one that says we should not steal. That was when I started to feel bad because our stealing habits had increased. I loved feeling special. I was the only one who went with Mama when she had stealing on her mind. She was on a mission and needed me to help her complete it, and I was very happy to do it. In those days, the stores were easy to hit. Mama taught me everything: how to hide clothes, put two to three dresses or whatever we were trying on onto one hanger. So if they were taking count of three outfits, it would really be six to nine. I also learned if they were taking count, nine times out of ten, no floor walkers were watching. If floor walkers were working, they didn't count your outfits before you went into the dressing room.

I learned how to steal clothes and then take them back to exchange for the things we couldn't steal: dishes, paint, bedspreads, sheets, contact paper for the walls, vases, ashtrays—whatever Mama needed to complete the house, even roach and rat killer. I won't say that all I did was steal with Mama because I also did things that little girls did to have fun. My cousin, Cathy, lived a few streets away from us when we lived on Newberry Street. Vanessa and I would spend some weekend nights at her house and have lots of fun.

Aunt Mabel was the third sibling out of Mama's five sisters and brothers. Mama and Aunt Mabel were very close; all of them were. Aunt Mabel was married, and her husband was not like Daddy. Uncle Ben was for no nonsense. Whenever he was around, the atmosphere changed. I always felt safe at my cousin's house. Even though Mama told me that Aunt Mabel was cheating on Uncle Ben, and at times they argued, it was nothing like at home.

I always worried about what was going on at home whenever we spent the night at Cathy's house, but we still played and played and played—you know, girls love to play! We never discussed what was going on in our home; we just played. We usually spent the night with Cathy on Fridays. That way, we could be home on Saturday to get ready for church on Sunday. Daddy and Mama often fought the night before; but come Sunday morning, we all went to church like one big happy family.

As we started to adjust to our new life on Newberry Street, I went to school daily with a lot of hidden fear and emotional disconnection. I couldn't learn anything because my mind was always focused on what was going on at home. I've always been friendly, so I had several friends, some that truly liked me and some that were going through as much dysfunction at home as I was. One friend from school that I will never forget was Dolly. She was jealous of me because of the clothes I wore, but on the other hand, she liked me because she was able to tell me about the fighting her parents were doing. I never judged her. I also talked to her about some things that were happening in our home but never to the extent that she talked to me.

Dolly had similar issues that I saw in my eldest brother, Charles, Jr. One time she came up with this plan to destroy our teacher's grade book during our lunch break. She would get so mad with the teacher if she got an E grade on her papers. She wasn't the only student that received that grade. There were approximately five of us that didn't do well in class, a few because they were slow at learning and a few because they just didn't care, like Dolly, and a few of us because we just couldn't concentrate on what the teacher was saying. Our mind was at home.

Dolly said to me, "Let's tear up Mrs. Wilson's grade book. She can't give us a bad report card if she has no book." Knowing that it was wrong, I still agreed to tear it up. When the classes were released to go to lunch, Dolly and I went to the restroom instead of the cafeteria. The plan was to stay in the restroom until Mrs. Wilson came out of the class to go eat her lunch. But she was taking too long, so Dolly and I became restless. Dolly said, "Let's stuff the toilets with paper towels and flush 'em." I agreed again, though I really didn't want to do it. We stuffed so much paper towels into the toilets that when we flushed them, the toilets overflowed. We took off running to the cafeteria!

When lunch period ended and we returned to class, we saw water all over the floor in the hall coming out of the restroom. We also saw the janitor cleaning up the mess. Dolly started laughing. I felt very bad when I saw him cleaning up our mess. As we made our way back to Mrs. Wilson's class, Dolly said, "We'll get the grade book tomorrow."

I never said a word, but when lunch time came the next day, we went to the cafeteria only to sneak out after we saw Mrs. Wilson come inside. We knew better than to go back to the restroom, so we went directly to her classroom and grabbed the grade book and destroyed it! Then we left the room. When lunch was over, everyone in the cafeteria returned to class. As we entered Mrs. Wilson's class, she had just learned that someone had ruined her grade book. She instructed everyone to be seated. Then she left the room to get the principal. After a few moments, they both returned. The principal firmly said, "Whoever did this will be expelled from school as soon as I find out who would do something like this!" Dolly and I acted like we knew nothing. Once the principal assisted Mrs. Wilson with replacing her grade book, he left the room. She proceeded with the next assignment for the class.

A week had gone by, and nothing else was said by the principal or Mrs. Wilson. The Es continued with Dolly and I. Once again, Dolly came up with the bright idea to destroy the grade book. This time, the principal and Mrs. Wilson were waiting for us. Dolly picked up the book. I stood there. Then I heard a door open. I looked back, and it was the principal and Mrs. Wilson. They were hiding in the closet. "Both of you, to the office," said the principal. Mrs. Wilson didn't say a word.

While waiting in the office, both of our parents were called, but they were working, so Dolly and I were on our own. Dolly was suspended for the rest of the semester. The principal felt that Dolly was the mastermind of our actions. As for me, I was suspended for a week. Daddy was very disappointed in me. I cared very much about what Daddy thought of me. Mama didn't respond like Daddy. She told me that I couldn't go outside for that week, but I believe that the only reason she did that was to satisfy Daddy. During that week of punishment, I stayed at Granny's house. I remember being so bored. Once I went back to school, I missed Dolly. Her grandmother lived in back of our house, so I would see Dolly at the fence whenever she was there.

As for home, things were never normal—whatever that was. I judged what normal was by the family next door, the Kings.

They seemed to be a happy family. Mr. and Mrs. King went to work daily. Their kids never seemed to get into trouble like us. They didn't live a life of chaos like our family. Mr. and Mrs. King had a friendly relationship with Mama and Daddy, but they lived differently than the way we lived. Even though as kids we were taught not to tell nobody what goes on in our house, some things didn't have to be told, it showed, like the fights they had that could be heard around the block. The police was at our house every other weekend.

By this time, going to church on a regular basis was falling off. Mama and I were hitting the stores at least four out of seven days a week. Mama was good at building up my courage. She would say, "Bean, let's go to the store after dinner." She never mentioned what we would be doing at the store, but I knew. Vanessa never wanted to go because she knew what Mama and I were doing. Mama didn't want her going anyway; she would have just been in the way! We stole so much that after a year or so, our home was starting to look spectacular!

Mama was beginning to act a little happier. She always stopped at a certain house on our way back home from stealing. I knew that there was a man that she was stopping to see. I stayed in the car while she went inside. "I'll be right back, Bean," she'd tell me. She would be gone so long that I would start talking to God. I was scared, not just because I had been in the car so long but because I knew that what Mama was doing was wrong, and I feared Daddy popping up or finding out. I never feared him finding out about us stealing, only about the men Mama would stop and see.

Then a pattern emerged. Mama and Daddy would only fight when one of them had been cheating on the other. And from what I saw, it was mostly when Mama had cheated. I'm not saying that Daddy didn't cheat on Mama. I'm only saying that whenever Mama went out on Daddy, the fistfights would take place. Whenever Daddy cheated, Mama would hunt him down. She would make all of us put on our clothes at eleven o'clock at night, and we would be on a mission to find Daddy. Mama would tell us everything Daddy was doing while we rode along with her:

"Your daddy is hoe hopping again. He'll be broke by the time he gets home. Your daddy is the reason we have no food. Your daddy didn't pay rent again. Your daddy keep lettin' them hoes clip him."

She told us so much about Daddy's wrongs that as children we felt everything that was wrong with our family was Daddy's fault. We loved our dad, and we were convinced that every fight, every wrong thing, was only because of him. If he didn't drink and get drunk, we would be okay; that was what I felt. Not one time did I give thought to the fact that not only was Mama stopping at other men's houses but she also had me out stealing. My siblings had no idea what Mama was doing. Mama would share with me when she was going out on Daddy, "Bean, I need something to wear this weekend. We're going to go the store Thursday evening after dinner, okay? I'll take care of your Dad." And that she did.

Daddy never said a word when I was with Mama. She always collected bags, and whatever we stole, we would put into those bags to take inside the house. Sometimes I had to sneak the bags into my room so Daddy wouldn't see them. Vanessa never asked why she didn't get anything because she knew Mama and I were stealing and she felt it was wrong. Sometimes we stole an outfit or two for her. Mama shopped for the boys whenever they needed something. Sometimes the money would come from the refunds we received when we returned the stolen clothes to the store. Mama had a system going that was not only keeping us dressed nicely but that filthy house we moved into was also totally redecorated. Charles, Jr. did the painting and all the home improvements Mama wanted done.

Whenever Daddy wasn't drunk, he taught Charles, Jr. a lot. Daddy was a man of moral character when it came to working. Auntie raised my daddy to value hard work, to be a man of his word, and to be honest. "You keep your word when you tell somebody you will do something. Your word is all you have," he would say. I loved being around my daddy whenever he was sober. He taught me a lot also. He taught me what it meant to be dependable, to take pride in anything I did. He had no idea, in the beginning, that Mama was teaching me just the opposite. I learned self-discipline from my daddy.

Not only did Daddy teach me what he had learned in the navy, but he also made me earn any money he gave to me. He tried to teach me what it meant to save money. My Mama would say, "I ain't thinking 'bout your daddy. You might be dead tomorrow, so you better spend that money today." So I did. Daddy would ask why I spent the money. He would get upset with Mama because she told me to spend it.

By this time, going to church on a regular basis was a thing of the past. Some weekends we went to Detroit to visit Mama's family. Mama was obsessed with making her family think that our lives were the best. She would give the four of us children instructions on how to behave when we arrived at our grandma's house. She spent the entire drive from Flint drilling us, which was nothing compared to how she drilled Daddy. "Charlie, don't you start drinking before we get to Charles's house." That was her elder brother. He had the same name as my daddy.

No playing and no talking until she called us to speak to our grandma. We were required to sit on the couch like mannequins, but we would get restless and start playing with one another, and our uncle James, or JayJay, would let us. He was Mama's youngest brother and lived with Grandma. She treated him like he was her baby. I guess he was. You could see that he was very special to her.

JayJay had it made. Grandma or Mama didn't say a word if JayJay was playing with us. We loved going to see our uncle James. He was cool. Somehow Daddy and JayJay always made their way across the street to the store, even though Mama had already told Daddy not to start drinking. Uncle James never let Mama stop him, though, and he always invited Daddy to join him.

Once they got started, Mama would hurry up and find a reason to leave Grandma's. She would say, "I'm going to visit Uncle Charles. I'll be right back." She never made it back on that visit because once you got to Uncle Charles's house, it was party time. Her sisters, Aunt Penny and Aunt Mabel, would be there with their family from home, and Aunt Felicia would also come over. Uncle

James would be with us. I'm sure, after so many times of being told that lie, Grandma knew we wouldn't be back until the next visit.

I enjoyed going to Detroit because I got to wear pretty new clothes! Coming back home was never fun, though, because Daddy would always be drunk. I would be so scared! I would get on the floor of the backseat of the car and cover my head. Daddy would be driving all over the road. Mama would pinch him on his face every time he swayed out of his lane. Sometimes she pinched him so hard that he would bleed. "God, please get us home," I would desperately say to myself. My siblings would also be lying on the floor. Every now and then, we would rise to see how close we were to being home. Mama always fussed because Daddy was drunk. But I always wondered why she just didn't drive? She knew Daddy was drunk. By the grace of God, we always made it home safely. My daddy wrecked a lot of cars in his lifetime. He was involved in so many accidents that I now understand why the support groups against drunk driving were formed. Our cars always had a dent some place on them because of his drunk driving.

If it was Sunday when we returned home from visiting, there would be no fighting that night because Daddy and Mama had to work the next morning and we had to go to school. Everyone prepared themselves for our week to come. Nothing more was said about the commotion of the week. We just kept it moving.

Nothing changed at school. I never felt like most girls felt at school, happy or excited about learning. In fact, the only thing that made school bearable was the pretty new clothes I wore. Looking gorgeous was something that I looked forward to being. At this time, I started having crushes on boys. I met more girls in school after Dolly went away. I could befriend the "good girls," the ones that had normal lives at home with parents that cared about what happened with their children in school and how they progressed. I could also befriend the "bad girls," the ones that had a life at home like mine—very dysfunctional. That's what made me different. I was able to fit in on either side, although the so-called bad girls didn't really like me. They always felt I thought I was prettier and better than them. If they had only known what was really happening in my life—a lot of turmoil!

I remember the Saturday Mama was at work and Daddy had already left home on his weekend mission. My brother, Charles, Jr., was cooking pancakes for us. We were all sitting around the table waiting for him to give us pancakes. I was sitting at the head of the table. I watched Charles, Jr. as he picked up the kitchen towel and stuck it in the fire on the stove as he waited for the pancakes to cook. I wondered, *What is he doing?* My sister, Vanessa, was sitting around the table with her back turned toward Charles and the stove. After the towel started burning, Charles grabbed it and stuck it to Vanessa's ponytail!

Our hair wasn't as long as some girls', but it wasn't short either. Her hair quickly started burning. I yelled, "Vanessa, your hair is burning!" Then Charles, Jr. quickly dropped the towel on the floor and stepped on it to stomp out the fire. Then he grabbed the same towel and patted it on her head to stop the fire from spreading. By this time, it was too late because most of her ponytail had been burned off. I was shocked! I looked at Charles, Jr. and thought, *What in God's name is going on with him?* Vanessa got up from her seat and went to the bathroom to look into the mirror to see what was left of her ponytail. Charles, Jr. calmly turned back to the stove and flipped the pancakes. Vanessa was in the bathroom crying hysterically. Charles, Jr. assuredly said, "It's gonna grow back."

My brother, Johnny, sat there quietly and waited for his pancakes. He was never a problem; he was very quiet. I got up from my seat and walked toward the telephone on the wall. "Beanie, ain't gonna do nothing but tell Mama," Charles, Jr. said. The phone number to reach Mama at work was always posted on the wall next to the phone. We could only call Mama at work if there was an emergency. The number was probably used more than she wanted. I practically called her every weekend because Charles, Jr. usually did something he wasn't supposed to do.

When Mama came to the phone, I told her what happened. "I'll be right there," she said.

Vanessa waited in our bedroom for Mama to come home.

"You always call Mama and tell everything, you know," Charles, Jr. said to me.

"You shouldn't have burned Vanessa's hair!" I told him.

They would double up on me sometimes for calling Mama, but I didn't care. Somebody had to keep things in order for Mama while she worked. Finally, Mama came home and checked Vanessa's hair. Then she started hollering at Charles, Jr. She grabbed whatever she got her hands on, which was usually a broom, and hit him. "Go to your room!" she said. Then she checked Vanessa's hair to see how much damage was done. Mama was good at making us feel like everything was okay when we were little girls, even if it was a lie.

Then the telephone rang. Mama answered it. I heard her say, "I had to leave early. My daughter was sitting too close to the stove, and her hair caught fire. Thank God my son is a Boy Scout! He was able to quickly put out the fire." I was listening to her talk and questioningly thought to myself, *Put it out quick? He started it!* Mama always covered up the truth. Sometimes I questioned why she did some of the things she did when it came to Charles, Jr., like how she continued to send him to the store to get her a pop every day and every day he would come back without the pop.

"Where's my pop?" Mama would ask.

He'd say, "I dropped it."

Then Mama would start hollering and hitting. Although this continually happened, she constantly sent him to the store and still said, "Don't drop it either!" Of course, I thought, *Why does she keep sending him to the store?* But what did I know? After all, I was only a child.

After we had settled down into our house on Newberry Street, my grandma Ann became a part of my life. She was a beautiful woman. Daddy forgave her as much as he could for abandoning him when he was a baby. My grandma Ann was a "woman of the streets." She always had men and alcohol around. I can still vividly see a picture of her coming through the front door.

Daddy and Mama would be talking about her: "It's bad enough for a man to be a drunk, but a woman?" he said. Yet he still loved her. Her beauty was breathtaking. Grandma Ann was the prettiest dark-skinned woman I'd ever seen. She wore a wavy hairstyle. She had a very strong character, and she certainly had her way with men.

I remember this particular visit because it was a holiday. She wasn't the type of grandma that put you on her lap and taught you about God. She partied. Grandma Ann showed me lots of attention whenever she was around, but when she was done greeting me, she would say, "Go on now. Stay outta grown folks' business." As the day unfolded, Daddy and Grandma Ann were drinking liquor. Mama didn't drink; she would be cooking and doing what she did best: impressing you with the material things she had.

I watched them all, the way they behaved. I was fascinated with them. I always did what I was told, to stay out of grown folks business, so at a distance, I watched. My siblings would be playing, but I was too busy watching the "grown folk," as my grandma Ann put it. Then I watched their behavior gradually change. What started off as a family affair was shifting. Daddy and Grandma Ann were getting drunk. Mama was trying to hold things together. She'd say, "Charlie, don't burn the meat. Charlie you've had enough!"

Grandma Ann got upset with Daddy for drinking the last drink. In return, he brought up the past about how she was never there for him as a child. The next thing I knew, Grandma Ann hit Daddy and they started fighting. I couldn't believe my eyes! This wasn't a petty fight. Grandma Ann actually shoved Daddy's head through the window on the back door. Blood was everywhere! There was broken glass all over the floor. I remember thinking, *Is this real? Am I really watching my daddy and my grandma fight?* Grandma Ann no longer looked beautiful. She was a drunken mess. Mama was the stop-it woman for now.

That was the end of one of the many family affairs that always ended with violence. Some of them didn't even make it to the actual holiday, like the Christmas Daddy was so drunk that he fell on to the Christmas tree. I was heartbroken! The Christmas tree was propped up against the wall on Christmas Day. Don't get me wrong. We had many Christmases that were good. Mama and I hit the stores hard during Christmastime. We had to. Daddy was getting clipped by his hoes, and Mama was not about to have the things she desired for herself and her children compromised on Christmas. I always knew what gifts everyone would receive ahead of time. I always got what I wanted, which were mostly dazzling clothes. It was part of the deal: If I helped Mama, I could get whatever I wanted.

Vanessa and I loved dolls. I remember the year we first received black dolls. We loved playing with them. One day we went out some place with Mama and Daddy. While we were gone, we pretended to put our dolls to sleep and laid them in our beds. We made sure they were warm and covered. When we returned home, we were anxious to wake them. We went into our bedroom, pulled the covers back, and screamed!

To our surprise, our brother, Charles, Jr., had put dead mice on our dolls and placed the covers back on top of them. Vanessa and I were horrified! She no longer wanted her doll and never played with it again. I told her to wash the doll, but she didn't want to do it. But I washed my doll off. I wasn't about to throw it away! Charles, Jr. and Johnny thought it was very funny. Actually, it was.

> Dear God,
>   I'm sorry for being so bad. I was wrong for telling a story and tearing up the teacher's books. I feel so bad for flooding the bathroom. I deserve to be punished. I don't know why I'm being so bad. Please don't stop helping our family, God. Amen.

Foolishness is bound in the heart of a child; but the rod of correction shall drive it far from him.
                                        —Proverbs 22:15 (KJV)

Withhold not correction from the child: for if thou beatest him with the rod, he shall not die. Thou shalt beat him with the rod, and shalt deliver his soul from hell.
                                        —Proverbs 23:13–14. (KJV)

Chapter Three

DEAR GOD, I KNOW YOU LOVE ME

Mama and I had become road dogs. We plotted and planned our week while we drove to one of the stores. I counted on Mama making what we had planned come to pass. She took care of Daddy so he wouldn't be a problem when it was time to hit the stores in the evening. We were a team. We stole just to be stealing at times. I didn't know it then, but Mama used going to the stores as a way to cope with the drama at home.

One fight in particular that affected me for a long time was when Mama came in after 2:00 a.m. one day. She used to get Daddy drunk on purpose on Saturday nights so she could sneak out after he passed out. This particular night she didn't make it back home before Daddy woke up, and he was waiting for her. I always heard every movement in the house after we were in bed. I woke up when I heard Daddy arise. Instantly, I became afraid for Mama. I knew that Daddy not only was sobered up but had also figured out that Mama got him drunk on purpose, and he was steaming mad!

Mama walked through the door, maybe a half hour later. My heart was beating so fast. I was scared for her! I frantically prayed, "God, please help us. Help her, please." Then I heard Daddy say, "Where have you been?" Mama made up a lie that he probably would have believed had he still been drunk. "Pow!" I heard. The fighting got louder. Charles, Jr., Johnny, and Vanessa woke up from sleeping.

All of us were crying, except Charles, Jr. He would tell Johnny to lie on the top bunk bed in his room. "Come on, girls," he'd compassionately say to us. "Get on Johnny's bed and cover your ears with the pillows." We did whatever he told us to do. But I always uncovered my ears to hear whether they were done, if Mama was still hollering or if she was dead. Then I would still hear the commotion, so I put my head back underneath the pillow.

The fighting escalated and moved into the kitchen. Mama tried to escape. Vases and ashtrays were being broken as they fought their way into the kitchen. I peeked out from underneath my pillow and saw that Mama was naked. Daddy was beating her senselessly. Then the fighting stopped. Sometimes I believe Daddy stopped hitting her because he realized we were crying and that he was scaring us. After they stopped fighting, Daddy would walk back to his bedroom most of the time. Mama would crawl into the bottom bunk bed and lay alongside us.

This time I believe Daddy felt bad that he had his home in such an uproar, that he was trying to make things right. So he asked Mama to come to bed. My siblings had fallen asleep. I lay there awake. Then I started hearing faint sounds coming from my parents' bedroom. It sounded like they were "doing it."

Eventually, I fell asleep and woke up the next day to find Mama and Daddy getting along, like nothing happened. Even though I was a child, I began to feel like sex was the answer, so I asked God to "Please let them have sex tonight." Daddy beat Mama until she was swollen, crying, and bleeding. We would put ice on her swollen lip to stop the bleeding. This violence went on weekend after weekend.

Our entire family began to feel the effects of such violence. Our hearts were hardening. We never talked about it. We went on with our day at school and work like nothing happened until the next weekend. School had become just a place to go to wear my nice new clothes because I wasn't learning anything. I spent my day at school playing with other kids who weren't interested in learning anything either. I was placed into a special reading class because I wasn't keeping up with the other students.

The first day I entered this class, the teacher asked what my name was. I said, "Lavinia." She said, "Spell it." In three syllables, I said, "La-veen-ya." She said, "That's not how you spell your name. That's how you pronounce it. Your name is spelled L-A-V-I-N-I-A, not la-veen-ya." I was crushed. I felt like a fool. I didn't even know how to spell my own name.

I went home and told Mama what the teacher said. "It ain't," Mama said. I thought, *Why, in God's name, would you let me say that's my name, if it isn't?* I never stopped saying that my name was La-veen-ya, even if that wasn't the proper spelling. It's all I've ever known, who I felt I was. But I still passed through school feeling dumb because every time the school year started and I had a new teacher, I always said that my name was "La-veen-ya." Whenever I did, I felt like someone was saying, "That's not your name."

My brother, Charles, Jr., made me feel like everything was going to be okay. He loved us so much. Just like Mama felt about her siblings, Charles, Jr. felt, because he was the eldest, he had to take care of us. And that he did. One day, as the fighting went on at home, Charles, Jr. couldn't take it anymore. He jumped down from his top bunk bed and told my brother, Johnny, to stay up there. We did our routine of putting the pillows over our heads.

Where are you going? I thought. I watched my brother, a child, walk out of the room. I was afraid for him! *What if he couldn't stop Daddy from hitting Mama?*

Charles, Jr. told Daddy, "Stop hittin' my mama!"

My daddy said, "Go to your room, Charles, Jr.!"

"No!" he replied. "Stop hittin' my mama!"

At that point, Daddy realized that fighting Mama as usual had just gone to another level, a level that he wasn't ready to accept the blame. Oh, but it was too late. Things would never be the same.

Most Fridays after school, I spent with my cousin, Cathy. Sometimes, when her dad brought me home, he would come in and speak with Daddy. They were close friends. Whenever Daddy got drunk, Uncle Ben would come over and put Daddy in check. I loved to see him crack down on Daddy. I knew he was going to straighten him out.

In the meantime, my brother, Charles, Jr. was getting older and stronger. I remember the day I rode my bike to the store. On my way home, one of the Samson boys saw me getting onto my bike and started pushing me down the hill. He was known to be the worst one out of all the Samson kids. There was a very steep hill on Bay Street.

"Stop, don't do that!" I told him.

As I rode down the steep hill to return home, I started going faster because he kept pushing my bike. I was riding so fast. It was scary! I kept telling him to stop, but he wouldn't. I tried to push him away. I had a small bag in my hand with candy inside. I dropped it, and then I lost control of my bike. Thump! I hit the curb! I flew into the air at least ten to twelve feet and landed on the ground. I fell so hard that I couldn't get up.

A lady witnessed it and came out of her house, picked me up, and carried me home. I had hurt my knee. I couldn't walk. When we got to our house, Mama opened the door, and they sat me on the kitchen table. The lady told Mama what happened, and Mama thanked her. Charles, Jr. was listening. Mama was bandaging my knee. The pain was excruciating! I was crying uncontrollably!

"Where does it hurt?" she asked as she looked up at me. "Bean!" she yelled.

"What, Ma?"

"Your mouth!" she said.

"What, Ma?"

"Your teeth are gone!"

"Which Samson boy pushed you, Beanie?" asked Charles, Jr.

"That bad one," I said.

Mama was comforting me: "It'll be all right, Bean. We'll take you to the dentist. Your dad has good insurance. We'll get your mouth fixed, Bean. I promise."

"I'm going outside to play," Charles, Jr. calmly said.

"Be back before dark," Mama told him.

Later Daddy came home from work. "Let me see your mouth, Lavinia Lynn. How did this happen?" he asked Mama.

"Some boy pushed her down the street while she was on her bike," Mama said.

"What was she doing at the store alone?" Daddy asked.

"Charlie, it's done now," Mama said as she looked at Daddy with a mean, nasty look in her eyes.

Mama finished doctoring my knee, and I sat on the couch to rest. I could hear them talking. Daddy said, "Get her a dentist appointment tomorrow. Find a good dentist. My insurance will pay for her to see a good dentist."

Well, the evening had changed to dusk. Charles, Jr. came home and into my room. He said, "Beanie, that Samson boy that pushed you off of your bike, you don't have to worry about him no more." Charles, Jr. would do things that made me worry about him. One day he was outside playing and he froze a cat in a bucket. That scared the daylights out of me! His behavior was becoming more aggressive. Not toward Mama or even Daddy, if he wasn't fighting Mama but if anyone did anything to me, Vanessa or Johnny, Charles, Jr. wasn't having it. I loved my brother, and I always felt protected whenever he was around. As a child, I had so much fear that I felt a need to be protected, and he fulfilled that need. I never asked Charles, Jr. what he did to the Samson boy. When Vanessa came home from school the next day, she told me that all the kids were talking about what happened to me and how Charles, Jr. had beat up the Samson boy.

I missed a week or more of school while I healed. The Samson boy apologized for what happened when I returned to school. I felt he was sincere, but he was still a bad boy. I actually became friends with his sister. Their family reminded me of mine, only they were buck wild all the time. Our family was only buck wild on the weekends, whenever Daddy was drunk.

Even though Mama and I were stealing every chance we got, there were still civilized days in our home. During these times, Daddy spent time teaching Charles, Jr. things that a man needed to know. Johnny was just a little boy, and Charles, Jr. took time out with him. During our years as little children, Charles, Jr. was put in a position that no little boy was mature enough to handle. He was so burdened that he would twist his hair to the point of having bald spots on his scalp. He would bite his nails until they bled. He was a nervous wreck! We all were.

Mama started seeing more of her father. She told me that she will never forget how he used to cheat on her mother. But because he had a decent job and wanted a relationship with his grandchildren, she was going to get all she could from him. So he became a part of Mama's plan to get everything she could from whomever she could by any means necessary. Whether it meant the stores, Daddy, Granddaddy Frankie, the strange men, whomever— it didn't matter. And all the while, she's planting in our heads that everything was Daddy's fault: "If your daddy wasn't drinking, hoe hopping, or whatever, we wouldn't be in the position we're in, and I wouldn't have to do what I'm doing." I was told this almost daily.

Mama also had a way about her that was kind, giving, and nonjudgmental. Once, she told me that I had too many clothes and to give some away to a little girl who needed them. Vanessa and I dressed alike on Sundays, but she didn't like wearing dresses as much as I did. Mama told me to give this little girl the clothes privately. One day I waited until school ended and took the clothes to my cousin Cathy's house and gave the clothes to the little girl next door. Mama told me to never say anything regarding the clothes if I ever saw her wearing them. And I didn't. She said if you give from your heart, never brag about it. "God is the rewarder," she said.

She used God's name in a lot of areas, like when Vanessa and I kept her house clean. She'd say, "Cleanliness is next to godliness." To this day, I agree. Daddy was the one who introduced us to church, but Mama also spoke of God, even if it was during the time we stole the stores blind. "God protects his children, Bean. He ain't go' let you get caught." Still, I would be afraid. What I had learned from Daddy and the church was instilled on my mind and heart, yet I continued to listen to Mama.

Dear God:

I know you love me because the Bible tells me so. I don't feel loved. I just don't know of anyone else who would care about what is going on in my life. I pray that you are here. I pray that you do love me. That promise is all I have. Amen.

He said unto them, Give place: for the maid is not dead, but sleepeth. And they laughed him to scorn. But when the people were put forth, he went in, and took her by the hand, and the maid arose.

—Matthew 9:24–25 (KJV)

Chapter Four

THE BEAUTY OF CRYSTAL

By this time in my life, stealing, Mama and Daddy's fighting, and Daddy's drunkenness on the weekend had become the norm in our home. I had learned to go through it on the weekends and shut my feelings down by Monday morning because we had to return to our weekly routine of work and school. After the trauma took place, it was never mentioned again. There were no hugs given or any "I love you" spoken. I grew up in a home that was filled with lies, deceit, broken promises, mistrust, and dishonesty—a very dysfunctional environment that had become what I had accepted as normal in my life. I knew no other way.

My brother, Charles, Jr., always made life bearable for me as a child. No matter how deep the trauma became, he made the times we shared at home alone fun for us. He was very creative and made up a lot of games that we would play for hours. In between the trauma, we endured. We would have fun until Charles, Jr. broke something.

"Don't tell, Beanie!" he would say.

"I ain't."

But as soon as Mama came home, I would hurry up and tell, "Charles, Jr. broke your curtains down today!"

Mama would holler, "Charles, Jr., I told you no playing. Get the belt!" Mama would start whooping him with the belt, but he never cried. Then she would grab the broom. Charles, Jr. never budged.

Then Mama would get angry because he seemed unaffected, physically, that is; and she'd say, "Get outta my face!"

Charles, Jr. never said a word to me after that ordeal was over until Mama and Daddy both were gone: "Don't play with Beanie. She ain't go' do nothing but tell Mama everything." But he didn't stay mad with me long. If I promised not to tell, he would play with me again.

Well, it was Friday night again. Daddy didn't come home after work. Mama made us get into the car and go with her to search for him. Seemed like we were riding for hours looking for him! Then all of a sudden, Mama said, "There's your daddy, riding his hoes around again!" I sat up in my seat so I could see him. He was sitting in his car at a stoplight. Before I noticed him, my eyes focused on the woman who was sitting in the passenger seat of his car. She was very pretty. Her complexion was light brown like mine. Her hair color was red. I also noticed her hairstyle.

Then I looked at Daddy. Mama blew her car's horn. Daddy heard it, looked over at us, and drove off in his car. We couldn't follow after him because we were at a red light. Mama got so mad that I began to worry. "Beanie, do you see that mess? He took off after he saw us! I'm taking y'all to Granny's for a little while," she said. "Why?" I asked. She said that she wouldn't be long and took us there, told us to go to bed, go to sleep, and that she would be back soon. Granny always got out of bed whenever we came to her house late at night. My cousin, Angie, was always there whenever she wasn't at our house or Aunt Mabel's.

We loved visiting Granny and playing with Angie. But this night I didn't want to stay. I didn't want Mama to leave either. I had trouble sleeping, so I just lay there and prayed that Mama was okay. Well, a few hours passed and Mama came back. Someone else brought her home because she said that she saw Daddy and was trying to catch up with him, but she was in an accident and hit another car and totaled her vehicle.

"Your daddy saw me hit that car, but he just kept going!" Mama was very upset. I felt sorry for her. I was glad she was back and safe though. Then she lay in bed alongside us. Finally, I fell asleep, only to wake up the next day scratching and itching. There were bedbugs in our bed. Daddy came and got us from Granny's house. When we got home, the name-calling and arguing went on all day long. Daddy started drinking. Mama would be the one hitting tonight. She got revenge on Daddy whenever he was drunk.

Mama was violent and angry. If you shamed her, she didn't take it too kindly. Embarrassing Mama was something you just didn't do. "I'll let y'all get away with a lot at home, but in public, you will act like you got some sense. Do you hear me?" You knew Mama wasn't playing by the way she said it. I never got a lot of whoopings. Charles, Jr. did though. I never did anything to make Mama angry. I always wanted to please her. Plus, I was with her so much that I learned how to make her happy. Daddy didn't start the fighting tonight because he was too drunk.

The next Sunday morning, Mama came into my room and said to me and Vanessa, "Get dressed. After you eat your cereal, we're going to get Granddaddy Frankie and go to Detroit." She went inside the boys' room and said the same. I was so excited! I loved being with Granddaddy Frankie. He made us laugh. He was like Grandma Ann in a lot of ways. He didn't sit us on his lap and tell us stories like other kids' grandfathers did. He drank and told us jokes, but he never took a drink before seeing his mother.

There were some new dresses I hadn't worn, so I went to my closet to pick out one. Putting on new pretty dresses always lifted my spirit. As I was getting dressed, I heard Mama, "Charlie, you've had enough drinking this weekend! Don't you get with Frankie and start drinking." Daddy never said a word. After everyone was dressed, Mama always made her rounds to see how we looked and put the finishing touches on us. She would tell Charles to change his pants because she didn't like them and made sure Johnny's hair was brushed. She never said a word to Daddy about how he was dressed. Daddy already knew how to dress with style. He was very conservative and not into fads.

On Sundays, Daddy wore suits and hats. He polished his shoes. All the items in his dresser drawer were neatly folded and lined. If you touched anything in his drawer, he knew it because of the way he kept it. My daddy had it going on as a young man! He wore ties and cufflinks, jewelry and watches. He only wore his best on Sundays when he was with his family. That was a good thing because he got clipped so much that it all would have been taken while he was drunk. Mama dressed the way she felt was respectable for her grandmother, but as soon as we got to Uncle Charles's house, she would change into her party clothes.

All of us were dressed and ready to hit the road. We picked up Granddaddy Frankie. He even tried to look presentable for his mother. As soon as he got into the car, he started with the jokes. "Y'all look like you're going to a funeral!" he said. It wasn't what he said. It was the way he said it. The sound of his laugh was so funny to us! I really don't know whether I loved Granddaddy Frankie. Mama told me so much about why she resented him that I believe it affected how I felt about him.

Anyway, Daddy drove to Detroit as usual. Mama sat in the front seat between him and Granddaddy Frankie as always. We sat in the backseat and played a game called "That's my car!" Every time we saw a fancy car on the highway, you had to be the first to say "That's my car!" We played that game every time we went to Detroit while Granddaddy Frankie told his jokes.

I enjoyed seeing Mama's family. We had fun once we got past seeing our great-grandma. This time Daddy got so drunk with Uncle James that Mama became very upset with them, but neither one of them cared that she was angry. They didn't care that they were drunk in Grandma's presence. JayJay lived with her, and he didn't really care, so I didn't understand why Mama was letting it get under her skin. I do know that impressing Grandma was Mama's number one priority. For some reason, she had a need for her approval.

Our visit was cut short, and I was glad. I looked forward to going over to Uncle Charles's house. The music was always jumping and party atmosphere welcoming. This was during the Motown years, and there were a lot of popular Motown artists that recorded great songs. Their music was always playing on the stereo. Once we arrived at Uncle Charles's house, Mama couldn't let the fact go that Daddy had "clowned" on her, as she put it, at her grandma's house. She wasn't feeling the party scene, so we didn't stay at Uncle Charles's house very long.

Daddy and Granddaddy Frankie were tore up by this time, so it was time to go home. I knew this was going to be a very dangerous ride home. Daddy was too drunk to drive, but Mama always let him. She pinched and threatened him while he was driving all the way home. The car was swerving all over the road. You could hear the sound of other cars' horns blowing because Daddy was in their lane. My siblings and I got off the backseat and on to the floor because we were scared. We would sit back on the seat whenever we heard Mama stop with the threats. Then we heard her say, "I'm killing you tonight, Charlie!" She often threatened him whenever he was drunk, so it didn't faze me. I found myself praying while I was on the floor, "God, don't let us die tonight." Thanks be to God that we always made it home safely.

When we got home, we did our usual routine of preparing for the week ahead and letting go of the past. Daddy changed into his pajamas (while bumping into everything) and got into bed and fell asleep in a matter of seconds. The boys did the same. Mama, Vanessa, and I took a little longer to prepare for bed because we had to prep our clothes and hair for the next day. Mama was not her normal self. She was very quiet. She put away the clothes we had just taken off. "Good night, Mama," I said, but she didn't respond. I thought she didn't hear me, so I got into bed and silently prayed, "God, thank you for getting us home." Praying was my secret. Then I fell asleep.

At 2:00 a.m., I turned over in bed and opened my eyes. I saw a light on in the kitchen. I got out of bed and went to see what was going on. Mama was in the kitchen. A large pot of water was boiling on the stove. A black frying pan filled with oil was also heating up on the stove. She was holding a glass that looked like it had wine in it.

"Whatcha doing, Mama?"

"Gettin' ready to burn your daddy up. Sit down and have some wine with me," she calmly said.

I sat down at the kitchen table, and Mama placed a beautiful crystal wine glass in front of me. The glass was so stunning that I couldn't take my eyes off it. Mama poured the wine into the glass. The color was dark, like purple grapes, and the scent was very strong. I'll never forget how the presence of that wine glass made me feel. I sat there. I stared, hypnotized by the crystal. I sipped the wine. The taste was delightful! I began to fantasize: I'm rich! I'm socializing with my rich girl friend. But in reality, I am only a child drinking wine with her mother.

"Mama," I said, "that water's not hot enough." I was stalling because I didn't want that moment of fantasy to end—alone, sipping wine with my mama. Because I was a child, my mind hadn't grasped the fact that Mama was about to burn my daddy literally. Mama turned off the knobs on the stove. She picked up her glass and drank a sip of wine. We talked some more. "Beanie, you gotta go back to bed. You have school tomorrow." Then she turned toward the stove. I watched her put on an oven mitten, wrap a kitchen towel around the black frying pan, pick up the black frying pan, and say, "Here goes . . ."

She carefully and slowly walked out of the kitchen, through the dining room, through the living room. She didn't want to spill the grease. When I saw her walk into their bedroom, I braced myself. I finally understood what was about to happen. A few seconds later, I heard piercing screams, so loud that it frightened me! I jumped out of my chair. The screams got louder and louder!

Charles, Jr., Vanessa, and Johnny were awake by now. All of them ran into the kitchen. They curiously looked at me. "Mama just threw hot grease on Daddy!" I said to them. We all were crying, except Charles, Jr. Then Mama ran from the bedroom and headed toward the front door, never looking back. She ran out of the door so fast and left us standing there while Daddy was in the bed screaming. I can't say for sure, but I thought I heard him yelling, "Hot! Hot!"

Then I remembered seeing that pan of grease on the stove and how it was smoking hot! I know that must have hurt because I had experienced a little hot grease popping on me as I stood by the stove while Mama cooked. Then I reacted. I thought, *Cool him off!* I filled a pitcher with cold water and quickly walked toward their bedroom. I'm glad Charles, Jr. was with me because I was afraid to go in the room. I had to help Daddy though. The bedroom light was on. Charles, Jr. and I entered the room. Daddy was in a lot of pain and agony. I can't recall what I saw when I looked at Daddy, I may have blocked it from my memory, but I do remember throwing the cold water on him and running out of the room.

Anyway, Daddy kept screaming. I couldn't take the noise. Charles, Jr. told us to go to bed and cover our ears and head with a pillow. Then he climbed onto the top bunk and did the same. The level of fear I experienced that morning as a child was too much. It would affect me the rest of my life. Finally, Daddy stopped hollering. I thought he was dead. *Where's Mama?* I thought. Then I heard the front door open. It was Mama and Uncle Ben. I heard him say, "The ambulance is on the way." He must have called them before he left home. Mama had run all the way to her sister's house. She was in shock after she realized the severity of what she had done. Uncle Ben told us to stay inside our bedroom.

The ambulance arrived. I heard the paramedics, but I didn't hear Daddy though. But I knew he was still alive when I heard the paramedics say they had a pulse. As they transported Daddy by ambulance, Mama and Uncle Ben followed. Mama said to us, "I'll be back as soon as I can. Stay home from school today, and I will call y'all." Uncle Ben said, "Don't let nobody in the house!" Charles, Jr. began to comfort us. Afraid but feeling better, knowing that Daddy was going to get help, I found myself secretly praying, "God, please don't let Daddy die. Help him, God. Save my daddy, please. Help Mama, God, to be able to deal with what she has just done. Help our family, God. Amen."

A new day had begun. Daylight slowly revealed itself. Charles and I got rid of the pot of water. I washed the wine glasses and tried to put our house in order. Vanessa helped. We never talked about what happened earlier that morning. Never.

Dear God:

Please help us. Help Mama get through her day at work. Thank you for loving the little girl that called on you when she felt alone and scared, the little girl whose only hope was to believe the words she learned in church: Jesus loves me. Yes, he loves me, for the Bible tells me so.

Thank you for hearing my cry for help. Thank you for never leaving me nor forsaking us, for stationing your guardian angels all around us like a protective hedge and being the light that chased away the darkness in our lives. Thank you, God. Amen.

But whoso shall offend one of these little ones which believe in me, it were better for him that a millstone were hanged about his neck, and that he were drowned in the depth of the sea.

—Matthew 18:6 (KJV)

Chapter Five

THE ICING ON THAT CHRISTMAS

Daddy was in the hospital. I went to school that day. We didn't discuss our home life with anyone because Mama firmly instilled in us "Don't tell nobody what goes on inside this house! I don't care who it is!" Situations at home were causing me to lose focus. My grades were falling, but I never flunked. I didn't learn very much in elementary school. I don't even know how I was able to comprehend the little knowledge that I had gained.

It was very quiet in our house while Daddy remained in the hospital. At that time, kids weren't allowed to visit patients in the hospital, so I depended on Mama to tell me daily how Daddy was doing. Each day she not only told me how he was healing, but she also shared everything with me. Mama said the police wanted Daddy to press charges against her, but he wouldn't do it. In that day and age, police didn't take it upon themselves to charge the victim, if the victim decided they weren't going to prosecute an alleged accuser, so the case was dropped. Daddy told the police that he couldn't do that to his children.

Daddy had been hospitalized for several months. One day Mama came home and said, "Your daddy is doing very well. His ear was badly burned. He will never hear again in his left ear." Then she said, "Bean, the doctor said that if you hadn't thrown that cold water on your daddy, his ear wouldn't be damaged the way it was." When she said that, I started to cry. I felt it was my fault that my daddy couldn't hear. I loved Daddy, and it was at that point that I felt I had to take care of him.

"Mama, when is he coming home?"

"Soon," she said.

Then Mama and I were on a mission to have the comfort in our home that we felt Daddy needed when he was released from the hospital. We were hitting the stores every evening. Both of us felt guilty. A few months later, Daddy was finally coming home. Mama left home early that morning. Vanessa and I cleaned the house as soon as she left. We wanted everything to be just right when Daddy got home. The boys also did what they could to stay out of our way while we cleaned. They stayed in their rooms and played. When we were done cleaning, we dressed for the day. Then we patiently waited for Daddy and Mama to come home.

I was standing in the kitchen when the door opened. What I saw would never leave my mind. Never. My daddy walked through the door. "Oh my god!" I said to myself. I was hurting to the core of my being. My daddy's face and neck was pink. As I got closer to him, I saw that his ear was burned so badly that it had shriveled up like a piece of burned bacon. He didn't look like the same handsome man that I saw four months earlier.

"Hi, Daddy!" I said with tears in my eyes. He looked at me and said, "Hi, Lavinia Lynn." That's what he called me. Then he went into his bedroom. We didn't go into their bedroom often, so I didn't follow him. I went into my own bedroom. I couldn't stop thinking about how Daddy looked. "Why, God, does my daddy's face have to look like this? Why?" God had become my only friend. I didn't understand why I spent so much time with God, but I always felt better whenever I did.

It was this tragedy that would start the behavior of knowing how to separate myself from true feelings and become that other person needed to handle the situation. How to survive—it was this tragedy that would take the stealing to a level that only God could get the glory for me coming through! This is where I learned how to smile and act as if everything was good. In fact, I was messed up completely after this. Yet you would never know it by looking at me.

I didn't know what I could do or say to my daddy to make him feel better. I wondered how he was feeling about me and Mama. I would never know as a child because, as always, we never discussed it. Our lives started over from that point on. Mama and Daddy's relationship improved after Daddy got out of the hospital. Mama stayed home more. She didn't visit other men's homes, and Daddy stopped gambling and hoe hopping. I went to school with a clear head for once in my life.

Charles, Jr. was spending time with Daddy a lot after Daddy got well. Daddy taught Charles, Jr. how to fix and repair what was needed in the home and how to care for the yard and car. Mama and I even stopped stealing for a few months. But that didn't last long because Christmas was right around the corner.

Our life was so different from our next-door neighbors, the Boldens. Mama and Daddy played cards with them, and we played outside with their children regularly. After Daddy was burned, I started thinking we had a family like the Boldens. The chaos I was used to was now a thing of the past, and it felt good! Daddy's skin was healing. His complexion was returning. He was darker than he had always been, and you could tell that he had been burned, but he didn't look half as bad as he could have.

Although his hearing didn't improve, his ear didn't look as bad as when I first saw it. The average person that would have suffered that kind of burn would have looked a lot worse than the way Daddy did. Daddy wore a lot of caps and hats to hide the scars, but he was my daddy, and I thought he looked great! He hadn't drunk any liquor since the incident, and you could tell. He even started smiling again. My daddy didn't eat sweets, so his teeth were perfect. Whenever he smiled, all you saw were pearly whites! He didn't like Mama giving us candy all the time either.

Daddy learned that Grandma Ann was sick during this time. She had developed tuberculosis and was in a special hospital designated for patients with this illness. When we went to visit her, we had to stand on the lawn outside her room window, and she looked out at us. Daddy told me that the reason for this was not just because kids couldn't go inside hospitals to visit but because we could also catch what she had. I was sad that my grandma was sick. Even though I didn't really feel close to her, I didn't have any other grandma. The only thing I was told about my other grandma was that she got sick and died with the same illness.

Grandma Ann was a lot kinder after she became ill. She was treating me like a real grandma treated her grandchildren. She no longer drank. She made me and Vanessa the prettiest dolls before she died. I'll never forget when Daddy brought them home to us. Mama said they were special dolls, and we were not to play with them. We could only look at them and sit them at the head of our beds, against our headboards. I had no problems not playing with my doll because I felt she was just too beautiful to play with anyway. Grandma Ann died soon after she gave me my doll. That's all I ever received from her. The doll was an honor to have for years.

Daddy began to spend more quality time with us, the kind of time that he had spent with us before. During this time of my life, Daddy took us to play at the parks, to drive-in movies, and to visit relatives on his side of the family. His eldest brother, Ted, lived in the projects with his wife and family. To me, they didn't seem to have a close relationship; something was missing. They never got together as a family like Mama and her sisters and brothers did. I was never close to my cousins on my daddy's side of the family like I was with my first cousins on my mama's side.

We visited Daddy's aunt. We called her Auntie. Daddy told me that her husband built the house she lived in when they relocated from Tennessee to Michigan. They were freed slaves, and she was in her sixties when she began to raise Daddy. Her husband died before I was born. She had a sister named Betty that lived with her. Betty had some mental challenges.

Their house did not have an indoor bathroom. We used an outhouse. Whenever I knew we were going to Auntie's house, I would use the bathroom at home. We didn't like the looks or smell of that outhouse! Sometimes we would laugh at how disgusting it was! Sometimes Mama would pull out the slop jar from underneath Betty's bed and let me use that instead of going to the outhouse. There was no privacy in her house. There weren't any doors to close. Auntie hung blankets all over the place to create some privacy.

Auntie was an elderly woman. Daddy went to help her at least once a week. Betty was also aging, but she was ordered around by Auntie like she was a child. I liked Betty. She was funny, almost like having another friend. Because of the stories Daddy shared with me, I always felt like I was experiencing as much as I could of how the first freed slaves lived whenever I was at Auntie's house. She was one of the first ones to move to Michigan.

Auntie's house resembled houses that were depicted in a famous movie about slavery that aired on television in the 1970s. Daddy also took us to visit his other brother, Kevin. I was always scared of Kevin. He wasn't very nice. He had one eye and was taller than Daddy and Uncle Ted. Mama told me that Uncle Kevin lost his eye when he and his woman were fighting in the car and the car crashed.

Whenever I visited my grandfather on my daddy's side, I was always told how to behave, like at Grandma Ann's house. But this was different. Something about my grandfather reminded me of being around white people. He had a very nice home with a huge yard. All sorts of trees were planted in his yard: cherry, nuts, apples; even grapevines were growing all over the place. I loved playing in his yard. I remember feeling free and running around. There was a lot of space.

Whenever we went to our grandfather's house, it was always on a Sunday. We were dressed to impress. Daddy and Mama would always be together when we first arrived. We'd walk into the house together as a family. After a short while, we would go outside to pick fruit from the trees. Mama would end up outside with us. She would lean against the car and yell at us, "Don't get dirty!" We always had lots of fun there, even though we didn't go often.

There were other relatives on my daddy's side that I would see every now and then, but none of them were ever close to us. There was one relative, my grandfather's sister, who had a piano inside her home. She gave me piano lessons. Mama paid her for the lessons. I got a stick of Juicy chewing gum as a reward for playing the piano well. Mama and Daddy were doing so much better than they were before the burning incident. As a matter of fact, I will say that I felt a peace of mind that I had never experienced.

One day, when I returned from school, Mama told me that we were going to move. After living on Newberry Street for four and half years, I don't know whether I was happy to hear that news. Mama and I had a lot of new things to get for our new home, so before I even knew where we were moving, the stealing resumed. I don't know where Mama told Daddy we were going every other evening, but he never said a word about our coming and going. When we left home, we always came walking back through the door with bags full of merchandise, so I'm sure Daddy thought we bought what we had. Mama was very excited that we were moving. She told me that we were moving to The Valley. I know that made her feel important. We were moving up into a better neighborhood.

At this point, my parents were still getting along quite well. Although Mama started back making her stops at that man's house whenever we were out hitting the stores, I never told a word. I didn't want Mama to get caught. Besides, Daddy had been through enough. Not only were we moving at the beginning of the upcoming year, but it was also the Christmas holiday season. That meant Mama and I had to hustle overtime to get the gifts and other items she wanted for her new home. We got new curtains, bedspreads, rugs, vases, ashtrays, dishes, and much more. If we couldn't steal those things, we stole clothes and exchanged them for what we wanted and needed.

Just like a doctor or lawyer went to school to learn their profession, I was learning how to become a professional booster, except Mama was the teacher and I was the student. She taught me that book of knowledge, and then I did my internship at the stores. There was never a time when I wasn't afraid that I would get caught, but I felt I had to do the job in order to please Mama. I didn't want to disappoint her, so I prayed when it was time to walk out of the door of the stores: "God, please don't let them stop me. Please." I was so nervous. My body would be shaking so bad that once I made it to the car, it took a minute for me to calm down. But after I looked at the pretty dresses I was going to wear to school and over the holidays, I got excited and quickly pulled myself together.

I remember all my Christmases being full of all sorts of exciting presents. Mama and Daddy made sure we always had holidays to be remembered. For years, I believed in Santa. Then one year Mama told me that Santa did not exist. After I found out there was no Santa, I always went with Mama whenever she shopped for gifts. Daddy often gave Mama some money to purchase gifts, but it was never enough. Mama always felt she had to have more. After all, she had to impress her family every holiday.

There was never a dull moment during our holidays. I remember one Christmas when Daddy was so intoxicated that he fell on to the Christmas tree. We always had artificial Christmas trees, and Mama always decorated them so beautifully. We would help her hang the bulbs. After Daddy fell on to the tree, we propped it up against the wall. That certainly ruined my holiday spirit that year! Mama tried to make the best of it, for our sake, but I could tell that it put a damper on her spirit.

So much violence had taken place in my life as a little girl that I was a nervous wreck by the time Mama told me we were moving. *I won't fit in with the new kids at the new school*, I thought. I didn't think any other child experienced the trauma I had gone through. I also had a complex about my front teeth still being knocked out. The roots were still in my mouth, and the third tooth was broken in half. My mouth looked horrible! Yet in those days, I was still too young to have them fixed. The dentist said I had to wait until I was twelve.

During this time, Mama and Daddy were away from home all day long. They always had to take care of some business. We were home alone every day. We got ourselves off to school, and when we returned home from school, we watched television. Charles, Jr. was always in charge. He always made sure the doors were locked and we stayed indoors. If someone knocked on the door, we were not allowed to open it. We would change from our school clothes and into our play clothes. Charles, Jr. would help make us a sandwich to eat. We had fun and played until Charles, Jr. did something wrong. Then he would say to Johnny and Vanessa, "Beanie ain't go' do nothing but tell it." He was right. That's how I got my brownie points with Mama.

Our school had a Christmas musical program that year, and our class sang three songs there. I had never been in any of the Christmas programs at school, so I was excited to participate. Plus, I was relieved that there wasn't any drama going on at home. My whole family came to watch me sing in the program. It felt good knowing they were sitting in the audience. I found the prettiest dress to wear, and Mama styled my hair. I felt so beautiful that evening.

As a child, I always heard that the birth of Jesus was the reason for Christmas, and even though I loved the many gifts I received, knowing that Christmas Day was the day that God sent us a Savior meant a lot to me. By this time in my life, Jesus had become my friend. I never told anyone how much I talked to him. Singing "Go Tell It on the Mountain That Jesus Christ Is Born" had meaning to me, even as a little girl. The Christmas musical was just what we needed to put the icing on that Christmas. It was the first Christmas that I ever remember having as a child that Daddy wasn't drunk. It also would be the last.

As the New Year set in, Mama and Daddy were finalizing the paperwork for our new house. Mama was so excited! She couldn't stop talking about how she wanted each room decorated. When she came home in the evening from work, she would prepare dinner. After we finished dinner, the two of us would hit the stores and steal what we needed for our new house. I learned a lot about exchanging clothes for other household items during that period. We kept everything for the new house on the front porch. Mama wanted new furniture, but Daddy had recently bought new furniture for the living and dining rooms, so she didn't get her wish. But if Mama and I could have stolen some furniture, we would have.

The closer it came time for us to move, Mama and Daddy started having disagreements about money and business. I didn't know everything, but I could hear enough at night as I lay in bed to know that the harmony I was experiencing was breaking up. Anyway, the moving day was here. I said goodbye to all my friends at school and had mentally prepared myself for this change. Like Mama, I was looking forward to moving to The Valley.

Dear God,

Thank you, Father, for being my friend. Thank you for making me feel better when I'm hurting. Thank you for saving my daddy's life. Please help our family to keep loving each other like we do right now. Thank you for making Mama happy by giving her a new house to move into. God, please don't stop helping our family. Please let the kids at my new school like me. Watch over my sister and both my brothers, dear God. Amen.

Then shall ye call upon me, and ye shall go and pray unto me, and I will hearken unto you. And ye shall seek me, and find me, when ye shall search for me with all your heart.

—Jeremiah 29:12–13 (KJV)

Chapter Six

THANK YOU, GOD, FOR MY NEW TEETH

I will never forget that first day of school in The Valley. The kids at my new elementary school were different from most of the kids at Willow. All of them wore clean clothes, and their hair were neatly combed. None of them looked poor. I felt I fit right in, in the grooming area at least. I didn't want to smile because I felt my mouth was jacked up, so I learned how to smile without showing my teeth. I would stand in the mirror for hours and practice smiling. I learned how far to extend my lips to smile before you could see that my teeth were not only broken off but also the little that was left of them had started to rot. I hated how my mouth looked, but I dealt with it.

The kids were very friendly. I was able to mix with the girls that were popular and the girls that weren't very popular. They all liked me. I found that with my home life now being at peace, I was feeling good. I was even able to concentrate on being taught in class. For the first time in my life, I wanted to learn. I could actually hear what the teacher was saying. I liked my new school. I also liked our new home.

Mama and Daddy worked a lot. Johnny and I were home alone in the mornings until it was time for us to leave for school. Vanessa and Charles, Jr. were in junior high school, so they had to leave home at least forty-five minutes before we left. Life was good! God and I talked daily. Not only did I say my prayers before going to sleep, but I also woke up talking to God. I asked him to give me what I needed to get through the day. I told God whenever I was afraid, and I asked him to help me that day and protect me and my family.

I'll never forget my last year in elementary school. The classes were in different rooms with one teacher instructing in math, another in English, and another in history. My history teacher was a black man, named Mr. Taylor, who took a special interest in the black students. He pushed me to do my best. He told me that I was smart and could do anything I set my mind on doing. I believed him. He gave an assignment that would be the biggest assignment of the sixth grade.

The class had a choice of learning and reciting one of four speeches. The longest and hardest speech was Dr. Martin Luther King's speech. You had to recite the speech word for word, as Dr. King said it, not leaving out one single word. *If I could pull this off,* I thought, *I could bring up my final grade.* I cared about my grades during this time of my life. I also wanted to prove to myself that what Mr. Taylor said was true. I would receive three As if I did it. The other two speeches were worth two As, and the shortest speech was worth one A.

There were only three of us who chose Dr. King's speech; the other two were bookworms. We had four weeks to learn our speech. I spent a lot of time locked in the bathroom at home practicing. It was the only place in the house that had privacy. Whenever someone had to use it, I would come out long enough for them to go. Then I would go back into the bathroom and lock myself inside. This went on every day until it was time to say the speech in class. Mama and Vanessa would let me practice in front of them day after day.

Whenever I got it wrong, I would stop and go back into the bathroom to study. I worked hard on getting that speech right. I felt a sense of pride whenever I practiced it. It wasn't very many years before that Dr. King had been killed and the riots in Detroit had taken place. I remembered Mama talking to her brothers and sisters on the phone and sharing with me about the violence that was going on in Detroit. I also remember watching how his death affected us as a people.

Anyway, the day came when it was time to stand before the class and Mr. Taylor and recite the speech. Mr. Taylor came from behind his desk and sat among the rest of the class. Then my turn came. I stood up. I left my papers at my desk. I started shaking inside. I was so nervous. I knew this was it—there was no turning back now. I had to say the speech. As I spoke, my voice shook. Almost like I was about to cry, but I kept on speaking. I was nervous throughout the entire speech, but I finished it—all of it! I didn't leave out one single word.

Mr. Taylor stood up and clapped his hands when I was done. I hurried back to my seat and sat down. All the kids in the class were staring at me. I felt they were thinking, *She was scared to death!* But one by one, they started telling me that I did good. I said, "Thank you." Later Mr. Taylor put the finished report paper on top of my desk. It read, "Excellent job! A+ A+ A+." When I saw that, I felt a feeling that I'd never felt before. I liked what I was feeling. It was even a better feeling than I got from wearing new pretty clothes.

When school was over, I couldn't wait to get home to tell Mama and Vanessa. But when I got there, no one was home. Johnny came in right behind me, so I told him, "I got three A+s!" Johnny said, "No, you didn't!" I showed him the paper and said, "Yes, I did!" Then Vanessa and Charles, Jr. came home, and I shared my good news with them. We didn't have to complete our homework as soon as we got home. That was never a rule in our home, so we always found something to eat and went straight to the television. If I did homework, it was because I wanted to do it. One rule that we did have was that Vanessa and I had to make sure Mama's house was clean before she came home.

Charles, Jr. did all the outside work. He took out the trash, shoveled the snow, cut the grass. Johnny helped him. Mama wanted not only the inside of her home neat and clean, but she took pride in the yard as well. She bought small shrubbery that Charles,

Jr. helped her plant in the yard. During that time of my life, we couldn't go outside until Mama and Daddy got home. When Mama got home, I told her about my speech and how scared I was when I said it and that I didn't miss a word. Mama was proud of me. I believe once I started to take an interest in school, I inspired Mama to take some night classes at the high school in the evening. She never graduated though.

We were all doing good. Daddy was promoted at work. He was a printer by title. He was a perfectionist. He printed all the signs on the roads and street by hand. There was no modern machine to do the job back then. The local newspaper wrote an article about my daddy. His picture was in the paper. The article talked about how straight the lines were that Daddy made in striping the streets.

I liked going to his job. Whenever I watched Daddy work, I could see that he was a man with lots of knowledge. Not only was he smart and had lots of friends and coworkers who called him to talk, but they also learned from him. Daddy was liked by many people, whenever he wasn't drinking. I liked listening to my daddy as well. I learned a lot from him. He was very proud of me when I said the Martin Luther King, Jr. speech.

Daddy gave me my first job. I ironed all his shirts and work clothes for two weeks, and he paid me on his payday. Mama and I had let up on the stealing. I didn't care because I had so many clothes that I didn't need any more. I also started pressing and curling Granny's hair every two weeks, and she paid me as well. Mama stopped doing my hair the year before because I was old enough to do it myself.

As a family, we became very popular in The Valley. Everybody liked us. We lived next door to a white family, the Smiths. Mr. Smith was a nice man. He had a snowmobile, and in the winter, he would take us for rides on it. It was fun! I never liked the cold weather though.

I had been going to Northpoint School for a while now. The year was coming to an end, and next year I would be in junior high school. I already knew a lot about the school because Vanessa would tell me about it when she came home. We talked a lot at night before we went to bed. Vanessa always said that I was fast. She was quiet and shy. I teased her about being so dark-skinned: "You ain't my sister. Mama and Daddy found you in the sewer." I didn't realize that I was causing her to have a complex about her skin color.

In all actuality, I thought my sister was gorgeous. She resembled my grandma Ann, and I'll never forget how beautiful she was. I loved Vanessa, but there were days when she was mean to me though. We never liked doing the same things. I was a girly girl that was into looking pretty, and she wasn't. She was more of the jeans type. Our relationship was different from most sisters. We talked a lot at home. I did most of the talking, mainly about boys. I had liked boys since the second grade.

I remember when Dolly and I would go to the pencil sharpener to meet these two boys in Mrs. Wilson's class. They would put their hands underneath our dresses. As the years went by, I started letting this particular boy I liked put his hand in my panties. I never told a soul what I was doing back then because Charles, Jr. would have beaten him up had he known what I was doing with this boy. I felt I could trust Vanessa, so I told her just about everything. She would listen and say, "You so fast!" Vanessa didn't like boys. Heck, she barely liked girls! She loved me, though, and I loved her. We shared a secret life of trauma that other kids knew nothing about.

Well, it was summertime, a get-to-know-the-neighborhood summer. As kids in a new neighborhood, we made friends with other kids that were our age and enjoyed doing things we liked. Charles, Jr. quickly became popular with the boys his age. I too became very popular. Johnny had his own set of friends as well. With him being the youngest, he had friends, but Charles, Jr. was his idol. This would be the summer that we had fun, not just in the neighborhood but as a family. Mama spent her free time bringing the family together.

Summer holidays were always big at our house. Daddy sho' could cook some ribs! Mama's sisters and brothers and their kids and another cousin of Mama's that she was close to, Jeff, gathered at our house. He was a small handsome man. He reminded me of Daddy. Daddy's coworkers would also stop by the house.

The Fourth of July—what a holiday! Even our friends from the neighborhood would stop over. There was a popular song about family reunions always playing on the stereo around this time. Days before the reunion, Mama would let me go to the record shop with her. From the moment we got there, I liked watching the interactions of not just Mama but of everybody in the shop—from the saleslady playing the different hits to the different people buying the music—it was a "black thang." Back in those days, we as people listened to music and spent lots of money setting the atmosphere with it, whether it was for your night with your lover or Sunday at church.

We loved music. The 45s and albums were always playing on the stereo at our house, especially Fridays, Saturdays, and Sundays. Mama played all the popular R&B artists' songs, especially whenever she was about to step out on Daddy. Daddy listened to his favorite blues songs while she was gone. It was about this time when Daddy started drinking again. First, it was a little beer. I watched him as he started to change. Whenever I heard his favorite blues song playing, I knew Mama had hurt him with her lies to get out of the house.

This was the summertime, though, and every summer at our Veron Street home was filled with barbequing in the backyard and music. The fad for dressing that summer was bell-bottoms and hot pants. And not only did I wear the latest fads, but Mama also stayed on top of how she dressed. We loved clothes, so the stealing was on again. Mama couldn't afford to live the lifestyle she wanted to, so we did what we had to do to stay on top of the latest styles we loved so much.

We became that family that was the talk of the neighborhood. All the girls wanted to know Charles, Jr. and Johnny. All the boys wanted to know their sisters. Charles, Jr. wasn't having it though. I became close friends with this one girl named Tammy, who stuttered. She was so funny! Not just because she stuttered but she made me laugh. She shared personal things with me also. She told me that she hated the police, how they had killed her father. She made me feel like I could be myself with her.

The other girls that had befriended me were girls that were very pretty and dressed like I did. But their parents were professionals. They had no idea of the life I had come from. I had to hide too much whenever I was with them. When I was with Tammy, not only did I laugh a lot, but I could also be me. She had a twin sister and another sister that was a year younger than us. Actually, there were six of them. Their mother was a strong woman who didn't take no mess from them. They called her Princess Ann. She worked a lot and was never home during the early evening, so their house became a hangout for me.

Princess Ann let them have me and Vanessa over whenever she wasn't home. They took care of their younger sister and brother. Their aunt's daughter lived with them also. She was just a baby. Princess Ann's sister was a drug addict among other things. She only came to their house every now and then. I didn't know much about drugs back then, but Tammy talked to me about her aunt. She told me that she shot heroin.

I knew a little about people that used drugs like that because Mama had told me about her youngest brother. He started shooting up when he went away to the war in Vietnam. Uncle James was my favorite uncle, even though I knew what he did. When I was a little girl, Mama spoke of Aunt Penny's issues with drugs also. When I was a little girl, Mama supported their vice.

This was the Fourth of July Mama wanted to celebrate with her siblings. Besides, this would be the first gathering among many that she would get to show off her new home. I had fun that summer, as it was coming to a close.

Well, the fall season had begun, and I was about to enter junior high school. I was more than ready, or so I thought. Vanessa had spoken of her first year at Bristol Junior High School all the time, and I was anxious to go to school with the older kids. I had to get my clothes together to start junior high, so Mama and I went to the stores on a regular basis after the Fourth of July.

I thought there were a lot of white kids at school when I first went to Newberry School, but I remember my first day at Bristol, thinking, *I've never seen so many white kids in my life!* I'll never forget walking into my homeroom class on the first day of school. There were only about eight or nine black kids in the class. Three kids I'll never forget: Gwyn, Michael, and Bruce. Bruce was a white boy. I'll never forget him because he liked me.

Michael was a black kid that went to Newberry with me. He used to follow me home from school the first year. He never said he liked me, but I knew he did. He always tried to talk to me when no one else was around, mostly walking home from school. Then there was Gwyn. She was different. She was a girl with a personality like a boy. I started to talk to her first. She had on a skirt that first day, so I didn't see anything different from any other girl that first day of school, other than the fact that she had a heavy voice.

Bruce told me that I had on a pretty dress. "Thank you," I said. *He's so nice*, I thought. Most boys didn't tell me I looked pretty, the black ones anyway. Charles, Jr. would give me compliments sometimes, but he was the only black boy to say that I looked pretty. He was my brother, and I knew he always tried to make me feel better, especially after the fights that Mama and Daddy had. I don't know what I would have done if it hadn't been for Charles, Jr. He made things bearable in my childhood. He protected me from everyone and every situation he could. Now here was this white boy telling me how pretty I was. He followed me from class to class that day. I was very scared. Not only didn't I know where my classes were located, but I also had this white boy following me around school. It just so happened that we had the same classes.

I never had any white friends. The year before, there were some white kids at my new school, but they played with and only talked to the white kids. The other black kids played and talked with one another. Now that I was in junior high, things were different. We all talked to one another. I was a bit frightened the first few weeks. I feared being among the older students. I also feared not being able to keep up in class. As weeks turned into months, I became comfortable with junior high school. I actually liked it. My grades were never As and Bs, but I was able to keep average grades.

Well, the year that I had been anxiously waiting for had arrived. I was twelve years old. I could finally go to the dentist to get my teeth fixed. I couldn't wait! Mama took me back to the same dentist that told her there was nothing they could do until I was twelve years old. By this time, the kids had started to call me green mouth because the decay on what was left of my front teeth had turned the color of green. Kids can be so cruel to one another. Most of the time, it was all done out of fun—we teased one another to get a laugh, but some of us didn't think the jokes were funny, even though we laughed at them. It took some months to finish the work in my mouth because I had to get a root canal and fillings in some of my other teeth. By the time the work was finished, it was the beginning of spring that year. I met so many kids that year. Among Charles, Jr., Vanessa, Johnny, and me, we became very popular at school. Everybody wanted to hang out with us.

I remember the first day I went to school with my mouth fixed. All my friends were saying, "Let me see. Smile. They look so real! You look so different!" Tammy would say, "You look pretty." Then she would start stuttering. Sometimes I would copy her. Then she would laugh. I loved Tammy. We had fun together. We all walked home from school together. Although we broke off into our own small cliques, we were still together. As my first year in junior high school came to an end, I had no bad feelings all bound up in the pit of my stomach, like so many times in the years before. I felt like life was finally good to our family.

Thank you, God!

Thank you for hearing my prayers and helping our family. I am so grateful for how happy I feel! Thank you for making Mama happy—she loves her new home! Thank you for stopping Daddy from drinking. Thank you, God, for my new friends and allowing me to be liked by so many kids.

God, thank you for Mr. Taylor. If it had not been for him telling me that I can do whatever I set my mind to doing, I never would have tried to say the Dr. Martin Luther King, Jr. speech. Saying that speech gave me a confidence that I will always have. Thank you, God, for my new teeth. Please, God, continue to look out for Charles, Vanessa, Johnny, and Mama and Daddy. Take care of all my relatives and friends, God. Amen.

Even a child is known by his doings, whether his work be pure, and whether it be right.

—Proverbs 20:11 (KJV)

Chapter Seven

THE VALLEY

It was my second summer in The Valley. By this time, I'd adjusted to my new life. As soon as I felt that the chaos and fighting of the past was over, Daddy started back drinking to the point of intoxication. Our weekends always started off with plans of Daddy barbecuing, like he did every summer. Mama had her family over quite a bit this summer. It would be the entire English clan. Every time Mama had her family over, she would always set herself up to be disappointed. I found that I fed off into the same behavior.

As I helped Mama with her plans for the weekend, not one time did we stop to think that all that planning and stealing didn't make sense, especially when Daddy wasn't going to do nothing but get drunk and break everything! It happened every time. It never failed. Mama and I replaced a lot of vases and ashtrays that summer. Daddy had a routine. First, he would be in a good mood. He'd start the ribs to cooking after Charles, Jr. would help him cut the grass and get the fire going. Then once the ribs were cooking, well, he'd take his first sip of beer.

There were stages to Daddy's drinking. When he first started, he would be in a pleasant mood. He was nice to us. He even talked to us kids. I enjoyed listening to him. He spoke about his job and his coworkers. He talked a lot about racism on the job. The one thing he said that I never forgot was that they needed him. He had a skill that no one else in the paint and sign shop had. He had to teach the white man how to do the job. He resented the fact that he never made to be a supervisor. He did become the assistant supervisor but felt that was because they needed him to teach the supervisor. My daddy was a man to be honored when he wasn't drunk.

I learned from my first cousin that it was Daddy who their mother called upon whenever she needed something for them as small kids. It was Daddy who took on the responsibility of his eldest brother. When she told me this, it didn't surprise me. My daddy was a provider. Mama just could never have enough; she always wanted more and more.

This would be a summer that shook Mama up dearly. Her cousin, Jeff, was killed. He and another man were having sex with the same woman. Jeff went to see the woman. He had a gun on him. Jeff and the man got to fighting, and the other man was able to get the gun out of Jeff's hand after he pulled it. The man shot and killed Jeff. Nothing was done to the man. He never did a day in jail because Jeff was the one that pulled the gun on him. Mama was devastated!

Once the funeral was over, I would hear Mama and Daddy talking some nights. I heard Mama say, "We're going to lose the house." When I heard Mama say that, I became all ears. I listened to Mama. "Jeff's wife don't like me. She's gonna take our home." I found out that our house was in Jeff's name. After Daddy lost his first house, he had bad credit. Mama talked Jeff into signing for our house. Daddy not only paid the money it took to close the deal, but he also paid Jeff for using his name.

One night I heard Daddy say, "We're going to go to the VA and tell the truth."

"The truth?" Mama said. "Have you lost your mind? Them white folks don't care about us. You're gonna make things worse!"

"What other choice do we have?" he said to Mama.

She didn't agree with Daddy, but she had to admit that he was right. In the meantime, they went to Jeff's wife. She told Daddy that she didn't want his house. Daddy told her that he would be getting the house out of Jeff's name as soon as possible. I can't say for sure because he didn't talk to me about it because I was a kid, but I believe my daddy prayed to our Father, God, that he was able to get our home in his name.

That Monday morning I'll never forget because they both stayed home from work. Mama and Daddy went to the Veterans Administration. I was worried about them all morning long. I tried to go on with my morning, but I found myself thinking of what would happen to us if we lost our home. *What would that do to Mama?*

After a few hours, they returned home. Mama was all smiles. "They did it!" she said. She was so happy. I felt her joy! I too was very happy! Vanessa and I had cleaned the house from top to bottom. That was something I did whenever I was nervous, sad, scared, or worried; I cleaned Mama's house. Cleaning up her house was also a way to make her smile. She loved for her home to look spotless.

After our home was officially Daddy's house, his drinking got even worse. He was drunk every weekend. He didn't hang out in the streets like he did when I was a little girl. He got drunk at home, and while he was drunk, he continued breaking everything in sight by either falling on it or dropping it. Mama wanted me to go with her to the stores to replace the vases, plants, ashtrays, glasses, plates—you name it—because Daddy broke it on a regular basis.

Life was a mess in our home. We all had started to act out. Charles, Jr. was breaking into all the neighbor's houses. He used Johnny sometimes to go through the window and let him in through the door. The fighting between Mama and Daddy reached a peak this year. They were at it every weekend. Vanessa would have anxiety attacks whenever the fighting went on. I always watched her because I knew any second she would start shaking uncontrollably. I would holler, "Daddy! Mama! Look at Vanessa!" She would be freaking out. Then they would stop fighting for the time being, and Mama would get Vanessa to a hospital.

Johnny was very quiet. Charles, Jr. protected him, kept him out of harm's way. I always had to do first aid on Daddy. He would be bleeding from being cut with glass. This went on every weekend. Then came Sunday evening and we would focus on Monday morning. Mama and Daddy had to go to work the next day, so the chaos would calm down for the next few days.

This particular summer was coming to a close. School was about to begin. This year sports became a big part of my life. Charles, Jr. was a very good athlete. He not only wrestled, but he also ran track. I watched him practice with his friends. The first year I watched, I learned that I could run. One of his friends named Edward was fast. I mean very fast! Out of fun one day, we raced against each other. I didn't beat him, but I was able to keep up. That was the talk of the neighborhood: how Charles, Jr.'s sister kept up with Edward in a race. Edward was fast! He and another boy from our neighborhood were among the fastest runners in the city at that time.

After that, Charles, Jr. and every other kid were telling me to try out for track that year. I did, and I made the team! As a matter of fact, there was only one girl that could beat me, and I hated that she was faster than me. But it was all good because we were teammates. Vanessa made the team. She was fast too. It was four of us girls from The Valley, and we were fast! We went on that season to take first place among all the junior high schools in the city—so did the boys' track team. Charles, Jr. and the other boys from the north side were good in all sports.

We started to make lots of enemies that year. Kids from the east side started to talk about us. We all hung out together after practice. Walking home, we joked and laughed at one another. We had lots of fun! The black kids stuck together. We supported one another in different activities. When track season was over, a talent show was being planned. Charles, Jr., Edward, and one other friend of theirs were going to be in the show. I couldn't wait to see it! They were very talented. They wore eye-catching jumpsuits in the show. Charles, Jr.'s jumpsuit was light brown on one side and dark brown on the other side. Charles, Jr. and his friends learned to perform like one of those famous Motown groups. Girls always fought over Charles, Jr. and Edward. Charles, Jr. became "that guy" quick.

That year I experienced my first death of a friend. Charles, Jr. and his friends always went out on devil's night and threw eggs, among other things, at houses and cars. This year Mama told us to stay home. She was going out partying, and whenever she did, she tried to keep us in the house while she was gone. (Tried, I said.) Charles, Jr. chose to listen this time. Johnny stayed home also. He always did whatever Charles, Jr. did.

This year Charles, Jr.'s friends did what they always did on devil's night without him. An hour or so after they all went out, Edward came and knocked on our door.

"Charles, Jr.!" he frantically said. "Linda's missing! We threw eggs at that house on the corner right before The Valley and started running up the hill in back of the school. We heard a gunshot, so we kept running. When we got to the schoolyard, we noticed that Linda wasn't with us anymore. Can you go back with us and help us look for her?"

Charles, Jr. looked at me and said, "Beanie, ain't go' do nothing but tell if I leave."

But after hearing what happened, I said, "No, I won't. Go ahead."

Charles, Jr. returned a while later to say that Linda was dead. Edward had asked Charles, Jr. to go back with him because he knew that Charles, Jr. wouldn't be scared. That's how my brother was. He always stepped up and showed courage when needed. I could tell that this had messed up my brother. Vanessa was also hurting by the news because Linda was her friend. The entire neighborhood was shaken up. This was unreal. The man that lived in that house on the corner was known for disliking blacks. It was never confirmed that he did it because to this day, the police say they found nothing on him to prove it, so Linda's death was never solved. Every one of us left school to go to the funeral. It was packed. It was a very sad funeral.

I sat in the back with my friend, Tammy. I watched Linda's family enter the church and walk toward the front of the church to be seated. Linda's boyfriend, Larry Parker, also walked in with them. He was a very popular teenager from the east side. His family was known to have money. I watched his every move. I was very impressed with his clothing.

By this time in my life, clothes were a real big deal. I studied how a person dressed. I took how I looked very seriously. Mama had created a fashion nut. Linda's family cried uncontrollably. Her elder sister and her boyfriend embraced each other throughout the service. I felt sorry for her boyfriend. He became my focus of attention after the funeral. I had seen him before and heard some talk about him, but after seeing him at Linda's funeral, my mission began.

His uncle had a skating rink built in our neighborhood. It became the place to be for all the young people in the city. It was exciting! I loved roller skating. I learned to skate when we lived on Newberry Street. I was a Girl Scout for a short period when I was a young girl. On weekends the leader of our troop would take us roller skating at the community center on the west side. It was fun learning how to skate! Once I learned, I wanted to go every weekend.

Throughout my teenage years, I roller skated once or twice a week. I became a regular at the Parker's skating rink. Linda's boyfriend was also a regular. Now I was able to see him all of the time, and as always, he was dressed sharp as a tack. Not only did he dress, but his cousin and another young lady who worked at the rink also dressed. I loved going to see what they were wearing. They were much older than me, but I studied them whenever I wasn't skating. I'd just sit on the bench, while everyone else skated, and watched Larry and his family. I don't believe I was the only one watching them—every one of us wished our parents had the money Frank Parker had.

I remember when I was a little girl and Daddy bought the fuel to heat our house from Parker's Fuel Oil Company. They were one of the first blacks to own their own business in the city. I also remember the corner, a small section on the west side, that had several other businesses that were owned by blacks. One business that I remember well from those days was Club 77, a bar that Daddy would go to while he left us inside our car on the backseat.

I remember it being dark outside. I was scared to death waiting for him to come back. Even though he locked us inside the car, we still got down on the floor and hid. From time to time, I would peek out of the window to see the many different interactions among the people. One time when I saw Daddy come out of the bar, I got happy thinking he was on his way to the car, but he didn't come to the car; he went inside a place next door to the bar. I learned later that he was going to the hoe house that was next door.

One night our car was parked right outside the hoe house, and when I saw this man going inside, I saw that you had to walk up some stairs as soon as you entered the door. I always wondered what Daddy was doing up those steps, even though Mama had made it a point of telling me everything whenever she got mad at him. One day she even rode by the corner to show me which business was which—all the way to the "numbers house," which was no more than a block from the Parkers' home. Black people, back in the day, played the numbers daily. Sometimes Daddy would hit the numbers and win some money.

This would be the year that I began to see that lots of girls disliked me. I started to see how the girls from the east side looked at me whenever I was at the skating rink. There was this girl that also lived in The Valley who came to the skating rink every Friday like I did. We started to skate together. People often said we looked alike. Her name was Lisa. We became good friends. Lisa's family was just the opposite of mine. Her father was the principal at the junior high school of the kids that didn't like me. Those kids didn't like her either. The two of us loved doing our hair, putting on makeup, and boys! She was fun to be around. I started hanging out at her house all the time. I often spent the night there.

Lisa's mother was one of the people who did the hiring for jobs at the local hospital. She was never home. With both of Lisa's parents being professionals, she didn't have the issues in her life that I had. Her life was so healthy that at times I would get bored at her house. It was too quiet—not enough chaos for me! I was shocked when I learned that her parents were divorcing and she would be moving to another city with her father that next year.

Our friendship was put on hold at that point. I started going over to Tammy's house again and going skating with her and her sisters. Vanessa also liked going skating. We loved it! Mama even started going because she wanted to learn. She finally learned how to skate without falling down, and then after a while, she stopped going. I continued to see Larry every time I went skating. I didn't have the nerves to say anything to him.

As the year went on, I started seeing that there were girls even at Bristol that were jealous of me and wanted to fight. Gwyn and I were friends, though, and she always put them in their place. "You gotta fight me first!" she would say to them. She could see how nervous I was. I would actually shake to the point that you could see my hand shaking. I prayed all night, asking God not to let them touch me the next day. Some days I didn't even want to go to school. I would be talking to God in the mornings. He always made me feel like I could do it. I always felt his presence whenever I was scared.

I finally got enough courage to say something to Larry at the skating rink. He noticed I was following him one Friday night, so he spoke to me. We started to talk to each other that night. I had already started having sex by the time I was in the seventh grade with boys that I thought I liked. Every time I did it, I walked away feeling used. Boys at that age are very childish. They would always tell other boys or never called me again.

I started to like boys that were older than me. I found that the boys who were three or four years older were more mature. Larry was three years older than I was. Besides, my brother Charles, Jr. had already checked all the boys my age by now. They were all scared to say very much to me and Vanessa without sneaking around Charles, Jr., but when he found out about Larry, he didn't say anything. I often wondered why.

By this time, Charles, Jr. was off into some heavy crimes. He used to ask us what we wanted to eat every weekend when Daddy was drunk and Mama hit the streets. I would always name something that I didn't get to eat on a regular basis. "Shrimp!" I would holler out. "Or steak!" Vanessa would say what she wanted, so would Johnny. Charles, Jr. would leave home and come back pushing a shopping cart full of food. He would break into the grocery store that was three blocks from our home.

One night, Charles, Jr. broke into our next-door neighbor's house. He had Johnny go through the window for him. That night there was a knock at the door. I answered it. It was our neighbor, Mr. Brown. He was very angry! He asked for Mama or Daddy. Daddy was in bed drunk as a skunk, and Mama had sneaked out on him to go partying after getting him drunk. I told him that Daddy was asleep and Mama was gone.

He said, "I know it was your brother that came in my house. You tell him I called the police."

Charles, Jr. was right down in the basement playing the albums that he had stolen from Mr. Brown. I'm surprised Mr. Brown didn't say anything about that. I was shocked! I know he heard his music playing.

I asked Charles, Jr., "Why did you do that to Mr. Brown?"

"I ain't did nothing," he said.

"Whose album is that you're playing?"

"Mind your own business," he told me.

Once Mama and Daddy were done fighting that night, and Charles, Jr. had stopped them, they questioned him about breaking into Mr. Brown's house. Charles, Jr. looked at Mama like "I don't know what you talking 'bout." Mama hit him with things like a broom or a stick. Charles, Jr. would just stand there. He never tried to hit Mama back or move. He would just stand there with no emotions. Daddy didn't push Charles, Jr. either. He said, "Did you do this, Charles?" Once he said, "No," the subject was dropped. Needless to say, Mr. Brown and his family stopped speaking to our family. Daddy tried to talk to Charles, Jr. about it, but it wasn't reaching him. Charles, Jr. went buck wild. He became very bitter toward white people. He wasn't the only one.

A few years before, there was a killing in The Valley. A teenager who was a couple of years older than Charles, Jr. murdered the paperboy who was white. Charles, Jr. and his crew came up with a plan to write this white man who was one of the few white families left in The Valley. After the paperboy was killed, most of the whites moved out one by one. Charles, Jr. and his crew wrote a note to this white man telling him that he had to pay them to continue living in The Valley.

Extortion was the charge. This stuff was a whole lot deeper than going after the neighborhood bully for knocking out my front teeth. I'll never forget the morning I skipped school because I wanted to sleep in. I heard Charles fumbling around downstairs, but I just thought he had skipped school too. I heard him leave out the back door. I got up a few minutes later and looked out of the living room window, something I did every morning. I'd check my surroundings, the weather, whose car was still home, and who could tell Mama that I didn't go to school, whatever. I had a habit of looking out of the window in the mornings.

Anyway, after staring out of the window for about ten minutes, I got back in bed. About fifteen minutes later, someone was banging on our door. It scared me! It was at the back door. I looked out of my bedroom window. White men were standing all around our house with their guns drawn. I could hear them saying, "Police! Police! Open up!" I started shaking. I knew I had to open the door, so I went to the back door and opened it.

"Who's in the house?" they forcefully asked.

"No one!" I answered.

They barged in like they owned the house. I followed them into the living room.

"Have a seat," they said. I sat down on the couch, shaking.

What's going on? I thought. *Where is Charles, Jr.?* I got up to call Daddy and Mama at work.

"You're under arrest," they said.

"For what?" I asked. Then they proceeded to tell me that I was the lookout person.

"Lookout person? Lookout for what?" I said. "You can't arrest me. I'm only thirteen years old!"

That's when I heard them talking on their walkie-talkies. "No one's in the house but a female, approximately fifteen years old."

They were all over the basement. It didn't take me long to figure out that Charles, Jr. had done something, something pretty bad for the police to be walking all through our house like they were.

"Cuff her," he said to a detective.

Wow, talk about being scared, this topped the cake! Yet the fear wasn't for me as you would think it should have been. I knew I hadn't done anything—the fear was for my brother. *Where is Charles, Jr., and what are they gonna to do to him?* I'd heard so much about how the police were trigger happy from Tammy and my uncles from Detroit. I couldn't get out of my mind what I saw when I looked out my bedroom windows. They had their guns drawn like something I'd seen on television. *God*, I started to pray in silence, *please don't let them kill my brother.*

I was taken to the police station. Once there, I was allowed to call Daddy. While waiting for him to arrive, I saw a group of cops enter the booking area. As I looked at what was going on, I caught eyes with Charles, Jr.; he wasn't dead. When Charles, Jr. saw that they had me, he started to raise his voice. "Let my sister go! Let her go now or you get nothing from me! She had nothing to do with this!"

When Daddy arrived at the station, I was released.

"Why aren't you in school?" Daddy asked me.

"I don't know. I didn't feel good," I said.

Daddy drove me back home. Charles, Jr. wasn't so lucky. He was arrested. This put a big strain on us as a family. We became the talk of The Valley. Come to find out, Charles, Jr. and his gang had the man he was extorting money from drop the money at a fire hydrant across the street from our house. When I was looking out of the window, the police thought I was the lookout person. I had no idea that anything was going down like this.

I couldn't sleep at night after Charles, Jr. was arrested. I prayed for our family every night. I prayed for Charles, Jr. Daddy did all he could to help him. With Daddy working for the city, he knew several players at the police station and city hall. Sure he was embarrassed, but this was his eldest son—that son that he went after when he was born to stop him from being adopted, that son he didn't want to grow up abandoned like he did. Charles, Jr. wasn't your average teenager gone bad. He had more good qualities than bad ones.

I remember when he got his first job. He worked as a dishwasher at a restaurant not far from home. I remember Mama talking about him dropping a few dishes, but that didn't surprise me. After the pop incident, when we were smaller, dropping a dish here and there was nothing. I always worried about Charles, Jr. when we were younger. He used to bite his fingernails until the tips of his fingers bled. He also used to twist his hair until he had bald spots at the back of his hairline. We all had nervous conditions. We experienced so much trauma in our young lives. Anyway, Charles, Jr. worked a good while at this restaurant.

By this time, though, busting dishes was a thing of the past. Everything changed so quick with Charles, Jr., from helping Daddy with the yard, learning how to work on the first car Daddy had given, wrestling, talking to girls, riding his mini-bike with his best friend Edward, hanging out with his buddies on the corner after school, to hanging with the boys from the east side and the ones from The Valley that went for bad. His whole attitude changed. He was robbing whatever he could rob. He didn't set a very good example for Johnny. With Johnny being the youngest, he was the one that got the short end of the stick. He looked up to Charles, Jr., so before long, Johnny was following in Charles, Jr.'s footsteps.

God,

I just want to say thank you for allowing me to feel your presence. Thank you for your comfort. Without the time I spend in private with you, God, I couldn't make it. You always make me feel like everything is going to be okay.

I'm worried about Charles, Jr., God. Help him. Thank you for not letting the police kill my brother, God. Things are falling apart, God. Help us, Lord. In Jesus's name, do something, God. Mama is starting to go out a

71

lot. Daddy is drinking again too much. I feel like we are in trouble, God. Save us. Amen.

He that deviseth to do evil shall be called a mischievous person. The thought of foolishness is sin: and the scorner is an abomination to men.

—Proverbs 24:8–9 (KJV)

Chapter Eight

MAMA WILL BE
MAD IF I DON'T

Charles, Jr. had been in jail for a long time. While he was locked up, I started to spend time with Larry. We talked on the phone every night. He cut hair in his mom's basement, so most of the time I was waiting for him to finish cutting hair. I enjoyed his company. He drove his mom's car in the beginning so we went places, like to the movies. We would ride down to Detroit a lot. He would shop there. His mom gave him money to buy clothes all the time. I loved the way he dressed.

I was starting to get serious about him. I had been with other boys, but it didn't last. Larry and I were becoming a couple. When I wasn't with him, I was with Tammy and her sisters or at Lisa's house, planning what we would wear to the skating rink. Even though Vanessa was my sister, we didn't hang out together. She had her friends, and I had mine. Vanessa and I didn't get along, to be honest. We argued almost daily. I had been picking at Vanessa since we were little girls. She used to wear sandals with white socks. I thought that was the weirdest thing. "You scared to show your feet?" I'd say to her. She was very quiet. Me, I was just the opposite.

We shared a bed together. I loved making her angry. Even at a young age, I let my sinful nature overtake me. Sometimes I would stick my hand in my panties and then stick it to her nose. "Smell my hand," I'd say. Then I would laugh at her. She always said that I was fast. "You and Lisa are so fast. You go' get beat up." But then I would say, "No, we ain't." This picking at each other went back and forth sometimes for hours or until Mama would say "Stop it!" or the fighting between her and Daddy stopped us.

Even though we argued a lot, Vanessa and I were rather close. When we were little girls, we played with our paper dolls every day. We were also a team in keeping Mama's house clean. I loved my sister, and I knew she loved me. We just didn't get along at times. She always wanted to wear my clothes. I would say that she couldn't, but I always gave in. "You can wear it if you don't get it dirty."

By this time, I had worked my first job. Daddy got me a job painting fences at the city's cemetery. I hated it. Not only was I hot in that sun, but I also didn't like getting that silver paint on me. Nevertheless, it was a job, and at the end of the summer, I didn't have to steal my clothes. I enjoyed going into the store to buy my clothes and not coming out shaking like a leaf on a tree. I also enjoyed going shopping with my friends.

I was so glad when that summer job was over. Daddy talked to me nearly every day about being on time for work and doing what I was paid to do without complaining and about doing the job well. I tried to make Daddy proud of me, and I feel I did. I didn't get fired. Besides, our supervisor was this young man that lived up the street from us. I learned later that he called himself liking me. I wish I'd known that when I was dying out there in that hot sun! Maybe I could have gotten some favoritism.

It was almost the next summer. Tammy's mom did house cleaning for a living. She cleaned the houses in Bloomfield and the surrounding areas. She taught us how to put an ad in the paper— the paper that the white people with money read. She taught us how to lie and say that we had experience. We used each other as references. I even lied and said that I was eighteen years old or sometimes sixteen. Once we got the job, we never told them that we would be quitting at the end of the summer. One thing about me and Vanessa, we had no problem working. We wanted nice things, and we'd work to get what we liked. Daddy and Mama worked daily, so we weren't a lazy family—none of us. We just wanted more than our money from work could buy, so we all had a hustle as well as a job. Even Daddy did odd jobs for people.

Daddy felt like we were crazy: "Just like your mother," he would say, especially when he was drinking. He meant that too. I used to think Daddy didn't know that I was stealing. One time, Mama stole some lunch meat from the local grocery store and got caught. I didn't take anything that day, so when the floor walker stopped Mama, I ran home to tell Daddy that they were taking her to jail. He didn't say a word. He just looked at me, so I went to my room.

After about thirty minutes, the phone rang. It was Mama. I heard Daddy ask her what she was doing stealing when we had a refrigerator full of food. I don't know what Mama's response was, but I do know that after a few moments, I heard Daddy say, "I should leave you in there, got my daughter out here stealing!"

When I heard that, I hurried out of my room into the kitchen where Daddy was hanging up the phone from talking to Mama.

"Daddy, please don't leave her in jail, please," I begged. "We won't do it anymore."

"Stop letting your Mama talk you into doing what you know is wrong," he said to me.

"Okay," I said.

Mama wasn't out a week and we were back at it. When I wasn't on the phone with Larry or in the stores with Mama, I was at Tammy and her sisters' house. All of them attended church. Their mom would take them there and pick them up. I started going with them. I felt the presence of the Lord every time I went. I couldn't explain why I felt I wanted to change what I was doing whenever I was there, but I knew that it was God working on me.

One Sunday I went to the altar and joined the church. After that, I got baptized. The pastor that baptized me was a well-known pastor in the city. The sound of his voice used to comfort me to the point that my eyes would start to water up. I fought back the tears because I couldn't let my friends see me crying like a baby. Sometimes I would get up and go to the bathroom to hide my emotions. But this particular Sunday, instead of going to the bathroom or out the door to the corner store, I went to the altar.

I'll never forget the night I was baptized. Mama or Daddy wasn't there, only my friends. After I was saved, I told Mama that I wouldn't be stealing with her anymore. I told Larry I would not be coming over to his mother's house to sleep with him anymore whenever she was at work. I told Tammy I would not be smoking weed with her anymore. Her aunt brought her weed when their mom, Princess Ann, was at work.

I did well throughout the summer, going to church with my friends and working. As the summer came to an end, things were about to change in the city schools. Segregation had begun in my ninth grade year, which meant I was going to be bused to an all-white school, along with the girls from the east side—the same girls that didn't like me. I didn't like this idea at all. I thought the school that I went to *was* segregated, so why did we have to change?

Anyway, the girls from the east side school were very jealous and envious of us. They thought, because we lived on the north side, we felt we were better than them. I never thought such a thing. However, I did feel that they liked to fight too much. They had that go-for-bad attitude. I acted too much like a young lady for that nonsense. Maybe that showed, I don't know. I do know that once I got to the new school, I caught hell on a regular basis—on top of the hell I went through at home!

"God," I would pray, "if they only knew that my life is worse than theirs. Help me, God. Protect me, Lord." I not only prayed at night in bed, but I also prayed to myself throughout the day. I always had a short talk with God, asking for his help. Then I kept it moving—with a lot of fear and pain. But God always came to my rescue.

Charles, Jr. had started to build a don't-mess-with-Charles, Jr. reputation in our neighborhood, but now we were dealing with the east side kids—different story. Plus, he was still locked up. I remember the first fight I got into at this school. This girl from the east side approached me in the bathroom as I was combing my hair. She came into the bathroom with about seven of her friends. Suddenly, the bathroom was filled with east side girls, but I had no idea they were all there to jump me.

"I hear you call yourself going with my boyfriend," she said.

"Who's your boyfriend?" I asked.

"Jimmy Brown," she answered.

"Jimmy told me he didn't go with you," I said. "Now would you please move out my way so I can finish my hair?"

As I was speaking, she and her girlfriends jumped me. Tammy was in the bathroom with me, but she didn't help me. She stood way back in the corner, hysterically crying, "Ya'll leave Beanie alone!" Not only were they hitting me with their fists, but they also had me on the floor, kicking me. The hall monitors rushed into the bathroom and broke up the fight. One of the principals of this school was a black man. He was one of the adults who rushed in. He grabbed this girl as the other girls were being taken out of the bathroom.

"Are you all right?" he asked me.

"No," I answered.

"Come with us," he said.

As I was leaving the bathroom, I saw Gwyn standing in the hall outside the bathroom. She didn't say anything then, but after this girl and a few of her friends got kicked out of school for two weeks and I was released from the principal's office, she had a lot to say. After this fight, I knew Tammy would never stick up for me. I didn't hold a grudge against her. I just knew she wasn't going to do nothing but talk. Instead of helping, she actually stood in the corner crying. I couldn't believe it! Gwyn, on the other hand, came up to me and asked what happened. I told her that the girl got suspended for two weeks. I knew Gwyn had my back. And because I was jumped for nothing, I was not the type of girl that liked fighting, but I also wasn't who they thought I was. I was Charles, Jr.'s sister, Patty and Charlie's daughter. I had been around fighting all my life!

This girl messed up, and I mean, she messed up dearly. I patiently waited until her two-week suspension was up, and the day she returned to school, then I had my day! Gwyn and I had already made the plans. If any other friends jumped in the fight, Gwyn would stop them. Trust me, no girl in that school wanted a beef with Gwyn. I always thanked God she was my friend.

As we changed classes after second hour, I saw that girl coming down the hall. I looked over at Gwyn when she gave me the eye contact. I took off! I ran as fast as I could toward that girl. I ran up on her and jumped on top of her. I whipped her tail, and I mean, I whipped her good!

During the fight, the same black principal pulled me off her. He was the watchdog for the black students. The white principals knew they couldn't handle the black students. He and a few more black teachers took us to the office. He already knew what this was about. He looked at me and said, "You feel better?" I confidently said, "Yes!" He knew those girls had no business touching me because I didn't bother anyone. I was a classmate of this boy we were fighting over. I didn't want him. Besides, he was too young. I liked older boys. These girls couldn't stop me from laughing and talking to whomever I wanted to. I bet they figured that out quick.

Living a godly life didn't last long. It wasn't long before Larry talked me into doing it with him, everything I said I'd no longer do. Tammy never tried to get me to smoke with them, but as I continued to go over to her house, one day I asked to hit the joint. Mama talked about the dances she would be going to and what she wanted to wear. After listening to her talk about her outfits for a while, one day I asked her if she was going shopping and I went back to stealing.

As this year continued, change in our family came back to back. Mama divorced Daddy that year. He moved out while Charles, Jr. was still locked up, only to move back in a matter of months. Mama told me that she and Daddy decided to try to make their relationship work, only to get back together and pick up where they left off—fighting—while Charles, Jr. was locked up. They didn't have him to stop them, so at times I thought they were going to kill each other.

Vanessa kept having anxiety attacks and shaking uncontrollably during the fights. Every time this happened, I always hollered for Mama and Daddy. This would get their attention, and they would stop fighting long enough for Mama to get Vanessa to the hospital. After two or three times of going to the hospital and them doing nothing when Vanessa got to shaking like she did, they would just stop fighting. Over a period of ten to fifteen minutes, Vanessa would calm down. I would also have nervous attacks. Mine were on the inside. Sometimes I felt sick in my stomach. Not only did I feel sick when the fighting went on, but I also felt this same sickness whenever I would walk out of the door of a store with stolen clothes underneath my coat. I had become a nervous wreck.

Before this year came to an end, Charles, Jr. got out of jail on bond. I was so happy when he came home! I prayed on a regular basis that he would get out. When he did, I thought life would get better. It didn't. As a matter of fact, everything got worse.

Mama met this woman that she got very close to named Lois. They both worked at the hospital. I hadn't seen any woman that close to Mama since she was in a women's club with her sister Mabel and some more women. Mama and Lois would dress alike and go out partying together. Lois was younger than Mama. She was also single. Mama started back to getting Daddy drunk so she could slip out with Lois. We were basically on our own. Charles, Jr. was getting serious about this girl from The Valley. She was Cathy's best friend. Vanessa, Johnny, and I were doing whatever we wanted to do.

One Sunday night Mama came walking through the door at three o'clock in the morning. She woke us up. A tall black man was with her. When I heard her talking to somebody, I got up. She called Daddy. "Charlie," she called out. Daddy got out of bed and went into the living room. "We need to speak with you," Mama said. She was standing next to this strange man. I was standing right behind Daddy, and Vanessa and Johnny were standing behind me. "Wayne and I are getting married. You have to leave, Charlie."

Daddy was afraid at this point. You could see that Daddy, being the little man that he was, felt intimidated by this tall black man. I felt sorry for my daddy. As I stood in the doorway of the kitchen and living room listening to Mama, I heard my brother Charles, Jr. getting up from the basement. I heard him loading a shotgun, but I didn't say a word. When I heard Charles, Jr. running up the steps, I stepped aside so he could get through the kitchen to the living room.

Charles, Jr. came through the kitchen and aimed his shotgun at Mama's so-called man. This man had a lot of nerves to come into another man's house at three o'clock in the morning. *What's really going on with Mama?* I thought. *They gotta be high or drunk!* As Charles, Jr. aimed the gun at this man, he said in a very aggressive voice, "Get the hell outta my daddy's house!" We were all looking at Charles, Jr. Wayne turned to leave out the door. Then Charles, Jr. looked at Mama and said, "You too, Mama. Get out!" Mama knew she had better not say one word because Charles, Jr. wasn't hearing it.

At that point, Daddy spoke up. "You heard my boy! Get out!" Daddy got instant courage when Charles, Jr. showed up. I don't blame him. He knew Charles, Jr. had his back. Mama and her so-called man both walked out of the front door. All of us looked at one another, not saying a word. Then we turned around and went back to bed. Later that morning, we got up for the day. Daddy got dressed and went to work. We all started our day off as we always did. No one mentioned Mama or what had happened some four hours earlier. Neither one of us went back to sleep that night, so we were tired all day long.

This wasn't the first time we hadn't gotten any sleep at night. Whenever the fights went on, we never slept, but I couldn't let that fact interfere with what I had to do when daylight hit. I had to put on that fake smile and that mask I wore daily and pretend that I was good. The clothes I wore helped me do this. People never took the time to see if I was okay. Everybody said, "You look pretty. That dress is so nice," never seeing that I was dying inside.

Anyway, I had just turned fourteen. I thought I was in love. Larry and I had been a couple for about nine months. I got pregnant by Larry. He was not the first, but he was the first one who made me pregnant. After I found out I was pregnant, I told Mama. She said that I had to get rid of it. This was a year before abortions were legal, so my first experience with an abortion was one that I will never forget. First, Mama had to come up with the money to pay for it. She knew better than to ask Daddy for his help. She decided she would go to Larry's mother and ask her to help pay—wrong move.

She went to their home and knocked on their door. I was with her. I tried to tell Mama not to do this, but she wasn't hearing me. Larry's mother answered the door. Immediately, I could tell that she was a mean lady. She said to Mama, "Who do you think you are, popping up at my house!" Mama told her that I was pregnant by her son and that I was too young to be having babies and that she needed her to help me get an abortion.

Larry's mom, Jenny, called him to the door and asked if he knew what Mama was talking about. He said, "Yes." Then she hit him upside his head and asked him where and when we were having sex. He said, "While you were at work." She kept hitting him until he finally moved out of her reach. She was so angry! She told Mama, "I'm not helping with nothing! Leave my house now!" Mama walked away from Jenny's house. I'm sure Mama felt belittled. After all, I told her not to do it her way. Being told by Jenny that she wasn't going to help didn't stop Mama though.

By the next week, Mama had come up with all the money. She took me to this lady she knew from work. The lady was a licensed practical nurse. I was scared to death when I saw all those instruments boiling in a large pot of water on top of the lady's stove. One was a wire hanger, and it was sticking out of the pot. Mama told me it wouldn't hurt, and it wasn't a baby yet because a baby doesn't start to develop until after three months. I believed her. The lady asked me to remove my clothes and get onto the kitchen table. Then she took the wire hanger from the pot and inserted it in me. She said this would allow air to enter my womb.

Later, around 2:00 a.m., I started cramping real bad. I got out of the bed and went into the bathroom. I was in so much pain. I felt like I was going to die! I tried not to wake Mama and Daddy, but I couldn't stay quiet because the pain was so bad. I started to holler out in pain. That's when I heard Daddy tell Mama, "You take my daughter to the hospital, and you take her now!"

On the way to the hospital, Mama gave me instructions on what to say and not to say. She worked at this hospital, and the last thing she wanted was for her daughter to tell that she had an abortion. Both the lady that did the abortion and Mama could lose their jobs and be prosecuted if anyone found out.

Mama looked at me. "Bean, don't you tell them nothing!" All I could think about, other than the pain, was Daddy. Daddy picked me up from home on the morning of the abortion on his lunch break. Mama had it all planned out. After he picked me up, he was supposed to drop me off at Mama's job.

On the way driving me to Mama's job, Daddy said to me, "Lavinia, you don't have to do this."

"Yes, I do," I said. "Mama will be mad if I don't."

"It's not your mother's baby," he said.

He didn't say another word, and neither did I. When we arrived at the hospital, I got out of the car and got into Mama's car. She was walking toward the car. She and Daddy didn't say a word to each other. Now I was wondering if I should have listened to Daddy, but it was too late. After I was examined at the hospital, the doctor entered the room and the first thing he asked was "Has anybody touched you in any way?" I told him, "No." He knew that I was lying, but I had to say what Mama told me to say. Then he informed me that I had just had a miscarriage.

After that experience, I became very depressed. I resented Mama, yet I never said a word to her about it. I went on with my life. How the girls at school found out about the abortion, I have no idea. But they knew. I never told them that it was true. I just let them talk. My closest girlfriends knew about it though. They would say to me, "I heard you were pregnant."

This year in school was a mess. The white people didn't want the black kids in their neighborhood. They bombed the buses one night. At least ten buses were burned down. That didn't stop the kids from being bused though. It only made the tension between the black kids and white kids worse. Daddy moved out after the abortion, this time for good. He moved into this apartment building that was not only in the worst section of the east side but it was also a hoe house. The owner of the building made Daddy an offer to buy the building. The hoes loved him. Daddy stayed so drunk that they never paid him rent. About this same time, Charles, Jr. got his girlfriend pregnant. She was Cathy's best friend. Even though there was a lot of chaos going on in our home, Cathy and Angie still came over to our house a lot.

Mama stayed close with her sisters and brothers. As a matter of fact, Uncle James moved from Detroit to live with us. That didn't last long. He didn't get along with "Super Fly," that's what we called Mama's new husband, Wayne. Mama married him not long after Daddy moved out. They were some real country bumpkins. He and Mama would spray paint their shoes pink, green, gold, or whatever color to match their outfit. I would say to Mama, "Why are you dressing up like that?" I couldn't believe they actually thought they looked good! They went out partying every weekend. Mama started smoking weed with him. He was a pothead. She even started smoking cigarettes. Mama never smoked or drank when she was younger. Now she was "Ms. Cool."

Charles, Jr. married his girlfriend only to get into trouble again. It was Christmastime, and his new wife was complaining that they had nothing for Christmas, not even a tree. Charles, Jr. couldn't take being pressured. He not only broke into the apartment of two white women, but he also raped them and took their car, tree, and presents.

It was my understanding, from Daddy, that Charles, Jr. came up to his job and told him to come look at the new car he just bought. Daddy said to me, "Lavinia, the boy thought the car was his!" I couldn't figure out what was going on with Charles, Jr. "Did he have blackouts?" Whatever the case, he was in jail again. His daughter was born around Christmastime. His wife did get her tree that Christmas.

By now, I was emotionally bankrupt. I spent lots of time with God. Our family had fallen apart. Vanessa was starting to come out of that shell she was hiding in. She was going with this guy that was on drugs. Johnny was hanging with the worse family in the neighborhood. After Charles, Jr. got locked up this time, we all knew he was going to prison. His wife was devastated. So was I. But by now, I had learned how to hide my true feelings. I smoked weed and cigarettes.

Mama was hosting fashion shows, and she had turned me on to taking valium. She wanted me to model, and at the last minute, I got nervous and told her to get somebody else because I couldn't do it. "Here, take this," she said. It was a little pill. I took it and swallowed it. My feelings started to change. I went from being scared to not only wanting to model my outfits but I also wanted to model everybody else's clothes. The next day I looked around Mama's bedroom for some more valium. I found a whole bottle of them on her dresser. I started taking them every day.

I still liked going roller skating, so I went on a regular basis. I loved looking cute, so I kept enemies. I even got jumped again. This time I have no idea why, other than the fact that I looked too good and the teenagers from the east side didn't like it—nothing but pure jealousy. This time Vanessa jumped in and got beat up with me. When she saw those broads take off running on the skating floor with no skates on, she knew they were headed toward me. Vanessa ran toward me in her skates and yelled, "Leave my sister alone!" They started hitting me. Vanessa took her skates off and started hitting them with her skates. The fight eventually broke up. Those broads weren't allowed back in the skating rink for years.

It took years for those east side broads and dudes to realize that just because we lived in The Valley, our family wasn't having their mess. Charles, Jr., Vanessa, Johnny, and I stood up for ourselves. I had to be pushed to the limit before I fought back; but once I reached my limit, I acted just like Charles, Jr.—I flipped.

Dear God,

Thank you for getting me through another day. Thank you for your mercy. Thank you for loving me, for allowing me to feel your comfort. For if it had not been for your strength, I couldn't have come through the things I'm going through as a teenager.

Sometimes I feel like it's too much, God. Sometimes I wonder, Do you care? If so, then why won't you turn things around for me? I want so bad to do what's right, yet I fall short. I pray that you understand because I don't. I pray for protection for my family and for Charles. Let him be okay in jail, God. Work things out for our best. Forgive us, Lord. Amen.

Fear thou not; for I am with thee: be not dismayed; for I am thy God: I will strengthen thee; yea, I will help thee; yea, I will uphold thee with the right hand of my righteousness.

—Isaiah 41:10 (KJV)

Chapter Nine

I DO

It was finally time for me to enter into high school. Tenth grade was off to a very good start. I hung out with all of the cool kids. I missed Charles, Jr., but I managed to get to class and do my schoolwork despite missing him. I worked cleaning houses all summer, so I bought some awesome new clothes.

Mama had totally abandoned us. She was so wrapped up in Super Fly that she paid us no attention, unless he had a problem with something we were doing, then she would call herself checking us. By this time, though, none of us listened to her. We felt she didn't care about us at all. She started letting Super Fly put locks on the freezer. We couldn't eat their food. Mama only cooked for him. We had to fend for ourselves.

Next thing we knew, Super Fly called himself remodeling our home. To me, he tore up the place. I didn't like any of his so-called remodeling. He had Mama buy this red velvet furniture that was trimmed in white. It looked like some kind of funeral home furniture. No class whatsoever! They had the nerve to think this mess was nice. Our house looked like it belonged to a junkyard owner. Now when we first moved into our house, it was nice.

Daddy's taste was all over it then. My Daddy was a lot classier than Super Fly!

I started dying my hair auburn a couple of years earlier; but this year, I dyed it lighter and lighter every time I touched up my roots. My hair was never the same color. I dyed it back to black once, and this funny kid that always made us laugh in the mornings on our way to school called me Little Richard. I always wore it cut short, and I wasn't too fond of him mocking me. I didn't see black hair again for many years, more than fifteen. I didn't like the black any longer, so I died my hair red.

This year I did one of the dumbest things I'd ever done in my life. I was on my way to gym class, and this kid named Thomas asked me if he could put a gun in my purse until after class. I agreed but was not really giving much thought to what I was doing. He put the gun inside my purse, and I put my purse in my locker. Then I changed into my gym suit and went to gym class. This girl I shared lockers with came into the locker room after me. She must have noticed that my purse was heavier than usual. She looked inside my purse. Then she told my gym teacher I had a gun in my purse. The gym teacher went and told the principal.

I was called down to the principal's office. The principal had the gun with him. I told him who put the gun in my purse. All three of us were kicked out of school and had to attend the IIP school: institute for ignorant people. We called it that because of the stupid things we did to get kicked out of regular school. I was kicked out the rest of the semester. Thomas was kicked out the rest of the year, and the boy that brought the gun to school was suspended for good.

I had to enroll in a school where all the bad kids went. I felt sick when I realized what I had done to myself. "Great! Now I'll be going to school with the very girls that hated me!" I spent a lot of time with God in the morning before I got up to go to school. Sometimes I'd cry to the point of being hysterical. I hated this school. I was so out of place, but I had to go there in order to graduate with my class. Larry would pick me up from school most days. The boys at this school didn't like him.

One day he picked me up and got into a fight with another boy who liked me. The girls were constantly picking at me. All of them liked this boy from the west side. He always tried to talk to me. His name was Charles, like my brother's. He would always stick up for me. Whenever the haters made their smart remarks about jumping me, he would tell them, "You better not touch her!" They would roll their eyes and say nasty things to me, but not one of them put their hands on me.

This boy, Charles, regulated them very well. He got on my nerves, but he was cool, how he protected me. If all these girls weren't fighting over him every week, he might have been likable. I did manage to get my credits and get out of that school—thank God! Once back at my regular school, I found nothing was the same for me. I no longer wanted to be "little miss schoolgirl." I started stealing a lot more and smoking and getting high all the time.

Mama was still giving fashion shows at the local clubs and churches. She asked me, Vanessa, and some of our friends to model. When it was show time, I got scared. I told Mama to get somebody else to model my clothes. She gave me another valium. Thirty minutes later, I started feeling good and started modeling. I met this girl named Rosie that reminded me of a black hippie. She wore the shingles hanging from the sleeves on her jackets, the jeans with the holes in them, and the scarves around her head like that black hippie that played the guitar in the late seventies. She hung around these white girls.

One day I asked her why she dressed like that and if she wanted me to show her how to dress. Not only did I teach her how to dress, but she also became my stealing partner. I put Mama down. Well . . . she put me down when she met Super Fly. She was too busy chasing after him to go stealing with me, but she was in my closet every weekend. "Bean, can I wear this?" We wore the same size for a long time. "Dog, Ma! Can I wear it first?" I always gave in and let her wear whatever she wanted, although sometimes I would just let her keep whatever she wore because I couldn't stand wearing nothing that wasn't new, especially if I didn't wear it first—I didn't play that. I stole it. I wore it first! Mama, I just let her keep what she wore because she always got it dirty or it smelled like her.

Anyway, this girl didn't need to be stealing since her parents were business owners. They had money already, but she knew her parents weren't going to pay for her to dress like I dressed. Even though we both had jobs, we still stole our clothes. She tried to go to the stores once without me and got caught. Later both of us got hired at a well-known department store—one that most couldn't afford to shop at. When she worked the dressing room, she would have what she wanted waiting for me. I would get her clothes and mine.

Vanessa had been to modeling school, so she taught all of us how to model. Mama would schedule rehearsals for us to learn how to walk and turn. Rosie started modeling with us. Rosie and I became best friends. We did everything together—work, party, steal—everything. We even threw parties and charged a fee to get in to make more money. We also sold refreshments. We always made money from our parties. I was learning from Mama how to make money and have fun at the same time. I loved it! Rosie became good at modeling. Most people would say she was a cloned Lavinia. I did teach her style, though. She was a long way from that black hippie I first met. I taught her how to sit, talk, walk, smile, and look good.

We had jobs as nurse's aides in a nursing home for a while. We were only fourteen, but we lied and said that we were eighteen. We worked from three thirty in the afternoon until eleven o'clock at night. Back then, it was easy to lie about your age. Vanessa and her friend worked as aides in the nursing home first. My friend Lisa also worked with us. All of us told the employer that we were eighteen years old.

I was very popular, I must say. People who weren't envious of me liked hanging around me. I loved being that "one"—the one all my friends wanted to hang around with. I was not only dressed to the hilt, but I also stayed high. The pills Mama had given me that Sunday to model sat right on her turntable where she kept her perfume on the dresser. Every morning before leaving for school, I would get at least four of them, two for me and two for Rosie. We would stop at the local store and buy two wine coolers and smoke a joint. Then we would attempt to go to school. Sometimes we would leave school after the second or third hour.

This was the year that Vanessa was graduating from high school. She was working and going with this dude that was on drugs from The Valley. There were three of them, all brothers, and every last one of them got high. Vanessa had changed by this time. She went from playing the clarinet in the marching band at school to getting high and going with a straight-up drug addict. All of us were getting high. There was no "say no to drugs" in those days. If you didn't use drugs, you were a square. Everybody used something. That was the norm for us. Life was fun, so we thought.

Charles, Jr. ended up going to prison for a long time. He was sentenced to twenty-five to forty years. His wife had a little girl right after he went to jail. The effect of Charles, Jr. going away was like one of us had died. Even though I'd never experienced the death of a brother or close family member, this was the closest I felt I'd ever come. I talked to Larry on the phone more and more about having a baby. I soon got pregnant again. This time when I told Mama I was pregnant, she told me, "Well, you'll just have to have it because I'm a Christian now, and I ain't killing no more babies." When she said that, I thought to myself, *You told me it wasn't a baby until after the third month!* I also thought, *I know you ain't because I'm older now and I'm not gonna let you.*

Besides, I resented Mama around this time. At times I felt like I hated her. She had no respect for us. All she did was stay in the room with the door closed with Super Fly. You heard the sounds of sex every day. It was sickening! I hated being home with them. "You and Larry will have to get married," she said. So I told him what Mama said and also called Daddy and told him. I loved Daddy and tried to include him in my life as much as possible. Sometimes I think I got pregnant just to hurt Mama.

Then I wanted to be loved and to love someone. I felt that my own child would provide that love. Then I also thought I loved Larry. Reality had not set in. I was all messed up. Our family had been destroyed. I wanted out. *I'm grown . . . She don't tell me what to do . . . She don't care anyway . . . All she care about is Super Fly . . .* is what I thought. After Mama said that we had to get married, Larry asked me. I said, "Yes." I thought I wanted to be a married woman. I learned—quick—that being married wasn't as easy as I thought.

It was the last summer before my twelfth grade year in school. I was working for this white couple in Bloomfield, cleaning their house. One day I called Larry from work when I was cleaning their bedroom. I always snooped through their drawers in their bedroom. Not that I had planned to steal anything, I was just nosey. This day I saw five $100 bills.

I said to Larry, "Man . . . it must be nice to have money . . . to be able to have hundred dollar bills just lying around!"

"Whatcha mean?" Larry said.

"These white people have five $100 bills just lying in their top drawer."

The bills were actually underneath the lining in the drawer. I was supposed to be cleaning, not on their telephone.

Larry said, "Take it!"

"No, these people might know that it's there. They may have put it there on purpose."

"I'll take it!" Larry said. "Just open the garage door when I get there and close it back when I pull in."

He knew where to come because he had brought me to work several times. I continued to clean after we hung up the phone. From time to time, I'd check to see if he had arrived. When Larry finally pulled up, I opened the garage door quickly so he wouldn't be seen by neighbors. Once he was inside the house, he put on gloves. I took him to the bedroom and showed him the money.

He took it, looked at me, and said, "Lavinia, if this money is here, there is a lot more money in this house."

Then he started destroying the house, looking for money. He stole everything, from watches to rings to money and the stereo system. If it fit into his car, he took it.

"No, stop! What are you doing?" I had let Larry in, and he went crazy!

Larry said, "You told me that this guy is a prosecutor, didn't you?"

"Yes," I said.

"I'll just make it look like somebody he sent to prison did this," he told me.

"What do you mean?" I said.

Larry left and went to the trunk of his car and pulled out a tire iron. He came back inside and hit the big fish tank that was in their den. Water drained from the tank all over the place. Then he broke dishes in the kitchen. He broke up everything in his sight. I was a nervous wreck. *I'm scared! What if they come home? What if the neighbors saw him pull into the garage?* All sorts of thoughts were running through my mind.

"Larry, what have you done?"

Then he took a crayon from the kids' bedroom and wrote on the walls BLACKMAN, I TOLD YOU I'D GET YOU.

After he finished, he said, "Let's go! Leave the door unlocked. Tell 'em you had to leave early because you didn't feel good. Leave a note."

I wrote a note, but before we left out of the door, he took the note and balled it up and threw it on the floor. Then we pulled out of the garage. I was praying that no one would see us. Once we were home, we took everything to the house of Larry's mother and put all the money and jewelry into a metal box in her attic. I said to Larry, "Don't tell nobody what we did or what's up here." He agreed. Then he took me home. I was very nervous, but I played it off.

Later, around six o'clock in the evening, Mr. Blackman phoned me at my home to question me. "I got ill and came home about noon," I said. He asked whether I locked the door and how I got home. I told him that I thought I locked the door and that my stepdad picked me up. Then he told me what happened, and I pretended to act like I was concerned and shocked. He was very upset about his house being destroyed. I could hear it in his voice. Plus, he had made it known.

A few days later, two detectives came to our house. Wayne and I were the only two at home. He answered the door. The police asked for me. Wayne called me to the door. The police asked me all sorts of questions. I told all sorts of lies.

"How did you get home?"

"My stepdad picked me up because I was sick. I'm pregnant, and Mama told me I had to quit."

They asked Wayne whether he picked me up. Without hesitation, he said, "Yes."

Why he lied for me, I'll never know. When the police left, Wayne didn't even ask me what I had done. He just looked at me and went to Mama and his room to smoke some weed, something he did all the time while Mama worked. The police never came back. Larry, on the other hand, didn't do what we said we were going to do. He tried to sell some of the rings. I don't know why because we didn't need any money.

About a week after the robbery, we went to the drive-in movie to see a movie that we had already seen for the third time. I'll never forget that night. After he dropped me off at my home and returned to his home, he called me, screaming, "Lavinia, Jenny's house is on fire! Jenny's house is burning down!"

"Go in and get our money!" I said.

"I can't, it's burning too bad!"

"What? What do you mean it's burning too bad?" I said.

I wouldn't imagine that the fire was that bad. That Saturday morning, Larry came and got me. The fire department said not to enter the house because it wasn't safe. Jenny had already been there. She had gone back to her mother's house, so we went inside the house. I wanted to see the attic. We made our way to the attic, and the fire was very bad. But metal doesn't burn, and the inside of that box was empty!

I said, "Larry, who did you tell about what we did?"

"No one," he said.

"You had to. Whoever did this was after the money we had. How did the fire start?"

"The firemen said somebody threw a bomb in my closet," he said.

I knew then that whoever set his mom's house on fire was making a statement to him. Larry wore very nice clothes. The fire started in his closet. That following weekend, we went roller skating. When Larry went to the snack bar, this dude came up to me and said, "I hear you and Larry are getting married. What ya'll go' do—live off welfare?" The look on his face told me that he set the fire. I told Larry how I felt, and he said to me, "You don't know what you're talking about, so leave it alone."

Everything changed after the fire. Daddy got sick, really sick. Both of his kidneys needed to be removed. He had no one to help him. He had to go to a hospital in Detroit daily to have kidney dialysis. I didn't think that I was the best driver, but I had no choice. I woke up every morning at four o'clock and got my daddy to the hospital. Sometimes he would just stare at me. I knew what he was thinking. He couldn't believe that the one child that he dogged throughout her childhood was the one who stepped up to the plate to help take care of him.

Daddy used to call me "your mama's pet." "You tell everything you know," he would say whenever he was drunk. Yet when he needed his clothes ironed every week, he hired me. Whenever he wanted one of his kids to take the city job for the summer, he came to me. Sometimes I used to think Daddy didn't like me. He didn't talk to any of us much, except for Charles, Jr. when he was teaching him how to do the work that men did around the house. Johnny was too young for Daddy to teach him the things he taught Charles, Jr.; Charles, Jr. was Johnny's teacher, and the things he taught Johnny led him right to the juvenile home!

Angie and Cathy were still close to us, and they continued to visit us. Even though Angie was rebelling at home, Cathy had Uncle Ben and his father. She would walk to their house whenever she felt too much was going on at our house. Even when they came over, Mama would be in the room with that door closed. She didn't even care about them hearing her having sex, and at three or four o'clock in the afternoon, you always smelled weed coming from their room. I always felt ashamed whenever my cousins came to visit.

At this point, Mama and her sisters were all dating no-good men. They were all single, except Mama, who would have been better off if she were. I was doing everything I could to get out of Mama's house as soon as possible. I didn't feel like I had a home. I continued to get up and get Daddy to the hospital. One morning Mama was up. She was going to the bathroom. She said, "Your daddy is a lucky man to have you, Bean." She had to get up much earlier now because she worked for a major car manufacturing plant. She had to clock in at 6:00 a.m. She made a lot more money working for them, but she blew it pleasing Super Fly.

My relationship with Mama was nothing like it used to be. I was very disappointed in her. In between taking Daddy to the hospital and having morning sickness, Larry and I got married. In the morning before we went to the courthouse, Larry asked me if I loved him. I wanted to say no because I really didn't, but there was no turning back now, so I lied and said that I loved him. We didn't have a place to live. We didn't have anything. Jenny didn't want any part of this marriage. She was disappointed about her house being burned down. She knew the truth. Everybody knew it but Larry. After the way he dealt with his mom's house being burned down, I started to see that I had no respect for him. *Charles, Jr. wouldn't let somebody burn Mama's house down* is what I thought to myself, but I married Larry anyway.

Daddy treated me and Larry better than everybody. He offered us an apartment in his building, even though it was infested with roaches and mice. I appreciated my dad. I was going to make the best of it. Larry and I bought paint and put down rat poison and sprayed roach killer inside the apartment. We did all we could to make this apartment livable. Day by day, I became more and more depressed.

As the months sailed by, Jenny's house had been rebuilt. Even though she had taken back the car she gave Larry for marrying me, she saw I felt that she could use us to keep her house from being burned down again, so she offered us a place to live, upstairs. It was a two-family flat. She didn't live at home because she took care of her mother who was blind. Jenny never even thought I was pregnant by Larry, so I knew the only reason she offered us a place to stay was for her own self-interests. She was a mean lady. She treated Larry like he was a kid. I didn't like this. Her house was very nice, clean, and neat though. Even before the fire, Jenny had a beautiful home. Now it was all brand new. From the house to the furniture, to me, her house was looking better than it did before the fire.

Now I had big emotions to deal with. I was pregnant and couldn't get high to cover up my feelings, and it hurt. For the first time, since that time when I was ten years old and wanted to be with a normal family because of Mama and Daddy's fighting and I went to live with Aunt Felicia for two weeks and went right back home because I felt like Mama needed me, I was moving out of the one place I called home. I was about to close this chapter in my life and begin to live the life that shaped me for the life to come.

> Dear God,
>
> I am so afraid. I'm so confused. I know that I have to move on to grow up. I'm about to be a mother, and I have to provide an environment for my child that is suitable. I'm stepping out on the hope that you are going with me. I don't know how I feel about my husband, but I do know that my child comes first and what's best for him. Continue to watch over me, God, as you have always done. In your precious son Jesus's name, I pray. Amen.

The Lord bless you and keep you; the Lord make his face shine on you and be gracious to you; the Lord turn his face toward you and give you peace.

—Numbers 6:24–26 (NIV)

Chapter Ten

THE WHITE FUR COAT

Once Jenny's house was totally rebuilt, it was gorgeous! I was seven months pregnant when Larry and I moved in. We lived upstairs. We bought a bedroom set for our bedroom. Jenny gave us the furniture that wasn't burned from the house fire: the living room set and the dining room table and chairs. Her place looked so nice. She must have hired an interior decorator. I loved her custom-made drapes. She had class. I liked her style.

Jenny didn't easily let people into her world. She didn't like me, and I could tell. Besides, she didn't have a problem with making it known right in front of me. She would say things like, "I don't even know if it's Larry's baby." Then she would look at me so viciously. It scared me. *Oh my god! This lady is so mean!* She was meaner than my daddy's brother, Uncle Kevin.

I always wanted her to like me, not because she was a Parker but because I really liked how she operated. She was a strong woman. She didn't take no mess from her sons or anyone else. She was her own woman, a controller; and I loved it! From the beginning, she didn't like me though. She thought I was a gold digger and was out to invade her space. I felt she didn't trust that her son was smart enough to know if he was being fooled or not. I think she remembered when Mama came to her door asking for money to pay for an abortion.

So Larry's mama, Jenny, as he called her, was about to let me into her world. I knew letting us move into her house was for her own benefit, not ours. I was beginning to have very negative feelings for her son, but I didn't say anything. I just continued to act as if I was happy, but I wasn't. I was pregnant, and how I felt didn't matter. I had to do what was best for my unborn child.

I couldn't continue to live in Mama's house. Super Fly ran that. I didn't want to live with the alcoholics and hoes in Daddy's apartment building either, so Jenny's house was the best place for a decent home for my baby. I was so proud to be pregnant. Everybody thought that I was happy because I married Larry Parker. I wasn't. My feelings for him started to fade after the fire. I didn't see that strength in him that I always saw in my brother, Charles, Jr., especially after Jenny's house caught fire. Larry didn't have that strength, and I was very disappointed in him.

At times I wondered what became of the white people whose home he destroyed. I knew when the fire took place that Larry was reaping what he had sown. Nothing was the same for him after that fire. Jenny never replaced the clothes he lost. He often spoke about that, how Jenny's insurance covered everything lost but she didn't give him a dime to buy more clothes. To be honest, I didn't blame her.

I could not believe that Larry tried to sell some of the jewelry and took some of his so-called friends with him to show them what he was trying to sell. We didn't need the money. We had money. So what was his purpose? Stupid move, in my opinion. But who was I? He thought he was the slick one.

Well, that dude from the snack bar at the skating rink was right. Larry and I applied for welfare. We had no choice. We had no jobs and a baby on the way. I knew of young mothers being on welfare, but to be married and my husband is on welfare with me? I wasn't feeling it. Daddy would never have applied for such a thing. My daddy said that a man was supposed to work for a living, be a provider for his family.

My daddy talked about how he used to be a garbageman and came home smelling so bad that he couldn't even come in the house. He took off his work clothes at the door and went straight to the bathroom to shower. My daddy said that a real man will do what he had to do to provide for his family. I was always proud of my daddy for providing a roof over my head, but he was sick now, and he needed me, and I wasn't going to let him down. For me, a seventeen-year-old, I had my plate full; but like Daddy taught me, I did what I had to do. Vanessa was off in some other state doing her thing. Charles, Jr. was in prison, and Johnny was still in The Valley with Mama and was terrorizing Super Fly.

I remember having my baby shower at Mama's house. Nothing was right. Vanessa wasn't there, and Mama was in and out of the house during the shower. She was too busy trying to follow Super Fly around. My girlfriends came and brought gifts, but I missed my sister. I missed my brothers. I missed my mama and daddy. I missed my family. What happened to our family? I knew how to put that mask on and pretend that I was happy at the baby shower, but I was actually hurting—just like I was hurting at my wedding reception that we had at Mama's church.

After Larry and I got married, my insides were screaming, "Help me! Somebody please help me!" Jenny came to the reception, but the vibe she gave me was not welcoming. This was before she invited us to live in her home. While I lived there, I tried to be a wife and a mother. My girlfriends made life a little easier. Rosie and Kim often visited. Kim was a friend that I went to grade school with, and I met up with her again in high school. She was in love with one of Larry's friends. We were both pregnant, and we enjoyed talking about our babies. We went through maternity school together, a school for young mothers back then.

I had my baby before she did. I had a son. He was so precious to me. I loved him as soon as I saw him. I remember when I got out of the hospital after I gave birth and Larry picked us up. "Take me to your grandmother's house," I said. Jenny was living with her mother at time. He told me that the doctor said for me to go straight home. I said, "No. Take me to Jenny's." He took me there, and when I got inside the house, I had my son in my arms. I spoke to Jenny. Then I placed my son into her arms. It was February and cold, so she had to unwrap the blankets from him. When she opened them, she was so excited. "Oh my god! My grandson!" She was so proud and happy. There was no more denying Larry Parker, Jr. He looked just like a Parker.

Anyway, I went home and got into bed with my new son right next to me. I loved my son from the very beginning. He was my son, and nobody could say that the love I finally felt, that I'd never felt before, wasn't real. Loving my baby had no conditions, just love. I didn't feel that sick feeling I always felt with love in the past. I wasn't home more than three hours, and Jenny popped up again. It was her house. She still lived downstairs. She wasn't home often. He came in with a load of things for her new grandson.

I mean, I had never seen such quality things before. The sales tags had famous name brands on them. She gave them to me, and then she picked up her grandson from off the bed. I got up and started going through all the bags. As I opened some of the packages, my first thought was *My god! This lady* do *got money! These things cost money, and I mean money!* Inside a box in one of the bags was a beautiful baby white fur coat.

After Larry, Jr. was born, Larry started attending barbers college. He was gone all day during the weekday. I didn't care because I enjoyed being home alone with my new baby. I still had to get Daddy to the hospital for his dialysis every morning before daybreak, so I bundled up my son, and off we went to pick up Daddy. He bought a car for me to get him back and forth from Detroit. We did this for at least eleven months. Larry started going to this lady's house when he was supposed to be at school. Her name was Rena, and she was a friend of his from previous years, but I heard it through the grapevine that he was going to her house and they were more than friends.

Anyway, I was spending most of my time being a new mom and taking Daddy to the hospital. I found myself liking playing house. I stopped stealing after I had my first baby. I learned how to sew in school, so I started making some of my clothes. Mama would bring me a pattern and some material every other week to make her something. She felt she could do that because she was the one who bought the sewing machine. Mama would come up with these weird ideas for her outfits. "Bean, I want you to leave this sleeve off the jumpsuit," or "One leg blue and the other leg white." I always called Mama and her husband country bumpkins. "Ma," I'd say, "that don't look right. Ma, you know that's some crazy mess!" But she was Patty, and whatever Patty wanted, Patty got.

I even found myself doing the best I could to get it right for her. Sometimes I would say to myself, "Lord, this suit looks like a clown suit." But when Mama saw the finished piece, she would proudly say, "I told you, Bean, you could do it." In her own little way, Mama made me feel like I could do anything I set my mind to do. I guess I could do anything, if I could dress her and she liked it. Super Fly would spray paint their shoes to match their outfits, and you couldn't tell Mama or him that they weren't sharp. They partied all day and night on Saturday and went to church on Sunday morning. Mama always wanted to take Larry, Jr. to church with her once he was a toddler. She loved him so much. I believe it made Mama feel a sense of pride that her grandson was a Parker.

Daddy finally stopped drinking after his kidneys were removed. The doctors said he would die if he continued. I started spending more time with my dad than I ever spent. He started to enjoy life. He had a new grandson whom he loved. Whenever I took Daddy to the hospital for dialysis, my baby was right in the car with me. I'd never seen my daddy with a baby.

When Larry Jr. and I went to Daddy's apartment building, I noticed how all the drunks and hoes acted around my baby. Larry, Jr. brought joy and life into their lives. Even the worst drunk among them, nicknamed Wine, from across the street, stopped drinking whenever we came around and didn't start back up until Larry, Jr. and I left Daddy's. The respect they had was amazing. It had been hard on Daddy, for him not being able to drink with his friends. My uncle James was living in Daddy's apartment building. He moved with Mama and Super Fly when Grandma down in Detroit died.

After a few months, Mama went to Daddy behind Super Fly's back and asked him if he would help JayJay. Daddy not only took him in and helped him get on his feet, but he also helped him get a job with the city. Uncle James was hired as a garbageman, like Daddy was when he started with the city. Uncle James kept the job and got his own apartment upstairs in Daddy's building. He stopped shooting up drugs, but he drank and smoke lots of weed daily. He was still my favorite uncle. He was cool. Whenever I wanted to get high, all I had to do was to go my uncle's house. He would smoke weed for hours.

Weed wasn't really my thang—so I realized. It made me feel weird, unless I had some valium and a wine cooler with it. I could never smoke it alone. I was a valium lover. It relaxed me. I was constantly on the move all day. I never slowed down until I went to sleep. Speaking of sleep, one night I went to bed after putting Larry Jr. to sleep. I knew I had to take Daddy to dialysis in the morning, so I went to bed earlier than Larry. This particular night I heard one of his friends knock at the door. They always came over to get high with him. I always woke up whenever one of them came over. Larry opened the door for them. I listened to hear who it was. It was his best friend. He had come to speak with Larry.

His friend told him the truth, the truth that I had already known. He told Larry that two of his other so-called friends threw that bomb inside Jenny's house. Larry got very upset when his friend told him the news. Then I heard his friend leave. I got out of bed and went to talk to Larry. He had tears in his eyes. Then he told me what his friend said.

I looked at Larry and said, "That don't surprise me. I told you this that night at the skating rink."

Larry said to me, "What should I do?"

"I don't know what you're gonna do, but I know what I'm doing. Me and my son are leaving!"

After that night, I no longer looked at Larry as a man that could protect me and my son. I felt he was too weak. No way would Charles, Jr. ever ask me what he should do! I didn't leave Larry right away, but after that day, I lost all respect for him as a man. I'd never felt I loved him since I married him. Sure, as a young girl, he was my first love—puppy love. Now I was a woman and a mother, and I needed a man. My problem was that I was screwed up by this time, so I started to creep on Larry. I felt he was doing the same thing to me whenever he would leave to go to school and never made it. I would call the school and checked, so I felt justified with what I was doing.

My friend, Kim, and I went out on weekends. She would ask her mom to watch her daughter. Larry, Jr. would be asleep when I left home to go out. His dad would watch him. I was attracted to another man that was a photographer at one of the clubs where Kim and I hung out. For weeks, we went to this club, and he paid me no attention. Then one night he took a picture of me and started talking to me. I instantly felt something wasn't right with this man, but the drugs and alcohol had me ignore that feeling.

He asked me to come down to Detroit that following week to see him. Kim and I planned for the visit on the way home. She said she would go with me, so the two of us went to visit him. We took our babies with us. We set out to leave that night after Larry left for school one day. We found the photographer's apartment down in Detroit. Kim and I frowned at each other and thought, *This building looks just as bad as Daddy's apartment building.* (The things we do when we are young.)

Anyway, Kim and I went inside. We took our babies inside this filthy building. When he opened the door, I realized that I wasn't feeling him like I thought I did at the club. He looked totally different. The way he carried himself was nothing like I thought he did when he walked through the club taking pictures. The lighting in the club deceived me. (Or was I too high to notice?) This guy was a two-bit hustler; I learned that quick. But still, I went into his bathroom with him while Kim watched our babies. His place was so small that it looked like we were inside a motel room.

He turned to kiss me. As he kissed me, I noticed that he was wearing a weave. That's what attracted me to him—his hair. In the dark, he looked like the *real* Super Fly, but in this bathroom, he scared the daylight out of me. He was a bum. He even stunk. I got out of that bathroom as quick as I could and got my baby out of that building in a hurry. What was I thinking? I didn't know anything about this man, yet I had my baby off in an apartment with a man I knew nothing about.

This was one of those nights that I spent time in prayer thanking God that nothing happened, thanking him for protecting my baby. I used very poor judgment that day. I continued to creep on Larry. I went out with my girls every weekend. We were young. We wanted to have fun on weekends. My other girlfriend and I made some of our outfits to wear whenever we went out. All along, I was planning to leave Larry. He was never the Larry I was attracted to again after that fire. He turned me completely off.

Had someone thrown a bomb into Mama's house, Charles, Jr. would be livid—an eye for eye—and quiet as it's kept, so would I. "Handle your business" is what I wanted to say to Larry, but I knew that wasn't his nature. So I had to go. I didn't feel protected. I didn't feel I was with a man. He had shown me that he was softer than me. I saw a glimpse of his weakness when he got into a fight in front of our house in The Valley.

I remember one of Charles, Jr.'s friends liked me, and he picked at Larry every time he came over and Larry was at our house. Larry always got into situations that he couldn't get out of. He started a fight with Charles, Jr.'s friend and got beat up. I was mad at Charles, Jr. for not breaking it up, for letting Larry get beat up. "It wasn't my business," Charles, Jr. said. "You could have helped him," I said. I was angry with Charles, Jr. for days after that happened.

Then there was the time we were down in Detroit at the movie theater. These dudes lined the wall of the entrance of the theater. One of them said, "You sho' look good, baby! Why don't you be with a real man?" Then he called Larry a punk. Larry hastily turned toward the dude. I said, "Just keep walking." Now what was he going to do with all those dudes standing around? I could never figure out why he always got into fights, knowing he was going to lose. I wasn't about to be fighting, that was not my style—I was a lady. Now if I had to handle my business, that was a different story; but if you are not a fighter, there's more than one way to skin a cat. Daddy taught me that.

One day, when Daddy and I got to the hospital, the doctor came inside the room. He told Daddy that a kidney donor had been found for him. I was so happy for him because earlier I had offered one of my kidneys, but it wasn't a match. After the transplant, the doctor told Daddy that he would have to go to a nursing home for a short while to recover if he couldn't get anyone to help him daily. I wanted a way out of my marriage, so I said to myself, "No way will my daddy be in a nursing home. Not if I can help it!" I suggested that Daddy sell his apartment building and the two of us could get a place together. He agreed.

Daddy often talked to me about my husband. "A man is supposed to work. A man is supposed to provide for his family. If you're not happy, I don't want you to live your entire life in misery like I did. Life is too short to be unhappy."

I was never dishonest with Daddy. I told him my plan—my plan to help him get well and my plan to go to cosmetology school. I told Larry that my son and I were leaving. I told him that my daddy needed my help, even though that was only part of the truth. I didn't want to just say, "I don't love you." I tried to spare his feelings. I knew that he was still dealing with the truth about Jenny's house.

> Dear Father in Heaven,
>
> I come to you asking for your forgiveness. I didn't realize that I was getting into a situation that you take very seriously. I pray that you continue to stay by my side and bless me and my son. Father, I pray that you help my son's father to find his way in life. I pray that Daddy gets the kidney he needs to live a long life. God, you are an awesome God! You have brought me a long way. Please know that I am so grateful for your love. I thank you, Lord, for your love. Amen.

Marriage is honourable in all, and the bed undefiled: but whoremongers and adulterers God will judge.

—Hebrews 13:4 (KJV)

Chapter Eleven

PLEASE FORGIVE ME

Daddy sold his apartment building. We moved into a townhouse on the north side, not far from the neighborhood that I grew up in where Mama lived. We moved in right before Daddy had his surgery. Daddy healed quickly after his surgery. Everybody in his life was always telling me how proud my daddy was of me. Daddy never thought I would stick by him like I did. I loved my daddy. As Daddy became stronger, he started cooking more and spending time with his grandson.

Then I decided it was time for me to go to cosmetology school. I had graduated from adult education right after my son was born in 1975. My sister and her friends graduated with their class from this same school. There were times that I wished I had been a part of my graduating class, but the choice I made to be a wife and mother stopped that, so now I was separated from my husband and looking forward to the future, a future for me and my son.

Larry became very bitter toward me. He came over to see his son one day and acted very cruel. I believe he realized it was over between us. He got all up in my face, and then he started to raise his hands to hit me, which he did, and that's when I grabbed a knife out of the drawer. When he tried to hit me again, I pulled the knife on him and told him that if he put his hands on me again, I would cut his throat. When he saw that I meant it, he backed off and started talking a lot of nonsense. I told him to leave, and he did. Daddy was home, but he was upstairs in the bedroom.

After that incident, I no longer welcomed Larry into our home. If Larry wanted to see his son, he would have to go to Jenny's. Larry, Jr. was with her all the time. Daddy was good to me and my son. He paid most of the bills, bought most of the food. Even though I gave him what we agreed to help out, and I was to pay for rent every month, he always paid the most and gave me my money back. That was his way of making it lighter on me financially.

I made sure Daddy went to each of his doctor's appointments, took all his medication, and everything was good with him. I made sure Larry, Jr.'s needs were met. I cleaned our home daily, but when the sun went down, I did what I did. I got high. I spent hours drugging. My girls and I loved to dress and drug. I had returned to stealing. At this point, I had a taste for the finer things in life, and I loved it! Whenever I went to the skating rink that Jenny's brother built, I would watch his daughter and other coworkers and how they dressed. I wanted to dress like them, so I stepped up my skills a notch as a booster.

I started checking out the Woodward shop. I branched off into Bloomfield and Birmingham stores. I loved the clothes! Just looking at those clothes gave me a feeling, to this day, I can't describe. It was a feeling that was better than a sexual climax. I had to have these clothes. I dreamed about how I was going to get inside these stores to get what I wanted without getting caught. I meditated on my plan daily. Patty had taught me well, and I was stepping off into the big league now. I had to know what I was doing. I knew that I stood the risk of getting caught.

Floor walkers would watch the merchandise big time! I would even go into the stores days before I hit them to check it out—where are the doors, what's up with the security, how's the layout of the store, how close is the fitting room, what are the sales employees' personalities like. I had to know what I was stepping into. I had to have an exact plan. This was my part-time activity.

Whenever I wasn't busy with my daddy or my son, I was on a mission. First, I made sure my Daddy's kidney transplant went well and he was good. Then I made plans to check out the school one of my friends attended. I used to let her do my hair when I wanted to step up my hair color from the auburns to the blonds. She had more knowledge than I when it came to hair coloring. I wanted to have a career in the beauty field since being beautiful was what I did. I felt this field would be a good one for me. Besides, I had started doing hair for pay when I was ten or eleven years old. I pressed and curled Granny's hair every two weeks. Then two little girls moved next door to us, and I did their hair.

When Mr. Smith moved out of our neighborhood, all the white families had also moved. He was one of the last ones to leave. I never knew of Charles, Jr. breaking into his house. I thought he moved up North because he always talked about buying more property there. When he moved out, a black family from the South moved in. I thought the way they talked was so funny. I babysat for them when they went out on the weekends. I learned early in my youth how to hustle up on money.

Mama's life was falling apart. Wayne was hitting on everything that wore a skirt. He would even get fresh with my friends. I hated going to my own mama's house. I noticed that she wasn't keeping her home half as clean as she did when I lived there. Not only that, I felt no love in Mama's house anymore. Her house was no longer home. It had turned into a house of dysfunction and total chaos.

Rumors were all over town about how sick Wayne and Mama were. They would have sex with a house full of people. I couldn't believe she was acting like this, him either. Mama gave all sorts of parties. Drugs were always a part of these parties. Wayne loved his weed. Mama loved her pills. Yet they both continued going to church on Sundays. Sometimes the pastor would stop by the parties. I couldn't believe that he called himself a man of God. After God exposed this man for who he truly was, he was put out of the church.

I spent a lot of my evenings nodding. I loved downers. I found myself so busy throughout a day that the only way I could relax and settle down was to take valium, drink a glass of wine, and smoke a little weed. I never bought weed because I really didn't like the high. But with a valium and a little wine, I could deal with weed. I supplied the valium. I took them from Mama's house, although they weren't as easy to get anymore with Super Fly being there.

We continued to party on weekends. One Friday night that stuck with me is the one when Rosie and I wanted to hang out at a club in Detroit. We didn't know which club we were going to; we only knew that we were tired of the local clubs. This night we were dressed sharp as always. Rosie loved to shop with me, or should I say shoplift. I taught most of my girls some of my skills. They never wanted to take anything, unless I was with them. If they got scared or didn't know what they were doing, I got their clothes for them. I always made sure I helped them.

First, Rosie and I were cruising down Woodward smoking dope, talking, and laughing. I had done what I was responsible for doing for Daddy and home, and Larry, Jr. was at Jenny's. This was my time. I always took out time for Lavinia. I loved dressing. It had become who I was. Mama's small fashion shows and what she had instilled in me as a child had produced a young lady that dressing meant everything to. I loved being the center of attention. I knew that whenever I came walking through the door at any affair, heads would turn. I got a thrill out of that. Only my God knew how much pain the clothes were covering up.

This night Rosie and I stopped at a red light. I was driving. Daddy had just gotten another car to get us around. He could no longer drive because he had ruined his driving privileges drunk driving and wrecking cars. He also had hurt several innocent people. It was only by the grace of God that he hadn't killed anyone. While waiting at the stoplight, there were two dudes standing on the corner. The windows were down because it was so hot outside. Air conditioners weren't used as much back then. This night we had the windows down by choice. The dudes hollered, "Where you two young ladies headed?" Rosie and I told them we were headed to the club. Rosie asked them if they knew of a nearby spot that was happening. One of them tried to give us directions to a nearby club, but we didn't understand the directions too well.

"Do you want us to show you?" they asked. The light changed to green. I pulled over so they could get into the car. We exchanged introductions. They pulled out a joint, and we smoked it with them. By this time, we were approaching the club. We had no idea where we were. I didn't know what streets we were turning on to. I didn't even know what street the club was located on.

Rosie and I shared with them that we weren't from Detroit. That was mistake number one. I felt Rosie was being a little too friendly, but I continued driving and said nothing. Once we arrived at the club, we partied with the dudes. We danced together. They bought drinks for us and were trying to hit on us. Rosie was eating up the flattery. I felt a tease, but I was too high, so I paid attention to what I was feeling and went along with the flow for the night.

It was 1:50 in the morning. The last call for alcohol had been announced. Rosie and I said good night to the dudes. "Can you drop us back off where you picked us up?" one asked me. Rosie agreed, but I wasn't feeling this move. Even still, I went for it. As we headed toward the door, a third dude that was inside the club came along. He said, "I'm going along with them, if you don't mind."

We were so high that we were making very poor decisions. All of us got into the car. I was driving. The friendliest one gave me directions on where to drop them off. I had no idea where I was going. One thing I did notice was that we were in a bad neighborhood, but it didn't dawn on me when I drove to the club. But now something wasn't right. Rosie continued to talk to the two dudes who weren't giving the directions.

All of a sudden, the one that was giving directions said they were getting out at their room up the street. I noticed motel signs, but I still didn't know what was really going on, and I wasn't liking the change in destination. "Turn here," he said. I turned, and then I started understanding what was going on. I turned into a row of motel rooms. As soon as I completed my turn, I felt a knife at my throat. "Keep going, tramp!" he said. Rosie started crying. She finally realized what was happening. One of the dudes said to Rosie, "If you don't wanna die, shut up!" I couldn't move my head to look at Rosie, so I kept driving down the narrow drive that had rooms on both sides.

As we approached the end of the row, the dude giving directions said, "Stop! Get out. Get out, I said!" with the knife still to my throat. "You heard me! Get out!" My thoughts were *When I get out, I'm gonna run."* Then I thought of Rosie, and I couldn't run off and leave her, so I decided I had no choice but to ride this thing out. I couldn't run off and leave my friend, so I turned the car off and took my keys out of the ignition.

"Leave the keys," he said.

"For what?" I asked.

Then he told the dude that sat in the middle of the backseat, "Pull the car up and park it on the side of the building."

"Don't do anything wrong to my daddy's car," I said. "That ain't my car!"

Then the dude with the knife to my throat said, "Nobody wants your daddy's car!"

"Good!" I said.

The dude that sat on the passenger side of the backseat grabbed Rosie and told her to get out of the car. She was still crying; but me, I never cried. I didn't feel there was time for us to cry. My thought was that I needed to study these dudes and figure out how to save my life. I wasn't about to give up like that! By now, my high was blown. As these dudes ushered us into this filthy motel room, my soul began to mourn. I already knew what was going to happen, but my concern was not about that, rather how to stay alive and live to talk about this someday. God was right there. Today I know that he is the only reason I stayed cool, calm, and collected.

Anyway, the dude that had the knife on me was very tall—a big dude. The dude that moved Daddy's car was short. He wasn't bad-looking either. I could tell that he wasn't out cold like the other two. He was the one that joined us later at the club. Once inside the motel room, the dude with the knife grabbed Rosie and pushed me in the back toward the other guy. He was a medium-sized dude, not tall or short. As I looked at him in the light, I saw that he had scars all over him, like he had been cut several times. He also had scars on his arms.

I had never seen heroin tracks, but soon I was about to find out what they looked like. He grabbed me and pushed me into the bathroom. Rosie was crying uncontrollably by now. The big dude with the knife had pushed her on to the only bed inside the room, which was filthy. Once inside the bathroom, the tall dude hollered out, "Bring her in here so she can shut her friend up!" So the dude that had me inside the bathroom said to me, "Come shut your friend up before both of ya'll die!"

I started to walk back out of the bathroom with this dude right beside me making sure I didn't try anything. Rosie was on the bed. I felt so sorry for her. "Rosie," I said, "please, there's nothing we can do. Please, if you keep crying like this, they're gonna kill us. Please, Rosie, try to stop crying!" Rosie looked at me. I really think seeing me made her feel a little better. She never completely stopped crying, but she quieted down. I began to wonder why no one came to our rescue. I knew that somebody had to hear Rosie crying or the loudness from the dudes ordering us around, even though we were in the room on the end of the row.

Eventually, the one dude came inside the room after parking Daddy's car. The tall dude that I saw at this point was not only very ugly; he was cut from head to toe, even in the face. He was scary-looking! Then he forcefully started to penetrate Rosie. She was hysterical! There was nothing I could do to help her.

The other dude pushed me back into the small bathroom. The dude with the cuts on him also started to unfasten his pants. *Oh my god!* I thought. Then he pulled out his penis. It was so large that I felt like I'd rather them kill me! He looked at me and said, "I know you can't take me penetrating you. No woman can. But you can do something else." Out of fear, I proceeded to do what he requested. I had never done anything like that in my life.

No! No! I thought. Then he hit me upside my head. I was wearing a hat. He hit me so hard that it fell off. Then he pushed me to sit down on the toilet, and the rape began. It felt like filth had entered inside my mouth. I wanted to gag, but I couldn't. Both of these dudes were calling me everything but my name. One said, "I bet in that world you came from, you never thought you'd be in a predicament like this—that's why y'all need to keep yo' butts outta Detroit! I bet you'll stay home now!"

When I heard him say that, I had hope. I felt he wouldn't have said that if they were going to kill us. Besides, I began to see that he was the one in control, not the tall dude. Once he had relieved himself inside my mouth, he told me to spit it out in the shower. I guess he had a little compassion on me by letting me spit. That was my clue. After I spat into the shower, he asked for my purse. "Ya'll think you go' spend our money up on drinks, then just take yourselves back home . . . Gimme all your money!" he said. I only had about $20, which he took. Then I started talking to him, nicer this time.

Rosie was still in the other room crying. After that dude raped her, he also took her money. I said to him, "You don't have to do this. I have no intention of giving you any trouble. Take it all, but let us go. We won't tell nobody what happened!"

He said, "You ain't going nowhere 'til I get my dope!" Then I realized the scars on his arms were tracks.

"Oh my god—ain't no telling what we caught!" All along, I'm thinking and praying for God to do something.

"Please," I begged, "go get your dope."

"Yeah, and I'm gonna go get it in yo' car!" he said.

"You can't! I told you that's not my car. You do something to that car and my daddy will come after you!"

"I told you *nobody* wants yo' daddy's car!" he said.

The dude had the keys to the car, so he was still in control. "Come on!" he said. He let me out of the bathroom.

"Put your clothes on!" he said to Rosie. "And come on!"

He got the money his friends took from Rosie's purse and told the other dude that they were going to the "spot."

"Come on!" he said to Rosie after she was dressed.

One of the dudes stayed in the room, while the other two led me and Rosie to the car. The one that raped me said, "I'm driving."

I got into the car next to him. At that point, I felt that he was going to let us go as long as we didn't give them any trouble.

Rosie's crying died down to a whimper. I think she realized we were going to be freed. "Are you okay?" I asked her, but she didn't answer.

When all of us got inside the car, the one dude drove off. The one that raped Rosie was sitting in the backseat next to her. When we got to the "spot," as they put it, the one driving got out, while the other dude remained in the car to watch us. He took the keys with him. When he returned to the car, he drove to Woodward. I knew it was Woodward because he said, "When you get outta this car, go straight ahead and don't look back. Don't stop and you better not tell nobody about tonight! You hear me? I *can* and I *will* find you if you call the police!"

"I won't say a word. Just let us go," I said.

Then we came to a stop, and both of them jumped out of the car. I quickly moved over into the driver's seat. Rosie stayed in the backseat. I pulled off in a hurry, shaking like a leaf. I drove away and then stopped and told Rosie to get into the front seat. She was crying again, but this time I believe those tears were because we were on our way home and not dead! When I got to Rosie's house, she went inside and woke up her parents and told them what happened. I was envious of Rosie because her mother got dressed and took her back down to the Detroit police station.

Me, I went home. Daddy was asleep. I got into bed and started crying. Finally, I could. I called out to God. I didn't even shower. I got with God. I cried, and I cried. He gave me the strength to get up and take a shower. I used Daddy's mouthwash to rinse out my mouth about four times. Then I went back to bed and let God put me to sleep.

I knew I had no one to tell but God. My mama was wrapped up into Super Fly; she didn't care. My daddy wasn't able to help me either. He had started drinking again, no more than nine months after his kidney transplant. I found myself missing my brother, Charles, Jr. I knew if he was out of prison, he would do something.

I would have told my brother. I missed my brother. I needed my brother.

> Father God,
>
> I humbly come to your throne. Dear God, I need you. Help me, God. I'm hurting. I'm hurting, God, and I need you to lift me up. In Jesus's name, God lift me up. This hurts. I feel unclean. I feel like filth. Please, God, stop the pain. I'm ashamed. Stop the shame, God. I can't tell anyone but you, God. I have no one else. Help me, God. Help me to face tomorrow. Amen.

These six things doth the Lord hate: yea, seven are an abomination unto him: A proud look, a lying tongue, and hands that shed innocent blood, An heart that deviseth wicked imaginations, feet that be swift in running to mischief, A false witness that speaketh lies, and he that soweth discord among brethren.

—Proverbs 6:16–19 (KJV)

Chapter Twelve

··

BEAUTY SCHOOL

··

Rosie and I moved along with our lives. She seemed to be holding up pretty well. I still used mouthwash daily and scrubbed my skin as close to being off as I could. I had secret issues, yet I hid them quite well.

Anyway, there was an upcoming concert in Detroit, and Rosie and I wanted to go. We discussed it and came to the conclusion that we would never see those monsters again in a million years, so we went to the concert. We were sitting in the car in the front of the theater. Lots of people were walking by the car, making their way inside. We were thinking about where we should park. All of sudden, I see him! It was the dude that raped Rosie. Just as plain as day! He looked like he had been in a meat grinder. His face was all cut up. I wondered sometimes why we never noticed how sliced up he was that night at the club. That's what drugs do to you, deceive you.

"Rosie, look!" I said.

She looked up. "I'm getting the police!" she said.

Rosie was nervous. I wanted to tell her that they weren't going to do anything, but I didn't want to scare her into leaving. When that dude spotted us, he took off running like the coward that he was. When I saw that, God placed peace within my heart and soul, and I knew that we would be okay. These cowards would run every time they saw me. I knew that God had shown himself strong. He exposed them for who and what they were—nothing and nobody!

The cops finally came. After Rosie spoke with them, we went inside to be seated. I enjoyed the concert as much as I could. I must say that at times I found myself looking to see if I would ever see him again. I never saw either of them again in my life. We never did that dumb move again either. If Rosie and I went to Detroit, we never stopped for anyone on the street.

A few months later, I started cosmetology school. I really liked learning about hair. Actually, I couldn't learn enough. Jenny kept Larry, Jr. most of the time, but Daddy would be home in the mornings, so Larry, Jr. stayed with him if Jenny wasn't able to babysit. Daddy was screwing up though. He would come and get me from school with my son in the car. The students would say, "Lavinia, Lavinia, your daddy is out there on the sidewalk." I would go outside and Larry, Jr. would be sitting on the armrest in the car. Daddy would be so drunk that he didn't even realize that the car was on the sidewalk instead of on the street. I had to be out of my mind for asking Daddy to babysit, but by the grace of God, my son was never involved in an accident whenever he was with Daddy.

Although I left my son with Daddy when he was sober, whenever I returned home, Daddy would be drunk. "Daddy, what are you doing? The doctors said that if you started drinking again, you would be dead in a few years." Sometimes Daddy acted like he didn't hear me. Sometimes I felt he didn't care. I didn't understand the disease of alcohol addiction. I was young, living my life. There's something about being grown. It makes you feel like you have to explore life, test the water, do things that you've watched so many grown folks do.

I hung out in the wee hours of the night a lot. I loved to party. One night I was at a party at the place of business of Rosie's parents. They had a vacant spot next to their company, and Rosie threw a party there. I came with another one of my girlfriends. Keep in mind I was in beauty school at this time. I wore a short afro with a blond star right in the center of the back of my head. I didn't dance at the party. I didn't dance often. I wasn't about to blow my high by dancing. I was too cool for that, so I observed a lot.

This particular night I was doing what it was I did, and a dude walked up to me and said, "What's up, star! You wanna dance?"

I looked at him and said, "No, thank you."

"Why not?" he said.

"For one thing, it's too hot to be dancing!"

He continued talking to me, but I wasn't interested. I really wasn't. He was a tall dark dude, and I loved dark dudes, but there was something about him that I was not feeling. The jeans—he had on blue jeans—and I wasn't feeling him. I never danced with him that night, but when he asked me for my phone number, I was sick of him and just wanted to get rid of him, so I gave him a phone number. Whose number? I have no idea. I made one up. I felt he wasn't going to take no for an answer.

We lived in a small town, a town where everybody knew everybody. I had to ask some questions about this dude. I had never seen him before. He looked older than me. When my girlfriend and I left the party and went to the car, she said, "Do you know who that was trying to talk to you? His name is David. My elder sister used to go with him. He just got out of prison."

Great! I sarcastically thought. Some women go for bad dudes from the projects and penitentiary. But me, I wasn't interested. I'm glad I gave him the wrong phone number! Anyway, my friend and I finished up our night. I dropped her off at her home, and then I went home and got into bed. Larry, Jr. was at his grandma's. I had to go to school in the morning.

The next time I went out partying, I went to a bar that was the spot at the time. I was sitting at a table close to the entrance of the bar with a couple of my girls. We were laughing and drinking. We had already had our dose of street drugs before we entered the bar, so we always came inside high. The drinks were to maintain the buzz we already had. Life was fun, even though whenever I was alone, past hurts always showed up. I learned how to shut the feelings down quick. I was still ashamed and hurt from what happened to me down in Detroit, but I could never tell anybody. I even lied to all my friends and told them they only raped Rosie but not me.

Anyway, there was a group of dudes who came walking through the door. One of them was the dude from Rosie's party. He came straight over to my table and said in front of everybody, "Here she is, man. This is that broad that gave me the wrong number. How she go' play me?"

"Did I give you the wrong number?" I said. "I'm so sorry."

"You know you did. If you didn't want me calling, you should've said that," he said.

"No, it wasn't that," I said. "I didn't realize I gave you the wrong number."

I liked his style—the fact that he had the nerve to confront me the way he did. *Who is this dude?* I thought. I took a second look at him. He looked good. I could tell he was high, but he had swag about him that I was digging. All my girls looked at me like what was I going to do. I wrote down the right phone number and passed it to him. "Sorry, if I got it wrong the first time," I said; but I wasn't talking about the phone number. I was referring to the impression I got of him.

Anyway, I partied that night with my girls. Halfway through the night, he came back to my table and asked me to dance. I really wasn't the type that stayed on the dance floor. I danced to a few records because I didn't want dancing to blow my high. Plus, I wasn't going to sweat my style. Whenever I was with several of my girls, we sat at a table. Whenever I was with one of my girls, mainly Rosie, we sat at the bar. Men bought us drinks whenever we sat there. I loved being told that the gentleman on the end wanted to know what I was drinking. I had no problem telling him that I drank the finest cognac on the market at that time. If I were buying my own drink, I would settle for less. At any rate, I was on the floor dancing but not with him. I liked the way he moved. He was smooth. I was wrong about this dude. He told me, "I'll call you in a few days." I said, "Cool," and left the dance floor.

The next day I went to cosmetology school. I was still sleepy, but I went. I had a client scheduled that evening at my home, and

I needed to wake up and get myself right for the day, so I popped a valium. When I made it home, I had to be a mom, so I spent the evening with my son. To my surprise, David called and asked if he could see me that night. I was so excited! I ran out to get some wine for the evening. I agreed to meet him at nine o'clock. My son would be in bed by then, and I would be done with my client's hair.

When David arrived, I wasn't finished with my client. Daddy and Larry, Jr. had gone to bed. I dimmed the lights in the living room and had music playing. I asked him if he wanted some wine. I poured some into a glass for him to drink while I finished up with my client. After I finished my client's hair and let her out, I went into the living room to sit and drink wine with David. We talked for hours. The wine was also talking, and David started to look better and better. His rap was smooth. I ended up in bed with him that night.

I was confused though. I didn't know whether to feel shame or tell myself "You go, girl!" Men always got off knowing that I got that the first night. Well, some of us women got that same feeling. Plus, it was good. David knew what he was doing, and I liked how he took control in bed. I didn't like having boring sex. If a man acted like he didn't know what he was doing, he would never see me again. That was another reason why I left Larry. He didn't have enough experience in bed.

After I left Larry, I met a man who was approximately the same age as my daddy. He was my secret, and I would meet him between 2:00 a.m. and 4:00 a.m., in the wee hours of the night. Nobody knew about this score I hit. I still had hang-ups about the past that I was holding on to that nobody knew about. I loved going to see this old man, although I had no intentions of being with him otherwise. I loved the way he made me feel.

Now I was hanging out with David, and things were quickly turning serious. I hadn't seen the old man in weeks. David and I went to the bar, and of course, who do I run into? It was the old man, and he had been drinking. When David left to go to the bathroom to smoke some dope, the old man came up to me and said, "I wanna talk to you."

"We have nothing to talk about," I said.

"You got yourself some young punk and you stopped calling?" he said.

"You knew there was nothing serious between us," I told him.

He continued talking his drunk talk. David came out of the bathroom and saw what was happening. He walked up to the old man and said, "You hear the lady! She said she's got nothing for you! Besides, she's with me. So whatever ya'll had going on is dead now."

The old dude says, "I ain't looking for no trouble, man."

"Good. Won't be none if you leave the lady alone like she asked!" David said.

So the old man moved on, and David asked me to dance.

The next day I met up with David at his mother's house. He lived in the projects. I had been to the house of Daddy's brother and his auntie's house in the projects when I was a child. I never had any friends or boyfriends who lived there. When I arrived at his house, I was surprised by what I saw. Roaches were everywhere. I was scared to sit down to wait on him. He took a shower first. As I sat on his bed waiting for him, I heard the front door open.

"David?" It was a woman's voice. I couldn't tell if she was drunk. She came upstairs and realized he was in the shower. She entered the bedroom. I was very edgy, moving around every time I saw a roach.

"Hi, baby, what's your name?" she asked me.

"Lavinia."

"That's a pretty name. I'm Mrs. Brooks, David's mama," she said.

"Nice meeting you."

To be honest, I was wondering if she was looking at me or the roaches. She was cross-eyed. She was far from the prettiest woman I had ever met. After meeting the rest of his family, I wondered how David got to be so fine; but after getting to know them better, they were the nicest people you'd ever meet. His mother was such a nice woman. His whole family were good people. Even though they were poor, they knew what it meant to love one another. They were a close family that loved David. I was impressed at how they treated him. Them roaches had to go though.

Soon David and I became a couple. Daddy had been drinking so much now that it was time for us to part. I spoke to Daddy and told him David and I were going to live together and that he needed to get his own place within the same complex. He moved right down the street from me into a one-bedroom townhouse.

I was still at Daddy's place daily doing everything I always did for him. The only difference was that we didn't live together anymore. David moved in as soon as Daddy moved out. I was still in beauty school, so things for us were tight in the beginning. Daddy helped us all the time, even though he complained about David not working. By this time, Mama's world was falling apart. Her husband, Wayne, had been in so many disagreements with my brother Johnny that things came to a head one weekend. Johnny had a big fight with him down in in the basement of Mama's house. I was not there, but I had been hearing so much about my mama's house that nothing at that point was a surprise.

Wayne's name was all in the streets for hitting on the young women to how much dope he smoked. Mama was on every pill you could name. She always told me she was a legal junkie. She kept the Vicodin and valium and many more pills. I didn't have to go far when I wanted pills. I wasn't into pills at this time in my life though. I had been turned onto getting high on cough syrup.

David's ex-woman who was from the projects had followed him to River Trail. She actually moved into our neighborhood, one street from us. Then she started being nice to me. One night in the bar she came to me and offered me an ounce of this really potent cough syrup. I looked at David when she made the offer. He nodded in agreement, so I accepted. It wasn't the first time I had drank cough syrup to get high.

Vanessa went from being the square of the neighborhood to using lots of drugs. She started dating the man who supplied the cough syrup himself. She would travel and come back from New Jersey, South Carolina, North Carolina, and New York selling books. She was a totally different sister from what she used to be when we were growing up.

Charles, Jr. had been in prison for some years now. He was making a name for himself in prison. He was a boxer inside. Charles, Jr. was the first prisoner to turn pro as a boxer in the Michigan prisons. He had a very promising chance at becoming a light-weight champion, but he couldn't stop robbing and went back to prison after he was released the first time. He had three straight years as a Golden Glove state champ. The administration allowed Charles, Jr. to have the first and only professional fight at the Michigan Reformatory at that time. Charles Jr.'s name was known all over town as being a very good boxer, but I was not surprised that my brother was that good. We were just good at sports. It was in our genes.

After Super Fly left Mama, Johnny was at the house with her, and Vanessa returned home. I didn't really know how bad it had gotten at Mama's, but I do know that Johnny was out cold. He was using heroin and stuck up every dope man he could. Vanessa was also hooked on cough syrup. All of us got high, except Charles, Jr.

Mama began to act strange, I mean *strange*. At first, I didn't think it was no more than the pills she was taking. I didn't even know that Mama was losing her house. I should have, though, because she was also out cold. Super Fly was taking her down too fast in my opinion. By now, she was smoking cigarettes and weed, on top of taking all kinds of pills.

Daddy was a drunk. Johnny was a heroin addict. Vanessa was a syrup head, among other things. I was a syrup head and a valium freak. Mama was a pill head and a sex addict. Charles, Jr. was in prison, a gambler, and a fighter. What a family mess! But the worst was on its way. That day came when it finally happened. Mama lost the house. She hadn't paid a house note in over nine months. She was evicted. That put the icing on the cake. Mama lost her mind. Daddy was still in love with her, so he took her in. Although I loved my mama, I was very upset with my daddy.

"Why would you do this to yourself, Daddy?"

"I just love her," he would say.

I knew he deserved better. Mama dogged Daddy. She was totally out of order. One day she came over to my house, and it looked like she had gained weight. Then I realized she was wearing several layers of clothes. She was also talking out of her head.

"Mama, why do you have on all those clothes?" I asked. "What's going on with you?"

"An outfit a day," is what she told me.

"What?" I asked.

"You heard me. I just peel off an outfit each day. When I've peeled off six, I'll be back."

"Mama, where are you going?"

She also lost her car while dealing with Super Fly, so she left walking.

"Mama, where are you going?" I asked again.

She didn't answer. She walked out of the door. I didn't see Mama again for six days. When I finally saw her, she had on the last outfit, and she came back to Daddy's to change into seven more outfits, and I hope she took a bath. Anyway, I was getting worried about her. She was having a nervous breakdown right before my eyes. I felt helpless. I didn't know how to help her, yet I knew I had to be the one to help her. Who else would take on this responsibility?

Nevertheless, through all the pain I covered up so well, it was time to do something to help Mama. Even though I was very angry at Mama for getting into this predicament, I had to let all that go and get my mama some help. This weighed heavily on my heart. "God, help me take care of her. God, where is she going all of those days? What is she doing?" She had lost so much weight. My mama was so sick mentally. I cried a lot whenever I was alone. The cough syrup helped me cope. But even being high wasn't deadening the pain.

I called the courts to find out what I could do and how to go about getting Mama some help. Her world had fallen apart. She had lost everything and couldn't deal with that fact. My mama had checked out mentally. That was her way of coping with what was going on in her life. What was I to do? Charles, Jr. would have helped me, but he was in prison. So I had to put on my big girl shoes once again, just like I had to do for Daddy when he lost his kidneys.

Dear Lord,

As I come to you in prayer, I humbly repent, for you are the Almighty God. You already know every sin that I am partaking, not just me but my entire family. We are trapped, dear God, in the trick of the enemy. Help us, God! Help us see the path we are on and the darkness that we are allowing to consume us.

O Lord, hear our prayer. We need you, God. Help us realize this before it's too late. Thank you, God, for hearing my prayer. Thank you for giving me the knowledge to help my mama, for I know it is you once again. Thank you for guiding me. Amen.

For we wrestle not against flesh and blood, but against principalities, against powers, against the rulers of the darkness of this world, against spiritual wickedness in high places.

—Ephesians 6:12 (KJV)

Chapter Thirteen

SHINING IN THE WORLD

Mama's behavior had gotten so bad that as she walked about the state of Michigan, I worried about her daily. Yet I continued to take care of my business with the courts, go to school, and be a mother. Now I was hanging out with David, partying at least three nights a week, and I was drugging every night. I did it all. I did what I had to do. I never took the time to feel the pain. That was for the weak. The strong sucked it all in and took care of the business at hand. I did get an order from the court to have my mama put in a mental institution for help. The only way I could get this order was to prove that she was a threat to her own safety or someone else's. I proved them both. Not only was she not eating, bathing, or living in her own home, but she was also cock strong. One day she grabbed my wrist and started twisting it.

"Mama!" I yelled. "What are you doing?"

She scared me. "You can't get loose, can you?" she said.

I really couldn't get loose, and the look in her eyes was so glassy. Now the problem was getting her to stay in one place long enough to serve her with the court order. That didn't happen. But that winter, she walked all the way to the top of the thumb. I was home when the phone rang.

"May I speak with Lavinia Reynolds?"

I didn't know how to respond because I thought it was the police looking for me because I was stealing.

"Who's calling?" I asked.

"This is the police station. Do you have a relative named Patty Frank?"

I knew this had something to do with Mama.

"Yes." I said. "My mother."

"Well, she's being held at the city jail. We need you to come and get her. She used your name as an emergency contact. She ate at a restaurant and walked out without paying. We feel that there's something mentally going on with her. You need to get her to a hospital ASAP."

"I'll be right there," I told them. "I have a court order to have her placed in a mental hospital for evaluation. I'd like to come and get her."

"Sure, ma'am."

When I arrived, I couldn't believe what I saw. Mama was acting like a mad woman. She looked like she had been foaming at the mouth.

"Miss, we feel you need to transport your mother by ambulance."

"No, she's all right. It's my mama. She's gonna be all right. We'll be okay," I said.

Little did I know Mama was a lot worse than I thought. My sister, Vanessa, was with me. Mama was handcuffed to the bars on the cells. She was sitting in a chair. She had destroyed the chair, so she was sitting on the floor. After they took off the cuffs, she was released to my care. At first, she acted real cool. When we got into the car, I made the mistake of letting Mama get into the backseat. She always rode in the back, even when she wasn't tripping. She used to say, "Bean, chauffer me. If I want to be chauffeured, I can. I'm the mama. Just do it!" Rather than argue with Mama, I just did it, but this time it was poor judgment to let Mama get into the backseat. As soon as we hit the freeway, she started.

"You think you go' lock me up, don't you? You just want my money, that's all! I tell you what, before you lock me up, we all go' die!"

I tried not to say much because she was right. My plan was to take her straight to the mental hospital, but she wasn't having it. As I drove on I-75, at least seventy miles per hour (the speed limit was fifty-five miles per hour back then), Mama sat up on the seat and grabbed me around the neck. She was so strong! I couldn't do anything. The car was swerving all over the freeway. Thank God it was after 2:00 a.m. and the road was clear. Vanessa started screaming. I was trying to gain control of the car while Mama held my neck in a lock.

"You wanna die?" Mama said to me as she was laughing strangely. "If I go to the nut ward, you're going too."

Finally, I was able to pull the car over on to the side of the highway and stopped. I was shaking like a leaf.

I said to Vanessa, "I saw one of those phones back a little ways. Go and call for help!"

"No, I'm scared," she said.

"Vanessa, this is *not* Mama we're dealing with! Get out of the car right now and get help, or we are gonna die!"

Vanessa looked at me, and then she jumped out of the car. Mama's arm was still around my neck. She was talking a whole bunch of nonsense.

"Uh, huh, you can't get loose, can you?"

All I could say to myself was "Oh my god, what has happened to Mama?" I had never seen anything like this in my life, except on television, yet I was smack dead in the middle of this nightmare. Wrapping my mind around the fact that this was not a dream was mind-blowing. This was my mama, and she wanted to kill me. Wow!

She finally let go of my neck. I remained still. I didn't want to set her off again. She started jumping around on the backseat like a monkey or something. I kept still. Vanessa made it back to the car. She was scared to open the door. She wanted me to know she had reached help. She cracked the door to tell me. Mama didn't attack Vanessa. As a matter of fact, she didn't say much of anything to Vanessa. I was the enemy. She saw me as the one trying to harm her. Once help arrived, they didn't try to force Mama out of the car. They talked to her. I had my window down, so they approached my side of the car.

"What's her name?" they asked me.

"Patty."

The officer turned to Mama and said, "Hi, Patty!"

Mama didn't speak.

"Patty, we are here to help you get to the hospital for help."

"I don't need to go to no hospital! If you want somebody to go to the hospital, take her," Mama said as she was referring to me. "She's the one that need to be in the hospital. She just wanna lock me up so she can take my money! That's all she wants!"

"Mama, nobody wants your money. I just wanna help you," I calmly said.

The paramedics talked to Mama for at least a half an hour. Then she opened the car door, after which time they walked her to the ambulance. I followed them in the car to the county mental hospital. Aunt Mabel worked there, so I felt she would see to it that Mama got proper care. Even though I felt very hurt that my own mother was talking to me and treating me like I was the enemy, I felt better knowing that she was on her way to get help. After Mama was evaluated, they took her to a judge whose decision was to place her in the hospital to stabilize her mentally. He felt she was a threat to herself and others, and I was about to learn to whom.

Anyway, I continued with beauty school, took care of my son, and visited Mama regularly. Things were very disappointing when it came to her progress. Johnny as well as other family members visited her. Even though Mama talked a lot of nonsense, she still managed to control her own income. She was on paid sick leave from the automotive plant, so when her checks came, she gave me instructions on what to do with her money. If Mama told me to pay this bill or that bill and bring her the rest, that's exactly what I did. I don't know why I was giving her all that money while she was mentally ill. That was poor decision on my part. I hadn't realized the seriousness of this thing called mental illness.

She used the money to control. One time Johnny came to see her. She told him that if he brought her a knife she would give him $300. Johnny was on drugs at that time, and I don't think he realized just how sick Mama was either. He took the knife to her one Friday. She gave him the money. When I came to visit Mama, I didn't know that her plan was to use the knife on me. I watched her come to the visiting room and sit down. She didn't look very well. She was looking at me like she did that night up north at the jail. Hate! She looked at me like she hated me.

"Hi, Mama, how are you doing?" I pleasantly asked.

Mama looked at me. If looks could kill, I would have been dead right then and there.

"You think you go' keep me locked up and take my money!" she said.

"Mama, ain't nobody trying to take your money—what money?" I said.

Mama had a purse that she carried with her all the time. There was nothing in it but a lot of loose papers that had no meaning, so I thought. She always dug in it. Looking for what? I couldn't tell you. This time, when she put her hand inside the purse, I didn't think anything of it. She took her hand out of her purse, and in it was a butcher knife. She rose from her seat and headed straight toward me.

"Mama!" I hollered. "What are you doing?"

I saw that she wasn't Mama at this point, at least not the mama that I knew—that mama that told me, "Bean, you can do it now. Make this outfit . . . Bean, I need you to model . . . Bean, you have to get an abortion . . .," that mama who, in her own sick way, protected me. She was out to stab me, and I saw it.

Fear surfaced in me as I realized that my own mama wanted to kill me! Wow! This was mind-blowing. I had to do something. By the grace of God, I was able to rise from my seat and make it to the intercom system and push the button for help. The staff came immediately. They disarmed Mama. I couldn't believe what just happened. I looked at Mama, and I didn't know what to say or do. I watched them take my mother out of the visiting room.

At this point, she was wearing a straightjacket. I was so hurt. I felt like she had cut me, not with the knife but she cut me in places that I couldn't deal with. I refused to feel this cut. I couldn't. I had to take care of my son, my daddy, my new man, and myself. No time to feel this cut. Drugs—that was the answer. Drugs—drugs made me forget about it. Even though I prayed in the wee hours of the night, I didn't feel I could stop this pain. Besides, I wasn't praying for him to stop my pain. I prayed for Mama. "God, do something! Look at my mama. Don't let this be, God. Help her."

I was told by hospital staff that it was best that I didn't return for a while for my safety and for the progress of my mother. Now I was feeling like it was my fault that Mama wasn't getting better. So I did as they requested. I stopped going to see her. This hurt, though, but I continued on with the other responsibilities I had. I did, however, check Johnny when I learned that he had been to the hospital that day twice. I knew she got the knife from him.

He laughed and said, "I just wanted the money. I didn't think she was really gonna use it."

"What do you mean?" I said. "She's in the state mental hospital!"

I, for some reason, was able to understand Johnny's explanation because I too couldn't grasp that Mama was gone like this. I was in denial big time! Johnny was my little brother, and I always felt sorry for him. I felt that he was that one that was left behind, by not just Charles, Jr. but by Mama and Daddy. I felt I was showing him that I cared by letting him have his way, even though I knew I had no business giving Johnny some of the things he asked me for, like using the car that Daddy had bought for me.

Johnny would get me every time. "Bean, I promise you I'll be back by 2:00 a.m."

"Johnny, Daddy go' be mad if he knew I let you take the car."

"I know, Bean. He won't know."

But every time, Johnny stood me up. He never made it back. I would be out at two-thirty in the morning looking for him. My girls would ride me around. While I looked for him, we got high. Whenever I rode up on the car and Johnny, the car would always be wrecked. This went on until Johnny landed himself in prison along with Charles, Jr. Johnny was not only drinking and drugging, but he was also involved in a lot of robberies. Johnny had become a menace to society.

I became pregnant with my second child in the midst of this fiasco. David and I were living together, and I fell for him hard. He had become everything to me. I was in love. We spent a lot of time together. I went to his mother's house with him just about every Sunday. She cooked soul food for her family every week. Our family had fallen apart right before my very eyes. I wanted to feel a part of something. I needed a family, so I dove into his. I continued to go help Daddy daily, but he was getting drunk daily, so when I went there in the mornings, he would be trying to get himself together from the night before. When I went back at night, he would be pissy drunk.

I was worried about both my parents. I had a load on my back, yet I kept doing what I had to do to hold things together as much as I could. I will say that there were times when I was with David that I felt happy. We made plans for a future. He was interesting. What I liked most about him after being with Larry was that he didn't depend on his mama. She depended on him for her happiness. Actually, the entire family looked to him for their joy. I liked that—a man in control. I learned quickly that David was a man that lots of women felt the same way I did about him. Not only was he very popular among his friends, but women were also all over him. Yet in the beginning, he made me feel I was the only woman for him.

I continued to go to school while I was pregnant. I had to quit using drugs, like pills. I did, however, smoke weed from time to time and drank at the bar, but overall, I let the drugs go.

After about three months, Mama called one morning. "Bean."

I was so excited. I hollered, "Mama, you're better!" She began talking to me as though nothing had happened. This was good! Mama got out of the hospital shortly after that.

In the middle of the summer, I had a healthy baby boy. He was a joy to all of us! Even Little Larry loved having a baby around. I finished school and got a job working in the hair salon. David was working for the city. Things were good, so I thought. That feeling didn't last long though. There were the women from the beginning, yet David always found a way to smooth things over me, but this time I wasn't buying it.

One day he told me that he was going to Pittsburg to visit the grave of a good friend that had been killed while he was in prison. He said he would be back on Sunday. While he was away, I worried about him the entire time. When he returned that Sunday evening, we argued about him not calling me while he was away. Later that night I picked up the telephone to call my girlfriend. David was already on the line. I wasn't intentionally listening to his conversation, but I heard him say to his friend, "Man, come get me. I'm sick of this mess."

When I heard this, I listened more intently.

"You still over Mandy's house?" his friend asked.

Mandy? I thought. *What's going on?* Mandy and I were supposed to be friends. She came to my home when our son was born. "You and David make such a good couple," she said to me as she leaned over my son's crib and I lay in my bed. Well, it sounded like she had crossed me, and I mean *double-crossed*! How dare you come into my home and smile in my face knowing all along that you were after my man! I had a problem with that, not just with his betrayal, which was another issue, but her—what she did, in my opinion, was worse than what he did. I was fighting mad at her! I felt there were certain things as women you just didn't do to each other. If I wanted your man, I wouldn't associate with you. I couldn't bring myself to grin in your face while plotting to sleep with him. "What a snake!" is how I felt. As for him, "How dare you lie to me like this?"

I remember when I was in the hospital after giving birth to our son. As they wheeled me out of the delivery room, David asked me why our son's complexion was so light, but that fact never crossed my mind because he was such a blessing to me. I was in love all over again with another gorgeous son. "I don't know," I said. I wondered why he asked. David left the hospital. His mother came shortly thereafter to see me and my baby. After she saw my baby, she knew that it was David's son. I went through some physical trauma during this period when he clowned on me. I couldn't move my body for a whole day or more. The doctors couldn't figure out what was going on with me. David's mother kept saying, "You will be all right. You've been through a lot. Try not to worry." Eventually, I started to feel the movements in my body returning. David returned to the hospital after a couple of days, after his mother told him that David, Jr. was his son. Wow! I should have known then what was ahead. Daddy, in between his drunken days, always tried to talk to me about my life's choices, but I chose not to listen.

A lot of broads were hating on me because of David. I couldn't keep up with them. But Mandy—I thought we were cool. I never felt so betrayed in my life by the both of them. That's when the hurt started to turn into that need-to-pay-David-back-I'll-show-him.

After that, I started stealing like crazy. I stole a lot. A friend of mine who was strung out on drugs also stole with me. She was shot heroin. I worked in the hair salon during this time. I got Daddy's Social Security and welfare and stole clothes. Now I had begun to sell the clothes that I had stolen. I was bold! Satan had me thinking that I couldn't be touched. I dressed to the hilt! Clothes meant everything to me at that point in my life. As always, they hid the pain I was suffering. What the clothes didn't hide, the drugs hid.

It was so ironic because the friend I was boosting with was Mandy's cousin. She even shared with me that David took sex from her one morning after she let him into her house after we had argued. I wondered why she was just now telling me, but I didn't buy it. I was no fool. I was, however, on a path with Satan that I had opened the door to many, many years before, but I couldn't see it. I was "Ms. Lavinia," the one who had it all together. When I wanted to show Mandy that I could get him whenever I wanted, I stole clothes for him and took him to Canada on vacation with me.

When I was alone, in the night hours, I couldn't deal with the hurt anymore. I found myself drinking liquid drain cleaner to get high. I had no regard for my sons. I felt like their grandmas would take care of them. Things were calm with Mama and Daddy, so I thought, but right when I was ready to check out, the phone rang. It was Mama. She was living with Daddy. He always took her in whenever she fell and had no place to live. She said that Daddy's neighbor, Josh, sexually abused her while Daddy was drunk.

At this point, I didn't feel like killing myself, but I had already drunk the drain cleaner. My throat felt like it was on fire. I told Mama to call the police, but she never did. I had to get to the emergency room, so I drove myself. The doctor at the emergency room x-rayed my throat. He said that my left lung and throat was damaged. He also warned me to stop smoking. I had been smoking cigarettes for eight years. Stopping was out of the question. I had also gone through my fourth abortion. I was all messed up, yet I masked it very well as always. No time to feel pain. I had to keep our family above water because we were sinking fast.

After I left the hospital, I was on a new mission. With my throat feeling raw, I continued to smoke cigarettes and dope and drink cough syrup and take pills. I was a functioning drug addict. The drugs kept me going. I wanted to pay David back for betraying me, so I set my eyes on this dude that worked in the salon. I had been told by my girl, Tina, who had been working at the salon before both of us, that he had been to prison for many years.

One day we were hanging out, and she said, "Beanie, that's him . . . He's the dude that started work the same day as you." I looked at him, and for some reason, I felt some negative feelings, but I chose to ignore what I felt. I said, "Not bad." I was referring to his outer appearance. He was dressed nicely, and his hair was relaxed, styled like a woman's hair. The first time I saw him in the shop, he talked with Tina and I, but he made it known that he was a married man, yet he knew I was flirting.

Now I had a plan to get David back for crossing me with Mandy. Every time I was out partying and saw him and Mandy, I had to let her know that what she did to me was scandalous. I felt that as a woman, if I set my eyes on your man, I'm supposed to respect you enough that, number one, I won't be grinning in your face like we are cool. I can't be phony like that. I stay outta your face. If you ask me what's up, I will let you know that I want your man, just like I did when Felix's wife called me at the shop one day.

She told me that she wanted to talk to me because she felt something was going on with me and Felix. I told her straight up that I had an interest in her husband, but he told me that he was a married man, so I backed off. I also told her that she had him, but if she continued to be insecure about me, she was chasing him to me. And she really didn't want to do that. I kept it real with her. She knew just how I was laying. I didn't do that fake mess to her. Understanding is the best thing in the world.

Anyway, I busted the lights out on Mandy's car on my way to the bar every time I felt like it. One night she pulled out a knife and stabbed my sister Vanessa right on the side of her eye. Vanessa was still getting into all kinds of trouble with me. One thing about my sister is that we may have argued among ourselves, but she was always down with me. She was the only one who really was at that time. Mandy messed up big time stabbing Vanessa. I called the police on her, and she was arrested. David called and asked me to drop the charges. "You can't get your woman? Bond her out and stop calling me. I ain't got nothing for you!" I told him. Eventually, she was released. I just wanted to inconvenience her.

Anyway, I was boosting so much that I decided to host a fashion show. Patty always gave fashion shows. I guess I picked up her ways. The show was off the hook! There were people everywhere, standing room only. And I got paid that day, so you couldn't tell me nothing! It was a hair and fashion show. My girls helped me pull it off. Clothes, drugs, and men—wow! I did it, and I did it well! I was making a statement: "I'm Lavinia. David, you messed up, and you will never find another Lavinia. And, Felix, you will wish you weren't married. Every one of y'all, eat your hearts out!"

Funny how when we think we are shining in the world, we forget all about God—God who?

Dear God,

When I'm alone in the middle of the night and I have no one to talk to, I turn to you. When life is overwhelming and it seems that I can't take anymore, I go to that secret place, and I seek you. Yet when I'm shining in the world and the enemy has his grip on me, I'm all in. Forgive me, Lord, for thinking that I am God. Forgive me for walking in darkness and loving it. Amen.

And the devil, taking him up into an high mountain, shewed unto him all the kingdoms of the world in a moment of time. And the devil said unto him, All this power will I give thee, and the glory of them: for that is delivered unto me; and to whomsoever I will I give it. If thou therefore wilt worship me, all shall be thine.

—Luke 4:5–7 (KJV)

Chapter Fourteen

PURE PANDEMONIUM

After the first of many fashion shows was over, even in the midst of my situation with Mama and Daddy, I was all-in with the enemy. If I wasn't giving the show, people wanted me to provide new clothes for their shows. If they had the money for my clothes, my girl, Mandy's cousin, and I were happy to accommodate them. I stayed so sharp that sometimes I would look in the mirror and wish I could kiss myself! Females were so jealous of me. Sometimes I found cigarette burns on my outfits or coats. I would be so high that I wouldn't even feel myself getting burned. Half the time, my so-called friends were the ones who burned my stuff.

"Who burned my coat?"

Then I would take it off and head to the dumpster.

"You throwing that away? Don't throw that coat away. I want it," someone would say.

"If you want it, get it out of the trash!"

I was a mess, but I was no fool. The next day I would go and steal another coat.

By this time, Felix and his wife were on bad terms with each other. One day at work he asked me if I was still interested. I told him that I was. He asked me to go with him after work one day, and I went. After that day, lots of changes began to take place at the shop. It finally closed. Rumor was that the owner owed Larry, Jr.'s uncle some money. I went to work at another shop for a short while, but I was making more money in the streets at this point, so I let go of working in the salon and became a full-time booster.

I had all kinds of customers: doctors' wives, professional business women, preachers' wives, etc. They were a trip, especially the preachers' wives. Don't let me be late with their merchandise and not have it by Thursday, or they would say, "I can't go to church on Sunday without my new dress on!" Well, of course, it would be unacceptable for the preacher's wife to not be the sharpest one in church on Sunday.

Wow! I was living the single life. I didn't have a man, so I did what I wanted when I wanted. I was very promiscuous and had two more abortions. One weekend my girls and I had been partying so tuff that we hadn't been to sleep in three days. I got a call from Detroit. I had met this cute dude, and he wanted to know if I would come down that night. I asked my girls if they wanted to go, and we decided to drive to Detroit. They went to a club and came back after the club closed to get me. We were in Tina's car that night. I was the only one who wasn't high, so I was the driver. We made it to Detroit fine, but it was on the way back home at two thirty in the morning that I had some problems.

I still wasn't high, but we forgot to keep in mind that I hadn't been to sleep in three days. I began to feel sleepy, so sleepy that I couldn't keep my eyes open. Tina's sister was in the front seat next to me. She kept turning the music up and talking to me, but that didn't last long because soon she fell asleep, and so did I. Tina and Vanessa were in the backseat nodding.

All of a sudden, the car went off the highway. I was traveling at least seventy miles per hour in a fifty-five-miles-per-hour zone. God had his angels carry that car across a huge drop off the side of the highway. All of us were asleep. When I woke up, all I saw were weeds. I was whipping through these tall weeds and knocking them down. I couldn't believe it. It looked like a dream. I had never seen anything like it. "Where are we? Oh my god! I went off the highway!" The car was moving so fast. My reflex was to stop the car, so I instantly hit the brakes! After the car stopped, Vanessa, Tina, and her sister woke up.

"What happened?" they asked.

"Beanie fell asleep," said Tina's sister.

"Where are we?" Tina asked.

"I don't know," I responded as I opened the car door.

When I looked back at the highway to see how far the car had traveled, I was so scared. I started shaking. *How are we alive?* I thought. *How?* When I stepped out of the car, the weeds were real high. They were almost as tall as I was. We climbed out of the car. We realized we had a long walk to get to the highway to get help. As we climbed our way through the tall weeds to the highway, we came to a drop in the land. We had to walk around it. *How did the car get across?* I thought. Then I let go of the thought and focused on the task at hand: "Lavinia, get some help."

All of us were in shock. I didn't even realize that my halter dress was down to my waist. As we approached the highway, I stood on the side waving my hands hollering for help. Tina laughed. "Beanie! Pull your dress up!" I said, "Oh!" I pulled it up, and all of us tried to flag down help. It was difficult because that time in the morning, people didn't know if they could trust anyone standing on the side of the road, even if they really did need help.

Finally, someone stopped. He was a trucker. He called for help. We waited for the police to show up. While we were waiting, I kept looking back at Tina's car. We were so lucky, I thought, but I don't know if luck had anything to do with what just happened. When the police arrived, they were quite amazed.

"Do you know how lucky you are? How did that car get down there? How are all of you alive?"

"Yes," I said. "The car must have slid down up the road because there's no way it could have jumped over this drop."

"Miss, I want to show you something," the officer said.

He took me to view the tire tracks. They showed where the car went down. I couldn't believe it! The car tracks were right at the drop. The car flew over the drop! Even after seeing that, I still didn't wrap my brain around the extent of what happened: God, the Supernatural.

And that wasn't the only time God protected me while I was in my pursuit of sanity.

Another time I was high and driving, I had to take all my girls home before I could go home. I had just dropped off Dolly. After our high school days, she turned on me, but we were back to being friends. She worked for a car manufacturing plant. She loved to dress and party just like I did. After letting her out of the car, I stopped at a red light. While I was waiting for the light to turn green, I dozed off.

When I woke up, I was looking at some boats inside a showcase. I mean, I was about one foot from the glass! The car had just stopped short of the glass showcase. I looked around and saw the traffic light far behind me. I had crossed over the intersection. By it being that late in the night, no cars were at the intersection when the car started to roll. My God had stopped that car, yet instead of me seeing that he was protecting me through my nonsense, I backed up the car and proceeded home. How I got home, I couldn't tell you. God did it all.

Anyway, I was seeing a lot of Felix by now, not just for sex but he was selling heroin. I had graduated to the big leagues! Cough syrup was becoming a thing of the past. Even though the cough-syrup days were the best, it was running dry. There were times during my cough-syrup days that I would hang around dudes that kept gallons of it. I was addicted as you can see, but if I didn't have a valium or two, the high wasn't complete.

This one dude that went to high school and wrestled with Charles, Jr. was a syrup head just like I was. He used to come over with gallons of it and get so high that he would pass out downstairs in the basement. That was our hangout. Much more happened in the basement. I always took his cough syrup while he was knocked out. Besides, he was always at my house. I know he didn't think he was going to nod all night at my house for nothing.

Anyway, one night he was asleep in the basement at my house. He woke up. My girls and I had drained the syrup jar, so to speak. He came upstairs asking for his syrup.

"I don't know," I said.

"You don't know? You don't know!"

Then I laughed. Next thing I knew, he had hauled off and slapped the mess out of me. "What the heck!" I turned to Tina who kept a small pistol inside her bra. "Let me see your piece, Tina!"

"No!" she said.

By this time, I'm on fire with anger, so I reached into her bra and grabbed the gun. I turned toward Tommy and aimed it at him. I never said a word. When you're really going to do something, you don't talk. You just do it.

Eddie, a friend of mine that was there and who also kept drugs, saw what was unfolding. He grabbed Tommy and placed himself in front of Tommy. Then he backed Tommy out of my bedroom as he stood in front of him, blocking my aim. I didn't want to shoot Eddie. God was using him to stop me from committing murder. I realized that while Eddie dragged Tommy down my stairs and out the front door. Meanwhile, I was moving around trying to get a shot, but I couldn't. Thank God that I didn't. God blesses his people for his purpose. Years later, Eddie died. Rumor was that he had a heart attack while he was driving his car and smoking crack.

As the Holy Spirit brings into remembrance God's many blessings and miracles in my life, there is one more miracle that surfaced in mind which is the one when I first shot myself. I had been dating Felix for a while. He was selling cocaine. He asked me if I would sell some to my friends. I didn't necessarily say no, but I found myself with a big sack of cocaine in my possession. I knew that I wasn't going to sell it, so another dude that had drug dealings agreed to buy the sack from me for one set price. That was good because I avoided having traffic to and from my house.

It was one thing to party with the dope man, but now Felix was trying to take me in a direction I wasn't feeling, so I gave the coke to Greg. That caused another problem. Greg's woman, Linda, was out of the box. She was sitting in front of my house one day when I pulled up. I wasn't aware that she had a beef with me. I knew her a couple of years prior. She and I crossed because she used to be sweet on David. He reassured me that they were done, but in my heart, I knew that she still wanted him. Yet by this time, we both had moved on.

As I got out of the car, she said to me in a friendly manner, "Lavinia, can I speak with you?"

"Yes," I said. "Come in."

My sister, Vanessa, said, "Beanie, don't let her in your house. She's got a gun."

I wasn't feeling Vanessa. I thought she was exaggerating, so I totally ignored what she said. "She's tripping. Nobody would be sitting outside my house, waiting to kill me." I couldn't wrap my mind around that thought, so I welcomed her into my home, my home where my sons lived and I was protecting them. I let her and her girlfriend, who also had an issue of jealousy with me, come inside. She was one of the broads that constantly tried to fight me at IIP. It was that boy, Charles, who kept those girls in line. Why he did what he did back then, I have no idea. I thought everything was over with them years before.

Once inside my house, I led them to the basement to be seated. The basement is where I took all my company. I bought a new living room set and put my old furniture in the basement to entertain. I could do that since I worked doing hair. When I was a child, Patty taught me not to allow people in my living room. The living room was to be decorated and looked at. At least I wasn't into putting plastic on my furniture like Mama was. You had to be real special to sit in my living room!

Anyway, the telephone rang right after Linda and I started talking. She asked if I was having an affair with Greg. I told her what was up, that our relationship was because of drug transactions and nothing else. After I answered the phone, I saw Linda reach her hand into her purse. I turned to hang up the phone, only to turn back around to see this big gun pointed at me.

"Hoe, you go' tell me 'bout you and Greg!" she said as she rose from her seat to point the gun to my head.

"What was going on? Oh my god!" Most women would have frozen at that point, but I didn't. Again, I had no idea why I remained calm or my thinking was so sharp. I glanced over at my son. He was in the basement with me. *What if I don't get this gun out of her hand?* I thought. *She could shoot my son.* Instantly, I grabbed the barrel of the gun. The two of us tussled over it. All of a sudden, I heard a loud boom! My adrenaline was working overtime. I didn't even realize I had been shot. I grabbed the phone to call for help. Meanwhile, I felt something running down the side of my face. I touched my face. *Am I bleeding?* I thought. She had shot me.

When I reached the police on the phone, Linda ran up the stairs. Soon after she heard the gun go off, she put it back inside her purse. She and her friend ran up the stairs as fast as they could. They made their way outside, got into their car, and quickly drove off. The police arrived shortly thereafter.

Once again, they told me how lucky I was. They showed me the hole in the basement wall. It was a cement wall. The hole was the size of a volley ball. Then they showed me the hole in the basement step. That hole was the size of a golf ball. They told me that the bullet ricocheted, hitting the wall, then the step, and then my head. The impact was slowed tremendously from the wall and step. Today I have a small dent on my head where no hair will grow, but that's nothing compared to what would have happened had that bullet missed the wall and step first. I would have been dead!

After the police conducted their investigation, they showed me the bullet that was found in my basement. The bullet was huge; she had a *big* gun! The police were on the lookout for Linda. After they found her and arrested her, the people on the street gave me a lot of trouble, especially Felix. "What are you doing? You don't call the police when you livin' street life!" I wasn't hearing him. Besides, this broad actually came into *my* home and pulled a gun on *me* in front of *my* little son! Had she approached me in the streets, I might have listened to what Felix was saying.

Linda stayed locked up a short while, and then she got out on bond. I was combing my hair in the bathroom of a club one night. I saw Linda when I first entered the club. I knew she was there. I didn't say anything to her. She followed me into the bathroom. A few minutes after I entered the bathroom, she came walking through the door. We were the only two in there. She came over to the counter where I was standing. Out of the blue, she dropped down to her knees and begged me to drop the charges. "Lavinia, please! Please don't pursue the charges. I'm sorry. I will never come to your house again. I don't know what happened to me that day. I don't go with Greg no more. I'm sorry that I went off in your house. Please don't send me to jail."

I looked down at her. As usual, I was high and dressed to the hilt. I said, "You know what? You just did the one thing that I wanted you to do. You are on your knees begging me, so get up. I won't show up in court when you have to go, but if you ever come anywhere near me or my son again, getting on your knees won't help!" Then I walked out of the bathroom.

Rumor has it that Linda was killed some years later. She was tricking and getting high at a hotel and found dead. Anyway, at this time, Mama and Daddy were struggling in life. I did what I could to help them, but you can't make somebody stop drinking. That dude, Josh, was robbing my daddy blind. He was raping Mama while Daddy was drunk.

One day, when I was at Daddy's house, Josh hit on me. "I got a lot of money," he said. He had been drinking. "I'll give it all to you if you have sex with me." I thought about all the money he took from my daddy and how he had dogged out my mother. I told him to put the money in the mailbox and that I would meet him later. He put it all in my mailbox.

After I got the money, I called one of my girls over. I counted it. It was over a thousand dollars. I knew that when I took the money, I had no intention of having sex with him. Actually, I had resented him. I knew if Charles, Jr. and Johnny were home, he wouldn't be messing over my mama and daddy. I told Josh I would call him in a few hours to come over.

When I didn't call, he came and knocked on my door. I didn't open it. He walked back down the street half drunk. He couldn't make too much noise because he already had a woman. Josh didn't want her to know he had tried to trick with their money, so he stayed cool for a few days. But that didn't last long. I was at

Daddy's house. Josh came walking through the door. Daddy had let him in. He didn't say anything to me at first, but when I went to leave out of the back door, he followed me.

"Where's my money?" he said.

"What money?"

"You know what money! You took my money, and I want it back!"

I didn't like his tone of voice. I was getting angry. "You been taking my daddy's money for years!" I said to him. "I don't owe you no money! The way I look at it is that I just got back some of the money you been taking from my daddy!"

He reached for me. I took off running. There was an elderly lady, named Mrs. Butler, who lived across the street. The door to her house was open. I quickly ran inside her house. I didn't even knock. She was at her kitchen sink. I said to her, "Josh trying to jump on me! You know him. He lives a few doors down from you!"

She yelled at Josh, "You get away from my house! You leave Charlie's daughter alone!"

He hung around her house until his woman pulled up in her car and they went inside their house together. I called my girls to come and get me. I left the car at Daddy's house. After my girls came and got me, I went home and called the airport to check on flights. I needed to leave this city for a while. Actually, the plan was to not come back when I left.

Larry, Jr. and David, Jr. were with their grandmothers and Vanessa. She lived with me during this time and took care of my sons when I was hustling. I took the money I got from Josh, and I went to Miami to see Aunt Felicia. I made sure I took plenty of drugs with me. Josh stayed away from me. Mrs. Butler told his woman what he did, so he was in big trouble, not just for trying to jump on me but for the money.

I left for Miami.

Heavenly Father,

I need you to help me. Satan has a grip on me, and I'm living too messy. The drugs rule my life. The stealing is out of control. The lifestyle is fun until tragedies hit. The chaos is addicting. Why wouldn't it be? All my life I've lived in chaos, yet by your grace and mercy, I've been able to maintain.

God, I know you hear me. Please don't leave me. I need you, Lord. I know that I am in deep, yet I don't want out. In Jesus's name, I pray that you continue to watch over me. Amen.

For they that are after the flesh do mind the things of the flesh; but they that are after the Spirit the things of the Spirit. For to be carnally minded is death; but to be spiritually minded is life and peace.

—Romans 8:5–6 (KJV)

Chapter Fifteen

MIAMI

I was glad to see my aunt Felicia. I hadn't seen her in a while. When she first left Detroit, I wondered why. When her husband left her and took their son, I wondered what happened to Aunt Felicia and Uncle Mike. Later I learned that my aunt had cheated on Uncle Mike. Looks like Mama and all her sisters had big-time issues with being trustworthy to their husbands.

When I arrived in Miami, I was a little shocked. My aunt was with a dude that I wasn't feeling. I felt like he was using her, but I minded my own business. I learned to do that the time Mama caught me in the bathroom one Sunday and said, "Bean, I love Wayne, and if you love me, you will accept him." I looked into Mama's eyes. I saw that she loved him. After that, I stopped making trouble for her and her man. I minded my own business. Besides, I just wanted Mama to be happy, so if Aunt Felicia liked it, I loved it! I had to get my own business.

The day after I arrived in Miami, I read the newspaper. There was an article about a hairstylist from Hollywood that was coming to Miami. They were promoting his return to Miami. I saw his picture and the salon where he was going to work. The next day I called the salon and asked to speak with him. I introduced myself and told him that I was from Michigan and a hairstylist by trade. I asked if I could come and watch him style on that day. I told him that I could learn a lot from him. "I read the article in the Miami newspaper about you yesterday. I'm very impressed with what the article spoke of you," I said to him.

At first, he was a little skeptical, and then he said, "Well, yes, you can do that."

"If you would be so kind, when you are on your way to work, could I ride with you? I'm not familiar with this city, and I have no idea how to locate your salon." I said.

"I suppose I can pick you up," he said hesitantly. I'm sure he was thinking, *Who is this woman that has the nerve to not just ask me if she can watch me but also ask me if I can pick her up?* I believe he agreed because he couldn't believe I asked. Anyway, the next morning I was picking out my outfit. I didn't bring my best clothes, so I couldn't dress the way I loved to, but I still wanted to look as good as possible. I brought some summer halter dresses and casual outfits. Aunt Felicia had also read the article. The article stated that he had styled some very well-known celebrities' hair and would only be returning to Miami for a short while, so I had to look my best.

Aunt Felicia still couldn't believe I had contacted this man and asked him to pick me up. She said that she could have dropped me off. "Why should I have you come out this early if you don't have to?" I said. "It's nice being here with you, Aunt Felicia, and you have been so kind, but I need to see Miami! I didn't come this far to stay stuck up under you and your man, so please don't worry about me—I'm good!" I put on a red and white halter dress. It was pretty, and I looked very beautiful, if I'd say so myself! I told Aunt Felicia I would call and let her know that I was okay.

Soon the hair stylist pulled up in his car and into the driveway. I looked out of the window before I walked out of the door. He was driving a really nice expensive car. It was green. Mama had this same kind of car when she was working in the automotive plant. Super Fly put an antenna in the window of her car so that people would think she had a television on the inside. I walked up to the hairstylist's car. He got out of the driver's side and came around to the passenger's side to open the door for me. *Thank you! You need to teach the men at home how to treat a lady*, I thought.

"Good morning, I'm Theodore . . . and your name again?" '

"I'm Lavinia, and good morning to you!"

I got inside the car, and he closed the door. I was impressed already! On the way to his place of employment, I was amazed at what I saw of the city—I was loving it! *This man ain't half-stepping*, I thought. I checked out his clothes, his rings on his hand. I didn't like his style of dress. He wore jumpsuits. I wasn't feeling him. He was a dark-skinned man, and he had wavy hair, like Super Fly. I could tell he was used to the finer things in life by the way he carried himself. As he drove to the shop, he asked me a lot of questions. I told a lot of lies. I was trying to build myself up to his standards.

I didn't share that I had just drank two ounces of cough syrup before he pulled up in his car. I brought a couple of pints with me when I left Michigan and flew to Miami. Airport security wasn't as tight then as it is now. They didn't inspect the luggage. I had also brought a lot of clothes with me. It wouldn't have been Lavinia if I hadn't! One thing I didn't do the entire time I was in Miami was steal one stitch of clothing. I didn't know this city, and I wasn't about to go to jail. Besides, I didn't want Theodore to know I was a booster.

I thought the city of Miami was gorgeous—just like I had seen on television! We arrived at the salon. It was a nice shop, but Tiger's shop back home, where I used to work, was nicer than this, I thought, and more advanced. The women who worked at this salon adored Theodore. He was a great stylist. He styled better than Tiger to me. For one, he made his own products. Two, he got client's hair straighter than I had ever seen anyone do. All his hairstyles were magazine-ready.

I was impressed, but now I was *really* impressed! I couldn't believe how talented he was. I asked him a lot of questions, especially about why he made his own products. We talked about the different climates in Michigan and Florida. He said that because of Florida's climate, store-bought relaxers were not strong enough to keep the hair straight. He was right! He did my hair. When he finished, my hair had never looked so sharp! I looked like

I had just stepped out of a high-fashion magazine. My hair was laid! I didn't want that day to end because I wanted my hairstyle to last forever. I always wore my hair short, but when he was finished, I couldn't believe how silky it felt. It was beautiful! At home, we did the blow-and-go to the hair, which was cool, but you couldn't do a blow-and-go here and have it last. This man was on to something.

He gave me a ride home after he did my hair. Again, I was able to see how beautiful Miami was as I rode along. He asked if I was going to come back tomorrow and said he would pick me up at eight fifteen in the morning. When I got home, he was a gentleman again and got out of his side of the car to open my door. I almost wanted to say to myself, "You don't have to get out." I was not used to this kind of treatment. It made me uncomfortable. Honestly, I didn't like it. I felt like he was making a big deal out of me, but I never said a word.

That night, I went to a club with Aunt Felicia and her man. It was a rinky-dink joint. I partied with the poor Miami folk, and I almost had the nerve to feel like I was better than them. Like the first morning I was there, I decided to go for a run, not that I exercised on a regular basis but I just wanted to show off my new gym shoes and my new pair of cute shorts. Aunt Felicia told me not to cross over into this particular neighborhood that was considered bad. I was supposed to turn around before I reached it. I did my little jog with my head down and didn't realize that bad neighborhood was such a short distance. I looked up only to realize that I was in what looked like a war zone.

"Oh my god, where am I? I need to turn around." It looked like a scene that I had only seen on television. It was very distressing. People were living in abandoned buildings. The windows were missing from the buildings. People were all over the streets, homeless. This scared me! Being poor in Miami was much worse than being poor where I came from back in Michigan. I am sure I stuck out like a sore thumb, wearing my new shoes and matching clothes. "God," I started to pray, "help! Get me back to Aunt Felicia's, and quick!" As I crossed back over into familiar territory, I felt a sense of relief. When I made it to Aunt Felicia's, I told her what I had done and how bad the area looked. I never jogged again the entire time I was in Miami.

I still partied in the hood with my aunt though. God always kept me, even when I partied in the ghetto in Miami, where I stood out, and the people could tell that I wasn't one of them. This particular night, I was high as a kite. Aunt Felicia knew I had brought my syrup with me. She asked me what it was the first day she saw it. I didn't lie. I didn't have to. I was grown.

Besides, her man was always higher than I ever thought of being. I danced on almost every song the deejay played at this club. I set my eyes on this one dude in particular. He was very handsome. I had to have him. He asked me to dance several times. I told Aunt Felicia that I wasn't going home with her and not to wait up for me. She told me that I was not in an area where I could trust people. I could tell that she was worrying, but she left me there at the bar, anyway, with the dude. She told me to call her if anything happened.

Anyway, I was on Biscayne Boulevard, the wrong end—I learned before the night was over. When the bartender said, "Last call," I went to a motel with this dude, not knowing anything about him, only that he resembled a famous movie star. I was so high that I couldn't tell you anything about the time I was at the hotel with him. I don't even recall whether he told me his real name. I do know that I passed out sometime during the night, only to wake up about seven o'clock in the morning alone in the hotel room. My purse was gone, so was mister. I had been robbed and no telling what else. I was so ashamed. I didn't know where I was, and I had to call Aunt Felicia.

"We're coming to get you. Where are you?" she said.

"I don't know where I am."

She told me to look at the street sign. I did.

"Lavinia," she said, "you are in one of the worst areas of Miami. It's a wonder you are alive! I'm on my way. You stand right where you are so people can see you."

I listened. She pulled up in her car a short time later. My high was worn off by this time, and I felt so small. I couldn't wait to get to Aunt Felicia's to get my cough syrup. Plus, I needed to call Theodore and tell him not to pick me up that morning due to an unexpected emergency. I couldn't watch and learn that morning. Theodore said that I could come the next day. I was glad because I slept all day.

Meanwhile, Aunt Felicia kept reminding me of how lucky I was to be alive. I did find myself calling on the Lord while I was alone in that hotel room. Luck had nothing to do with it. How stupid of me. This dude could have cut my throat and left me for dead. Who would have known? I didn't even know where I was, not to mention *who* he was—all for a booty call. It could have been a fatal attraction.

Anyway, I went to the shop the next day with Theodore. I didn't tell him about my experience the night before. He started telling me things about his personal life. Then I discovered why he had been coming to get me. His woman from the past was from Michigan. He showed me a picture of her. She was very beautiful, tall, and dark-skinned. She drove a fancy little sports car. I looked at the car and thought, *Girlfriend ain't just driving a car like this with no money. I wonder what she does for a living. She must be rich.* Then he told me that she was a high-class call girl. Wow! Her name was Katie. I was a long way from home, and I wanted to know more about this line of work, so I listened. I always wanted to experience that lifestyle. Being a long way from home, I was able to fulfill that fantasy.

Theodore told me about his ex-life. We took a break from work, and he took me to a well-known men's club. I was so intrigued when I watched the wealthy people interact with one another. They were all full of bling! I mean big time! I was loving it! The feeling was remarkable! I could live this life, and I mean, I could live it well! The people knew Theodore by name. White folks were speaking to him left and right. He knew everybody. *Long way from last night*, I thought.

After we ate lunch, we were on our way back to the shop. Theodore asked me if I could join him later that night because he wanted me to meet a friend of his. By this time, I was very interested in his friends. After his day was done, he took me back to Aunt Felicia's house. I shared with her my day. She could not believe what I was telling her. "He's coming back to get me tonight to meet a friend of his."

I spent my evening pampering myself, getting ready for the night. He picked me up about nine o'clock in the evening. I don't go any place without two ounces or more of syrup, so I drank two ounces before I left with him. My supply was low, and I wondered how I could get more cough syrup. When I got inside Theodore's car, he started talking about Katie. He finally told me that she was a call girl who worked alone, but he wanted me to ride with her tonight. When we arrived at her place, I couldn't believe my eyes. This woman lived in a penthouse on the top floor of a very tall building. When she opened the door, she was laced up and down in beautiful lingerie. I also loved wearing lingerie. I stole robes and gowns to lounge around in at home.

She was my kind of lady! I was really feeling this broad. I wished I'd live the life she was living. I wanted in. She talked with Theodore and me as she continued to watch me. She was very pretty. She asked Theodore if she could take a picture of me. I agreed. She took the picture and then excused herself to get dressed. She had two poodles that were walking around her penthouse. They were so cute. Their toenails were painted and pretty little bows that matched their toe polish were on their heads. She also had a fish tank filled with piranhas. She was one bad broad! I was fascinated with her.

When she came out of her bedroom, she was sharp as a tack! She couldn't touch me in the clothing department, though, but I still gave her props—she was sharp! She asked me if I wanted to ride with her. "Sure," I said. We walked out and got into her fancy little sports car. I liked her style, even though she was a white broad. Wow! I had formed an opinion about black broads: We were messy; we were not about business. This white broad now, she was on top of her game! She impressed the mess out of me.

As we rode through the streets of Miami, she spoke of how she didn't believe in a pimp. I felt the same, that if you were going to sell your body, you didn't need any help doing it. We saw several pimps that knew her car. They would pull up behind her car. She said they always tried to intimidate her or run her out of business if she didn't get on board with one of their teams. She wasn't having it though. This night she wasn't working; she was out to show me the ropes, to break me in, so to speak.

When you are one of God's chosen, you feel guilty when you know that you have turned totally away from him. I thought I had met the one connection I needed to get paid, yet in my heart, I heard the Lord, the Holy Spirit saying, "You have two sons. You need to go home." However, I chose not to listen. I asked her how to cop drugs. I needed a cough-syrup connection. She could get all the cocaine you wanted but no cough syrup. They were into cocaine in Miami. It was plentiful. Theodore would get me all the cocaine I wanted, but the problem was that I didn't want it. I wanted to nod, not be zig-ziggy-boom! I was already hyper. I didn't need any help. I wanted to be slowed down.

As the weeks went by, we needed more money. Theodore was working at the salon, but the life we were living doing hair wasn't creating enough money. I continued to stay in touch with Aunt Felicia by phone. I didn't really share with her what I was doing, but she was no fool. She knew I was sleeping with Theodore. We were staying at a luxury hotel, and Theodore's girl, Katie, hadn't brought me any clients yet. I felt she kept them for herself. I did learn that she was one of Theodore's women at one time.

One night Theodore asked me to go with him to a strip club. He knew the owner of the club. The women that were dancing were getting big tips. Theodore asked me whether I thought I could strip dance. I thought, *I'm in Miami. Nobody will know. I would fulfill the fantasy I used to have*, so I said I would do it. I studied the women as they danced. I learned quickly that the key was not to tire yourself out with a lot of dancing. There was no pole so they did a lot of walking on the stage like a model, squatting and bending from time to time. As the women paraded the stage, they undressed. They wore costumes that they stripped off. None of the men could touch them or go near the stage. I felt cool if I stayed high. No way could I have done that if I wasn't lit up, and I mean good and high.

I tried out. The owner liked me and asked when I could start. Theodore told him that I could start the next night. We left the club. I thought Theodore was weird because he treated me like I was his trophy to show off. At night he put the scarf on my hair to keep it perfect. He ran my bathwater, even telling me when to get in and how long to stay in. He's wasn't abusive. He treated me like an investment. I wondered whether he was looking for a replacement for his woman who left him.

I called back home often. Little Larry and David always asked when I was coming home. I often spoke of my sons around Theodore. He always told me that I should go see them soon and to give my sister some money for taking care of them. He never showed an interest in my sons though. The last thing he wanted was two little boys to cramp his lifestyle.

Now I was beginning to feel the real deal. One night at the club this man that had been giving me a big tip offered to give me a ride to the hotel. I thought it would save Theodore from having to take me there. I called Theodore to let him know that I had a ride. Theodore asked who the man was and told me to be sure not to go anyplace else with him. I told Theodore that I wouldn't. When the night was finished, the man gave me a ride home. He drove an expensive foreign car, but that didn't surprise me. With all the money he was giving me in tips, I knew money was no problem with him. *Must be nice*, I thought. He made small talk on the way to the hotel. Then he said, "I'm tired."

I didn't say much back to him. I told him where I was staying, and he said he knew the hotel, so I didn't see the need to talk a lot. At this point, my sons were on my mind, and I wanted to be back home.

This man proceeded to tell me about his wife. "She would love it if I brought you home for her."

"What?" I said. My only thought was that I had gotten into the car with a freak—him and his wife!

Then he says, "Your man, does he do men? I'll pay both of you well if you make it happen."

I thought that if he paid me well for dancing, then surely Theodore could make a lot of money. "I'll call and see what my man says."

So I told Theodore about the proposition. Theodore said, "No, I don't deal like that. Get rid of him!"

I'm thinking, *You don't deal like that? But I can dance every night for a bunch of dogs that look at me like I was their treat?* Meanwhile, I wasn't liking what I was feeling. I went inside the hotel room; all the while, this man was thinking that I was going to have sex with him, after I had just finished dancing for five hours, but I wasn't.

Whenever I wasn't on the stage, I never hung out with anyone. I spoke to them in the dressing room and started sniffing this drug that made you very freaky. We sniffed it right before we went on stage. Those broads looked good on stage, but when we got into the dressing room, under the lights, I could see all kinds of cuts and scars all over their bodies. My god! The stage lights covered up a whole lot. These broads were cutthroat-type broads. I was the only one who had a little bit of class, if you will. I noticed how they looked at me. I also saw how they made dates while they worked. When I got done, I said to Theodore, "Baby, I'm so tired. I just want to sleep and shower." He'd say, "Don't forget to put the scarf on your head." He wanted my hair to look good more than I did!

The next night, after I danced, that same man asked if he could take me home again. Theodore was never there when I finished dancing. I hated waiting for him. Besides, he couldn't find any cough syrup in the whole city of Miami, and I was sick of cocaine and him as far as that mattered. I missed my sons. I had done well in tips that night. I was also tired of using my money for Theodore to stay at this hotel. It was too much money, in my opinion, for me not to enjoy on myself. While I was riding along with that man to the hotel, he made sexual advances at me. He unzipped his pants and exposed himself. It was dark outside, but the lights along the streets and around the buildings lit up the night.

Well, I was not about to find out what he had planned to do next, so I quickly reached for the door handle and pulled it, and the door swung open. The car was moving but not that fast. I rolled out of that car and on to the streets. He stopped the car and told me to get back into the car and said that he would stop with the harassment. I picked myself up off the streets and moved closer to the sidewalk, and I told him, "No, thanks! That's okay! I'll get a ride." When I made it to the sidewalk, I was able to wave down a cab. I had made up my mind to go home at that point. I left all those spectacular clothes behind. Those clothes meant nothing to me at that point.

I heard God when he said to me, "You are a mother. You go home to your sons." I went straight to the airport. I called Aunt Felicia from the airport and told her I was going home. She showed me love. She never judged me or said anything to make me feel bad. She knew I had gotten off into something over my head. She told me to call her when I got back to Michigan.

She was like Mama. Mama wasn't judgmental when she was in her right mind. Mama loved people. God can touch your mind right in the middle of sin. I know because he touched mine and he softened my heart for my sons. He gave me the heart of a mother. I longed for my sons, and it was time to go home. My heart was changing. I was no longer drawn to this Miami lifestyle. I had to stop being that woman of the night and return to being a mother to my sons. I had fulfilled a fantasy I had dreamed about for years. I was swallowed up in Satan's world, but God stepped in once again.

> Father God,
> I humbly come before your throne. I ask that you remove all that is in me that is not of you so that you will hear my prayer. God, I have sinned before you over and over, yet you continue to protect me. For that, I say thank you. Thank you, God, in Jesus's name! Thank you for touching my heart and soul and allowing me to feel your presence. Thank you that I hear your voice even in the midst of my sin. God, I am so sorry that I put my

own desires before my sons. I do desire to make a new start, God. Help me. I know that I need to stop using drugs, Father, so please help me to do that. Amen.

Happy is the man that feareth alway: but he that hardeneth his heart shall fall into mischief.

—Proverbs 28:14 (KJV)

Chapter Sixteen

MY THREE SONS

Once back in Michigan, I felt good. Seeing my sons was the highlight of my return. I tried to be with them for days, and I did. Every time I walked out of my front door, Josh was outside lurking around, drunk. I felt threatened, so I called Felix. He was glad I was back from Miami. He said, "I'll straighten him out!" And that, he did. I was not there when Felix checked Josh, but I do know that I never saw him in front of my house again. I heard things he told other people about me, but he never called himself intimidating me again. He continued to clip my dad and sexually harass my mother, though never when I was around, but I heard rumors.

Felix started coming around often since my return. He kept drugs. He was known to be one of the big-time drug dealers during that time. He went to New York a lot. One time he called me from New York to tell me that he wanted me to try something when he got back in town. "Okay," I said, not knowing that this would be the beginning of one of the worst nightmares of my life.

I had been back home for a while now. I was starting to get bored. I needed to be busy. I needed a project. I came up with this idea to have a hair and fashion show while nodding that night with my girls. Dolly dated a man that was well-known in town for promoting dances and drawing in the crowd. I spoke to the man. He guaranteed me a full house and live entertainment for a set price. I couldn't beat it. I knew he was giving me a deal because he was sweet on Dolly, and it worked for me.

I used all my girlfriends for the modeling. They all dressed spectacularly, so most of them modeled a lot of their own clothes. I supplied the clothes that they didn't have through boosting. The deal was they could have the clothes for their pay for modeling. Vanessa would give us all modeling lessons through the night as we got high. Tina and I did the hair. Tina was the commentator for the show. The day of the show, I got paid big time! I didn't think I was going to make that much money. I made so much money that the security of the club had to walk me to my car. A lot of hard work had paid off, and I mean, it paid off! I was very pleased with what I had done that day.

My girls started this nonsense that they felt they should be paid, since I had made so much money.

I said, "Okay, I'll pay you. Give me back everything I stole, and I'll give you cash."

"That's okay. We wanna keep the clothes."

"That's what I thought!"

Who would take money when you got over $500 in free clothes a piece? That was a lot back in the day. I was no fool when it came to making money! Even the promoter came with the same nonsense. I did give him more than we agreed because he did his job over and above his calling. Once all the business was taken care of, it was time to take the party to a higher level. We had drugs big time! Anybody that was somebody in the dope game stopped by that night, except Felix who was still out of town. He did, however, make it back by the next day.

The drugging continued. Felix came over with some cocaine. He had some drug paraphernalia and some rum. All of us sat at the table and watched him cook up this cocaine he had. I asked lots of questions. This was something new to me. I'd never seen anything like this before. Once he was done with cooking the cocaine, its form changed. It was no longer powder. It was now in the form of a small rock. I was amazed at how it now looked.

Nevertheless, he cut the rock with a razor, and then he placed it on the screen that was on the pipe. He hit it first, and then he passed the pipe around the table. When it became my turn to hit it, I was a little hesitant because I liked downers, and I had already had a dope man in my life that supplied cocaine, and even though I could snort all I wanted, I didn't want it. That's why Miami didn't turn me on. "Where are the downers?" I like to nod. I did enough in a day. I didn't need anything to boost my energy level. I needed to come down. I needed to relax and nod.

I remember one night nodding with my girls. I was so high and felt so good that I heard myself say, "Umm-umm-umm!" That's how good I felt. I was not feeling this freebase mess Felix was introducing to me, but I still hit it. I'll never forget how it made me feel. Oh my god! I loved it! Talk about leaving your troubles behind! This freebasing was awesome. Wow! I became addicted to Felix *and* his drugs that day.

Later that week, when the partying slowed down, I had to take care of what I considered a minor issue. I was pregnant again. By who? I figured it was between the one night stand in Miami and Theodore. It didn't matter to me because I knew what I was going to do about it. I had hardened my heart to even feeling anything about getting abortions by now. When I was alone, I thought about it. But when the guilt showed up in the middle of the night, I drank cough syrup or blew more heroin. Now I had found a new high—freebasing. That put the icing on the cake. I had learned how to change my mood, my feelings, and my mind quick; and it worked for me.

Now Felix was "the man." He kept what I had to have. The drugs had become my god. The drugs meant everything to me. The more I drugged, the more I saw of Felix. One day he asked me if I would be his woman, and I said, "Yes." Although I loved the drugs he supplied, I didn't feel for him what I felt for David. I didn't really like his personality. Felix was too serious to me. He didn't know how to laugh and have fun, yet I ignored that because he had the drugs.

It wasn't long after the abortion that I was pregnant again, this time by Felix. When I told him, he wanted me to keep the baby, which meant I had to stop using, at least the heavy drugs like heroin. I did slow it down a lot. I was still boosting, though, and I mean, I was getting some *bad* maternity clothes. I hit Bloomfield's maternity shop. I wore silk maternity dresses. This was during the summer months, so I even wore halter maternity dresses. I looked cute, if I might say so myself!

One day Little David broke his leg at his grandma's house, and I had to go take him to the hospital. Felix took us there. David walked into the emergency room. When I saw him, I knew I still loved him, but my pride had allowed me to disregard my true feelings for him. We discussed our son. Felix waited in the waiting room. When Little David had his cast on and we were ready to go, David left the hospital. I watched as he was leaving. I don't know if Felix could see what I was feeling or not. I do know that once we got home, after I put my son to sleep, I was standing in my closet, about to change clothes, and I felt this sting come across my back. It was so painful that I fell to my knees. I knew my sons were in the other room, and I didn't want them to hear me scream, but I couldn't hold it in. The pain was so severe that I couldn't get off my knees. I looked around, and Felix was holding a wire hanger. He had struck me across my back with a wire hanger! "Why you flirting with David?" he said out of anger.

Here I am, five months pregnant and on my knees, in the most pain I've felt since that night in the bathroom when I had my first abortion. I heard what he said, so instead of realizing then what I had gotten myself into, I went on a guilt trip because, in my heart, I did enjoy being in David's presence at the hospital. The way he used to look at me turned me on. It had only been a few months earlier when David's woman and I got into a fight, right in his mother's living room, because I felt she had hurt Little David's feelings by saying, "Mrs. Johnson is going to our house for dinner," like Little David wasn't invited.

I said to her, "Well, my son wants to be with his grandmother, so guess he's going to dinner too!" The look she gave me was out of order. Don't treat my son like he's not wanted. I jumped her, and then I said, "Now take my son to his daddy!" Felix ran up to us in Mrs. Johnson's house and broke up the fight. He never said anything about it, but now I was his woman, and I was about to see his true colors.

Once the pain let up from my back, I rose to my feet, crying. He handed me two ounces of cough syrup. After telling me that I better not ever leave him waiting while I flirt with my ex, I denied his accusations; and once the two ounces kicked in, I was no longer upset with him. He helped me get my dress off and put first-aid cream on my back. The cough syrup had stopped the pain. I nodded the rest of the night, but before I got into bed, I checked on my sons to see if they were asleep. I never wanted my sons to know that I was being abused. Felix wasn't very nice, I came to realize.

I carried my baby through the summer, but I wasn't feeling very happy. I didn't feel like I did when I was pregnant with David, Jr. David and I were always together, laughing and spending time with our friends clubbing. Felix was so into drugs that not only did he use them but he also sold them. Sex became a big part of our relationship. He continued to go to New York regularly. One day he came back saying that he wasn't going to sleep on a mattress that my man and I had been on. He cut the mattress up with a knife, and then he made me sleep on it. He was mean and cruel to me. I wanted to ask him what he was talking about, but he would just go on and on, so I let him because I was tired of arguing with him.

Soon I delivered another blessing, a son. When he was born, I felt tired. I had lost that job I had. Sure I loved my son, but my soul was in pain. My heart was broken. I wasn't happy. I hadn't been high in a while, and I felt it. Without the drugs, I was miserable. Felix was so controlling. I was losing my grip on my self-esteem. I continued to help my dad. That was about the only thing he didn't argue about. But even when I went to Daddy's, Felix accused me of seeing Josh.

This son, just like my other two sons, spent a lot of time with his grandmother, Mrs. Black. She was a Christian. She never stopped talking about the Bible. Whenever Felix went around his family, he deceived them. He lived a life around me that he kept from his mother. I had never been around people like these. Mrs. Black owned her own foster-care home, and she loved doing things for people. She never talked or acted negative. She was a praying woman. She was a much older woman, yet I enjoyed listening to her talk about the Lord.

She loved my son. She loved her son. He was everything to her. She spent a lot of her money on Felix. When he got out of prison for something to do with a man being killed, she helped him get on his feet. He had been to cosmetology school before I met him. He lived in this house that she had put him in. She owned a couple of homes. I never told her in the beginning that her son was beating on me. I never even told Mama, yet she didn't like him. Daddy despised him. Daddy had already watched me be a fool for David a few years before, like the time he bought me a car and I took it and put it down as a deposit on a car that David wanted only to watch him and Mandy ride in it. Now that hurt my pride. She enjoyed it. She knew she was throwing rocks in my face. That's why every time I saw them, I started an argument. I couldn't take the embarrassment because I still wanted him.

I sometimes felt Felix was jealous of me. One day he was in the bathroom with me when I was combing my hair, and he arrogantly said, "Lavinia, I look better than you." What kind of man thinks he looks better than a woman? *Wow!* I thought. But I was in love with the drugs.

After Felix had lived with me for a while, he started telling me that he wanted us to move into his house. This house was on the east side of town. I refused to move at first, but after a week or so, I missed the drugs. He was my dealer. He had what I felt I needed to survive. I was a mess at this point, so I moved in with him. I took my three sons with me. I couldn't let go of my townhouse though.

Besides, Mama needed a place to stay, so I agreed to let Mama pay the rent and live in my place. I moved all my furniture with me. Felix's mother bought supplies for me to strip the floors and fix up the house. I was not used to living in a house that was in such bad shape. I did all I could to fix up this house. I enjoyed hearing that David had lost the car I bought, but the damage was done to me and Daddy. I hurt my daddy by allowing the men I continued to put in my life misuse me.

I realized that I was sleeping with the enemy, yet I did nothing to stop him because he had the drugs I felt I needed to live. After Calvin was born, I got two more abortions, back to back. I was so sick at this point that I was aborting babies like it was nothing. Felix was out cold. He sold a form of heroin that he cut up and called mix-jive. It had more garbage in it than heroin, yet the drug addicts loved it. He kept the best at that time, so he was making good money. He treated me up well.

Daddy had to go into the hospital after I moved in with Felix. He was having complications from drinking. He did, however, get better, but the hospital didn't feel he had recovered enough to go home, so I put a hospital bed in the bedroom with Baby Calvin. Daddy came to Felix's house with me. Daddy wasn't comfortable in Felix's house because Felix continued to fight me, even with my Daddy there.

Once we were high and Daddy was drinking, Daddy always got nasty whenever he was drunk. He said something out of the way to Felix, and Felix actually hit my daddy. It didn't take Daddy a second time. He moved back home the next morning, even though he wasn't supposed to be alone. I went to check on him as much as I could.

The drugging and fighting went on the entire time I was at Felix's house. His business selling mix-jive had fallen. He counted on his mother's money and the little hustling I did in the stores. The moneymaking booster days were over for me. I felt it was because he blocked my action. No one wanted to fool with us by now. Felix had run everybody off. I missed the fashion shows and the partying and the clothes. Felix had cut up everything I owned one day when I went with my girlfriend. She went to cop drugs, and when we returned home, all my clothes were cut up and on the floor at the top of the stairs. He didn't cut the suits I stole for him though. I was devastated! I had some *bad* clothes, expensive too!

I remember that day I was watching a famous daytime soap opera, and one of the actresses was talking to one of her many men on the show. I looked at the TV—I was so excited! She had on the very outfit I wore the night before. I started hollering, "Vanessa! Come look!"

When Vanessa got to the television, she said, "Man, you had that on last night!"

I proudly said, "Yes! I have arrived!"

Now all my clothes lay cut up all over the floor. All I could do was get high. Living in Felix's house was a nightmare. He fought me almost every day. My sons lay in their beds when they were home and listened to this monster abuse their mother. One time he came home when I was taking a bath and said that I was standing in the window to give the men across the street a show. The curtains were open, but I just didn't pay any attention. The men were not right outside the window. I checked before I even ran the bathwater. He beat me until I was in the closet in the dark, trying to dodge the blows.

I became hysterical and started to panic. The entire left side of my body stiffened up on me. I couldn't move it. "My arm, my leg, my body," I hollered, "I can't move my arm!" He stopped hitting me and saw that I was serious. Then he started trying to help me. "Calm down and breathe. You are worked up. Relax, try to calm down." I did what he said, and my arm started to move. The calmer I got, the looser my body got. Within a few minutes, I could move my entire body.

The fighting stopped for that day. He had already gotten the drugs, so immediately after I could move, we got high and nodded the rest of the day. Later I had to cook dinner for my sons. I was in pain, but the drugs always deadened the pain, so I could continue with doing everything I had to do for my sons. This type of unhealthy living had to be affecting my sons, yet I never thought about that. Praying was of the past, except when I prayed for my sons. I no longer felt I was worthy of God's help, but I knew how he was right there when I was a little girl, so I knew he was going to answer my prayer for my sons. I knew God loved his children. My mama told me that.

Felix had a sexual addiction as well as a drug addiction. He liked having sex after fighting. I also was sick in that area. After that night as a child when I heard Mama and Daddy being intimate after they fought one night, in my sick thinking, the sex was more intense after the fighting. Satan had total control of me.

One night Felix was dealing with this woman on the drug tip and we started arguing. I became very agitated, not because I was jealous of the woman but because I was sick of living the way I was. Day after day after day, we did the same thing, getting worse through the years. This night I slammed my right hand through the glass of a china cabinet. As the glass broke, a piece fell down and cut my wrist. The cut was very large. Blood was everywhere! Felix wrapped my wrist with a towel and rushed me to the emergency room.

Once at the hospital, I had to get ninety-two stitches. The cut was so deep that eighteen of the stitches were underneath and seventy-four were on top. The doctor said if the glass had cut any deeper, I would have severed a main artery. Basically, I could have been dead, but I didn't even care. I was trying to end my life, anyway, but not over Felix. I didn't care for him that way. This woman had nothing to do with me cutting my wrist; I was just tired and felt trapped. Something had to change quick! I felt my sons would be better off with their grandmothers. Felix knew I wanted out. He felt we needed to move to Houston and start over. I was foolish enough to listen to him. He and his mother sold the house, and off to Texas we went! I placed my sons with their grandmothers.

While we were in Houston, not only did the fighting continue but so did the drugging. Both of us got jobs at a convenience store that was right across the street from the apartment building we moved into. It was a nice apartment. The family of Felix's mother also lived in Texas. I didn't really like his cousin because she was one of them broads that drove a fancy foreign sports car and bragged about it every time she opened her mouth! "You still gotta pay for it" is how I felt, "and until you do that, it ain't yours!"

We didn't even work a week before Felix quit. He came up with this mess about the manager was trying to set him up. I kept working, but I was taking money from the cash register every day. We had smoked up the money that Felix got from selling the house. By now, Felix loved smoking cocaine. That cough syrup we used to drink had been taken off the market—hmmm . . . I wonder why. We left Michigan with a heroin habit, so in Felix's bright mind, we could kick the heroin habit by smoking cocaine. He loved drugs. I had done it all with Felix, even tried to shoot heroin one day.

A friend of mine that shot dope came over one day, and she and Felix were shooting up. Felix asked me if wanted to try it, and I did. Felix spent so much money that day trying to get me high, but I never felt the drugs. Felix eventually said, "Screw you, Beanie! You just ain't go' get high." I looked at that as being God. He knew I didn't need to be shooting dope, so I never tried it again with them. I would blow my heroin while he shot his. Sometimes he would blow his too.

After a few weeks of me stealing from the store, Felix became very paranoid. He went to talking about the police was building a case on him. He actually said that we had to leave Texas because he wasn't going to jail, so back to Michigan we went. I was ready to go home anyway. Every time I called home, Daddy and Mama talked about how I needed to be with my sons. They were right! I missed my sons.

> Father God,
>
> I humble myself and come before your throne. I know that you are God Almighty, King of Kings and Lord of Lords. I don't feel worthy to come into your presence. I'm sinking, God. Satan has a stronghold on me and my life. I know, God, that you love your children. I come to you for the sake of my sons. God, help them. Help my sons. I know that I am not the mother they deserve.

I ask that you place my sons in a loving environment, a stable environment. I've put them in such confusion and chaos. They deserve better, God. Protect my sons.

Why, God, do I want to be with them yet I can't stop what I'm doing to be a better mama for them? I feel like their lives would be better off if I was dead. I've allowed Satan to have his way in my life. He rules today, God, and I don't feel I can do anything to stop him. Help my sons, God. Amen.

For I am about to fall, and my pain is ever with me. I confess my iniquity; I am troubled by my sin.

—Psalm 38:17–18 (KJV)

Chapter Seventeen

THE STREET LIFE

When we got back home, Felix continued the same paranoid foolishness that he was talking in Texas: somebody's trying to set him up and get him locked up. He started selling heroin, not mix-jive but straight-up heroin. The mix-jive brought certain types of drug addicts that people like me looked down on and thought we were too good to be around. Now he sold to the people that were on our level of drugging, so to speak. He was more leery of these addicts than the less fortunate ones. My sons lived at home while I allowed a drug dealer to use their home to deal.

Even though Felix took the drugs to most of his customers, my sons were old enough to know what was going on. I was older now, and I didn't have the company in my home that I used to. Besides, Felix didn't allow people to come to our house. He copped his drugs from Detroit. He had met a man that had given him a deal and was selling him drugs that were so good that he could put a cut on them and triple his money.

Life was good, or so I thought. I got high as much as I wanted. My sons continued to go to their grandmothers' every week. I enjoyed being high, even though Felix was still beating on me. I had a routine: get high, get beat, have sex, get an abortion. The cycle repeated itself over and over and over again for years. Then Felix started to ask me if he could have sex with some of the women in my life, from my best friend to my cousins. The more he used the drugs, the sicker he got, which, in turn, meant the sicker I got.

I no longer spent time with God. I would go boosting from time to time, but I wasn't that "pro" I used to be. I got caught several times, which meant that I caught a couple of cases with the court. I was doing dumb stuff, like the time Felix was mad at his "connect" for selling him drugs that were cut. Felix felt it was this man's fault that his business had fallen off, so he was mad and came up with this bright idea to stick up the dope man. How I allowed myself to get involved in a robbery shocked me! Felix said that if I knocked on the door, the dude would open it.

"He likes Lavinia," he said to his cousin who was planning the stick up with him.

His cousin said, "I feel we need another man."

I said, "Another man for what?"

Sarcastically, Felix said, "You go in since you think you know so much."

"I will," I confidently said.

After I said that, I started to feel sick to my stomach. I had just volunteered to be in on a robbery, something I'd never done in my life. Felix asked his cousin who he had in mind for the third man. His cousin said, "Charles." Felix said to call and see if he can get out the house. His cousin said, "Charles do what he wanna do. He ain't gotta ask no woman if he can leave!" So Felix's cousin set it up for Charles to be the third man. I hadn't seen Charles in a long time. He had a few dealings with Felix in the past, but the last time I had any dealings with him was at the IIP school when he stopped the east and west side girls from fighting me. I was pleased with the choice of the third man. I knew Charles was no punk.

I went back inside my house and started cleaning. Whenever something was bothering me, I would clean up. I found that as I cleaned, I was able to spend time with God. During this period, I no longer had that contact with God that I had when I wasn't living a life of sin, but when things didn't set right with me, like they weren't right now, I would go to God. I asked God not to let anything go wrong. I had seen enough violence, and I knew anything could happen. I didn't so much care about myself as I did my sons. "What if I got killed? What if somebody else was killed?" All this I took to God while I cleaned up. I also got high. There was no way I was going to pull this deal off, unless I was on cloud nine.

Well, it started getting dark out. That was the plan. We would wait until nighttime. Felix was ready to go. His cousin lived down the street, so he walked up to our house. Once we were in the car, we went to get Charles who lived on the way to Detroit. They were making final plans. Felix told me, "When I knock on the door and the dude lets us in, get behind me and stay behind me at all times. I can't protect you if you get in front of me," like that made me feel better.

When we arrived at Charles's house, he came right out and got in the back with Felix's cousin. He spoke to them. He never said a word to me. Felix told both of them that another one of his distant cousins, the one that introduced him to this dude, had given a layout of the house. He also told him who would be there and when. He told his cousin and Charles that he would let them out at the corner and to walk around to the back of the house and come in through the window. He showed them which window on the plan he had. "When you hear my voice, come through this window," he told them.

Once we arrived close to the house, my stomach was turning flips! I was so scared. Felix let his cousin and Charles out of the car. He continued up the street to the house. Felix had a gun in his pants. His cousin also had a gun.

"You know what to do. Whatever you do, stay behind me," he said to me.

I said, "Okay."

We were in front of the house. We got out of the car together. Felix followed behind me. We walked up to the door, and I knocked. The dude came to the door. He was a small man, like my daddy. When he opened his door, the look on his face was puzzled. I was smiling at him while Felix said, "I'm sorry, man, I know your rule is to call first, but I was down here and thought I'd see if you wouldn't mind serving me now. Nothing I'll do again." When Felix said this, he looked at me and started to let his guard down.

"Sure," he said. "Come on in."

He had one of those safety-lock doors, so he had to unlock the door. While he was doing that, Felix was engaged in small talk with him. He couldn't even open the door from grinning at me. Once he got the door open, we walked in.

"Come on back," he said as he walked in front of us.

I followed behind Felix. I watched him pull out his piece. I was so scared that I was shaking and thinking, *What in the world am I in the middle of? I can't bail out now. I gotta go through with the plan. I could be the reason somebody gets killed if I don't*, so I kept my mind on the task at hand.

When I followed behind Felix, he shoved his gun in the man's back. "Keep moving," he said. "You know what time it is!"

I followed behind Felix. When we got to the den, I saw another man. He saw his boss's hands up. He instantly moves away from the drugs.

Felix said to the dude, "You know what you did to my business! I made you, and then you call yourself shuttin' me down!"

When Felix said this, his cousin and Charles came through the window. It had to already be open because they had no problem coming in. Besides, it was summertime, so it had to be up 'cause it was hot. Once the two of them came through the window, I watched this dude, and his eyes were on this gun that was at the center of the room on a table that sat low. When I saw him, Felix was still checking him for cutting his business.

I started to panic! I felt threatened. I felt that if he got his hands on that gun, somebody was going to die, so I started hollering, "Kill him! Kill him!"

Felix's cousin said, "No, don't kill him. We ain't trying to get no murder case!"

I calmed down and moved quickly from behind Felix and grabbed the gun and handed it to Charles. Then I stepped back behind Felix. He picked up the sack from off the table. I remembered what I had to do. I left the room and started searching the house to look for anything of value. As I searched, I opened a closed door because I thought it was the bathroom. But once I opened the door, my heart sank. "Oh my god! It's a young boy!" He couldn't have been any more than eleven years old, and he was scared to death! I felt like a piece of crap! I just finished yelling about killing the boy's father or grandfather.

"Nobody is going to hurt you," I said. "Stay in here, and don't come out, you hear?" He nodded. I immediately closed the door. Felix's cousin walked out of the den and started going behind me, checking out the house. He headed toward the bathroom as he reached to put his hand on the door knob. I hollered out, "Don't go in there!" He looked at me, and his eyes were asking why. I never took my eyes off him. "There's a child in there!"

Felix's cousin could see that I was hurt. He walked away. He headed toward the master bedroom. I went back into the den. Felix was wrapping up the robbery and telling the dude that he had messed up by crossing him. Then he took the butt of his pistol and hit the dude over the head. Blood quickly gushed out all over his head. Felix turned to leave the room, and I moved quickly to the front door in front of Felix. His cousin followed, and behind him was Charles, who hadn't said a word at this point, just his presence said enough.

Once at the door, a woman in a white uniform came up the walkway. I knew it was his wife because Felix had told me months ago that the dude's wife was a nurse. She saw the gun and turned and ran down the sidewalk, hollering, "Help! Help!" She fell to the ground. I watched her and felt her terror. I and the rest of my crew continued to run to Felix's car. We got inside the car, and he pulled off quick! We traveled about three miles toward home, and Charles impatiently said, "What we waitin' for? Set it out!" We got high in the car on the way back home.

Once we arrived home, we all went inside the house. Felix divided the drugs into three piles among us. I didn't say a word because his cousin and Charles were watching him. Charles had this look of distrust on his face, but Felix did not cheat either one of them. I felt that he should have given them less than what he kept because it was his job and I was with him. "Where was my cut?" I waited until the two of them were gone, and then I said something, "That gun I handed Charles was mine. I just let him use it. I want it back!"

Felix said he would get it back, so I let it go. We got so high that we didn't even go to bed that night. I had been nodding a lot of years now, and as I said, I loved it! I smoked a pack of cigarettes a day. Well, I lit a pack; most of the time the cigarette just burned. If I wasn't holding it, I dropped it on my chest from nodding. My chest would be burned before I even felt that I had dropped the cigarette.

Felix was back in business, selling a better sack, but he was using so much that he barely made any money, not only was he using but I had a habit also. We were both full-blown addicts. His cousin and Charles were doing well, I had heard. This made Felix jealous. He had gotten the gun back, but now he decided that he wanted them to give him some of their drugs. His cousin gave him what he wanted. Charles, on the other hand, gave him a sack full of mix. That was funny to me. I laughed to myself.

He, on the contrary, started saying that I wanted Charles because I made an issue over the pistol. He actually jumped on me when Charles gave him a sack of mix. When he called Charles about the sack, he didn't answer the phone, but he kept hearing in the streets that his cousin and Charles were making money. It was his own fault that he chose to blow his sack up. After that, Felix's luck started to change, so did his behavior.

I had been through so much with him by now that I was losing my strength. I still had the courts to deal with, and I had a serious habit. I checked into the local hospital for the first time. While there, my sons stayed with their grandmothers. I stayed in the hospital for ten days, and while I was there, I had my eleventh abortion. I was so depressed. Mama and Daddy were so disappointed in me. "What has happened to Bean?" Not only had I been enslaved to addiction, but my mama and daddy were also struggling with their own demons. Mama had at least two more nervous breakdowns by now, and Daddy was killing himself, drinking himself to death right before my eyes. He would tell me,

"I've got nothing to live for. What do I have to live for?" I would say to him, "Stop saying that, Daddy!"

All Daddy every talked about is how much he loved Mama. I would tell Daddy that there ain't that much love in the world and that Mama didn't love him. The only time she came around was to use him. Daddy would let her stay with him, and she would have her men pick her up from his house. "You're always there for Mama, yet she always disrespects you, Daddy," but the real choice of words that I used were not so nice. I cussed, and I cussed a lot, every other word, to be honest.

"Lavinia Lynn, you got a mouth that is too filthy to be a woman. You cuss like a sailor!" Daddy would say to me, but his language wasn't too clean either.

"No joke!" I'd say. "I wonder where I got it from."

Daddy would just say, "Forget it!" Then he would get up and stumble on down the street.

I loved my daddy, even though, by now, I was putting my addiction before him. The boys and I would walk down to his house and check on him daily, but both of us were in our addictions, and things were changing. Daddy always told me that I deserved better and said that a man is supposed to work a job and be a provider. I knew he was right, but a man with a job didn't make enough money to support my drug habit! I felt I had to have a street man, not a man that worked a nine-to-five.

Felix was on a down period. He was changing from that get-paid-man to that stay-high-man. He had become his best customer. I was being pressed into bringing in more money. I hustled a little, and then I put an ad in the newspaper in Birmingham and Bloomfield for housework. Even though I made money cleaning, something I could do with my eyes shut, I stole from the homes I cleaned. Diamond earrings were what I set my eyes on. I learned that wealthy people had a safe for their best jewelry but kept the okay stuff, the not-so-expensive jewelry, right in the jewelry box on their dresser, which was enough to get me and Felix high. I got the jewelry, and he sold it in the streets once I returned home.

Court was a place that I called my second home. I stayed in trouble. Felix had started calling me a snitch because I never went to jail or prison. I wasn't a snitch. I just had a God in my life that was directing my path, even when I didn't know it. He placed people in my life like the probation officer that I got honest with and told about the drug habit, the shoplifting since I was a child, the rape, the abuse, and the sons that I loved so much; so whatever is good in me is because of them. I got so real with this man that he felt my pain and he wanted to help me. He tried to help that little lost girl that I didn't even know, let alone know who I was at this point in my life. He never recommended prison for me.

One time he recommended treatment for six months at a rehab center that was into degrading addicts. When I got there and saw a patient technician put a grown man in a corner, and he told him to face the wall for two hours with a weird hat on saying, "Since I act like a child, I need to be treated like one." I watched that happened, and I thought, *I'm not feeling it. What is really going on?* That night, after I prayed for my sons, I thought about the exit signs I saw in the hall right outside the room I was stationed in.

When everybody was asleep, I got out of bed, gathered my belongings, and got dressed. About 3:30 a.m., I walked out of the door. I walked all the way to the probation department. When Mr. Max got to work, I was standing in front of the building waiting for him. I didn't know whether he was going to send me to jail, but I do know that place was not going to be better. If anything, I would have caught another case when the tech called herself placing me in some corner. I knew I had to leave that treatment center, and that was what I told Mr. Max. "If you are going to help me, then help me." That was not help, in my opinion.

At times Mr. Max didn't know what to do with me. Felix accused me of sleeping with Mr. Max and said that was the reason I wasn't sent to prison. I did not sleep with Mr. Max; we had a professional relationship. He was just one of many people God placed in my life. He recommended that I be sentenced to outpatient treatment, which was much better because I was able to stay home with my sons.

Although I continued thinking I was the smart one and my gift of gab had gotten me out of another situation, not one time did I give credit to God or even speak about how I spent the hours in the middle of the night with him. I was sick. To be honest, my entire family had issues, from my mama and daddy to my sister and brothers, to my aunts and uncles, to my cousins. Some may have been sicker than others, yet we were all struggling with issues.

I didn't see a lot of my family now. I didn't want them seeing how sick I had become. My aunt Mabel would come and let me do her hair every two weeks, but I struggled to do it. Half the time, I was sick due to lack of drugs. My cousin, Cathy, brought her son to get his hair cut by Larry, Jr. also, but I felt so distanced from my family. My cousin, Angie, had found the Lord, and she would come and share about Christ with me. I enjoyed listening to her, except when she called when I was about to get high. Then I couldn't wait 'til it was time for her to leave. As far as materially, my aunt Penny was doing well, but her name was ringing in the circles I hung in at times. My uncle Charles had moved from Detroit. He was hanging with Aunt Penny. He was also drinking and drugging. The difference between us was they weren't in the street like I was.

Being in the streets wasn't an easy life. I became enslaved to the lifestyle. I woke up in the mornings plotting who and what to hustle up on that day. My cousin Chris, Angie's little sister, was in the streets also. We were in different company. She was younger than I was, and from time to time we crossed paths, and whenever we did, we gave each other the family respect as much as we could. I mean we were *in* the streets. I tried to stay away from my family because I chose not to dog my own family; I thank God that I didn't go there.

I missed my family because as kids, we were close. My little cousin Dennis, Cathy's brother, was special to me; we had fun together. I hadn't seen him in years. Dennis was no longer a little kid. I thought of him when I reminisced about my childhood: Cathy and I used to dress him in girl clothes. Aunt Mabel laughed when he went upstairs to show her how he looked. When Uncle Ben came home, we would hurry up and take them girl clothes off him. Today I don't know why he lives the way he does, but I sometimes wonder if Cathy and I had a part in it.

Uncle Charles's kids now lived up the street from me with him, but Felix was jealous of them, so whenever they tried to visit me, he treated them so nasty that I felt uncomfortable around them. My family had totally fallen apart. Satan was having his way in my life.

> Heavenly Father,
>
> I come before you and I repent. I'm lost, Father, and I have strayed away. I live an unholy life, yet I can't stop. I no longer hear your voice. All I hear is the voice of the devil. Are you here, God? Have I lost your love? I've done things that I am ashamed of—things that I don't feel you will forgive me for doing. I worship man. Drugs is my god. I know I'm out of order, yet I can't stop. I need you. Thank you, God, for even allowing me to come before you, for you are God Almighty. Help me, in Jesus's name. Amen.

So, as the Holy Spirit says: "Today, if you hear his voice, do not harden your hearts as you did in the rebellion, during the time of testing in the wilderness.

—Hebrews 3:7–8 (NIV)

See to it, brothers and sisters, that none of you has a sinful, unbelieving heart that turns away from the living God.

—Hebrews 3:12 (NIV)

Chapter Eighteen

TELL HER I LOVE HER

As the getting high continued, so did the drama. I was so scandalized that Daddy decided he wasn't going to give me any more money. He said he was tired of giving me money and buying things for me and my sons, especially when I continued to keep a man in my life that contributed nothing to the household but drugs. Daddy was right inside my heart. I knew this. Yet Felix felt he was contributing to the household—his mother doing for her son and giving him money to use on buying drugs was his way of thinking that he was doing something to help.

Felix was sick. He always found a way to speak negative about my mama and daddy. "Your daddy ain't go' do nothing but let Josh take all his money. He might as well give it to you!" He would always say something to make me feel as though Daddy owed me, like how he would always put his own mother on a guilt trip. I never knew the extent of his family issues, but I saw that the dysfunction and enabling was also in his family.

When I went to give Daddy a ride to the liquor store, I asked him for some money. "No," he said, but I couldn't accept that.

"Why not? You ain't go' do nothing but get drunk and let Josh rob you," I said.

"Whatever I do, it's my money! If I drink it up and piss it out, it's my money!"

He was not going to give me a dime this month, I could tell. He had already started to drink enough, so I could just take it, like Josh did. This time he fooled me. Right in the car, Daddy started defending himself from me taking his money. I tried to take it out of his pocket, but I ripped his pocket. Daddy might have been a small man and sick, but he fought me back. I felt so bad. I was totally out of order stealing from him. *What am I doing? This is my father. He has done so much for me. Even if he never gives me another dime, I should appreciate all that he has done.*

Anyway, I pulled back and apologized to my daddy. "I don't know what's going on with you, Lavinia Lynn." He was shook up so bad that he was trembling. I had no business doing this to my own father. I began to feel hate for Felix. *It was his fault*, I thought. I never would have done anything like this if it wasn't for him.

As I drove my daddy home, there was silence in the car. When we arrived at this particular house, he got out of the car and said, "I'll get somebody else to take me to the store." Once I got back to my house, Felix was anxiously sitting up in my house waiting. Knowing that I had some money, he was ready to go get some drugs.

"I didn't get any money," I said.

"What?" he said. "Whatcha mean?"

"Daddy wouldn't give me any money," I said. "He's sick of us, and I don't blame him!"

Felix called his mother up and fed her some lies, so she told him to come over and get some money. When we got to her house, she was listening to a Christian television preacher named Billy Graham. She listened to him every day. I used to listen to what he was saying on the television whenever I was at her house. Felix did the same, but he was only doing it so that he could get the money. Sometimes I felt she gave him money to keep him away from her because he was trouble for their family. He pressed his mother for money, and she eventually gave it to him. She knew that we were on drugs, yet she still gave us money.

During this time, I still checked on Daddy every day. This time, he didn't look too well. I got the mail out of his mailbox for him, and there was an advertisement for some life insurance in his mailbox. By this time, he had cashed in his life insurance policy, so I said, "Daddy this advertisement said you can get life insurance for $1." He didn't say anything. He just looked at me. "I'm going to send it in for it. You never know when you might need it." I knew that if something ever happened, it would be my responsibility, so I just thought I'd try to get it since I was sitting there. I filled out the application and mailed it in.

A week or so later, I got a policy in the mail. Daddy was covered, they said. All I had to do was send in the $1. I continued using. I never got around to sending in the $1. I did, however, check on Daddy daily. One day when I went down to Daddy's, I found the heat in the house at eighty degrees. That would have been cool if it wasn't eighty-five degrees outside!

"Daddy, why do you have the heat up so high? Why are you still in the bed?"

I noticed that there was a fifth of gin on the floor underneath the end table. That was not like Daddy. He never saved liquor. Most times, he couldn't even wait to get home to drink it up. He would pop the top and start drinking in the car.

"Daddy, what's wrong?" I asked. But he didn't answer, he just stared at me. "You got the heat on eighty degrees, and you're all covered up, and you haven't drunk your liquor. Why?" He still didn't answer. "You need to go the hospital, Daddy! I'm calling the ambulance now."

"No!" he said. "I'm not going. For what, Lavinia?"

"So they can check you out."

"I said no, Lavinia!"

"Okay, Daddy, I turned the heat down, and I'm going to fix you something to eat."

I made him some food and told him I'd be back to check on him tomorrow. "If you're not feeling better, I'm calling for help," and I left the room. I went back to the kitchen. Roaches were everywhere. The townhouse complex where we lived was changing. Most of the people that lived in River Trail Townhomes were from the projects or on housing assistance. River Trail was now the *new* projects. Daddy called to have his place exterminated a few times, but the roaches came back. It was a constant fight to keep those roaches away. I had to go home and get some bug killer before I could get into Daddy's kitchen. They were making their way into my townhouse also, so I stocked up on bug spray.

Once I returned to Daddy's, I started to gather my belongings to leave. Josh came to the door. "Daddy's not feeling well," I said to him. "He's in bed."

"I know," Josh said. "He's been acting funny the last couple of days."

"He'll be fine," I said. Then I closed the door to go home, but before I left, I told Daddy to eat.

My boys were still at their grandmothers, so that left me time to drug. But something wasn't right. I couldn't get my mind off Daddy. I told Felix what was going on. Felix always told me that my daddy didn't want to live anymore, but I didn't want to hear that or feel it, so I just kept using the rest of the day. When the night came, I felt so much pain. I prayed for my daddy. In my heart, I knew Daddy had given up. I just couldn't face the truth. I was in denial. "Help my daddy, God. When I get there tomorrow, let him be up, and whatever is going on with him, let it pass."

I didn't really sleep that night. I couldn't wait to get back down to Daddy's house to see if he was better. When I got back to his house that morning, not only was he not better but he also still hadn't touched the fifth of gin. The food was still sitting there, and the heat was back on eighty. This time I didn't ask him whether he wanted to go to the hospital; I just called the ambulance to come get him.

"Daddy," I said, "the ambulance is on the way. They are taking you to the hospital to get you some help." Daddy didn't say nothing; he just looked at me with this look, a look that I'd never seen before. It was a long look that said to me with his eyes, "Lavinia, leave me alone."

I couldn't. I couldn't. I had to help my daddy. I thought, *You can't just give up. You have to fight, Daddy. You've never fought for anything. I need you to fight for your life!* I didn't say it, but I felt that way. *You can't leave me. I need you, Daddy. Please don't do this.* As I watched the paramedics lift my Daddy onto the stretcher, I knew that Daddy had given up, but I just didn't want to accept it. Drugs meant so much to me at this time in my life that I didn't even go with Daddy to the hospital. I went home and got high. This was too heavy for me to deal with, but I needed to deal with my emotions. I had to put on my courage.

Once I was good and high, I went to the hospital. It wasn't good. In the little time it took me to get to the hospital, Daddy had slipped into a coma. They were doing tests for hours, but it felt like days. When the medical staff came to speak with me, Felix had already left and gone home. I had been calling Mama, who was doing well at this time. She was living with Aunt Mabel. She had been through so much. She had been raped and had a couple more nervous breakdowns, but she was on her medication and doing well. She had even returned to work. I called and told her that Daddy wasn't doing well. She talked with me, but when I hung up the phone, I knew I was in this one alone. The doctor told me the truth that Daddy's pancreas had failed, and nothing could be done about it.

"He's on life support for now," they said.

"What do you mean there's nothing you can do? You can do something!"

"I'm sorry, miss, but you have to give your consent to have your Daddy removed from life support."

"No," I said. "No, you do something! You save my daddy!"

The doctor said that he would let me think about what he had just told me. At that point, I started crying. I went into the room, and I just stared at Daddy. I was so angry with him. "What are you doing, Daddy? How you just go' check out on me?" I needed some drugs. I couldn't deal with this pain. I felt too weak. Weakness was not an option. I left the hospital and went home and got so high that I don't even know how I was able to stand on my two feet. I did this day after day after day. Each day God was speaking to me right through the high, but I wasn't hearing him, so I used more drugs, trying to shut the voice of the Lord out.

After about fifteen days, in the middle of one night, the Lord got my attention. I cried, and I cried. God said to me, "You are being very selfish. You are only thinking about yourself and what you want. Your daddy is tired. Let him go. There is no more life in your father."

That morning I got up and got dressed. I didn't even get high first. I went straight to the hospital. I went to the room he was in to say goodbye. I didn't speak very loud, but I knew that God felt me letting my daddy go. I came out of the room and told the staff, "Turn the life support off."

"You're making the right decision," they said.

"Why doesn't it feel like it then?"

I left the hospital to go get high. Felix knew what I had done, so upon my return home, the drugs were waiting. My boys were still at their grandmothers, so I had plenty of time to be in another world—any world other than this one. I didn't go back to the hospital, but after about eight hours or so, the phone rang. I still remember the call. I walked to the telephone to answer. I knew my daddy was gone.

"May I speak to Lavinia Reynolds?" they said.

"Speaking," I responded.

"This is St. Mary's Hospital, and we need for you to come in as soon as possible."

I knew what they were going to say to me, but even knowing, I didn't want to hear it. I called Mama. This time she went with me, and so did Felix. The staff led us into a room. and we all sat down.

"Ms. Reynolds, I'm sorry to inform you, but your father has passed away."

Mama shook her head in disbelief. I felt tears rolling down my face, which was out of order since I thought I had enough drugs in me to stop the pain, but I was wrong.

"Can I see him? I know he's gone, but I need to see him."

I believe in spirits. I believe that my daddy's spirit was in that room waiting to comfort me to say goodbye.

"Sure," they said as they led us back to where he was. Mama looked at him quickly, and then she left the room. Felix asked me if I needed some privacy, and I told him I did.

My daddy looked good, peaceful. I had never seen this peacefulness on Daddy ever. I got into the bed with him and just lay there. I cried and cried and said to him, "Daddy, I pray that God gives you the love you've longed for all your life on this earth. I'm sorry I was so selfish. You had been telling me you didn't want to be here any longer, so now you have what you wanted. I'm okay, Daddy. I'll make it. I promise you. I love you, Daddy."

I lay in the bed with him for at least forty-five minutes. I felt so at peace. I didn't want to leave that room. Felix came back in and asked if I was all right. I nodded. After a short time longer, I got out of the bed and made it to the hallway. Everybody was staring at me. I felt strong. I felt like it was time to go and plan a funeral. It was time to take care of my daddy one last time. God gave me the strength I needed, even though at the time I thought the drugs were doing it. I went home and contacted the funeral home. "My daddy is at St. Mary's Hospital. He just passed away. Would you transfer his body to your facility? I will call in the morning to schedule an appointment for the family and to meet with you."

I asked Mama to go to the funeral home with me. She couldn't because Granny had also just died, and Mama went with her sisters to make arrangements for Granny's funeral. Both bodies were at the same funeral home. Daddy's eldest brother and my cousin, Bo, came to the funeral home with me. The funeral home director called the insurance company that I had filled out the application for insurance with Daddy five weeks prior. The insurance company told them Daddy's funeral expenses were covered, so I was shocked that the letter I got in the mail stating that Daddy was covered was actually the truth, especially since I hadn't mailed in the dollar.

The funeral home had also called the city since Daddy worked for there for over twenty years. They also told the funeral home that Daddy had a funding that would be paid out. It was a funding that Daddy had paid into while he worked for the city. The funeral home chose to go with the insurance policy. They chose to release the money from the city. I didn't even know anything about a funding that Daddy paid into for twenty years.

When I met with the funeral home and was told that the insurance would pay for the funeral, I picked out the best of everything. I picked out a bronze casket, and I put on my daddy a navy blue suit. Blue is my favorite color. I put a tie on him, and the flowers were also blue. I had the funeral at the chapel in the funeral home. I asked a friend of Felix's mother, a pastor, to do the eulogy. Daddy's friends from work were to speak and be the pallbearers.

When I returned home, I got high. Then the phone rang. "May I speak to Lavinia Reynolds?" the white lady asked. On a regular basis, I would have told them they had the wrong number. I didn't take calls from white people because it could have been the police or a bill collector. But this time I felt in my spirit that this call was about my daddy, and I was right.

"This is the city hall, and I would like to know if you would come down in the morning. I need to speak with you about your father."

"Sure, I'll be there," I said.

Turning to Felix, I asked, "Felix, what do you think the city wants?"

The funeral home had not told me that they contacted the city. They only said that they were going to be paid by the insurance company. I found out later that they had called the city.

"I don't know, but you gotta be there in the morning?" Felix asked.

I arrived at the city hall, and the lady said to me, "Your daddy was a very good man. I knew him personally. He was always in here talking about his daughter, Lavinia, and how he appreciated you taking care of him. He talked about how he hadn't been feeling good and wanted to check on his death funding and change his beneficiary. He told me he wanted his daughter to have it. He said, 'Give it to her, and tell her I love her.'"

At that point, I began to cry. All I could think about was how Daddy would say to me, "I ain't leaving you nothing! I'm spending my money now! It's my money. You can put me in a cardboard box for all I care. I won't know. I'll be dead!" His words of choice were a little different though.

Now for this woman to be saying to me what she said, I was so emotional that I felt like a punk. I began to realize that I was out of order, so I stopped crying and straightened up quick. She handed me a check. As she handed it to me, she said, "This is for you and only you. Your father wanted you to have this. It's not as much as his insurance policy that he cashed in on a few years before, but it's a few thousand that he saved for you."

I was so proud of my daddy. I felt like I had something that no one had. I had a relationship with my daddy to remember. I knew him. I knew how he felt in his heart. I had something that no one could ever take. My daddy was a man that lived his entire life in pain—first, mental; then in the end, mental and physical. He never knew what it felt like to feel joy or happiness to be alive. My heart hurt for him, but at the same time, I felt proud of him. I was never the selfish type of person. Even though I knew the money was left to me, I thought of my sister and brothers. I sent Charles, Jr. and Johnny a couple of hundred to the prison they were in. Then I gave my sister a few hundred.

Mama, unfortunately, started a rumor that Daddy had left his insurance money to his kids and that I kept it all. Mama always had me and my sister and brothers arguing. I felt she loved the chaos. I'll never forget the time she told me something that my sister said and told my sister something else. When we got together, Vanessa and I started fighting right in front of her, two grown women fighting in my house while she hollered, "Felix, stop Lavinia! Help! Stop Lavinia!"

For one thing, if Daddy had left some money to the four of us, the insurance company would have split it among us. I wouldn't get their money. Besides, there was no money to get. I even wanted to spend some of the money to get my brothers to the funeral. They both refused, saying that they had a funeral in their cell. That hurt me too—to know that neither one of them wanted to come to their own daddy's funeral. I tried to understand when Charles, Jr. said that he didn't want to come in handcuffs and with prison guards.

Vanessa came to the funeral. She had just given birth to her first baby, and she was going through her life drinking and drugging, but she was there also. During this time, Vanessa was out cold. I couldn't count on her for any support either. I was starting to wonder what was going on with Mama. She said that she would go with me and support me, but she never showed up.

Mama had a way of turning us against Daddy when we were kids, saying that it was all his fault that they fought. I thank God I learned that it was both their faults. I learned that Mama nor Daddy didn't know how to be parents. I learned that they couldn't give what they didn't have to give. Both my parents had been through very traumatic childhoods themselves. Daddy had more of a sense of what was right than Mama did. Now he's gone.

The funeral was very nice. All of Daddy's friends from work were there. I'd never heard so many people tell me how proud my daddy was of me. I was proud of myself, proud that I was standing on my own two feet for the first time without Daddy, proud that I had allowed God to give me the strength to let him go. On the other hand, I kept looking around for Mama. She told me she would be there. She told me that she would support me, but she never showed up. Daddy's family was there though. His father had died not long before him, but his brothers were both there. Uncle Kevin even had the dinner afterward at his house.

When the funeral was over, I walked behind the casket. As I was leaving out of the door, I looked to the parking lot. I saw Mama's car at the back of the lot. As I looked closer, I saw that she was in the car. *What is she doing?* I thought. *She couldn't come into the funeral? Why is she sitting at the back of the parking lot?* Leave it to Mama to do something like this. She couldn't come and pay respect to the only man that ever loved her, the only man that would take her in and do for her no matter what she had done. I was very upset with Mama.

Once I had Daddy placed in the ground and went to Uncle Kevin's because I felt I had to for Daddy, I ate a little something, and then I left, and I went straight to get high. Larry, Jr.; David, Jr.; and Little Calvin didn't go to the funeral because I didn't want them to see Daddy dead. I wanted to protect them, on one hand, but on the other hand, I was exposing them to other ungodly things that no child should experience, just like I went through. I too was as sick as Mama and Daddy.

> Dear God,
>
> As I humble myself to approach your throne, I repent, for I know that you are Almighty God. You made me, and you are the only one that can help me right now. Only you know why it was time for Daddy to die. I know that he no longer has to suffer, yet I miss my daddy. God, I need you to comfort me in a way that these drugs can't do. This hurts, God, and I mean, it hurts bad! Take away my sorrow and give me the peace only you can. Amen.

[Jesus said] And ye now therefore have sorrow: but I will see you again, and your heart shall rejoice, and your joy no man taketh from you.

—John 16:22 (KJV)

Chapter Nineteen

SLEEPING WITH AN ENEMY

After the funeral was behind me, I was blowing a lot of money. I was copping cocaine daily from the man that I knew from my cough-syrup days. He was now selling cocaine. He was also one of the undertakers at the funeral home. I had done business with him and his wife on the boosting tip in the past also, so he knew my track record, and I felt I knew his. He mostly dealt with Felix now, but he knew whose money it was. Felix loved to smoke cocaine, and at this point, so did I. This particular day somebody knocked at the door early. Felix opened it.

"Lavinia, Young Blood is at the door for you."

I went to the door, and Young Blood said, "I'm here on behalf of Hopkins Funeral Home. Mr. Hopkins would like to inform you that the insurance company called and said that a mistake was made, and they would not be covering your father's funeral."

"What?" I said. "What do you mean a mistake? How they go' say they go' pay and then say they ain't?"

"I don't know, but Mr. Hopkins would like you to pay on the bill with the money that your father left at city hall from his job," Young Blood said.

"That money is gone!" I said, and I was lying. I had some money, but I was saving it for later. "Can the funeral home dig my daddy up and take the casket if they don't get paid?"

"Between you and me, Hopkins Funeral Home has insured themselves for matters such as this, so trust me, they go' get paid."

"So they can't take Daddy out of the ground?"

Young Blood said, "No."

I said, "Cool. Tell Mr. Hopkins that I'm sorry. This is unfortunate, but the money that was left at city hall has already been spent, and I will contact him later."

"Okay, I will relay the message. Thank you," Young Blood said.

"Call us, Young Blood, when you get off work."

Young Blood was no fool. He sold drugs on the side. I copped from him. He knew that he had a choice of me paying off the funeral home or paying him for the drugs, which is why I asked him to call when he got off work. Yes, I used almost half the money my daddy left me to get high. The other half, I helped Felix buy a car that Jenny was selling. She took good care of her cars, so I knew I was getting a good car. Felix thought he had gotten over it, but he knew that she sold that car to me for the sake of her grandson. The other half of the money needed to buy the car, Felix's mother gave to him, like she always did. He got the car and treated me and my sons like it was just his car. He ended up reselling it to the car dealer because some broad told him that I had told her I paid for half of the car. He jumped on me and sold it and took every dime of the money and bought drugs.

We lived to use and used to live. Every waking moment consisted of drugging, yet I still did what I had to do for my sons. On the outside, they looked good, but on the inside, I was destroying them, just like I had been destroyed. My sons never kept it to themselves whatever was going on in our home, like I did. I don't believe they told about how much Felix was beating on me though.

193

Young Blood did call after he got off work. That night I got so high that my heart was beating so rapidly. Somebody knocked at the door to bring Felix a downer. The freebasing had us going zig-ziggy-boom! We needed a downer to mellow out. As he went to answer the door, he said, "Go 'head and hit that again."

People have always told me that I was greedy when it came to drugs. I put a hit in that pipe so big that I was in a hurry to hit it before Felix saw what I had done. I stuck the torch in the rum, and then I lit it. I started to pull the coke, and I pulled hard. As I was pulling, I hit the floor. I hit the floor so hard that even I heard the loud bang once I hit the floor! I didn't waste any time getting back up. I also held on to the glass pipe when I hit—can't break the pipe up now, can we?

When I stood on my feet, with pipe in hand, I never even gave thought to the fact that my heart could have burst. Not once did I even wonder how I was able to stand right back up. I know Felix had to be embarrassed when he and his company heard me hit the floor. When Felix made it back up the steps, he asked, "What was that noise?" I said, "Nothing. Can I have another hit?" We smoked all night and the next night and the next night, having sex every night when the coke was gone.

Getting abortions were now a part of the long drawn-out routine of getting high. By this time, I checked into the hospital to get them done. They would put me to sleep for the procedure. That was the best high. When I was told to count backward from ten, by the time I reached seven, I was lit up, and then boom! I was out as quick as a light being turned off. When I awakened, I was no longer pregnant. This went on for six more abortions after the eight I already had. I admit I was as sick as they come. Sure I would give thought to the fact that I had really turned my back on God, but whenever my heart started to eat at me, I got higher.

Once all the money that the city had given me was smoked up, my life started deteriorating quick. All I did was use drugs and listen to Felix verbally abuse me. I started working the midnight shift off and on as a nurse's aide to bring in more money so that I could buy things like Christmas gifts for my sons. Felix's mother gave him money every month for him to smoke up. That's all he did with his money—smoke up. I kept him in my life for that purpose. The drugs had me. Felix was no longer buying cocaine. He started buying the new form of cocaine: crack. It was cheaper, and it was already rocked up. But what it really was was a bunch of garbage mixed together. Today I can say that crack was like the mix-jive Felix used to sell: a little coke and a lot of mess!

As this went on for several years, my brother, Charles, Jr., was released from prison, about a year and a half after Daddy died. Charles, Jr. lived with Cathy. After doing nine years, when Johnny got out, he went to a halfway house. Neither was out long. Charles, Jr. had a beef with Felix about drugs. Felix lied and told Charles, Jr. that I had used up his drugs. One evening I went to Detroit with Felix to cop and left my sons home alone. I told them not to open the door for anyone and that I would be back soon.

While I was gone, two men came through a basement window on my sons. When Larry, Jr. and his brothers heard them coming up the stairs, they were scared and started crying. The men wore masks, but one of them said to my sons, "Nobody is going to hurt you. If you're scared, get under the cover and cover your heads with the pillow." When Larry Jr., told me what happened, I said to myself: "It was Charles, Jr." I knew this was true because that's what he told us to do whenever Mama and Daddy fought.

Larry, Jr. told me, "It looked like Charles, Jr."

"How do you know?" I asked.

"His eyes," Larry, Jr. responded.

Felix checked our bedroom to see what was missing. Nothing of mine was gone, only Felix's pistol and drugs were gone, and he was hollering mad. "Your brother did this!" It was too late to go to Cathy's house, and I couldn't leave my sons alone again, so I waited until the next day. When I got up, I fed my sons and did my household responsibilities. "Take me to Cathy's," I told Felix. I had been thinking about this since I got home. I knew I had to confront my brother. I was mad! I don't care what Felix messed up. You don't traumatize your own nephews! When I got to Cathy's house, she wasn't home. Charles Jr. was there alone. I knocked on the door. He answered. I checked him—you just didn't check Charles, Jr., but he listened to me for some reason, more than others, or maybe I just had more nerves than others.

"What's your problem? You came in my house last night on my sons. You knew you were wrong. Why would you do something like this? I don't care what Felix did. Scaring your own nephews was out of order, and you know it!" I was cussing and speaking to my brother in a way that you just didn't do. He just stared at me. His look was so chilling that it scared me. I saw that he was getting very angry, but he never said a word. I shut up as his eyes started to have this cold look about them, and then I said, "I'm your sister—don't come in my house and kill me tonight!" Still, he never said a word.

I walked out of the door to leave as Cathy was coming in. When I got to the car, I said to Felix, "Charles is out cold!" I felt very uncomfortable the rest of the day. That night I didn't leave my house. I even found myself looking out of the window from time to time to see who might be out there. I didn't sleep all night. I prayed, "God, don't let my brother do nothing stupid," and then I thought about the time when I was fifteen years old and Charles, Jr. had just got out of jail on bond. He messed up the kitchen after I had just cleaned it, and I asked him to clean up the mess. He looked at me and started walking away. I said, "You make me sick! I wish you had stayed in jail!"

Wrong thing to say. Charles, Jr. picked me up off my feet and threw me from the kitchen to the living room! He was steaming mad! He didn't talk; he just reacted. Wow! As I tried to get up, I didn't say another word about him cleaning up after himself. Super Fly came walking through the door, and I told him, "Wayne, Charles just put his hands on me."

He looked at me and looked at Charles, Jr. and told him, "Don't hit your sister!"

Charles looked at Wayne like "Who are you? You need to shut up, or you'll be next!"

Then Wayne said to him, "I'll have to tell your mother!"

Charles, Jr. was staring at Wayne like "What is she go' do?"

Wayne shut up from talking. Charles, Jr. turned and went into the basement. I became absorbed in just how angry my brother can get, and it was very scary, so every time I heard a noise that night, I jumped.

Charles, Jr. never retaliated. He wasn't out of prison for long before he went back. Both he and Johnny were released a couple of times but ended up going back. When they were out, our lives were so full of chaos. Charles, Jr. had been taken into custody once for suspicion of murder of this woman's man. Charles, Jr. was sweet on her. She was a drug dealer and an addict. I saw that. I couldn't understand why my brother couldn't see that, but Charles, Jr. never used drugs. He was the only one of us that didn't, and he never did. Sometimes I felt like he was worse off than any of us. At least the drugs kept me from losing my mind. After watching what mental illness did to Mama, I used to pray that I never lost my mind. I would ask God to keep me from having mental breakdowns. If she didn't take her medication, she lost it, and I mean quick! I remember when Mama would take at least twenty pills a day.

Anyway, my brothers were into crime so much that when they were out and I heard on the news or read in the paper that a store was robbed, I would try to figure out where they were on that night. I received calls about Johnny stealing brand new cars off the manufacturer's lot, Charles, Jr. dealing with Cubans, murder, Johnny sticking up after hours joints. You name it, we did it! I told a lot of lies, covering up for my brothers throughout my life, but now I was falling apart. I had become a crackhead. Nothing about my life was pretty. I looked horrible! My lips kept burns on them as did my fingertips. I had lost so much weight that I would wear my youngest son's jeans.

My sons were getting older and Larry, Jr. started confronting me about my addiction. He had just experienced a tragedy in his family. His uncle had been killed by his other uncle over an argument that involved his grandmother. This was a very tragic time for Jenny. She had to help her son, and she couldn't be in Larry, Jr.'s life at that time like she had been. Now *that* was the tragedy of the city: Frank Parker—dead. People talked about his funeral for weeks. It was something to see. He had white horses and a carriage carry him in his casket through the city, and everybody lined the streets to watch. Wow!

Larry, Jr., wanted to be with Jenny, but she didn't feel her life was stable at that time. It was so sad how the love of money destroyed their family. I was worried about Jenny. She had become a woman in my life that I respected and cared about. Larry, Jr.'s uncle was only about sixteen years old when all this happened. I felt sorry for my son because he loved Jenny and wanted to be with her. His father was never in his life like he needed to be. David was in David, Jr.'s life more than Larry was a part of Larry, Jr.'s life. Sometimes I just thought Larry was like Daddy who let things happen and never stood up for his children to put his foot down to protect us.

All three of my sons were getting older right before my eyes. Larry, Jr., started his first job working on a golf course, caddying. He worked all summer, saving his money. When September came, he bought me a beautiful watch that I was so proud of. Then one day, while I was smoking crack because the other drugs were gone, I let Felix talk me into pawning my watch. "You can get it back as soon as Mama gives me my check the first of the month." I was high, and I did it. When the high wore off, I felt so ashamed. If I could have put my head in a hole and never showed my face again, I would have. It wasn't just this one time, but I continued to betray and steal from my own son.

Uncle James got sick one day and just died. He had stopped using heroin before he died, but he still drank liquor and smoked weed daily. He still worked for the city. Daddy got him that job when he moved in with him when Super Fly didn't want him at Mama's house. He had an insurance policy in Mama's name, so after he died, she bought Larry, Jr. a moped as a gift. Not only did Felix and I resort to riding it to cop drugs, but I also pawned it at the end of summer for little or nothing.

I had done so much to hurt my sons. I hated myself. The drugs had total control of me and my life. I used drugs so much that it was starting to affect me mentally; nothing else mattered.

The drugs were in total control, and since Felix was the one who kept the drugs, he was in control of my thinking. Today when I think about the many things I did while high off crack, I am overwhelmed with gratitude because I am sane and still alive.

Felix was also losing his mind. He was so paranoid that he accused me of letting people into my house while he went to get more drugs. One night he took a knife from the kitchen and just cut up the couch. I actually sewed that couch back together! Then one time he bought an 8-ball of cocaine, which wasn't cooked up. He did that whenever he had the money because it was much better to smoke cocaine rather than crack. We didn't have any baking soda, which is what was used to change the cocaine into rock form, so Felix told me to ask my neighbor for some. I called my neighbor, and she said she had some. Felix told me to tell her that he had some for sale. I told her, and she came by and bought a fifty while we were smoking. Felix served her up well.

As we continued to smoke that night, the neighbor came back for another fifty. By this time, Felix was quite high. By now, he was picking up crumbs off the floor, thinking they were hits. He also kept accusing me of stealing his drugs. When the neighbor came a third time, he gave her a small fifty, and I mean small. I kept quiet because the last time I said something about what he served a person, he accused me of being against him, so I never said a word, especially when he was this high. Felix acted like a madman whenever he smoked these drugs. The fifty was small, but I stayed out of it.

When the neighbor called to complain, Felix went off on her, telling her there was nothing wrong with the rock and that he wasn't giving her anymore. Then when he had smoked up most of the 8-ball, not selling any of it other than what was sold to the neighbor, he had the nerve to tell me to ask my neighbor again for some more soda. I was high, so I never thought she was pissed enough to do something as dirty as what she did. This time she gave me the whole box when I knocked at her door all zig-ziggy-boom!

Biting on my lips and paranoid, when I took it back to Felix, he cooked up the last of his drugs with it. As we started to smoke, the hits tasted nasty. *What's wrong with this dope?* we thought, yet we kept on smoking. Felix accused me of tainting it, but I didn't really care what he was saying. At this point, we had sat at the table and smoked up an entire 8-ball while my sons slept upstairs. The arguing probably woke them several times, but then again, they may have been used to the arguing and slept right through it.

Felix became very violent, ranting and raving about me putting poison in the baking soda. Then as I was pulling a hit, Felix was behind me, and all of sudden, he threw a plate and hit me in the back of the head with it. Blood squirted out of my head and down to my clothes and on to the floor. I looked at the clock to see how long before my sons had to get up to go to school. It was 4:00 a.m., enough time for me to sleep for a few hours. I didn't clean the blood. I didn't even stop the bleeding. I kept hitting the pipe while Felix called me pitiful, yet he kept putting more drugs in the pipe. He wanted me to keep smoking because he thought I poisoned the dope. Anyway, I kept smoking and looking back at the blood all over the floor from time to time, thinking to myself, *I gotta stop before my sons get up for school.*

After about two hours of sitting there, I looked back, and the blood not only was dried up but it also had started to crawl together. I thought I was seeing things. The blood on my head also had dried up. My clothes were dry and full of blood. The hits were so nasty, but I couldn't turn them down. I smoked right up until 6:00 a.m. The dope was gone, and I had a mess to clean up before my sons got up. I got up from the chair, looking horrible. I felt my head, and there was a large lump on the back of it, which wasn't the first time. I was used to having knots upside my head. When I felt my head, it felt so cut and lumpy. At that point, I knew my days of modeling were long over.

As I looked down at the floor to see what I needed to get to clean up the blood—mop, bucket, rag, or whatever—I was blown away! The blood was in a pile, like flakes in a pill. I thought, *What? Does blood do this—pile up, dry up, and come together like this?* I didn't have time to evaluate, so I got the broom and the dustpan from the broom closet and swept up the pile of blood into the dust pan, but I noticed the floor was clean. I wondered, *How can this be? How can blood just do that?* I kept looking at the floor, which, by the way, was white. I never mopped anything up. I went upstairs to shower. Felix had shut up and gone to bed. He never wanted my sons to see him out of order either. (The youngest was his.) They all knew what was going on.

Once I got out of the shower, the alarm clock went off, and the boys got up to use the bathroom. I got into bed, but before they came out of their room, I thought about the blood that was all over the floor. Felix was touching me, and I told him I didn't want to have sex while they were getting dressed for school. I was sick of him touching me anyway. I no longer enjoyed having sex with him. I just didn't, never did. He had gone from sleeping with one of my friends to having me ask my cousins to sleep with us. He was pathetic, and I knew it.

It was the drugs that had me, not the man. He kept the drugs, though, so that meant he was like a leech—I couldn't get him off me. It didn't stop there either. It got worse. After that, we started taking rocks from petty little drug sellers off the street in the middle of the night. Once, after telling a dude I wanted a twenty and him putting it into my hand, I handed him a folded up $20 bill of fake money, and Felix quickly drove off. Then all of a sudden, I heard the dude shooting at the car, but that didn't stop me.

Sometimes Felix would be so high that he would have stupid attacks. One time I told him to go to the projects so I could get what I needed. It was 3:00 a.m. I spotted a target. I told Felix to make sure he didn't stop under a streetlight and that it had to be a dark spot so they couldn't see that it was fake money. He stopped right under the light, and I asked for a twenty from the dude. As the dude went to hand it to me in the car, he saw that the money was fake.

Pow! He socked me in the mouth so hard that my teeth went through my bottom lip. Felix asked the dude, "Man, what did you do that for?" I hollered to Felix, "Pull off!" He drove off, but there was no way I was going back home with no crack. Even with my mouth all busted, I needed a hit, so I found another target. I scored and went home and smoked the twenty. My lip could wait 'til later.

I took drugs from dealers for a while, not even realizing that it was God that kept me from being killed while I was out there. I was out cold, and I had no one to stop me. I no longer felt the presence of God. When and if I prayed, I felt nothing. I just prayed because I knew I needed to. I had totally walked away from God.

> O God! Lord Jesus, help me! Help me! I have sinned over and over. I am a disgrace in your eye. Psalm 52—I practice deceit. My tongue plots destruction. It is like a sharpened razor. I love evil rather than good, falsehood rather than speaking the truth. I'm consumed with doing that which does not please you. I can't sleep, God. I sometimes wonder if you still hear me, or have you turned away from me? I need you, God. Come and see about your child right now. In Jesus's name, Amen.

The evil deeds of the wicked ensnare them; the cords of their sins hold them fast. For lack of discipline they will die, led astray by their own great folly.

—Proverbs 5:22–23 (NIV)

And do not give the devil a foothold.

—Ephesians 4:27 (NIV)

Chapter Twenty

A GLIMPSE OF JOY IN TOTAL DARKNESS

Talk about a full-blown crackhead, you couldn't have told me that I was one because the drugs had my mind very distorted, but I was. I had lost so much weight that my cousin Cathy told me I looked like a little girl. She was a Christian now, and she would stop by at times to talk to me about God and the Bible. Believe it or not, when I talked with Cathy, I always cried because, in my heart, I felt him tugging at my soul; yet I had no time to fall for that weak stuff. I had to focus on the task at hand, and that was smoking dope. Sometimes when I knew that Cathy was coming over, I would impatiently say to myself, "I'll be glad when she hurry up and come so I can get on with my day!"

After I visited with her for a while, Felix would always get me started. He was no good for me. In my heart, I knew that, but I was sick mentally, and I couldn't leave him alone. Once the smoking started, he always, as I said before, bought the first rock. Once we smoked that, we wanted more. One thing about crack, you could never stop. You smoked every dime you had and then did whatever it took to get more. Even though I did whatever it took to cop drugs, one thing I never did was sell my body to get it.

When we were high, I even had Felix stealing rocks from dope boys in the middle of the night. One night, after we smoked, it was too late to try and gank another young corner dope seller, so we went to bed. You couldn't sleep after smoking all night, so Felix was still into sex to come down. I hated having sex with him, but it didn't stop me from twarping (uncontrolled movement of the mouth). This particular night after sex, we fell asleep. There was a loud knock at the door. It was the fire department. Felix's car had been set on fire. The crack I had taken that night was from, believe it or not, this young dude that wasn't having it. He went to the dope house that he saw Felix come out of and asked who we were. It turned out that he was the brother of Mama's stepsister, and on the straight of knowing me, he said that's why he didn't set the house on fire and burn me, Felix, and my sons down.

When I realized who I had taken from, I was like, "Oh my god!" I immediately went to him and told him I was sorry, I didn't know it was him. He let it go. Felix, on the other hand, had to ride around in a car that was so burned up on the inside that the seats and dashboard looked horrible! The car was still drivable, so he drove it until he convinced his mother to buy him another car. That still didn't stop me though.

Next, I started calling my cousin, Chris. She knew several young ballers, and she turned me on to one of her connects. It was the beginning of the month, and Felix's mother had given him his monthly stay-away money, so we started buying from the young dude. When we had smoked up the money, we got scandalous. I called and ordered a sixteenth. He had us come meet him, and when he put the drugs in my hand, Felix pulled off without paying. I had to be out of mind to even think he couldn't find out where I lived! Everybody in the city knew me and Felix.

Anyway, I got back home, and we were smoking the dude's dope when, all of a sudden, I heard a loud bang! I just about jumped out of my skin! I was already paranoid. I opened the door of my bedroom and ran down the steps. Felix was having a stupid attack. I noticed that whenever trouble hits, he's never around, so he stayed inside the room. By this time, Larry, Jr. had moved his bedroom to the basement. He ran up the basement steps.

When I saw that this dude had thrown a large brick through my living room window, I still didn't stop what I was doing. I looked at the damage. It was severe. The entire window was out. Larry, Jr., looked at me. I'm sure he saw that I was high. He shook his head at me and went back into the basement. He never said a word. I turned and went back upstairs.

When I got to my bedroom, Felix was on the floor looking for crack. Why? I have no idea. It wasn't like the sixteenth was gone. My thinking, at that time, told me that the window's broke now, so I may as well keep smoking, and that's exactly what Felix and I did. Felix had put his hands on me at least twice before we were done. He felt I had stolen his hit. Go figure.

My life was a total nightmare. I had been on some type of drugs since I was thirteen years old, but this crack thang was different. I saw crack as Satan himself. Crack hadn't just taken over me and my life; America was in *big* trouble. I felt the government knew what was going on. I felt that this crack epidemic was allowed to cripple a generation—and that's what it did! Some of the best of us were out of control: mothers selling their babies, men selling their bodies, kids selling crack. Satan was on top of the world.

I can remember when I let Felix talk me into moving to New Orleans years before after we stuck up that dope man in Detroit. I actually sold everything I owned for no more than $600. "We needed to start over" is what he said. However, we weren't in New Orleans no more than twenty-four hours before we found the drugs. When you have an addiction to anything, I don't care where you go, the addiction follows. I hated New Orleans, but I did find out why Mama loved the excitement. When I was a kid, she went every year for a few years with her women's club members.

Anyway, Felix got a job doing hair while we were in New Orleans. While he was working, I stood in the middle of the bed of our place because mice were everywhere, and I was scared to get off the bed. I went to some of the nastiest places with Felix. He had some relatives down South that lived like animals.

I'll never forget when we went to one family member's house. It was so nasty that roaches were actually inside the refrigerator.

The bathroom was so filthy that I wouldn't let my dog take a bath in that tub. I cleaned the bathroom and had Felix go and buy new shower curtains and rugs. The house made my skin crawl! I had to get out of that house only for him to get an apartment in the city of New Orleans that was rat-infested. New Orleans, just like Miami, is no place to be if you didn't have money. The poor lived in such a way that I just couldn't handle.

I'll never forget how disappointed I was in myself that I had made such a big mistake. I returned to Michigan with nothing. I had even sold my sons' beds and everything that Daddy left when he died. Drugs and the love of drugs had me making poor choices. Now I was at what I felt my worst. I told Felix several times that I didn't love him. I never did. He was such an evil man that he actually locked his car doors after pulling off the road and threatened me for hours. This was one night after we couldn't find anyone to take drugs from. After Felix knew that I wanted out, he got even more scandalous.

Mama could come over and visit me now. He didn't treat her like he used to. I realize now that it was because she worked for the automotive industry and had money—money that he no longer had.

One day Mama asked if she could see what the high felt like.

"No, Mama," I said.

"Let her hit it," Felix said. "Just don't give her a big hit."

He knew that once Mama hit it, she would be just like us and spend every dime she made on crack trying to capture that feeling of that first hit. I felt so ashamed of my behavior. I was smoking crack with my own mother. While I was smoking it, I would ask God not to let anything happen to my mama. I knew about people having heart attacks. I knew how "out of character" crack could have you. I knew how Mama clowned on me when she had nervous breakdowns, but you know, not one time did the crack take Mama to that place the mental breakdowns took her. She never once wanted to kill me or take off walking in the dead of winter and not return for days. No. Crack didn't do that to Mama. That was weird because as insane as crack made me, it made Mama act just the opposite. She was cool, calm, and collected whenever she smoked with us.

After smoking with us the entire summer, Mama called one day and said that she would no longer be smoking crack. I was glad she stopped, even though I knew that would put a dent in the free high Felix and I got. Once Mama stopped, Felix and I went back to snatching dope out of those young boys' hands in the middle of the night, only this time I said, "You take it. I've always been the one to do it." I was tired of getting socked in the mouth while he watched. It wasn't enough that Felix was beating the crap out of me, I was also getting beat up by those young dope boys.

One night Felix played the wrong dope boys. A month had gone by and he didn't know that they were out to get him. When Felix and I went back to buy a dime ($10 rock), the young boys attacked him. They had been looking for him all month. We were in Mama's car when we ganked them. Mama never told us that they stopped her one day, so when we went to cop the dime, they pounced Felix.

I knew something wasn't right when the dude told him, "Get outta the car. My man will be right here." Felix had already been smoking, so he had a stupid attack. He got out. When he opened the door, I thought, *Why does he want you to get outta the car?* But I didn't say a word. As soon as Felix stepped out of the car, about six or seven young dudes ran up on him and started hitting him upside his head. He lost the $10 as he took off running, and I immediately locked myself in the car. I saw one of the dudes look at me. As I locked the door, he saw that he had no trouble out of me as long as I didn't have any trouble out of him.

God was with me yet again. Felix, on the other hand, got the dog crap whooped out of him. They beat him so bad after they caught him. I leaped onto the driver's seat and followed in the car as Felix ran. I watched as he was being beaten. I, in no way, was going to get out of the car to help him. As a matter of fact, I enjoyed watching it. As many times as he had beaten me up, I had no compassion for him. All I needed was some popcorn, and then I would have felt just like I was at a good movie.

After they had beaten Felix unconscious, the young boys took off running down the street. I waited until I was sure they were gone, and then I rolled down the window and yelled out, "Felix, Felix!" As he started to wake up, I hollered, "Get in the car! Get in!" He staggered to the car. As he fell to the seat, I could see that he was in no shape to go home with me.

I knew that the last thing Felix wanted was for my sons to see that he had gotten the crap beaten out of him, so I asked him, "Where do you want me to take you?" He said, "Take me to my niece's house." I took him there, and she began helping him immediately. She helped him get inside the house with the help of her girlfriend. Felix stayed with her for a few days. I told the boys that Felix was at his mother's. Rumors started to fly. Everybody in the city learned what happened to Felix. He may have had a reputation at one time in his life but not anymore. These young dudes today could care less about who you used to be. Today he was a crackhead who took their dope, and he had to be dealt with.

When Felix recuperated and started looking better, he came back to my house for a while. After the beating, Felix started acting like he had some mental issues. I no longer trusted him to get high in my house. He began to let the drugs take him places that all I could say was wow! He would be all over the floor looking for crack. He would even think crack was in my hair. He always spoke of the beating he got. He would go from me saying that I enjoyed watching them beat him (which I did) to him saying he's going to kill them! After that, he put his hands on me for the last time because I started working on the midnight shift at this nursing home, so I didn't need him to get me high anymore.

Drugs were being sold in the entire townhome complex. River Trail was now crack city. All the adults smoked, except a few; and all their sons sold it. I had dealings with the young boys that no mother should have had. I ganked them and told them I was just taking them to school. Somebody was going to do it, might as well be me! At least I wasn't going to hurt them. I made so many of them angry that one of them actually brought a gun to my door. I got with him on that too. "Are you crazy?" I said. "If you pull a gun on somebody, you better make sure you're prepared to use it because if you pull it on the wrong person, they'll make you *eat* that gun!"

There were so many kids out there that had no idea what the streets were really about. The streets were no joke. The street life was no game, and it wasn't for everybody. Truth be told, it really wasn't for me—I just got caught up. It was God that kept me protected. I know this today. God was like a bodyguard to me. He was right there. With Felix out of my house, I was able to work at night.

My sons were old enough now that I didn't need a sitter. Larry, Jr. was fifteen, and he was changing. Mama had given him several sips of alcohol by now. Even though I would say, "Mama, don't give him that!" she would say, "It's his birthday. A sip won't hurt him." She didn't know the harm she was doing. Me neither. Larry, Jr. went from an A and B student in school to dropping out. He had watched his own mother spend her whole check with his friends. Larry, Jr. saw the neighbor's son make money and buy himself a car and run thangs at his mama's house, so he wanted in. He was definitely a Parker.

Larry, Jr. came home one day while I was smoking with Felix. He had bought a small pill bottle of crack. I'll never forget that day. He called me into the bathroom. "Look, Mama," he said. "Where did you get that?" I always said I'd never let my son sell drugs, I'd never allow him to destroy his life like that; but when my son told me to look, I said to him, "Sell me a twenty!" Wow! I had lost all the morals and values that Daddy once taught me. I was all-in and anything went.

Well, I had Felix locked up. "Felix, you're not only getting outta my house, you're going to jail for putting your hands on me." His mother kept saying that I was wrong. I felt she was a godly woman and thought she was weird because, all day long, she watched Billy Graham on the television. I didn't understand how she was always so calm, like nothing ever knocked her off her square. She was part of the reason her son treated me like he did, so I wasn't hearing what she was saying either. He stayed locked up for at least ninety days. By the time he got out, Larry, Jr. was rolling big time. I had gotten pregnant by Felix before this though. He was still into the sex when the drugs were gone, and it did calm me down, so I did it with him.

I got pregnant for the fifteenth time, and as usual, I was going to get an abortion. I was working, and I had lost the Medicaid insurance, so I had to pay for the abortion—the first one I would be paying for because the state paid for all the rest. I never got the abortion, though, because after Felix got out of jail, we kept smoking up the abortion money. I also thought when Dr. McWilliams said I could never carry another baby full term and that I would abort this baby anyway. But at five months pregnant, I realized that Dr. McWilliams was wrong. I had to stop using drugs because I was about to have a baby. I stood alone with this baby. I worked a few more months through the pregnancy, but once I stopped using drugs, I started to feel God's presence again, like I hadn't in a long while. I felt more peace in my life now than I'd had in a long time.

Felix was out of my home, and I loved it! Larry, Jr. and David, Jr. were teenagers now. Even Calvin was old enough, and he and David, Jr. got off into sports. They didn't say anything negative about me being pregnant. I think they were just glad that I wasn't using drugs and Felix was out of their home. It had been ten years since a baby was in my life, but I began to look forward to this baby. Back then, they couldn't tell you what you were having, but I felt in my heart it was a girl. I was the only female in my life for a lot of years, and I really didn't want no girl. Females were a headache. I didn't think I could share my space with another female.

Eventually, I was starting to see that this pregnancy was a blessing. This baby saved my life. I slowed my roll quick. I hadn't been high in three months, which was God's grace because I could never stop before, not even when I knew I should; but I never continued using drugs when I was pregnant.

One night Satan told me that no one would know and to go ahead and get high. "You got a month to go. By the time the baby's born, you will have the drugs out of your system." Unfortunately, I fell for the lie. I smoked crack that night. I only hit it one time, and all of a sudden, my water broke. *Oh my god!* I thought. *Well, I may as well finish. It's in my system now.* I didn't even call a ride to the hospital until I was done smoking the dope. It was about 2:00 a.m. I called my aunt Penny. She came and took me to the hospital. By the time she got to my house, the high had worn off.

When she pulled up to the emergency area, she said, "You don't need me to go in with you, do you? You've done this many times, right?" I said, "No, you don't have to come in." I got out of the car and walked up to the front desk and told the receptionist that my water broke. I felt contractions at that point. I sat down in a wheelchair, and they wheeled me up to the delivery ward. I was all alone, so I called Felix, but he acted like he didn't care. He really didn't believe that I was pregnant by him. He was just that sick that he was still telling himself that I was sleeping with other men, so he never came to the hospital. I was on my own.

When Dr. McWilliams came into the room, it crossed my mind to say, "Dr. McWilliams, I thought you said I'd never carry another baby. I guess you were wrong," but I didn't say a word. I only wanted to deliver. When I did, I was so happy! She was gorgeous. She was fat. She was baldheaded, like I was when I was a baby. She was a doll! Princess is what I called her when I saw her for the first time. *I finally have a best friend*, I thought. *We will be friends forever.* I was in love again, just like I was when I first saw all my three sons. Only this time she was me and I was her. My daughter, Katrina, wow!

As soon as I brought her home, Felix realized that it was his daughter. He had never had a daughter, so he started to show signs of his controlling behavior right away. I resorted to using drugs with him again. Even though Felix didn't live with me, he came over with the drugs. Larry, Jr. was old enough now that Felix could no longer get away with the things he did in the past. Now when Felix started to get ugly, like he was going to hit me, Larry, Jr. would check him. One time Larry, Jr. came running from the basement with a baseball bat. "Hit her! Hit her! I've been waiting fifteen years to do this!" Felix knew Larry, Jr. was not playing, so he backed off. Then Larry, Jr. ran out of the front door and destroyed Felix's car. He broke out every window and light on it. Felix didn't carry his butt out there to try to stop him either. He had the nerve to say to me, "Stop your son!" I said to him, "You bad . . . You stop him!"

Felix was no fool. He knew that he had better not do anything to my son. That was the one time I would have hurt him. I took the abuse, but put your hand on my kids, I flipped! Once before, when he called himself angry at Larry, Jr. and acted like he was going to put his hands on him, I went straight to the knife drawer to grab the butcher knife. I was going to cut his throat. "Don't touch my kids, and I mean that! If it ain't your child, don't touch him." I was no fool. "You can't make me think you love my son, you're jealous of his family, and in David, Jr.'s case, you still think I want his daddy."

Felix started to see that his authority, as usual, was done and over. My son wasn't having his mess. Larry, Jr., as I said earlier, was about to become a drug dealer. After Princess was about six months old, Larry, Jr. started selling. I picked up where I left off when I quit because I was pregnant; and I deteriorated quickly. I was right back in the madness I had left alone. The only difference was that now Felix didn't live in my house and my eldest son had lost his mind.

> Dear God,
>
> I bow before you. I am so full of sin. When I wake up in the morning, my day consists of evil. In my heart, I know what I am doing is wrong, yet I continue to do it. Satan has full control of my life, God. I cannot fight him. God, I need you to help me. I don't have the strength it takes to turn from my sin. I am in the prison of sin. It rules over me, yet I seek you, God. I always seek you. I love you, God. I just can't stop what I'm doing. Only you can stop me. I need you now. Thank you, God, for the glimpse of joy when my daughter was born. Thank you for allowing me to feel love, to feel you, for you are love. Amen.

What a wretched man I am! Who will rescue me from this body that is subject to death?

—Romans 7:24 (NIV)

The wrath of God is being revealed from heaven against all the godlessness and wickedness of people, who suppress the truth by their wickedness . . .

—Romans 1:18 (NIV)

Chapter Twenty-One

A BAD DREAM

Charles, Jr. had got out of prison again for about four months. He just couldn't stay out of prison. Johnny got out too, but this time he did well. He worked a job, but he also sold crack on the side. He moved in with me for a short time, but as soon as I found his stash in my basement and smoked it up, he got mad and moved out. He rented a house not far from me. I was proud of my brother because he was doing something I'd never seen him do—he was staying out of prison, and he was not getting drunk or high. I was quite impressed. I was very happy for him. On the other hand, I was concerned because I knew, by selling, he was setting himself up. Selling drugs is also an addiction for those that get addicted to the lifestyle and money.

Mama had moved out of Aunt Mabel's house and into an apartment with a man she'd been seeing for a while. He was an alcoholic, but he didn't act like my daddy whenever he got drunk. Mama was doing better than she had been doing in years. Vanessa was living a life that consisted of her and her children. She drank a little, but she was also doing much better. My life, on the other hand, was falling apart. I felt the presence of Satan daily. He was all over my home. He had control of not just me but he also had my son.

Johnny had started to use his own product by now, and he pawned his car to Larry, Jr. often after he started buying from him.

Johnny had married this white woman that he worked for, but that didn't last. Larry, Jr. took over the River Trail Townhomes quick, but the problem was this was not the same complex it used to be. River Trail was dangerous now! It was the new projects. All types of people lived in the complex—people that I didn't trust, people that envied and was jealous of Larry, Jr. All I felt in my home now was darkness. Johnny had given Larry, Jr. a gun, a gun that didn't work properly. He told him not to fire it because it might malfunction. "Just use it to front" is what he told my son. Larry, Jr. was only sixteen and didn't need a gun, in my opinion, but in all actuality, he did need it. He was a target in River Trail: a young kid making money with no man around.

I was so cracked out. I was looked at as a joke. That changed because when I was high on crack, I didn't let nobody come to my house. I tried to treat my house like a home as much as I could. My children were living there. Sometimes I would be so paranoid that I would wake David, Jr. up in the middle of the night and tell him we had to leave our home. "Something's go' happen," I'd say to him. "Ain't nothing go' happen, Mama," he'd say back to me, but never once did he not do as I said.

When I lay in my bed that night, I was so disturbed that I couldn't sleep. I heard people walking around outside. At times I would look out of the window and no one was there but I heard them talking. I felt demonic spirits all around me. I knew something bad was going to happen. I knew it. I became so uncomfortable in my own home that at two o'clock in the morning, I would hide in the shrubs with Larry, Jr.'s gun when he wasn't home. My little princess Katrina would be in the crib sleeping, and so would her brothers. When they were home, Calvin spent most of his time at his grandma's. Larry, Jr. and David, Jr. were always someplace in the complex.

I hated living in River Trail. To be honest, I was afraid. I would allow Felix to come over at times just so I wouldn't be alone. I had quit the midnight job by now, and Larry, Jr. was treating me like I was a dog. He let that crack money go to his head. Even though I was a crackhead, I felt he could have treated us as a family better than he did. He was very selfish. I sometimes felt that he hated me. Sometimes Calvin would get mad and strike out walking, saying he's going to live with his grandma. David Jr. was my only son that showed me any compassion. He just had a kind heart. He never treated me like I was nothing. None of my sons treated their sister any other way than with love and concern.

I didn't get high until Larry, Jr. was in the house in bed most of the time. He was drinking and when he had too much to drink in him, he would come home and go to sleep. Larry, Jr. was very violent when he drank liquor. We loved to check people that he knew had crossed him. He was like his mother. He didn't like people that would grin in your face and be plotting behind your back.

He kept his customers from coming to my door mostly, except for this one broad who just didn't want to listen, so when she knocked, I said, "Who is it?" When she gave me her name, I was zig-ziggy-boom. I was disturbed because she had messed with my high. I told her, "I don't care if you think you know me! Don't call or come to my house for Larry, Jr. He has a pager. Page him. If he don't call you back, I can't help you! This is my home, not a dope house, so don't come here!"

She would listen until she got too high and the drugs told her, "Screw you!" Then one time she knocked, and I opened the door. I had the gun Johnny gave Larry, Jr. in my hand. "Come on in," I said as I waved the gun. She stepped in. I could see that she was scared to death. "I told you not to come to my house, but you chose not to listen. Sit down!" I demanded. She sat in the chair a few steps from the door as I closed it. I was still waiving the gun in her face. I sat at the head of the table and put a hit in my pipe. I took a hit and said to her, "Since you can't stay away from my house, you can sit here 'til I'm done. I bet you won't come knock on my door again!"

She begged me, "Lavinia, I'm so sorry, please let me go. I won't be back."

"I know you won't 'cause you ain't getting outta here," I said.

And then I smoked at least twenty to thirty minutes more. I heard Larry, Jr. get up. He came up the basement steps to see what I was doing, and he said, "Mama, let her go."

"No!" I said. "I told her to stay away from my house, but she wants to do what she wants, so sit here!"

Larry, Jr. opened the door and said to her, "Get out. I told ya'll my mama's crazy. I don't know why you won't listen."

"Oh, they ain't gotta listen, just be ready to deal with me when they don't!"

Larry, Jr. shook his head and said, "Mama, you had enough! Go to bed!"

He went back down the steps into the basement. David, Jr. never woke up. Neither did my baby. Calvin was at his grandma's. He spent a lot of time with her, just like Larry, Jr. and David, Jr. did spend with their grandmas when they were younger.

Satan was busy this summer at my house. There was an incident every week at my house. Larry, Jr. had two girlfriends, and both of them were fighters. One fought him, and the other fought the one that fought him, so they were fighting every week. This week the one who wasn't having him seeing another girl brought a knife into my house, and while in the basement with him, she stabbed him right in his side. I couldn't believe that she had stabbed my son! But she too was a victim of what she had learned at home. It's my understanding that her mother cut her dad often. She flipped just like I used to do.

When I saw her eyes, I knew she was dangerous. I called the police, but she ran out of the back door. The police went to another townhouse looking for her, but she was nowhere to be found. Larry, Jr. had a bad dream in the middle of the night, hollering her name. I woke him up and asked, "You wanna drop the charges?" He said, "Yes." I could tell that he didn't want to cause her trouble, so I stopped pressing the issue. Both of them were acting like kids, and they always got started in my house.

Life for me was out of control. The next time they fought in my basement, I went down to stop it. I was pushed back into a glass mirror that broke, and as it broke, the glass slid down the back of my ankle and sliced the skin off so thick that I couldn't bend my ankle for over a month. I was the one getting the whooping trying to stop them.

After she stabbed Larry, Jr., the other girl jumped on her; all this happened at my house. No wonder the manager of the complex wanted to evict me. They didn't tell me I had to move. I had been a resident in the complex for fourteen years. I had always been a good resident. My name was never nasty. I was not the type of person that lived loose. I've always been a private person, but anybody can't just come to my house.

But now my eldest son had become a drug seller, and he was good at it. He was a Parker, and he had a business head on his shoulder. His thinking was more like his late uncle than any of his relatives. Haters didn't like that, how a sixteen-year-old ran the River Trail like he did. He was experiencing some of the same things in life that I had always gone through.

One of Larry, Jr.'s friends saw me leave out of the front door one day. I went across the street to borrow some sugar. While I was gone, his friend went into my back door and down into my basement steps and stole $800 from underneath Larry, Jr.'s pillow. He had a lot of nerve. What if I had come back in the front door? Obviously, he had been watching my house.

When Larry, Jr. got home, he asked me, "Did you take my money?"

"No. What money?" I asked.

"I had $800 under my pillow!"

"Wha-a-a-t?" I said.

"Did anybody come over here?" he asked me.

"No," I told him.

"Well, where's my money?"

"I did leave out once to go borrow some sugar. I left Katrina upstairs in her crib asleep. I know ain't nobody got the nerve to just come in my home," I said.

I was wrong. When Larry, Jr. went back out into my neighborhood, he learned that one of his so-called friends had just copped some drugs. This was a kid that had been in the complex for a while. They were cool. When Larry, Jr. came back to the house, he said, "Mama, I know who took my money." Now this was money that was underneath his pillow. I hadn't even mentioned the money he kept in his safe. Yes, he had a safe in the basement. He kept his drugs and money in there. He lived the street life. High school was a thing of the past. He had been hardened by the life. I had exposed him to the life that Felix, his uncles Johnny, Charles, Jr. and his late uncle lived—they all were hustlers. It was a curse in our bloodline, one of the many generational curses on us.

When he realized who had come into his mama's house, he was so mad! He knew he couldn't just let it go; or every time I left home, somebody was going to try him. I said, "Larry, Jr., it's not worth killing him for. We are not people that don't value life. Now if you want to beat the mess out of him, I can call and get Felix and some of his people to have your back . . . But handle your business!" I called Felix. All Larry, Jr. had to do was give him a twenty or two and he was there. Larry, Jr. got his baseball bat. When he got back in the house, he was breathing real hard. He didn't go out there shooting. Young people today have no value of life because they are not taught that God values human life more than anything.

I found all kinds of money in my basement. One day I was coming up the stairs after doing laundry, and I saw what I thought was a dollar under the steps. I said to myself, "Larry, Jr. dropped some more money." I went back down the steps and picked it up. It was a $100 bill—Christmas in July! I kept it. If you can drop a hundred and not miss it, you don't need it. I found money in all his pockets whenever I did his laundry. In the middle of the night, I prayed. Believe it or not, I was scared for my son, so I prayed a lot. I used drugs, and I prayed, talk about feeling the presence of darkness. It was a heaviness that I couldn't explain. I felt it. I felt it all day every day. It ate at my inner being.

One night I was sitting at the table waiting for Charles, Jr.'s daughter (my niece) to come over. She lived with her aunt, Lucille, at the back of us. She would come over and talk to me all the time.

I would tell her about her daddy. I told her how Charles, Jr. was and that he may be in prison but she meant everything to him. I told her how he had tried to be in her life, but her mother wouldn't let him be. Her aunt had a boyfriend named Amos that I didn't trust for some reason. Because of my niece, Lucille and Amos were allowed in our world. But I also knew that because of what Larry, Jr. was doing, everybody wanted to be my friend. I didn't trust *nobody* at this point.

This night I was out of cigarettes. My niece had been sitting at the table with me for about an hour. Larry, Jr. had come in and gone to bed. When Lucille knocked on the door for her, I asked her if Amos could give me a ride to the gas station to buy cigarettes. She said she would ask him. Lucille and my niece left my house. About fifteen minutes later, Lucille's boyfriend knocked at my door. She was with him. I wouldn't have opened the door if he had been alone. "You need a ride?" he asked me. "Yes," I said as I grabbed my purse. I left out of the back door, and as I was walking toward his car, I walked up on a man lying in the grass who looked like he was asleep or drunk. I wasn't feeling that thing yet because, as I said, River Trail had changed, and it was summertime, so it wasn't unusual for people to still be out and about at two or three o'clock in the morning. River Trail was crack city, so somebody was always out.

As I was walking to their car, I looked and noticed that the man had on a black trench coat. I didn't say anything. I got into the car and traveled for about a half mile from home. Then God said to me, "Go back home."

Instantly, I said to the dude, "Take me back home."

The dude looked at me. "Say what? I thought you wanted cigarettes."

"Take me back home!" I hollered.

He turned his car around. I didn't say another word. As he was pulling up to my door, I saw a man. It was the man that was lying in the grass. I got out of the car and walked up my sidewalk. "Can I help you?" I asked him. He was knocking at my front door.

"Is Marcus home?" he asked.

He probably made up the name because I had never heard of the person he asked for. "You have the wrong address," I said.

"Open the door, tramp!" he said as he pulled out a gun and pointed it at me.

"I don't have a key," I said.

I didn't because I left out of the back door, but I wasn't going to tell him that. Then he lifted his leg and took his foot and kicked my door hard. The door didn't open, so he raised his foot again. As he went to kick it again, God said to me, "Run and holler and wake up the neighbors." I did just that. I saw the car that I had just gotten out of pull off. I started hollering so loud, "Help! Help! Help!" I saw the lights going on inside the neighbors' homes. I kept hollering. I had awakened the entire complex. Then I heard, "Pow!"

"Jesus!" I said. "Please don't let this man kill my son!" The gunshot scared me so bad that I peed on myself—I couldn't stop it. I've never in my life been so scared—never! While I was peeing on myself, I heard my son's cry, "Mama!" My heart was rapidly beating. The neighbors came out of their homes, and then I saw David, Jr. jump out the upstairs window. I remember when David, Jr. was a kid, his brothers always called him a monkey because he could climb a tree in a matter of seconds. His monkey skills were paying off at this moment. He leaped out of that second floor window and ran toward me.

"David, Jr.!" I ushered him into a neighbor's house. Then the dude that kicked my door in came running out. Larry, Jr. was chasing him and shooting at him with his gun. At that point, I started to talk tuff to the dude. "That's what you get! You thought you was go' rob my house cuz I live alone and you thought my son was a punk! Now who's the punk?"

"Let him go, Larry, Jr.!" I hollered.

By this time, the neighbors had called the police. They showed up after the fact. I told them which way the dude ran. He left a blood trail, so it wasn't hard to find where he went. The dude ran through the back door of an ex-girlfriend's house and out of her front door. Even though the police went into the house the dude ran, they never caught him. The police, on the other hand, were no fools. They knew what Larry, Jr. was doing. They just didn't have proof yet. I got the word of who that dude was though. He even had the nerve to speak with Larry, Jr.'s father, telling him that he was told that somebody else lived at my house, that he didn't realize that he was trying to rob his son. Larry, Jr. called and told me that when the dude got down into the basement, he woke him up with the gun to his head and told him to open the safe. Larry, Jr. actually told me that he told the dude, "No."

"What?" I said. "Why would you do that?"

"I wasn't opening my safe! I told the dude he could have my gold chain."

Larry, Jr. said that the dude pulled the trigger, but the gun didn't go off. He grabbed for the gun, and the dude took off up the steps. Larry, Jr. had the gun and started shooting at the dude as he chased him out of our house. That's where the blood came from. God had not only been right there for me, but he also had my children covered. God was in that basement. I know this without a doubt.

Once that was over, Larry, Jr. didn't stop what he was doing. River Trail told me that he had to move. I wasn't being evicted, but my son was. I was called down to the office and told that Larry, Jr. had to go. I didn't tell him because I didn't want him to have the attitude (like most of the young boys did) of they're putting me out anyway, so I might as well get paid before I go. Sometimes I wonder if these kids realize what kind of a life they are stepping into.

Anyway, Larry, Jr. went back to bed and back to sleep. Vanessa's kids were upstairs asleep. They never woke up while this was going on. David, Jr. went back to bed. Calvin wasn't home. Katrina never woke up that night either. Maintenance came early that morning and repaired my door. They didn't talk to me like they usually did. Everybody in River Trail was disappointed in the young boys because they were out cold, and the parents were all on drugs, so of course, they were no help.

Father,

I come before you humbly, for I know you are Almighty God, King of Kings. You control everything. You are the beginning and the end. Satan cannot win if you don't allow him to. I say thank you, God. Thank you for your son, Jesus, for his blood, for protecting my home, my children, and myself when I couldn't protect us. Thank you for your grace and mercy. I know, God, if it had not been for your love for me, I wouldn't be alive. Thank you. Amen.

God is our refuge and strength, an ever-present help in trouble.

—Psalm 46:1 (KJV)

Chapter Twenty-Two

THE END OF A NIGHTMARE

So much had gone wrong in my home that I talked to God daily. Isn't it funny how we run to God when we can't fix things, but as soon as we think we got it together, we put God on the back burner? "I can handle it now, God, but thank you anyway." Well, I used to run to God all the time, but now I was running to him sometimes. I realized that this was bigger than me, and I had lost control of the situation completely.

So yes, I ran to God. "Please, God, help me! Get me out of this one. I have racked my brains, the little that's left, and come up with nothing. You've been there, God, my entire life. Where are you now? Why won't you do something now? I don't sleep. I hear and see demons all around me, God. I feel like not only have they taken over me but my sons as well. They're all outside my house. I hear them through the night. They're driving me crazy, yet I continue to face them daily. I need some rest!"

My friend, Carolyn, who worked at the nursing home with me started smoking crack with me. I let her come to my house because I felt I knew her. She was a good person. Besides, she had started pawning her car to Larry, Jr. She couldn't go home without her car, so I let her stay at my house. She also smoked her dope with me, and I smoked mine with her. We were dope partners. We both had kids, and her son went to school with my son Calvin. We thought we were being good mothers; how drugs deceive you.

Carolyn's boyfriend, Steve, had been seeing Larry, Jr. in her car. Her boyfriend knew what was going on because he had been in the game also. He wasn't going for what she was doing. One night Steve came to my door for Carolyn. He started fighting her outside my house. Larry, Jr. heard him from the basement and came up the stairs.

There were a couple of dudes that had moved in right in the back of us, and they also heard the commotion and came out of their house and asked Larry, Jr. if he wanted to take Carolyn's man. Larry, Jr. said, "Yeah!" Together, they went after him, but he ran off. Larry, Jr. came inside my house and went downstairs. I was upstairs, but God told me that it wasn't over, so I stayed at the window, hidden but there. I felt that Carolyn's man wasn't going to let it go down like this. I was right! I saw this car pulling up to my house. Carolyn's man got out of the car with a shotgun in his hand. Somebody in the car hollered out, "Come on out! You wanna get wit' me? Come on out!"

Larry, Jr. was in the basement and didn't hear Steve. I'm glad he didn't. I opened the window and called Steve by his name. "Steve, you don't wanna do this. I have kids in here. You have kids! You know you're wrong!" He got quiet, and then he turned and got back inside the car, and the driver drove off. Never again did I ever hear from him. Carolyn called the next day to apologize for his behavior and asked me not to retaliate. I told her that her man was out of order for bringing that nonsense to my house. I then let her know that I couldn't have him coming to my house like that, so we needed to end this now. She stopped calling.

I started to dip off into seeing Felix now and then, just to get high. He was like a bad cold I couldn't seem to get rid of. One day, after Larry, Jr. left the house, Felix came over. We smoked for hours. I had crack. Larry, Jr. left it all over the basement, so all I had to do was go down there and look. I would always find some down there. It never failed. Plus, he gave me crack daily. He was making a lot of money. When he cooked up his sack, he gave me the shakes (crumbs that hadn't rocked up). He copped drugs at least twice a week. He sold out quick because he sold double-up, which was two for the price of one. All the smokers wanted to get his dope.

There was no denying it. Larry, Jr. had a head on his shoulders. He just did the same thing his mama did. He let Satan control it. Larry Jr. hated Felix. He knew he was rotten and that he meant his mama no good. Felix would smoke dope and get so paranoid that he would take baby girl Katrina out of her crib in the middle of the night and leave out walking with her. I never did a thing to try and get my daughter. I'd just let him take her from me.

I shared the drugs I had with Felix, but enough was never enough. He would always start a bunch of mess. This night Felix started in on me about Larry, Jr. He said to me, "If it was my son, I wouldn't let him sell crack without giving me what I wanted. This is your house!" Larry, Jr. gave me drugs, but he didn't whenever Felix was at my house. As bad as smoking crack made me act, when Felix was around, it was worse. I had begun to think that crack was everywhere whenever I smoked.

One time I scraped the old grease off the wooden cutting board that was on the kitchen counter, thinking that the buildup of grease was crack. Not only did I scrape it up, but I also I smoked it! I couldn't tell you how many times I smoked whatever. Now I was twarping and listening to Felix put in my head that Larry, Jr. owed me. I started feeling like he was right. "This is my house! How dare he treat me like I'm the kid!" So I went outside and got a tire crowbar out of Felix's trunk. Larry was gone for the night, but he had been home several times throughout the day, asking, "Mama, when is he leaving?"

"Soon," I'd say. "You didn't give me nothing today, Larry."

"Mama, I'm not going to give you no drugs with him here."

My son knew that Felix was trouble. He had been trouble in my life for over thirteen years. I knew Larry, Jr. wouldn't be back for a while, so with the crowbar I got out of Felix' trunk, I carried it down to the basement while he cheered me on and broke open Larry, Jr.'s safe. It took a minute, but I got it open. I destroyed it! I didn't touch a dime of the money, but I took all the crack I wanted. David, Calvin, and baby girl Katrina were asleep upstairs. Felix was in the living room waiting for me to bring more drugs upstairs for him to smoke. We smoked until two o'clock in the morning when I decided it was time to stop because I felt Larry, Jr. would be home soon. I needed to calm down so I could talk to him about why I broke into his safe. I sat there for about an hour listening to Felix put words in my head about why I wasn't wrong for what I did.

As the high wore off, I was beginning to see that Felix was full of it! He just wanted drugs. He didn't care about Larry, Jr. or me as far as that mattered. I began to feel sick. I had made a huge mistake. I knew Larry, Jr. wasn't going to deal with this too well at all. It was about three thirty in the morning when Larry, Jr. came walking through the door. He had been drinking. He was always ready to fight whenever he drank. My high had just worn off. When Larry, Jr. came in, he said, "Mama, why *he* still here?" Felix was sitting there looking like a kite—high.

"He's getting ready to leave," I said.

Larry, Jr. continued walking to the basement. When he got there, he yelled, "You been in my safe?"

I got up from the couch and hurried to the basement. I knew my son pretty well by now but not well enough obviously. I already had the gun Johnny had given him at the beginning of the summer. I didn't want him grabbing it and hurting Felix. I wanted to say, "I kept telling you to give me my drugs, and you had the nerve to tell me no."

But instead I said, "This is my house, you've gone too far!"

He looked at me, and I could see that the alcohol had him not receiving what I was saying. He pushed me so hard that I fell down to the floor. As I was getting up, I felt so angry and hurt. Out of disbelief, I said, "You put your hands on me! I'm killing you!"

He, at the same time, said, "Felix—I'm killing him!"

He went to search for the gun, but it was gone. "Where is it at, Mama?"

I took off running up the stairs, and he chased after me.

"Where's is it?"

I had hidden the gun in the kitchen on top of the freezer that was in a corner. As I was running up the stairs, I came to my senses. "You don't want to shoot your son." So I calmed down, but he was still burning mad. As I reached to the top of the freezer for the gun, he saw it and reached for it too. I grabbed the butt, and he grabbed the barrel.

He was pulling one way. "Let it go, Mama!"

I was pulling the other way. "No, Larry!"

"Give it here!" he said.

"No!"

Out of nowhere was the sound of a loud POW! Everything from that point on seemed like I was outside my body watching a bad movie unfold. It was unreal. I couldn't wrap my mind around what just happened. My eyes bucked wide. I saw my son hit the floor. I frantically hollered out, "I shot my son!" I ran around in circles like I had lost my mind. My son, Larry, Jr., was lying on the kitchen floor, and I was freaking out!

Felix came down from upstairs and slapped me, "Lavinia, your son is dying. Get yourself together!"

I looked down at my son on the floor. "Jesus!" I screamed. "Jesus, don't take my son! Don't let my son die!"

Immediately, I saw Larry, Jr. get up off the floor. He went into the basement, holding his stomach. While he was going down the steps, I called 911. When the police answered, I told them that I had shot my son and to come and help in a hurry. When I hung up the phone, I saw Larry, Jr. coming toward me. David, Jr. and Calvin were downstairs now looking on. Katrina was still in her crib asleep. Larry, Jr. moved toward his brother. He had the money from the safe clutched in his arms, holding it close to his lower body where he had been shot. His body bent over in agony. He walked up to his brother and said, "Pooky," David, Jr.'s nickname, "you keep this."

Pooky looked at me. I nodded at him.

"Yes," he said and reached for the money.

Once Pooky had the money in his arms, Larry Jr. fell to the floor again. The ambulance hadn't arrived yet. I looked at Felix and said, "Help me save my son! It's taking them too long!"

Felix bent down and picked up Larry, Jr. from off the floor. Larry, Jr. was just as big as Felix, but Felix's adrenaline was working overtime. He carried my son out of the door to Larry, Jr.'s car. It wasn't a new car, but it looked new. It was a nice seventies ride. Larry, Jr. had bought it with his dope money. I took the keys out of Larry, Jr.'s pocket before Felix picked him up. Everybody in the neighborhood heard the gun go off, so all the neighbors were looking out of their windows. Felix carefully placed Larry, Jr. on the front seat. I sat on the backseat. Felix drove to the hospital as fast as he could, running lights and all. Larry, Jr. kept going in and out of consciousness.

Once, he woke up and turned his head back toward me and said, "You go' shoot your own son? I'll probably die."

"You're not going to die, Larry, Jr.," I promised him.

He went back out of consciousness. "God, please don't let him die," I was praying as Felix flew through town in the car to the hospital.

Larry, Jr. woke up again, and this time he said, "You got me getting blood on my seats."

Unbelievable. I looked at him and said to God, "What has happened to my son? He's more worried about some blood on his seats than his life?" Satan was showing himself strong early that morning. I felt the warfare between him and God, but God was right there again. When I called out, "Jesus," and my son got up off the floor, I felt the presence of God in all that chaos. God was in that kitchen just like he was in that car.

Anyway, Larry, Jr. lost consciousness again. "Hurry up!" I told Felix.

We pulled up at the emergency entrance. Felix got out of the car and ran around to the passenger side. He picked up Larry, Jr. to take him inside the hospital. Larry, Jr. woke up again. I jumped out of the car and ran inside the hospital, shouting, "I shot my son! I shot my son! Please help him!"

Felix was ushered into the trauma unit with Larry, Jr. I stopped at the door. "Help, I shot my son!" I cried out. I went to the phone to try to call my neighbor across the street. The police had arrived at my house, but we had already left and gone to the hospital. My friend across the street had already taken my kids to her house.

As I hung up the phone, Felix walked out of the doors of the trauma area. He looked at me and asked, "You all right?"

I shook my head. "No."

He said, "I'm going to get the kids and leave."

I picked up the phone again and called Jenny. I had to tell her that Larry, Jr. needed her. As I was dialing the number, the police walked in. "Come with us. You're under arrest."

"No, wait! I can't leave my son by himself. I have to call his grandma!"

"You need to come with us!"

As they turned me around to put handcuffs on me, I started crying. I was hurting and hurting bad. I felt like I was watching another bad movie, and I was the actress. Once they got me to the station, they took my fingerprints and booked me. I was allowed one phone call, so I called Mama. She treated me ice cold. She had already been informed about the incident. I understood that Larry, Jr. was her favorite grandson, but I was her daughter, and I needed her too.

"As always, I get nothing from you, Mama. Have you heard anything about Larry, Jr.? They were taking him to surgery when I was arrested."

"No, Lavinia," she said sharply.

"Mama, I know you don't think I shot Larry, Jr. on purpose!"

"I don't know what to think about you, Lavinia."

"Mama, will you please call Jenny and tell her to go up to the hospital where Larry, Jr. is. He's in surgery, and he's alone. Tell her, Mama!"

The police told me to end the phone call. I hung up the phone. I was taken to a holding cell. It was cold sitting on that metal and lonely. I started pleading to the Lord, "God, give me the strength to get through this. I'm weak. God, I don't feel I can get through this one. This one, God, is the worst! It's too much, God. I can't do it. Help my son, God. Save his life, in Jesus's name, save his life."

It felt like I was in that cell for days. After three or four hours, the detectives came and got me and took me to the interrogation room. I was asked all sorts of questions. I told the truth. I had nothing to hide because it was an accident. I began to question myself, "That gun. Johnny. Why did he give my son that gun? How did I get to this place, a place that I wouldn't have even had a gun in my house; a place where my son, the one I had big dreams for, was a dope seller?"

"What happened?" the detectives asked. "How did the 8-ball get under your mattress?"

"What 8-ball?" I said. "There were no drugs under my mattress. Why would I break into the safe if I had drugs?"

That stayed on my mind for days. Pooky had to have put it there. He never liked how his brother treated me. He knew the whole thing was over me breaking into the safe.

One of the detectives was a woman, and she said to me, "That Bible in your closet, you need to read it." I agreed with her. It was Daddy's Bible, and yes, I did need to read it. I asked how my son was doing. They told me that the bullet ricocheted throughout his body. He needed four surgeries, and his colon had to be repaired, his intestines, large and small, and his stomach also. I asked if he was going to make it, and they said they didn't know.

"You are being charged with attempted murder. If he dies, you will be charged with murder."

"This is unreal. God, wake me up any minute now, please," I said to myself. But this *was* real. This was no bad movie. I was taken back to the holding cell and stayed there for hours, all the while talking to God. Not one time did God make me feel that my son was going to die. As a matter of fact, in my heart, I felt that he was going to make it. I felt the peace of God, so I sat there until they came and took me to the county jail. The booking process at the county jail was a long drawn-out one. While waiting, I talked to some women who were also there, and they made me feel a whole lot better. *Total strangers made me feel better than my own mama. Wow!* I thought.

I was in jail all weekend, not knowing if my son was dead or alive. I let the Lord comfort me because I knew that on Monday morning I had to go to court to be arraigned for attempted murder. God was with me because I was shocked at how well I was handling the situation. As I was sitting in the holding cell, a court officer came. I thought that he was coming to get me to take me into the courtroom.

He opened the cell door and said, "You're free to go."

"What?"

I looked at him, totally surprised.

"Your son came out of the coma and said that it was an accident. You're free to go."

I walked out of that cell and courthouse, and I took off running. I ran all the way to the hospital. When I got there, security wouldn't let me in. "It's the mother! It's the mother! Stop her! I'm sorry, ma'am, but you can't visit your son at this time."

"Why not?"

"Excuse me a minute," the guard said.

"I've been released from all charges! This is my son. I brought him here, and I will take him out of this hospital if you don't let me see him!"

The guard made a phone call. When he hung up the phone, he said, "Let her see her son."

"Thank you!" I graciously said.

I walked into Larry, Jr.'s hospital room and couldn't believe my eyes. Tubes were everywhere in his body! I tried to act like I could handle it. I couldn't let him see how this had shaken me to the core. I was trembling and thinking, *Oh my god, Jesus, Jesus!* I looked directly into my son's eyes. He was hooked up to all kinds of machines and couldn't talk, but I could read his eyes. He was scared. He was angry. He was hurt.

As I began to tell him that he would be all right, the look in his eyes told me, "Screw you! I don't care. Look at me. I have a colonoscopy bag. How can I live like this? Screw you!"

I went to the nursing station and asked the nurse, "How is he?"

The nurse told me the surgery went well and that it was up to my son if he wanted to live. "He has given up. He's not trying. He won't respond to us. His girlfriend has been coming, but he won't even try for her."

"Thank you," I said.

Then I went back inside the room because I had to encourage my son. The only person that could get across to him was me, and I knew it. I went inside the room and looked him in the eyes and said, "Larry, what happened between us was an accident. You know and I know what happened. I'm sorry that it did, but it did. We are not quitters. We are fighters. You will not lie here and just give up, Larry, Jr. You fight for your life! They have dropped the charges on me. You have to fight, son. You have to fight for your life."

I didn't cry while I was talking to him because I had to stand strong, but when I left the room and got into the hallway, I broke down and cried like a baby.

After I said what I needed to say to my son, I told him I was going home to take a bath because I was still wearing the same clothes from when I was arrested. Dry blood was still on them. I left the hospital. While I was in jail, I promised myself and God that I would never use drugs again. But I wasn't home for ten minutes and I started back at it. I couldn't take the pain. I was dying inside from the pain. Just a little hit. I needed to numb my pain. My, I was so sick. I had to get help. I couldn't do this any longer. I called to see if I could get into rehab. I was told that a bed was available immediately.

So I moved everything I owned into Cathy's basement. Cathy had always been there for me. *What is it that makes my cousin such a caring woman?* I thought. *Thank you, God, for Cathy.* She never judged me. She was only there to help. I loved her. I called and met with all the daddies and grandmas to say, "I have done this by myself for years, and now I need help. I need for you all to be fathers and take your children so I can help myself." I knew it would be the grandmothers who would take my children, but Child Protective Services had stepped in because Larry, Jr. was still considered a minor. He wasn't but sixteen. The protective services worker had compassion for me and helped me get my children placed with their families.

I called the hospital to check on Larry, Jr. The nurse answered. She was very excited. "He's up! He's up! Your son is taking steps!" I smiled while she was talking. Now it was my turn to get some help. I never went back to the hospital. I was on my way to the treatment center within the week.

> Dear Heavenly Father,
>
> I come before your throne, and I repent. I ask that you remind me of your love for me, especially when I don't get the love I need from my loved ones or when I don't give the love I should. Heal my heart, Lord, for it hurts. This is the ultimate pain of my life! I can't bear this pain, God. I've lost control, God. I need you to direct me, for I know not what to do. I surrender, Lord. Help me. Help stop the pain. This time I don't feel I can make it through the night. This is a prayer of desperation. Save my son. Save his life. Save my life. Save our lives. We need you to help us. We need you. In the name of Jesus, hear my prayer, God. Amen.

In your anger do not sin. Do not let the sun go down while you are still angry, and do not give the devil a foothold.
—Ephesians 4:26–27 (NIV)

He heals the brokenhearted and binds up their wounds.
—Psalm 147:3 (NIV)

Chapter Twenty-Three

A BLEEDING HEART

I felt like I was in a trance. Nothing felt real. Maybe that's because nothing was familiar. I've never felt pain to this extent—never. It hurts so bad that the mental pain has caused me to hurt physically. I feel sick to my stomach. Every day I relied on God to give me strength. Without him, I couldn't have made it. He gave me the courage to make it, not one day at a time but one minute at a time. He carried me by the minute. I couldn't carry myself. I just couldn't. I cried anytime anyone looked at me. I was so ashamed of myself. I felt like everybody was looking at me, and they knew—knew that I had been the worst mother imaginable.

My name had been on all the local news channels for shooting my son over drugs. I was the top story in our local newspaper. Vanessa told me that I was paranoid, but I just knew everybody was judging me. "That's the lady that tried to kill her son for drugs," that's how the news tried to portray me, but they had it all wrong, and I was too wounded to defend myself. I had no more fight in me—none. I really wanted to die. I didn't realize it at the time, but it was God that kept me from blowing my own head off and ending it right then and there. I wasn't worthy to be alive. *Let somebody else be the mother*, I thought. I knew I needed help, and I needed it quick. I never told anybody how suicidal I was. Have you ever felt that you weren't even worth dying? Helluva feeling! That's how I felt when I arrived at the thirty-day treatment center.

For the first time in my life, I couldn't figure things out. I could no longer keep it together for my entire family, let alone keep it together for my children. I couldn't carry Mama or Daddy either, even though he was gone. I felt the weight of it all—Charles, Jr., Johnny, Vanessa—and I, for the first time, didn't have the answers and couldn't be the one to hold everything together for my entire family. I had to walk away from it all and admit that I was powerless and that my life was unmanageable, totally unmanageable. I had no more answers. I had been whipped. All I could do was call on the Lord. "Jesus, Jesus, help me! Help me. I need you. I can't take another breath without you. I need you, God."

As I stayed at the thirty-day treatment center, I didn't feel like getting dressed or eating. I didn't want to face anyone because I felt the guilt that a life of addiction had left me. I felt I didn't deserve to be helped, yet at the same time, I knew I had to get help because I was a mother, a mother who had committed the worst sin possible by shooting her own son, but a mother that knew she couldn't give up. For the sake of my children, I didn't cop out. I talked to God all day every day, like I did when I was a young girl afraid of the world. God strengthened me. I got stronger by the day.

The very first day I went to group therapy, or group as we called it, there was a man there that I had grown up with and had known since the second grade. When I saw him, I felt as though he looked at me like I was the worst mother in the world. He never actually said that to me, but I just felt that way. Finally, he started talking to me, and I wondered why because I didn't deserve friends.

After being clean for a week, I spoke to Jenny. Larry, Jr. was being released from the hospital. I was so pleased to hear that news because the doctors had told me before I left for treatment that he would be in the hospital at least six weeks, but he wasn't even there for two weeks. They said it would take at least ninety days for him to recover.

Within three weeks of Larry, Jr. being released, he was right back out there in the streets. That scared me because the police told me that when he came out of the coma and told them it was an accident, they told him that they were aware of what he was doing. They said that if he didn't stop, it would only be a matter of time because they were determined to stop him. Larry, Jr. didn't think he was touchable though. I prayed for my three sons and my daughter Katrina, whom I called Princess—my daughter that I felt had been taken from me by Satan himself. All I could think about was the many times Felix would take her right out of my arms and leave home walking with her and telling me, "I'm feeding her drugs." He would be high as a kite himself. He went from not wanting her because he didn't think she was his daughter to trying to take her to hurt me. I loved her, and I missed her so much. I missed all my kids. They were the only reason I didn't give up.

One day I was talking to Felix on the phone. I called him often since he had my kids. While I was speaking with him, Charles, from cosmetology school, walked through the door. At first, I felt ashamed because I was certain he had heard what happened—it was the talk of the town.

I said to Felix, "Guess who just got here?"

"Who?"

"Charles, your cousin's friend," I said.

"Let me speak to him."

"Felix wants to talk to you, Charles."

He looked at me as if to say, "Screw Felix and you too as far as that goes . . ."

Still, he reached for the phone. I stepped aside so he could have privacy. I heard him say, "Man, I ain't thanking 'bout what you talking. I'm going to the hospital."

Then Charles handed the phone back to me and rolled his eyes at me. I didn't see Charles anymore for a few days until he showed up in the group. He said he had a heroin addiction. He had to go to the hospital because heroin had him feeling sick. Crack didn't make you sick physically like heroin. All of us who were there from the same town talked often. After being there for two weeks, I felt myself getting physically strong, yet mentally, I was still in bad shape.

Still, Charles, who protected me from the girls that wanted to fight me in the tenth grade at the institute for ignorant people that I attended when I was suspended from high school for allowing a friend to put a gun in my purse, was always saying kind words to me, not trying to hit on me but words like, "You're gonna make it. Hang in there. Be strong."

Actually, he was quite nice. We communicated like we were longtime friends. He shared with me about his life, and I shared with him about mine. Since Charles was there and he was a barber, I asked him to cut my hair when we had free time. I've always liked it tapered in the back, but drug addiction had me in a space that I not only let my hair go ungroomed, but I also hadn't had my eyebrows arched in years either, so Charles hooked me up. Larry used to keep my hair cut. He was very good with clippers too. He did all those things with his clippers that I missed.

Anyway, I was done with the thirty-day treatment, and now it was time for me to see my therapist. She suggested I go through long-term treatment and had found a long-term treatment center in Lansing, Michigan. "Lansing?" I was not feeling her. I didn't want to go that far away. I didn't know how to live life without drugs, but I didn't have any place else to go. I had no home for the first time in my life, so as I talked to God that night; I felt he was telling me to go. The next morning I told my therapist I would go to Lansing. Charles was also told that he needed long-term treatment. He asked whether I was going, and I said, "Yes." He told me he would go after he was released from the thirty-day program.

I had a week before it was time for me to be at the long-term treatment center in Lansing. Angie welcomed me into her home while I waited. She was married at that time, and her then husband treated me very kindly. During the week I was at Angie's house, I was able to see my children. I didn't like going to see them at the house of Felix's mother because he felt I was supposed to have sex with him. He soon figured out that I wanted to see my daughter and son, not him! Them being in his mother's home made me feel a little better, but to be honest, I hated him. I knew he was still smoking crack. All I thought about was when I was in jail and I called home and Felix was still at my house smoking crack. I told him to get my kids out of that house, that their brother had just been shot in that house, but Felix was sitting there smoking crack. He finally took them to his mother's house.

I now had to tell all my kids and their grandmothers that I had to leave for six months. I was so nervous during this time. I was shaking so bad. I still cried if anyone looked at me too long. Angie had to be at work on the Monday morning that I needed to be in Lansing, so before I left the thirty-day treatment center, Charles told me to call the center if I needed a ride to Lansing. I called the van driver for the center and asked him to pick me up. Altogether, there was three of us that came to Lansing. Charles went to a long-term treatment center in East Lansing. He said that he would check up on me.

When we arrived at the long-term treatment center and the van driver brought my luggage inside, I said to him, "Don't leave me here alone." We hugged, and he left. I wasn't at that long-term treatment center for ten minutes and I already missed my past. I had no present, and I saw no future at this point. I did have about forty days with no drugs, and I felt so alone. I felt so hopeless. I was still crying daily. I did that at least ninety more days, especially during the group sessions we had.

All the women in the long-term center wanted a better life so badly, including me. I did whatever I was told to do to earn it. I worked hard during those six months. I struggled with the pain of what had happened with Larry, Jr.; and the more clean time I got, the more I started feeling emotions that I'd never felt before. I had no drugs to run to for cover, no clothes to hide behind. I had to face my issues head on. One issue, particularly, was that of the fourteen abortions I had over the years. For once in my life, I felt sad for the unborn babies I had killed. For the first time in my life, I felt like I had committed the ultimate sin. I cried for those babies. My therapist at that time told me to write a letter to each baby and ask for their forgiveness and then write a letter to God asking for his forgiveness. I did just that.

The very first abortion letter was the hardest to write. Some letters were written in detail, some letters I didn't have a whole lot to say. I couldn't remember a lot because I had used so many drugs that my feelings were dead. I couldn't connect with my feelings. I just knew what I had done was wrong. When I started writing the letter to God, which was about a month later, I could feel his presence in my life. I could hear him speaking to me, just like he used to in the past. I told the Lord that I would never kill another baby. I asked him to forgive me. Even though I had to go through the process of healing and forgiveness, I felt his comfort. I felt him forgiving me, not just for the abortions but also for the guilt I felt behind aborting so many babies.

Then there was the issue of Daddy dying. I had never grieved my daddy's death. I got with that pain too. I was angry with my daddy. I felt Daddy killed himself. He was so young, fifty-one years old. What would make life so bad that you would drink yourself to death? I couldn't understand it. I loved my daddy. I felt it was my fault he gave up on life. He was doing fine until I let David into my life. Then Daddy watched me destroy myself with the drugs and Felix's abuse. I felt we all had let Daddy down—from Mama to Charles, Jr., to Vanessa, to me, and to Johnny. What happened to all of us? How could a family that started out studying the Bible at home and going to church every Sunday destroy themselves like we did? All I kept hearing was Daddy saying, "All ya'll crazy, just like ya'll Mama."

Well, for the first time, I felt the grief I'd never allowed myself to feel after Daddy died, and it hurt—so much pain. This was very uncomfortable; a thirty-four-year-old woman that had never experienced what it felt like to be in this much pain, a woman that had done all she could her entire life to alter her mood, was in all this pain. Yet the fact that I had children that needed me gave me the courage to not give up. As painful as life was for me during this time, quitting was not an option. My heart was so wounded.

After the first thirty days there, I could receive phone calls. Mama and I talked, but I felt she was still disappointed in me. Everybody else could take a fall in life, even her; but when

I did, she treated me very cold at times. I know I dragged my kids through a lot of trauma and dysfunction, so I understood why she was fed up with me. That hurt too. I was the one that always held our family together after Charles, Jr. was locked up. Now I was the pitiful one. I felt like I had nobody but Angie. She was a married woman, though, and had her own life. She did, however, allow David, Jr. to come live with her. His grandmother just couldn't afford to keep him, and David was busy doing what he did (women). It wasn't working out at the house of David, Jr.'s grandma, so again, Angie stepped up to the plate. I felt so alone.

Charles kept his word. He called to check on me when the thirty days were over. I was glad he did. I enjoyed talking to him and seeing him at NA (Narcotics Anonymous) meetings. We were becoming friends. Not only did he start to make me feel like Charles, Jr. used to—safe, protected—but I also thought of how he protected me from the east side and west side girls when I was in the tenth grade. I could see the growth in Charles every time he came to NA. He encouraged me whenever we talked. We both had some clean time under our belts, and we were experiencing a new way of life—a way that at times felt pretty good then at other times felt too hard to live.

I was back in that place I was when I first started to change my mood with drugs. I had stunted my own growth emotionally, and I felt weird daily. I felt butt-naked. Then I started meeting women that could relate to me, positive women inside the center and outside. I was becoming a new Lavinia! God was carrying me. I felt his presence. I felt him placing my feet on solid ground one step at a time. I depended on God, something I'd been doing all my life. So how did my life get to this place? How did I end up in this state? I had hit rock bottom, but God was bringing me out slowly and surely. He was easing the pain day by day.

I continued to work hard on my recovery. I wanted it bad. I could not believe that the one thing I said wouldn't happen when I was a new mother had happened to me: I couldn't understand how any mother could allow her own son to sell drugs. I prayed that my sons would never go to jail like my brothers did. Now that's one thing about Daddy; he never broke the law, well, except drunk driving, and that wasn't a crime back then when he was getting into accidents. I thank God that Daddy never killed anybody! It was by the grace of God that he didn't. He sure hurt a lot of people with his drunk driving though.

My son, Larry, Jr., was not only drinking and drugging but he was also selling drugs after he got out of the hospital. When Larry, Jr. turned seventeen, I was allowed to have a small birthday gathering for him at the treatment center. I invited all my kids and Mama. Felix even came with baby girl. He still wanted to be with me, but I never loved him, and I knew it. I no longer was enslaved to crack, so I had no purpose for him other than the fact that he had my kids, and I loved them. Even Mama came. I was so disappointed that Larry, Jr. had stood me up, but I enjoyed my kids that did come. We celebrated without him. We ate dinner and Larry, Jr.'s birthday cake. I was hurt and happy at the same time.

Feeling the pain was still difficult for me. I hadn't forgotten how to put on the mask for my other kids. I couldn't let them see that, on the inside, I felt like a failure as a mother. They were scattered all over the place, and I was too sick to do anything about it. When they left that night, I spent the night crying and talking to God. "How could this have happened, God? Why? Why? So much damage . . . only you can fix the damage that was done to my kids. Oh my god, what have I done?"

In group that Monday, my counselor, Gladys, told me that I had to work through the guilt. I needed to let it go, but I couldn't. As hard as I worked to get better on the inside, I couldn't stop that feeling of guilt and shame. It was eating me up inside. When I spoke to Charles on the phone, he made me feel better than speaking with my new female recovery friends. We had to get a sponsor to help us along while we were in recovery, someone with more clean time than we had, someone we could learn from; my sponsor's name was Crystal.

Since I had an issue with women, I didn't really trust the new women that I just met. I've always felt that women smile in your face and stab you in the back the first chance they get. I learned how to read women quick in life. I smell fakeness a mile away! In the world I come from, women were real phony. Now I was in a situation where I was told that I needed the women from the recovery program. I needed to reach out to them and let them help me because we were there to help one another. I wasn't feeling this, but I wanted to stay clean, so I did everything I was told to do—everything.

For the first time in my life, I started to talk to women who had issues just like I did. I learned that there was one thing about women who hit rock bottom and had been through a lot of pain: We had hurt enough that we were ready and willing to reach out to one another, even take a chance at trusting one another. Actually, it was a beautiful thing, women with a common bond. After a while, I began to love the women I met in long-term treatment. We cried together and faced painful issues together.

Gladys was a black woman who said a lot of things to me that were hard to swallow. She told me that I needed to stop talking to Charles. She talked to me about putting down one addiction and picking up another: sexual addiction. I didn't want to hear what she was saying, but to be honest, she was right. Charles and I both started to feel emotions and have desires that drugs had suppressed for years. We often talked about sex. He was showing me attention that no one else had in years. He told me to stop holding back on my true feelings, that if I had something to say about how someone treated me, to tell them if I didn't like it. He said that pleasing myself came first. He told me to start saying what I mean and mean what I say. He saw that I had very low self-esteem, but he made me laugh; he had a sense of humor. I liked that. I liked how he made me laugh, something I hadn't done in years. It was like I began to blossom. I saw it every time I looked at myself in the mirror.

Well, four months passed by, and one night I fell asleep, and for the first time in a long time, I slept more than two or three hours. I slept all night. I woke up so happy! I slept all night—that was a *big* deal! An even bigger deal was when I stopped sweating from withdrawal throughout the night. Sometimes I would get so wet that I had to get up and change my clothes. This went on the whole time I was in long-term treatment. During this time, I was still struggling with what had happened between me and Larry, Jr. The nights when I did wake up and could no longer sleep, I still cried and worried about him. I prayed for him and all my children. I still couldn't talk about it without crying.

After all the work I had done on myself, I felt I still had an in-the-middle-of-the-night issue that I shared with no one but *God*. That issue was the fact that I had failed as a mother. I felt my children had lost all respect for me. I didn't deserve their love. I was unworthy to be a mother. I beat myself up whenever I was alone.

> Heavenly Father,
>
> I come before you, and I repent. I ask for your forgiveness. Please take away this misery. Make a way, God. Bring me out of this pain. I need you, God. I need the comfort of your son, Jesus. Give me strength, God, to face another day. I can't do this without you. I can't sleep at night, and when I finally do, I wake up drenched in sweat. I'm trying, God. Please lighten this struggle. In Jesus's name, I pray. Amen.

And our hope for you is firm, because we know that just as you share in our sufferings, so also you share in our comfort.

—2 Corinthians 1:7 (NIV)

You, Lord, keep my lamp burning; my God turns my darkness into light.

—Psalm 18:28 (NIV)

Chapter Twenty-Four

A NEW BEGINNING

Gladys had begun talking to me about getting out of long-term treatment. She felt that it would be a big mistake for me to go back home. She said me that since I was known at home as a drug addict and a booster, I should start over elsewhere. Gladys felt that the people at home would not let me change, that I was not strong enough to resist and would return to what was familiar to me if I went back there. I had met some new people in Lansing. I needed to stay here, but I was not feeling this at all. I wanted to go home, even though I didn't have a home. I told her that I would pray about it.

I started going to a church in Lansing with the tech, Paula, from the long-term treatment center. She would come and get me whenever she wasn't working. My counselor, Gladys, was a member at this same church. I enjoyed going with her. God has always been able to get my attention. My heart longed for him all my life, even when I was living a life full of sin. I was just caught up and didn't know how to get out of the trap.

The first thing I did was share this information with Charles as soon as I was able to use a phone. He told me I should stay in Lansing. He was in a longer-term treatment center, so he was not about to get out. I still felt guilty about staying, but the women in Lansing were such a big support. I was given information on housing and rehab. During that time, drug and alcohol addiction was considered a disability, so you were eligible to receive some financial benefits from the government. I was taken to the Social Security office where I applied to receive disability income. Even still, I was torn about staying.

I had feelings of guilt and fear. I was ashamed that I had no home for my children, but I considered staying in Lansing. I felt like I needed to go back and deal with the mess I had made. I didn't feel like I deserved to change for the better. I didn't feel like I deserved anything good. I didn't feel that I had the right to take care of myself. I've never taken care of myself. I've always taken care of others. That's who I was. I had grown up with the message that it wasn't okay to take care of "Lavinia," so I was very uncomfortable thinking about staying, but I took her suggestion and decided to live in Lansing once I had completed my six-month program.

I felt so naked when I got out of there and out into the real world again. I had never lived without drugs of some sort. I'll never forget the last conversation that I had with my counselor. She told me that she had a concern, actually two. She said that if I didn't let go of the guilt I was holding concerning the shooting of my son, I would use again. I was upset at what she said. To be honest, I was offended. "I will never use drugs again," I told her. "You'll see."

Then she spoke of the friendship between me and Charles. She said that I should not get into an intimate relationship for at least a year for a reason, and I knew the reason. She said I needed to stay focused. I told her that Charles and I were only friends. I lied though. I didn't tell her that we were talking about having sex as soon as I got out. I didn't tell her that he was the one who told me to stay in Lansing and get my own place to live.

One of the women in the program had offered me a place to stay at their home. Charles said that if I accepted the offer, he would not be able to visit me. He was setting up a place to go when he got a pass to leave his treatment program. He was thinking about the desires that had surfaced in his body, and so was I. We both wanted to have sex. Anyway, I found a one-room efficiency apartment listed in the want ads right around the corner from the treatment center. Paula gave me a ride to meet with the landlord.

He was a white man, and he took a liking to Paula. I guess white men were just attracted to her. (Her husband was white.) Whenever Paula could get time off from work, I would go to her home. She lived on the outskirts of Lansing. Her life was very boring to me. I couldn't understand how she could live way out in the boondocks.

Paula did impress me though. She and several other black women from Lansing had started a meeting place for women to support one another and share their experience, strength, and hope. They met every Friday night. I started going with them before I got out of the center. I became close to all the women at the meetings. One woman that stood out to me when I met her was Crystal. She was a woman that had a lot of knowledge. She worked at an automotive plant. I liked her style as well as Paula's.

I had also met another black woman who worked at the treatment center. She was from my hometown. I remembered her because she had crossed my path, and I used drugs with her. She also knew Felix. It was good to see her working at the center. She was very kind; all the women were. We supported one another— black and white. It was cool, the bond we had formed. I'd never been by myself, the real Lavinia, ever. It was very scary.

Anyway, I got a job working in a department store, but it only lasted about one month. I was afraid of the people. Plus, I kept hearing gunshots, whenever I was outside in Lansing, after I got out of the long-term treatment center.

"Where are they shooting at?" I would ask.

"What shooting?" my friends would ask.

"You don't hear them shots?"

"No," they would say.

They looked at me very strangely, but I know what I heard. This went on for several months.

Charles began visiting me on weekends. When he couldn't come over, we talked on the phone. I began depending on him to make me feel good about myself. He was becoming my new addiction. The sex was the only thing that gave me a good feeling. During that time, it altered my mood, just like the drugs did.

I had been talking to my eldest son, Larry, Jr., on the phone. He started calling me once I was out of the center. His grandmother had put him out of her house for selling drugs. He had no place to move. Larry, Jr. had money to get a place, but he wanted to come to Lansing. My second son was also having problems at my cousin's house. I couldn't leave my sons like that, so I talked to Larry, Jr., who said that he had the money for us to rent a place to live. I had to end the weekend meetings with Charles. Besides, he was starting to go back home more and more on weekends.

Right before Larry, Jr. and David, Jr. moved to Lansing, I learned that I was pregnant again. I was taking birth control in the beginning, but as always, I was addicted to chaos. When I missed my first period, I called Charles at his sister's house. He told her to tell me that he would get back with me. When he didn't, I called back. Charles finally came to the phone, and I could tell that he was with a woman.

"Lavinia, what's so important that you can't wait 'til I call back? Are you pregnant?"

"Yes."

"Then you'll just have to get an abortion."

It's funny how murdering babies came so easy for us when we lived a life full of sin. Charles went back home on weekends because he couldn't leave his past. He started chipping again (using drugs). I was in denial, but in my heart, I knew he was using again. Whenever he came to my house after he got back to Lansing and I thought he was high, I would make excuses for him. "Maybe he's just tired—yeah, right!" When he said he would pay for an abortion, I recalled the promise I had made to God. I knew I would never get an abortion, but I was upset that he had the nerve to be with another woman, even though Charles and I were not a couple and he had made it plain that he didn't know what he wanted to do with his life.

Me? I was stuck in la-la-land. I had turned the sex into something it wasn't. I wouldn't let Charles take me to get an abortion, and he wasn't just going to give me the money because

I would have kept the money. When I realized he wasn't going for my plan, I just told him the truth. "I have no intentions of getting an abortion. You go on and do you. Me and my baby will be fine."

I still called him often though. He was in barber school trying to get his license to cut hair in Lansing. I called the school daily. My two eldest sons finally moved to Lansing. We got a two-bedroom house that Crystal helped line up for me. She and I had become close friends. She was cool. She once told me that I was a functioning drug addict. I wasn't a sorry dope fiend. I was a productive one. I used drugs to function in my daily living my entire life. "Well . . . wouldn't you?" I asked her. I believe she was fascinated by my life. I told her a lot about where I came from.

No matter how much I shared with my new friends, I never shared everything. There were things about my family that I didn't share with anyone. I loved my family. I shared with Crystal that I had a brother in prison that I hadn't seen in years and would like to see him. She told me that she would take me to see him one day. *Cool!* I thought, but first, I had to get moved and make a home for my children again.

I started working for this rehabilitation agency that my counselor, Keith Davis, at the state vocational rehabilitation program placed me in to get me back into the workforce. Crystal and I hung out together almost like I hung out with my closest friends at home. She did all she could to help me. When Larry, Jr. and David, Jr. got to Lansing, she liked my sons. She also had a son who became friends with them.

I was also good friends with another woman I met in the NA program. She was younger than me. I felt she had never lived the full-blown street life I had lived, so she couldn't relate to a lifestyle of hustling. She was young and wanted to stop drinking and drugging. She wanted a better life for her kids. Her mother had died from acquired immunodeficiency syndrome (AIDS), and she didn't want her life to end like her mother's. I felt her. I liked her. She had a heart of gold. She also liked Charles as a friend. He liked her too. He would tell her that she was the only true friend I had. She didn't have a motive for befriending me; she truly was a friend. I listened to Charles, just like I used to listen to my brother, Charles, Jr., when I was a young girl. I missed my brother so much. I was looking forward to going to see him someday.

My past was coming back to haunt me. I was a woman that got welfare, boosted, hustled, and worked. I lied on job applications and did whatever to cheat the system. Now that I no longer lived that way and modern technology was advancing, I received a letter in the mail from the state welfare office referring to when I was working as a nurse's aide and didn't report it. Therefore, I had to pay the state their money back. I didn't sweat it because I thought about how much money I had stolen in one way or another and had never been in prison, so I really didn't having a problem with paying what I owed the state.

After we had been living in our house for a few months, my first grandson was born. Larry, Jr. was now a daddy. His girlfriend, Chantel, stuck by him—through all the other women, through all the drinking, and through all the recovery from the shooting. She was a pretty good girl. I remember one time when I was in a store back home and this woman asked me if I was Chantel's mother. I told her that I wasn't but that Chantel dated my son. Some people said that I looked like I could be Chantel's mother. I saw why my son liked her. I liked her too. She would come to Lansing and bring my new grandson to visit Larry, Jr. My grandson looked just like his dad.

I didn't see my daughter or Calvin as much as I would have liked. Felix was still that evil man he had always been, and when he learned that Charles and I were seeing each other, he flipped! Why? I have no idea. Why he chased and continued to think that I was his property showed that he was out of touch with reality. He used my kids against me, just like he always had. I wanted my kids to come with me, and he wouldn't let them.

Even though Felix was smoking crack, he wouldn't give me my kids back; so I prayed that God would open up a door for them to come with me, and he did. But before that, as I continued working on the job through vocational rehabilitation, my counselor, Keith, started to believe in me. He was a godsend in my life. He not only helped me get my first of several cars through the vocational rehabilitation program, but he also took up for me once when this manager of the plant where I was working kept telling me to sew on a machine that she knew was broken.

A lot of employees at this place were mentally challenged, and the manager could tell them some nonsense like that, and they didn't ask the questions I asked. I also told her that the sewing machine was broken, and if she wanted me to keep sewing on it, for her to sew on it first. She had a problem with me saying what I said, so she reported me to the head supervisor who, in return, called my counselor. I had to meet with the three of them, at which time I saw that my counselor from vocational rehabilitation was on my side because he knew that mess was stupid. "Lavinia, you can't talk to a manager like that," he said. My counselor told them to move me to another department. I was beginning to love my counselor. He never gave up on me. Never.

After I worked for several months, pregnant, God blessed me with a car. My counselor found me a car that was in excellent condition. An elderly lady owned it. It didn't have very many miles on it at all. Charles said it looked like an old lady's car. I told him that it was and that it was *my* blessing. I loved my car. Sometimes I would be driving down the street and talking to God like he was in the passenger seat. I had a constant contact with him that I prayed I'd never lose. When I drove by the neighborhoods that were drug-infested, I would thank God that I was no longer one of those people. Sometimes I'd cry whenever I thought about how far God had brought me. "Thank you, God" is all I could say.

Not long after I had my car, I was at work and felt weird, so I went to the bathroom, only to find myself spotting. I was nine months pregnant, so I automatically knew that it was time to deliver. I called Crystal. She came and took me to the hospital. She also stayed there with me. I took her through hell. I couldn't figure out why I was hurting so bad at first. Then it hit me—this baby was the first in a long, long time, and I hadn't use any type of mood-altering drug during this pregnancy. Crystal knew of my relationship with Charles, and she didn't have a problem voicing how she felt about him.

About a month before I had my baby, Crystal took me to see my brother. My god! It was good to see Charles, Jr.! I hadn't seen him in years, and I felt like a kid at Christmas! I enjoyed the visit so much. I've always been able to read people. I watched Crystal. She too was like a kid at Christmas. I could tell that she was digging Charles, Jr. Of course, who wouldn't? My brother was very good-looking. Women always had stupid attacks around him, including me, so I was feeling Crystal. Besides, she didn't rush me to end my visit. Charles, Jr. asked about all my children. He asked a lot of questions about my baby, and I told him that I was the mama and the daddy. I told him that if I had a boy, I was going to name him Charles, after him. At that time, I meant that.

Now it was time for my baby to enter into this world. As I prepared to go to the hospital, I called Charles to inform him that I was on my way to the hospital. He never showed up while I was in labor. He chose to stay at school. Although he came to Lansing daily, he didn't come to the hospital until the next day. He showed up with a balloon. When he saw his son who looked like him, he said, "Name him Charles."

Anyway, Crystal never left my side when I was in labor. When the pains started to get worse, I clowned. I couldn't understand why she didn't leave. She was a very good friend. I spoke to her very aggressively during labor. "Crystal, go tell them to give me something for pain! Tell them people that I can't take this pain!" (Fifth birth, nineteenth pregnancy, but I couldn't bear the pain? Yeah, right.) I was setting myself up for relapses then. I didn't know that, but I was.

Several hours later that day, I had a healthy baby boy! I had delivered a big baby—over eight pounds. He was gorgeous just like his other brothers and sister were when I laid eyes on them. Since I was older and in a state of mind that I'd never been in before, I had more patience with this baby. I didn't have the grandmothers to keep him on a regular basis. I had to be and wanted to be a better mother now. I had accepted the fact that his father chose to continue to be with other women and stay in the past. I had to let it go, so I did. Even though I spoke to Charles while he was in Lansing in school, he had another world that he lived in that didn't include me. He wanted his son to be in his life after he saw that there was no denying him.

Against my better judgment, I let my son spend the night with his father when he was only seven or eight months old. I called to check on him every five minutes. I knew that Charles was with another woman, so the first time I called and he didn't answer, I got into my car and drove over eighty miles to see why he didn't answer. Charles came out of the house to talk to me. I noticed that he was high, yet I chose to be in denial. I found myself making a million excuses why he acted or looked the way he did instead of being honest and getting my son. I worried until that Monday morning when he brought Little Charles back home. I wanted him to be a part of our life. He wanted to be a part of his son's life. I kept trying to get him to see it my way.

Anyway, I had become very well-liked by my new recovery girlfriends. I started doing their hair in my kitchen. We used the time to socialize. We enjoyed one another's company. My girl friends were a big help to me being able to move on with my life, but even more so than their help, Charles, himself, helped me let go. One day he needed a ride from the barber school because his woman at the time had car problems. He put the car in the shop and called me to give him a ride. I went and got him. I left Little Charles at home. David, Jr. was home. He was so good with babies. I watched how he interacted with his little brother, and I saw way back then that he was a young man that loved babies. He was great! Now Larry, Jr. didn't have it. He had a little son now, but he wasn't the care-for-babies type.

After I picked up Charles, he stayed with me until it was time to go back and get his woman's car. The problem was that he called her on his mobile phone while in my car and started talking to her as if I wasn't even in the car. I spoke out and told him to tell her who he was with. He didn't actually tell her. He put his finger over his mouth as if to tell me to be quiet. That didn't stop me. I got even louder. "Tell her who picked you up!"

He told her, "Just a minute," and laid his phone down. He hacked up some spit in his throat, and then he spit it out of his mouth and into my face. I couldn't believe it! I hadn't felt that humiliated in a long time. The spit ran down the side of my face. I got a tissue paper and wiped if off, but I couldn't wipe away the feeling I was having behind being spit on in my face. When he saw the look of surprise and pain on my face, he started to say, "Sorry, but I told you to be quiet." I saw that he was high, and I couldn't deny it. It hurt like I had just been stabbed in the heart. It hurt so bad that I could have dropped to my knees right then and there. But he was saying things that I wasn't hearing. I did, however, hear when he told me to take him back to the shop. On the way back to the shop, I felt like I was in a trance. I could not believe what just happened—he spit on me! Even Felix didn't do this. Wow!

After that incident I couldn't bear the pain that night, so I remembered this man that worked at the rehabilitation plant where I worked, and I called him. He was shocked that I had called him and asked, "Didn't you say there was a man that lived in your building who sold crack?"

"What?" he said.

"It's for somebody else," I said.

He made the buy for me, and then I went to get the dope from him. I didn't have nobody with me, so he stated, "I thought you said it was for somebody else?"

"It is."

"Then . . . where are they?"

He knew the truth, so as he gave me the twenty rock, he said, "Lavinia, I don't know what's going on with you, but this ain't go' solve it."

"Yeah," I said. "But it's gonna make me feel a whole lot better tonight, so give it here."

Once I got back home, Little Charles was asleep. I had done everything I had to do for my baby and home before I left. David, Jr. watched him while I made my run. Once I returned home, he and his brother, Larry, Jr., went out for a few hours. As soon as they walked out the door, I pulled out my rock. I looked at it for a minute, and then I, just like in the past, had to go use the bathroom. I never knew why every time I knew I was about to smoke crack, I had to have a bowel movement. It was like a mental laxative.

Once I was done in the bathroom, I returned to my bedroom. I looked over at my son sleeping. I thought I'd better get it done because he might wake up or his brothers might return, so I used a pop can to smoke it in, something I did before I quit using. Buying a pipe had stopped a long time ago. Nothing about smoking crack was pretty; in fact, it was so ugly; yet here I was ready to fire up my first hit in a couple of years. I was shaking as I took the pop can and crushed the middle of it so the center was flat. Then I put a hole in the center where it was crushed and flattened, and then I put a piece of a steel wool scrubbing pad in the center of the hole after I burned the wool pad first. Then I put the crack inside the steel wool and lit it up! I pulled the crack from the opening that was at the top of the can.

As I lit the lighter and pulled in on the crack, I anticipated that feeling I was about to have. As I blew the smoke out, I felt that feeling I longed for that night. There's nothing like that first hit of crack—I was up on the clouds. It felt so good. After that, I spent the rest of the time chasing the feeling of that first hit and never got that same feeling again (which is why people get addicted because they spend their time and money chasing after the feeling of that very first hit). By the time I was done, I was zig-ziggy-boom—mouth moving, paranoid, peeking out of the window—the whole nine yards.

The only reason I didn't go get more was because my son was sleeping and I was afraid that Larry, Jr. and David, Jr. would catch me smoking, so I knew I had to calm down. It took a while, but I did. Then I went to bed. Going to sleep was not an option that night, so I spent my night not just in the pain of being spit on, but now I felt guilty for getting high. I felt like I had just wasted all that I had accomplished in the program. All my clean time went out the window in a matter of one night.

Guilt and shame were kicking in. Now I understood why it was recommended that you didn't become involved in a relationship when you're new in recovery. My counselor came to mind. Her words when she found out I was pregnant, "Umm, just friends?" she interestingly said. Now I had her on my mind. I did, however, make it through the night. Once the high wore off, I got with God. Funny how I always ended up calling on him when I should have looked to him first. Now I needed him to help me face another day.

> Father God,
>
> I humble myself as I approach your throne. For you are the Holy One. Wash me, Lord. Cleanse me as I repent for all the sin I have done. I'm here, God, for I know that you are King of Kings, and I know that I would not have made it this far if it had not been for you. I love you, God. I just want to say thank you. Thank you for your son. Thank you, Jesus. Thank you, Jesus. I really love you. I thank you for the courage you've given me. Continue to help me. Give me strength to go on. Amen.

Therefore if any man be in Christ, he is a new creature: old things are passed away; behold, all things are become new.

—2 Corinthians 5:17 (KJV)

Chapter Twenty-Five

I CAN'T TURN BACK

God gave me the strength that I asked for. After that day, I started to change how I felt about Charles. I started spending more time with my sons and on my recovery. I had some girl friends that I trusted with some of my life, and I started spending more time with them as we grew together. While working at the rehabilitation plant, I met another girl friend who had four sons. Her name was Brenda. We talked a lot at work, and as struggling mothers, we support each other.

So much had transpired during my first two years in Lansing. I was trying real hard to stay clean. My two eldest sons were staying high off weed. David, Jr. stayed in trouble in school for smelling like weed. Larry, Jr. was addicted to the lifestyle of selling drugs, so he stuck up the weed man one night and went back home to make money. I'll never forget that night. I had company. My friend, Kim, was over. We were sitting in the kitchen talking, and all of a sudden, we heard gunshots. A short while later, Larry, Jr. come running through the door. "They shooting at me, they shooting!" I told him to call the police. They found a man with a gun in the neighborhood park and arrested him. Once the police left, Kim and I found out that Larry, Jr. had robbed the weed man. That's why he was shooting.

"Larry, it's time for you to go. I won't have that here."

"I know, Mom. I'm leaving in the morning."

"No, you're leaving *now*!"

I had a baby to protect. I thought of the life I left behind. I'd never live like that again. So in the middle of the night, my son loaded my trunk up with his weed and his clothes, and I took him back home. It was only by the grace of God that I didn't get pulled over by the cops with my trunk full of weed. I remember him asking me if I was scared. I had sense enough to be scared this day. "Larry, Jr., yes, today I'm scared—scared for my home, scared for my baby, scared for you!"

At that moment, I realized how drugs had taken me so far insane, that I lived a lifestyle that the average person would have been scared to death of living before I moved to Lansing. But now that I was here, I feared being a part of that type of criminal activity. I realized that night that getting out of the life I had lived so long was harder than I thought it would be because my sons had become a product of what I had lived, what I had put before them.

Larry, Jr. started more chaos while he was in Lansing. He called my friend, Brenda, one day. Brenda was a few years younger than me, but I didn't play that. No friend of mine got no business kicking it with my nineteen-year-old son! When I was out cold in addiction, I did so many shameful things, but I never shamed my sons by doing anything sexual with their friends for drugs. I wish one of them young boys *would* try to proposition me for sex! If a man, young or old, tried to put me down like that, my thinking said, *Take his dope.* I did that several times, but at least Brenda called and told me that Larry, Jr. tried to contact her.

Well, Crystal shot a move that I just couldn't believe: She was going back to the prison to see my brother with another one of her friends and never told me that she was going. Crystal was my sponsor, somebody that I listened to for advice, someone that I thought of highly. She betrayed me to the point that not only was she visiting my brother behind my back, but she also married him. Some sponsor, huh? By the time I found out she was married to my brother, he was on his way home to Lansing to be with her.

As I said, so much went on back to back during that time. Felix finally showed his true colors and pushed his own mother. She ended up in the hospital. She called me and said, "Lavinia, come get your kids." I had been praying and waiting for those words for months. I didn't feel complete with my daughter and son still with Felix. I knew he was using. It showed one day when I went to visit my kids and Felix answered the door with large knots upside his head. I heard he got a beat down from some young man over his drugs. Felix also tried to put his hand on me one time because I came to get my kids to visit with them. He wanted me to visit them at his mother's, but he wanted *me* to visit him—"I DON'T THINK SO!" Anyway, I told her I was on my way. I was there within the day.

Now all of a sudden, our house was too small for us. I was expecting to get my Social Security check any day. Larry, Jr., by now, had gotten busted for selling drugs. He called me from jail, asking me to help him. I went to Jenny and told her that if she paid the money for him to get an attorney, that I would pay her back when I got my money. She agreed. I called an attorney that went to school with his father. When it was time to meet with him, I went to his office with Jenny because she had the money. She took control of the situation when we arrived at the attorney's office. While in the waiting area, I heard Jenny comment about me: "I don't understand how a mother can let this happen." She even said, "I know I may never get my money back, but I gotta help my grandson."

That wasn't the first time Jenny spit venom on me. I will never forget when Larry, Jr. was a baby and I was driving her car and a lady hit me with her vehicle. Jenny never asked if I was hurt; she was only mad at Larry. "She's not on my insurance!" I never said a word when she made her little comment. I was taught by Daddy to respect my elders. I was not on drugs during this time of my life, so when I received my Social Security lump sum, I not only kept my word with Jenny, but I also moved into a bigger house. Calvin and David shared a room, and Katrina and Little Charles shared a bedroom. I had the entire upstairs to myself.

I talked with Charles every now and then, and when I did, I could tell that he was having problems in his relationship. He started sharing his personal life trials with me. I also shared with him that my brother, Charles, Jr., was out of prison and that he married Crystal. Not only were they married, but also they both now lived in Lansing.

All these issues weighed heavily on my heart. I could not believe that not only did my brother betray me, but I was also hurt to know that Crystal felt she had to hide the fact that she was visiting my brother in prison and that she had married him. Her friend from work knew of this marriage; she was dating Charles, Jr.'s best friend. They married also. He too was released to Lansing.

My brother, Johnny, was in Indianapolis on drugs, and he called Charles, Jr. to come get him. Charles, Jr. went to pick him up. Johnny came to Lansing for a short time, but he eventually moved to Jackson. I was able to talk to both my brother and his new wife about why they would keep their marriage such a secret. Crystal told me that she knew she had feelings for Charles, Jr. the first time she saw him. She felt it was best not to let me know. I told her that I needed to talk to her about something important, but she told me to mind my own business.

Charles, Jr. had told her everything about himself. I was in shock. But still, I had to mind my own business. She didn't know my brother, I felt. She didn't know about the issues he had, just like I did, like Johnny did, like Vanessa did. She couldn't even imagine the life we had experienced, and she certainly didn't know everything about our family. I loved Crystal, and I was hurt by what she had done. I felt she was in for the ride of her life, and she had no idea of that. I just wanted her to know what my life, our life, had really been like. As much as I loved Charles, Jr., I was going to expose him to someone I also loved—not to hurt Charles, Jr. but to warn a woman I thought was my friend and sister. "Mind my own business? Mind my own business I shall do."

Charles, Jr. told me that he didn't want nobody to know that he was going to be released until he was officially released. I wasn't feeling him either, but I let it go. Well, Charles, Jr. helped me move into my home. Calvin and Katrina lived in Lansing now, and it was time to move into a bigger house. I gave my brother $400 to move me and paint the basement in my new home. I couldn't stand how gloomy and old the basement looked. It looked creepy, yet I painted it black—go figure.

I was in my new place now. However, I needed more out of life. For the first time in years, I was back doing hair and wanted to take it to the next level. I had attended advanced cosmetology training at Dudley's University when Little Charles was about nine months old. I quit working at the rehab plant due to problems getting there on top of the many therapist appointments, NA and AA, and now a baby. I was never one that could work nine to five. Self-employment was for me. I didn't like anyone telling me what to do and when to do it, especially since I felt I could teach them a thing or two, so I set out to find a job in a salon.

First, I got a job at a salon in a mall in Lansing. I worked there part time, though still not satisfied because I had to punch a clock. When I got paid and started reporting my wages to Social Security, I didn't like the dent they put in my disability check. I was trying to make money, not get it taken from me. My thinking was so warped. I still had that mentality I practiced in the past: lie and get all the money I could. So I started looking for a shop to work in that had a booth rental. I called all the shops in the yellow pages that look like blacks were the owners based on the name of the shop. I had learned that when I dealt with my own people, I could cut all kinds of corners.

Even though God had placed a blessing in my life through my vocational rehab counselor, I still thought the same way I always had. My counselor, Keith Davis, was another person that God used to show himself and his blessing to me. Keith never said no to anything I asked for. With the state's money, he paid for at least three cars for me and paid for me to go to Dudley University in South Carolina.

Anyway, I came across a salon in the yellow pages called Chocolate and Vanilla Beauty Salon. I had a feeling it was black-owned, so I called the number.

A man answered the phone. "May I help you?"

"Yes, I'm calling to see if you are doing any hiring?"

"As a matter of fact, we are. May I ask your name?"

That phone call was the beginning of a dream I had since I started doing hair when I was twenty years old. I went to the shop to meet with the gentleman the very next day. He was an elderly man, a barber. His name was Anthony. No one else was in the shop, except him and a client whose hair he was cutting. I sat down and waited for him to finish. I watched him cut the hair on a client's head. *He's okay*, I thought, *but not half as good as Charles, and Charles is still in school.*

After I talked to Anthony, he explained to me that the salon used to be run by a woman named Michelle. Her husband, Tyrone, bought it for her. When their marriage went bad, she walked out. The shop had basically shut down, but there were a few stray calls that still came in from women wanting their hair done. Anthony said I could build a clientele from doing those clients. I was interested because I could see that I would be my own boss. I would set my own hours and my own prices. I was definitely feeling this offer. I did, however, wonder where the owner and his wife were, when I would meet them, and would they be a problem.

When I first started, Anthony liked me. He called me whenever somebody called the salon that needed a service that he couldn't do—mostly students from the university in East Lansing. The salon was close to the college. I agreed to pay for booth rental, which Mr. Davis paid for me through the state. He also bought all my equipment and supplies. All I had to do was show up whenever I got a client; I didn't have to clock in any particular time. I also started doing my recovery friends' hair at the salon. Plus, I was getting help from the government for my children.

I was doing fine, yet I longed for Charles. He was graduating from barber school and started coming over more often. He took our son home with him one weekend, and I almost died worrying about my son. So of course, I got dressed once again and drove over eighty miles to check on him. "That woman you got, better not be playing house with my son!" I said to him, so I went to see if she was, in fact, caring for my son. Actually, it might have been better if she had been. I got there, and Charles let me inside the house. He was so high. I saw that plain as day.

"Little Charles is going home with me."

Charles dissed me. "He ain't going nowhere! You can't take him. He's my son! He's with me!"

I was very upset, so I went to Mama's house. She had an apartment right across Charles's and his so-called woman who had more sense than I did, really. Charles's girlfriend was getting tired of him, so she dated another man on him. She knew Charles was using. She probably wondered why I let my son go with him. Anyway, Mama didn't talk much while I was there. She was on medication for mental issues, and sometimes she acted like a zombie. She just paced the floor while her hands shook. Her eyes were always glassy-looking. I sometimes would pray and ask God, "Don't ever let me end up like my mother and lose my mind."

Mama was living alone during that time. Her man got caught drunk driving so many times that he was put in prison. The state of Michigan was now cracking down on drunk drivers. Daddy got away with hurting so many people and wrecking so many cars; it wasn't even funny. He never once badly hurt himself though. Mama waited for her man to get out, and in my eyes, she was finally content and settled. She did say some of the weirdest things though: "Bean, I want to be buried in all white. I want to look like I'm sleeping." I would listen to her as she talked. "Mama, why you talking about dying?"

No time to think about dying today. Today I was on a mission to get my son back home. I called Felix while I was at Mama's. I told him what was going on. He asked whether I wanted him to talk to Charles. I said, "Yes." He spoke to Charles and ended up going to jail himself! I had called the police to get my son and was told there was nothing they could do because he was the child's father and was not harming the child. Felix and Charles exchanged words. Then the police asked for everybody's identification. Felix had a warrant, so he was automatically arrested. I left and went home without my son.

That Monday morning, when Charles was on his way to barber school, he brought Little Charles home. Charles left quickly so he wouldn't be late for school. When he was out the door, I quickly took off my son's hat and coat. When I removed his hat, I almost had a heart attack! Little Charles's head was twice as big as it normally was. "Oh my god!" I said. I put his hat back on and went straight to the emergency room.

While there, I called his dad. "What happened to my baby's head?"

"Nothing. His head's big as a basketball!"

"What? He has a fractured skull, and you are saying *nothing* happened?"

Charles came to the hospital before Little Charles was released and stuck to his story that nothing happened. The next day Child Protective Services (CPS) knocked on my door. The swelling on Little Charles's head had gone down, but the fact was the hospital had called them and reported the baby's head was fractured due to possible neglect. I opened the door and told them the truth that he was with his father, and when his father brought him home to me, his head was swollen, and I took him straight to the hospital.

CPS had driven over eighty miles to see Charles. He told them to leave his house because he would never do anything to hurt his son. He also told them they couldn't stop him from seeing his son. "That's *my* son" is what the worker said when she came back to see me. "I'm suggesting that you don't let the little guy go with his father alone again." I heard her, but I wasn't feeling her. I didn't feel Charles would hurt Little Charles intentionally either. I don't believe he realized that Little Charles had been hurt. I believe ignorance was the issue. Well, I didn't have to let Little Charles go with his dad again because a short time after that happened, Charles called me late at night and asked me whether I still wanted him to move in with me. "Yes!" I said.

How quick we women allow men into our home over our child just to say that we have someone, just so we don't have to be alone. He can be a lump on a log, and we don't care as long as a body is in our bed in the night hours because we don't want to be alone. We use sex to make us feel better. We both used each other to deal with the pain life dealt to us. We both had addictive personalities, so we fed off each other's sickness.

So even though I felt I had the drugging under control, I used other unhealthy behaviors to alter my mood and to make me feel good. I had found another way to get that quick fix.

> Dear God,
>
> I need you, Lord. I need you to take away the thoughts of self-destruction, my addiction to pain. I'm so thankful that I can call upon your love. When I am weak in the middle of the night, you build me back up so I can face another day. Your love is always there for me. For this, I say thank you, Lord. Thank you. I continue to allow unhealthy men into my life, like your love is not enough. I don't see how sick I really am. I need you to open my eyes, God. Amen

If you do what is right, will you not be accepted? But if you do not do what is right, sin is crouching at your door; it desires to have you, but you must rule over it.

—Genesis 4:17 (NIV)

You have been my defense and refuge in the day of my trouble.

—Psalm 59

Chapter Twenty-Six

I SET MYSELF UP

That night Charles was moving in. I was so happy. When he arrived, he was high, and I knew it. He was honest with me and told me that he didn't know how he felt about us. He didn't have anywhere else to go and didn't want to come to Lansing to live, but he had no choice. We had sex that night, and it altered my mood, so I was good. I now had a new addiction. For months, I allowed Charles to come and go from my home and back home, doing all kinds of wrong. His friend, the same friend that was involved in the stick-up down in Detroit that I was involved in, came up with this idea that while he and his family were away on vacation, Charles was to set the house on fire. All this was planned so his friend could get the insurance money off his home.

Charles told me that he knew a man selling an air conditioner for a hundred dollars. I agreed to give him the money for the unit. Then I learned that the air conditioner was the one he took from the house before setting it on fire. Charles was using drugs and getting money for his habit, a must. Surely I could understand that since I had been in the same shoes before. He began to tell me what he had done when he realized that his so-called friend had no intention of sharing the insurance money with him. He did, however, get him high. Charles was all-in. He had become a full-blown addict. Using was his purpose for waking up in the morning. It was his mission throughout the day, and I didn't do anything about it at first, as long as I had a man, as long as I was not alone.

Charles never gave me a dime toward any bills or food. This went on for months. Then I got tired of it. I told Charles to get his stuff together and leave. He didn't even try to defend himself. He decided to seek treatment and found a center near Atlanta. He caught the next flight there. While he was away, I realized how much he was pulling me down. I had enough problems in my life. David Jr. (Pooky) was getting kicked out of school for smoking weed. He made himself feel better by trying to tell a lie. "Mama, I didn't smoke weed today." I said, "Pooky, your clothes smell like weed." More and more, he hung out in the streets.

While Charles was away, I got a visitor at the shop one day. It was the owner's wife, Michelle. "If I come back to work, would you stay and help me build my salon back up?" I told her, "Yes, I'd love to!" Once she was back, Anthony, the barber, became ill, so we needed another barber. Charles had graduated from barber school a month before he ended up in treatment. I called him knowing that he was about to get out of treatment. I asked him if he wanted a temporary job cutting men's hair. He said he did, so when he got back to Lansing, he began working at the salon and cutting the hair of Anthony's clients.

Charles was clean now and totally different. Actually, he was back to that Charles who first came to Lansing with me when I got out of treatment. Michelle was quite impressed by him. His hair-cutting skills were remarkable. Plus, he just had a coolness about him that was confident yet a little arrogant. We became a team. Things were good at that moment.

My son, Calvin, was making a name for himself in Lansing playing football. He'd gotten so good that he was always in the Lansing newspaper. One time he had a whole page to himself. I opened the paper, and I was like, "Wow, that's Calvin!" He made me proud. His little brother looked up to him. During this time, my daughter Katrina was starting to act out. She did something out of order. "You are getting a whooping, Katrina!" I went to get the belt, and she ran right out of the back door. "Katrina get back here!" She kept running. *What the heck?* I thought. I couldn't believe she actually ran out of the house like she did. I told Calvin to go get her. She was up the street at the end of the alley, just standing there. She didn't get the whooping. I felt if it was that deep with her, I would just let this one go. Big mistake—I'd be letting bad behavior go for years to come.

I couldn't figure out why my daughter's behavior was so different from my sons'. I was puzzled. Mama and her daddy spoiled her every chance they got. He not only spoiled her, but he also spoke against me every time he saw her. Her daddy would say things like "Your mama cares more about Little Charles than you." Nothing was further from the truth. I loved my daughter. I can admit that I didn't know how to love her with a healthy love, just like I never gave any of my sons a healthy love. I couldn't give what I didn't have, what I'd never been shown myself. All my life, all I knew were confusion, pain, chaos, and trauma. How Mama and Daddy showed they loved me was with material things and money. I cannot remember one time Daddy saying "I love you, Lavinia." Mama either.

Now I was trapped in an unhealthy relationship once again, not realizing that I was teaching my daughter the same. I'd already seen the results of the lifestyle I put before my two eldest sons. I always said that my sons would never end up like the street penitentiary men I saw daily, yet I was teaching them to be just that. The men I put before my kids made an impact to their choices in life. That's just a fact. I couldn't change my behavior if I didn't first admit that it was wrong. I admit that I did not protect my children as I should have. I allowed my addictions to drugs, stealing, sex, clothes—you name it—to come first. The first step to change is to admit that what we have been doing is not working and is wrong.

Once Charles got going good in the salon, Anthony had returned to work. We both worked under Tyrone and Michelle. This went on for months. We both had the support of our vocational rehab counselor. Then the day came when everything started falling apart at the salon. Anthony was dying and had to stop working. Charles got all his clients. Tyrone and Michelle couldn't get along. She also started to get carpal tunnel in her hands. She walked away from the business again. As a result, Tyrone approached me. "Do you want the salon?" I couldn't believe what I was hearing! All my life, I had prayed for my own business, my own salon, and here it was dropped into my lap. Wow!

I went to my vocational rehab counselor, and we developed a plan for me to take over the shop. I saw the favor of God upon me. I thanked him for what he was about to do in my life. I often told him how I never wanted to lose the constant contact I had with him, especially whenever I rode past highly infested drug areas. "God, I thank you that you brought me out of that darkness. I never want to go back there." Yet I couldn't see I was setting myself up to be in the very place I prayed not to be. I didn't know anything different. Old habits die hard. All I knew to do in life was what I'd always done, so I always got the same results. I thought this time it would be different, but I was still making the same choices with people, places, and things in my life. I did well with the salon in the beginning, but little by little, I was returning to familiar behavior, stressed with all the responsibilities I had.

David, Jr. had moved his bedroom to the basement. I watched as he started drawing pictures of guns on the walls. He had a talent for drawing. To be honest, I enjoyed seeing his artwork. I not once thought about the fact that he was drawing guns on the walls. I pressured him into going to school. He decided to go to the Job Corps, but when that failed, he got a local job. After I told him he couldn't stay in my house and not work or go to school, he got a job at a fast-food restaurant. I thought he was doing well until Charles said one day, "You should check on Pooky." And that I did.

It was a rainy day, and I offered Pooky a ride to work on my way to the shop, and he said he wanted to walk in the rain. I thought about what Charles said, so I called the restaurant, and they told me, "David hasn't been to work in two weeks."

"What?" Pooky got dressed every morning like he was going to work. So when he came back home this day, I asked, "How was work?"

"It was okay. I'm tired."

"You should be tired—tired of lying!"

He said to me, "I'm not gonna keep lifting them big old heavy pots! I'm moving back home!"

Soon after, he did just that. I worried about him daily. Calvin, on the other hand, was on fire playing football. I was proud of his accomplishments. He was still making the news weekly.

Charles was also a better man and father now. I met his eldest daughter for the first time when he invited her to our home. I enjoyed meeting her. She was grown. She was also in college. It was the situation with his youngest daughter, Porcia, that was messy. He told me that he wanted her to live with him because of how she was being raised, so I agreed to let her come when her mother allowed it. This turned out to be more stressful. When Charles's daughter first arrived, Katrina enjoyed having her around. She now had somebody to play with. Little Charles was now able to share a bedroom with his big brother, Calvin, and he loved it!

We went to church as a family every now and then, but we were not living a godly life by any means. The biggest sin at that time was Charles and I not being married to each other; we were playing house. God was not blessing our union. The Bible talks about the sin of shacking up. We paid no attention to the fact that we were not accepted by Christ. It never dawned on me, in all the living-with-men I had done, that I was dishonoring God.

Anyway, when the grown children of Charles's ex-wife wanted their little sister, Porcia, they had no problem telling him that he wasn't married to me. And because I wanted to show them, I said to Charles, "I won't keep playing house and taking care of not just my kids, our son, and now your daughter . . ." And that situation was a total mess! But I have to be honest and say that I was addicted to chaos too. Sure I was. That's all I knew my entire life. I felt more comfortable when a bunch of arguing was going on. I insisted we get married.

Porcia's family was always calling and bringing her stolen clothes. While I lived to do the right thing, I didn't boost anymore, and I couldn't stand another woman bringing hot clothes into my home—that was an insult. After my own kids watched Porcia sport her new clothes, I told Charles that I was not going for this in my home. I demanded that he marry me, not because I started to want to please God but because I wanted to show his ex-wife and her family that they would not run my house or my man.

When we got married, I felt the difference in being under what God considered to be a covenant agreement. Our relationship had been taken to a higher level. I started to place all I had into this marriage. I saw a difference in Charles's behavior. He started paying all our bills, and he managed the money because I still had the mentality that Mama had embedded in me: "You better spend that money. You might be dead tomorrow." So I couldn't hold water. Charles was very good with money.

I'd never been happier with a man than I was at that time—not in any relationship. Charles was everything I ever wanted in a man. We worked together, and we were friends. We spent our evenings talking. The salon was doing well. I made good money there. On weekdays, the salon was slow to me, but the salon did extremely well on weekends. Charles opened and closed the salon daily. I did the home thing, and it was starting to affect me physically. I was very tired. I had too much on my plate. I began to feel depressed. Mentally, I was deteriorating. Charles and I continued to make plans for the growth of the salon, but so much was going on with outsiders, not just with his ex but with my family as well.

We started to feel each other's weaknesses. We started chipping on drugs, at first every now and then. His drug of choice was heroin. We started going to Detroit. It wasn't like we didn't have the money. Money was no issue in our lives at that time. I only meant to wet my feet. I didn't mean to take this nighttime chipping any further than an every-now-and-then recreation. I was playing with fire, and in my heart, I knew I was, but the stress and chaos that I carried every day was weighing me down.

We played with drugs for a year or more. During that playtime, we did things that the average family did. We went to all of Calvin's football games. We visited Charles's family on holidays.

One Thanksgiving dinner was held at our house. My family and his family were there. You could feel the separation in the families. My brothers were doing well in life. Both had jobs and were in relationships. I had accepted that fact that my so-called friend and sponsor, Crystal, had betrayed me.

I was happy that Charles, Jr. had a woman in his life that helped him. Crystal was very good for him. He reminded me of Daddy in a lot of ways. The only difference was that Charles, Jr. was in control. In our house, Mama ran things. Crystal surprised me. But I'd been there too. We as women let men totally run us. We let go of our own self-worth, at least women who've been taught unhealthy behaviors like me. Johnny was in a relationship too. He lived in Jackson. He would often bring his woman to our salon to get her hair done.

I had gotten to where I took my ability to do hair for granted. I remember when I first got back in the styling game. In treatment, I had several clients whose hair I styled. One of them pushed me to the limit. She was a very picky client. It took forever to please her, but once I got it right, it helped me stay focused and please other clients. But now I was losing interest in the salon. I was starting to smoke crack again, along with the heroin, along with taking Prozac. I had been prescribed it by my new therapist. I was slipping and couldn't feel who I really was.

Charles and I took the kids on vacation that summer to another one of his family affairs. We rented a car. Whenever we went out of town, it was to one of his family affairs, never to any of mine. Both of us were using drugs on the way there. Charles was driving on our way down this particular time, but out of the blue, he said, "Beanie you have to drive." He had been speeding and cut a man off on the road as he attempted to change lanes or something. I didn't see what actually happened. I was too busy smoking crack while our kids slept on the backseat. Charles and I switched seats on the side of the road, and I started driving. The police stopped me and said that he received a call that a man had been cutting drivers off in traffic. I lied and said that I'd been driving for a while and hadn't cut anyone off. He let me go and told me to drive carefully.

About twenty minutes further down the road, I realized the car had swerved off the road and went on to gravel. It scared me, so I hurried up and turned the steering wheel to get back onto the road, but I lost control of the car. It had turned completely around on the highway and was headed off the road down into the high grass, hitting big rocks and everything else that was in this undeveloped land. This was the second time that God saved my life like this. When I fell asleep on the highway when I was younger and with my friends, the same thing happened. We were stuck in the car, but neither one of us was hurt. Charles kicked the car door several times so it could open and we could get out of the car. The car was totaled, but we were all fine. God had protected me again, even when I wasn't even thinking of myself or my children.

This time in my life, I was so into getting high. I had just been in another accident a few weeks before this one. A big eighteen-wheeler had hit my car and ran me off the road while Charles and I were on another drug run. My car was totaled. That's why we were in a rental. Now the rental was totaled. Charles told the police that his back was hurt because of the accident and went to the hospital. My insurance paid him for a back injury that he never had.

When Charles started getting the insurance money, he really started to change. He began treating his daughter and me very bad. I started using drugs all day and arguing with his ex-wife about their daughter. I felt sorry for his daughter. When I talked to her, she wanted to be with her mother. Her mother touched my heart when we talked. She wanted her daughter back with her. I felt her pain. I knew what it felt like when Felix took my daughter and didn't let her come with me and put negative things and lies in her head about me. I couldn't do that to any mother, so I helped Porcia get back to her mother. Besides, Charles claimed he didn't want his daughter being in a home where drugs were being sold, yet he was starting to do the same thing.

We all had issues. Some of ours may have been worse than others, but we were all sick, and the kids paid the price for our sickness. The madness got worse over time for our entire family: Mama's man was catching drunk driving cases and ended up in prison; Charles, Jr. was gambling and making poor choices to support his addiction; David was smoking and on bad terms with his woman; Vanessa struggled with alcohol; I was drugging out. Charles, Jr. was arrested for driving on a suspended license around this time and sentenced to ninety days. While he was in jail, Johnny and Larry, Jr. moved in with me. Larry, Jr. had been getting into trouble and needed a place to stay. Johnny and his woman had called it quits, and Charles, Jr. was losing control in his life as well. He was in over his head with a gambling addiction.

One evening when I got home from the salon, Johnny said to me, "The police are at Crystal's house."

"For what?" I said.

"A man in Jackson got killed!"

"What? I'm going over there!"

No, Beanie, don't go over there."

"I'm going!" I said.

I went over there only to be met at the door by the police. They wouldn't let me in, but I could see Crystal standing in the background. Our eyes met, and I just stared at her. I could see in her eyes that she knew then, that she really didn't know everything like she thought she did when she told me to mind my own business about three years prior. This was some heavy stuff. What else could go wrong? A man is dead, and the home of my brother's wife is being searched. Charles, Jr. also had an apartment, but the police didn't know it. He stayed with Crystal whenever he wanted to. He lived in his apartment more because he always had a secret life.

I was starting to get that feeling in my gut, that feeling that I had gotten so many other times since the age of fourteen when my brother was first arrested. The fear I felt for him, I was feeling that feeling, and it was very uncomfortable, so I went and got drugs to make it go away. As soon as I left Crystal's house and got back home, I saw the same fear in Johnny.

Father,

I humble myself before you. I am your child. I have been depending on you all my life. I have felt your presence even when I was doing wrong in life. Your mercy and grace has been everlasting; yet when I want to please you, I find myself doing just the opposite. Help me, God! I'm slipping. I'm losing control. I can't do this without you. I need your guidance. I need you to come to see about me, in Jesus's mighty name, Amen.

He has caused his wonders to be remembered; the Lord is gracious and compassionate. He provides food for those who fear him; he remembers his covenant forever.

—Psalm 111:4–5 (NIV)

As a father has compassion on his children, so the Lord has compassion on those who fear him; for he knows how we are formed, he remembers that we are dust.

—Psalm 103: 13–14 (NIV)

....

Chapter Twenty-Seven

LOSING A PART OF ME

....

We all found ways to cope with our pain. That worked for us. Vanessa had gotten where she just totally chose to separate herself from what was going on. She didn't live in Lansing. My brothers never involved Vanessa in their criminal activities like they always involved me. We all enabled one another in one way or another. Mama taught us that "nothing and nobody comes before your family." Lying to help one another was just how it went—what family didn't? Charles, Jr. never involved me in anything that would jeopardize my freedom. Johnny had always been that little brother that I always felt I had to care for. I know today that my behavior was dysfunctional, but back then, I didn't see it.

Anyway, after the search happened at Crystal's house, my husband, Charles, got out of jail. He talked me into changing the locks on my doors. I knew he was doing this because of Larry, Jr. and Johnny; but to keep peace with him, I allowed him to do it, even though I felt there was a better way to handle the situation. Larry, Jr. became so angry at what Charles did that he got into his car and went to the salon and broke out the windows in my husband's car. Then he got back into the car and went home.

I told Johnny that he had to go before Charles got out. Johnny had worked a job for a few weeks, and when he got paid, he tried to give me $10. I gave him his $10 back and told him he had to go. He went to Charles, Jr.'s apartment until he made him leave as well.

I had no intention of putting my son out. I had some extra money, and the plan was to help him get an apartment, but after he busted up Charles's car windows, I took that money and fixed it because Charles was talking about hurting Larry, Jr. All this nonsense and I'm right in the middle of it—I kept me some drugs.

Charles, Jr. gave no explanation in the beginning as to why the police was searching Crystal's house. The police took a pair of pants from her house and sent it to the lab for testing. In the meantime, they had Charles, Jr. bring his truck into the police station to be searched. When they questioned him, he told the police that his brother had his truck on the day in question. The police let Charles, Jr. leave the station with his truck. Meanwhile, Johnny was tired of drugging and living on the streets of Lansing, so he flagged the police down and turned himself in for an outstanding warrant he knew he had for a drug case in Jackson. At least, in jail, he had a place to sleep and take a bath.

Johnny was detained for questioning about the murder of the Jackson man. Charles, Jr. not only told the police Johnny had his truck, but he also told Crystal he had it. She called me after the police came to her house and she spoke to Charles, Jr. She listened to Charles, Jr. and began to speak against Johnny. Because Johnny was using drugs, he became the target for Charles, Jr. and his many friends and wife. I, on the other hand, didn't say a word to Crystal about the issue. I was in a very uncomfortable position. Both of them were my brothers. I didn't want to put murder on either of them.

"God! This has to be a bad dream." I started to give thought to how serious this was. I wondered what I'd do with my brother being in jail for murder. I knew we were all dibbling and dabbling off into areas that we shouldn't have been but never anything like murder. Then I started to think of the past and the things I knew about the past, what I had already been through with Charles, Jr. and Johnny. I thought about how I felt the first time Charles, Jr. went to prison. I had gotten used to having him out of prison. I was starting to enjoy the fact that my eldest brother was home. Our family was starting to come back together. Charles, Jr. was like

Mama; he believed in family. He was the head of our family since he was a kid. I felt safe whenever my brother was out of prison. Now I was feeling like it was about to end again—nothing I hadn't felt before.

I was worried about Mama. She had been doing good for the past few years as long as she took her be-cool medication. Mama was just as pleasant as she could be. She was patiently waiting for her man to get out of prison. Charles, Jr. went to see her at least twice weekly or more. He was good to Mama. She loved having him home too. We all did. We even loved the fact that he was married to a woman that loved him. Charles, Jr. was on the right path; he was a family man. "What had happened though?" I asked the Lord to help us. I knew this was going to be a situation that was going to take our family to the breaking point. Mama was heavily on my mind.

As this chapter in my life unfolded, it got real nasty. Charles, Jr. stuck to his story that Johnny had his truck. The police were on us like white on rice. They camped out at the salon. As I styled my clients' hairs, the police would sit in the waiting room and wait until I could speak to them. I'm sure my clients knew things weren't right. The police looked like police—didn't matter if they had on plain clothes or not; they stuck out, especially two white cops in an all-black salon. Finally, I wanted to get this mess behind me, so I finished up my two clients and spoke to the police. I was asked questions like "Which one of your brothers wore a kangaroo cap? Which one of your brothers would murder?" My response was "I would like to think that neither one would."

I tried to help my brother, but what do you do in a situation that if you say something about one brother, you are hurting the other? How could Charles, Jr. do this to me? How could he expect me to lie on Johnny? I couldn't, and I didn't. Bad enough, I had to listen to Crystal talk about Johnny. She actually said she hated him for not telling the cops the truth. I wanted to tell her, "Shut up! You don't know us. You think you know our family, but you don't have a clue, so just shut up!" But I didn't want her to turn her back on Charles, Jr.; I knew he needed her right about now.

Things got even worse. When the police lab work was done, a small blood stain on some jeans that were taken from Crystal's clothes hamper came back positive for the dead man's blood type. A warrant was issued for Charles, Jr., but he was not about to just let them arrest him. He not only ran from them when they came to arrest him, but he also got away. When Charles, Jr. was finally arrested, he was in Louisiana. Crystal and Charles, Jr.'s friends hired an attorney for him. Once he was extradited back to Michigan, he was placed on trial for murder. Mama was holding up, but she was very worried about Charles, Jr. and Johnny because of the confusion.

Mama couldn't make sense of what was going on. She thought both of her sons were in trouble for killing a man. Mama had been through so much dealing with her sons and her daughters as far as that goes. We all caused her big heartaches I'm sure. We were one of the unhealthiest families I'd ever seen, always a lot of conflict and chaos in our lives, yet this one was the worst: two brothers that always loved each other and protected each other were in a predicament that tore our family to pieces. This was heavy. Wow! What had become of our family?

Charles, Jr. was desperate, and he was so out of character. He had called me while on the run. When I answered, he said, "Beanie, I can't go to prison the rest of my life. I'll never see you again, but at least I'm not in prison if I'm on the run." I didn't tell him to come back and turn himself in. I too was on drugs and sick. I said, "Go, Charles, Jr., go!" He hung up, and then I cried like a baby.

A few weeks went by and I received a call that he was arrested and waiting to be extradited to Michigan. Once he was back in Michigan, I began to be pressured by the police on one end and Charles, Jr.'s attorney on the other end. The attorney was being paid, so he would call and ask me questions that had me believing that he was actually trying to help my brother.

Johnny was released when the police felt confident that they had the brother that committed the murder. Charles, Jr. still stuck to his story that his brother had his truck on that day. Johnny went to Mama's house when he was released. The police tried hard to get him to go against Charles, Jr., but he never did. I knew he wouldn't. Johnny loved Charles, Jr. more than he loved anyone—always did. Charles, Jr. was his hero. That's why he would do anything to help him. He too had learned unhealthy behaviors as to what love was.

We were all codependent and dysfunctional. A curse was on our family that started back during slavery, not just on Daddy's side but Mama's too, from addictions to mental illness; and by the time I came along, this curse went rampant. It was full blown. All of us had been consumed by darkness. Mama was aging, and she daily had to face the results of what she had created. Charles, Jr. had spent more time with her in the past four years than he ever did. He took her to the movies, concerts, and dinners. He even rented a limousine once to take her to a concert.

Charles, Jr. also had been involved with several confrontations with Aunt Mabel and a few of our cousins. That was Charles, Jr.—he didn't have a problem letting everybody know that he wasn't going for anybody getting in his way. He took care of Mama when he was out, and that's the way it went. I believe Mama enjoyed it. She just loved having her eldest son out of prison. Now she knew that she stood to lose him again. She had to feel worse than I did. Not only was she about to lose her eldest son being a part of her life, but she also knew of the division between both her sons, yet she never told them to stop it. She never insisted that whoever was lying on the other to stop destroying our family. Not only didn't she, but I also didn't either. I really thought Charles, Jr. would recant his story.

The trial began soon after Charles, Jr. was back in Michigan. I had to testify for the prosecution. Johnny pleaded the Fifth. Mama got on the stand and did what she did. She acted like she didn't have a clue about anything, not even what day it was. Mama was good at getting up out of tight spots—she just nutted up on you. She told the court she didn't know anything, and she really didn't. Crystal got on the stand and tried to paint a picture of Johnny that was an outright lie. Charles, Jr. took the stand to testify on his own behalf, and when he did, I was blown away by what I learned about his lawyer. Charles, Jr., in my opinion, should never have taken the stand. The prosecutor had a field day.

Charles Jr.'s attorney, during a break, went up to the detective who had been in my salon trying to make a case and get to the bottom of which brother to charge with the murder, and said to her, "Did you see when I asked him that last question? He just sat there like an idiot."

He didn't see me sitting in the back of the courtroom. When he realized I was sitting in the courtroom, he walked down the aisle toward me smiling. He was trying to see if I had heard him. I just smiled back like I hadn't, but I heard every word. The other detective who sat with the prosecutor remained a little more professional. She didn't say much other than "yeah." I told Charles, Jr. that his attorney was not for him. He never asked the judge for a mistrial. The judge never allowed us to be in the courtroom. He would tell us to leave when we were done testifying. The trial was over in about two weeks.

When the judge released the jury, they were only out four hours. During that time, Crystal and I went home. When we got back to the court, we went inside and asked at the information counter whether the jury was still out and was told that the trial was over. My brother had been found guilty of first-degree murder, which carried a sentence of life.

Once again, I felt like I was in a bad movie. I couldn't believe what I was hearing. When Crystal and I walked outside, I had to stop a minute to absorb what I had just been told. I started crying, not just for me but for my brother. I'd never seen him broken like this case broke him. He was knocked totally off his square in this trial. He was fighting for his life, and he lost. Wow! This tragedy would tear our family apart for fifteen years or more.

During those fifteen years, the separation and resentment among us broke my heart. I felt Charles, Jr. had crossed his family. He flip-flopped in my opinion. He even stated several times that Crystal and his best friends were his family. I felt he crossed Johnny also. I felt it was Charles, Jr.'s fault that Crystal and I were no longer the friends we once were. I felt it was his fault that our mama lived the rest of her life watching the peace and love her sons once shared shatter. I couldn't make sense of why Charles, Jr. had deserted us as a family. Sure we didn't have the money that his friends had, but I believe to this day that had Charles, Jr. been honest, the truth would have set him free in more ways than one. Crystal, on the other hand, never apologized to Johnny for her role in the destruction of our family.

Mama often spoke about how she really felt about Crystal, yet she never told her. She would only talk to me about how Johnny and Charles, Jr. were brothers, and because of outsiders, Charles, Jr. had turned against his own brother. I was angry at both Crystal and Charles, Jr. My brother going to prison for life took a toll on me. I started using drugs daily.

In the middle of the night, I had my husband, Charles, doing things that made him angry at me. The crack had taken me back to the point of being so paranoid that I would hit it and hide myself in the attic. He would leave to get more, and while he was gone, I became spooked. I couldn't handle what crack did to me, yet I kept smoking it. I thought I was sneaking at night using drugs. It's funny how God will bring to light what we think we are doing in the dark.

I had been smoking one night, and I didn't want to stop. I talked Charles into going with me to the ATM to get some money and then on a mission to get more crack. This night it started to rain. As we approached the corner that drugs were always sold on, I let down my window. As I rode up on a young dude, I said, "Got anything to sell?"

"Yes," he said, but when he got into our car, he said that he had to go get it. "Can you take me to the south side?"

Charles said, "No."

"Why?" I said. "We can give him a ride."

Charles rolled his eyes at me. I gave the dude a ride anyway. "Tell me where I'm going," I said.

As I drove, he was talking to Charles. When I got to the south side, the dude said, "Turn on this street." And then he said, "Stop here."

When I stopped the car, out of the corner of my eye, I saw him pull out a gun. He said, "All right! Empty your pocket!"

Charles quickly reacted. He turned and grabbed the gun. I took hold of the steering wheel and moved the car around. Charles scared the mess out of that young dude! When Charles grabbed the gun, it fired. The bullet headed straight through the back of my seat. After piercing the seat, it hit me straight in the back. When it hit, I felt this strong burning sensation in my back. It was so hot that fear rose in me and I let go of the steering wheel and opened the door. I rolled out of the car while it was moving.

Charles was fighting with the dude as I got up off the pavement in the street and ran. I fell to the ground at the edge of a driveway. "Jesus!" I hollered. "Help me!" I got up off the ground and ran to the back of the house at the end of the driveway. I was in a lot of pain, but God had given me the strength to bang on the door.

The lights in the house came on, and I saw a white woman through the window. She was standing in her kitchen, saying, "I'm calling the police!"

"Help! Help!" I hollered.

I could see that she was very nervous. When she was done making the call, she said, "Help is on the way!"

I stepped down off her porch and crawled up in a fetal position in a corner at the back of her porch. I heard four more shots. "Oh my god, I think he killed my husband!"

Not even sixty seconds later, I saw two police cars go by on the side of the house where I was hiding. The house was on a corner. As I saw the police drive by, I rose. I was in agony, but I made my way to the front of the house thinking that Charles was dead. Then I looked up the street and saw Charles coming up the street toward me. He was just a cussing.

"Charles! Are you shot?"

"No."

The paramedics pulled up.

"Are you hit?" they asked me.

"Yes, in the back," I said.

"Lie down on your stomach, on the ground."

I did what they asked. They cut off my coat to get to the gunshot wound, and then they laid me on the gurney, and the ambulance driver drove off. When we arrived at the hospital, Charles, along with the police, walked in. The officer that I spoke to while I was on the ground said, "We caught him." They took me to have an X-ray to determine the exact location of the bullet. They had also pumped me with morphine, so I wasn't feeling as much pain. Actually, I was enjoying the high. I said to the officer, "Thank you," never once telling the truth about why the young dude was even with us. I told them that it was raining and we went to the store and he asked for a ride. I never said that I was looking for crack, so I felt like I got away with not getting exposed again, which told me I could keep chipping. And that's what I did.

After I was released from the hospital, I was in denial. I kept on drugging. I told myself that I could stop whenever I wanted to, but truth be told, I couldn't stop. I did everything I could to stop. I called the insurance company and told them that Charles's back was not hurt and he was still working. I thought if I could slow him down, that would slow *me* down. The more Charles used, the more his behavior started to change back to when he first moved in with me. I thought if we didn't get the extra money, we wouldn't be able to use so much. I thought I could control his addiction when I couldn't even control my own.

Things got even worse. We were both high and doing clients' hairs. I knew my skills were falling. Everything was changing in the salon. The clients, whose hair Charles cut, were straight from the streets. I could tell that Charles had gotten off into more than just cutting hair and drugging, so one day I followed him down into the basement. He would go there whenever he came back from Detroit. I felt uncomfortable being in the shop, and I wanted to know what was going on. When I got to the backroom that he was in, I saw drugs on a table. He appeared to be bagging the drugs.

"What are you doing?" I asked.

"What are you doing down here? Who told you to come down here?"

"You have lost your mind!" I said to him.

Charles wasn't listening to me. A little while later, I saw two white men sitting in a car at a car dealership directly across the street from the salon. I told Charles. He said, "They're just looking at cars."

"What?" If they're just looking at cars, then why won't they get out of their car? No. They are watching this shop!"

At that point, I got scared that if something went down, I was going to jail. The salon's lease was in my name. Charles and I were not getting along anymore. We argued daily. Sometimes we would actually destroy each other's equipment and get into fistfights right in the salon when there were no clients there.

By this time, I had been sent a summons to appear in court to prosecute the young man that shot me in the back. While in court, he hollered out, "I didn't shoot that lady! Her husband shot her!" That statement made me feel sorry for the kid. During the tussle between them when Charles reached to take the gun from him, the trigger went off and the bullet pierced the driver's seat and hit me in the back. Thank God for slowing down another bullet!

One evening, a stranger knocked at my door.

"Who is it?" I asked.

It was the voice of a male.

"We don't want any trouble. We just wanna talk to you."

Calvin was home and heard what was said. He put his jacket on and went outside on the front porch with me. Calvin never said a word; he just stood off to the side with his hands in his pocket. I saw that the young men were uncomfortable with Calvin standing there. I was very proud of my son that he didn't let me go outside alone. *Where was my husband?* was all I kept thinking. I couldn't do this to another son. I refused to ruin Calvin's life. He was doing so well in school. He was about to go to college, and because of me, here he was standing outside with his hands in his pockets like he's got a gun.

The young men wanted to know if the man that shot me could pay me to drop the charges. I wanted to drop them, not for the money but because I felt for his mother. I knew that pain of seeing your son in a courtroom and you can't do nothing to help him. That's a horrible feeling. I told them that I couldn't, and they needed to leave before my husband got home. They left. Calvin and I went back inside the house. Calvin never said a word, but I couldn't stop thinking of what I was getting my son involved in: "Not Calvin, Lavinia, he deserves a chance."

When Charles got home, he had the drugs with him. We did what we always did, but now I was starting to want "out" of the marriage. I was no longer in denial. I had to face the truth, and the truth was that my addiction was out of control. I had a decision to make. This would be the second time that I would leave my own home. I felt I had no choice. Once before, I went to the women's shelter for abused women when Charles, Jr. helped me move out. This time I knew I could not return, so I found a townhouse with the help of one of my clients.

I planned this move to a tee. My next-door neighbor helped me. Little by little, I had been putting boxes in the garage. I called and set up the moving truck for a Saturday. I knew I could pull it off on a Saturday because Charles would be at work. We never missed a Saturday because that was our busiest day. I played sick one Saturday, and with the help of my son Calvin and my neighbor, we moved everything out of my house and into the townhome within four hours.

When Charles got home after work, everything that was not his was gone. I used to say that I wish I could have been a fly on the wall when he walked into the house that evening. At any rate, I was feeling unsure of myself as I made this transition in my life. I knew I had a heroin habit, and I was smoking crack, but I felt I couldn't stop as long as Charles was in my life.

> Heavenly Father,
>   I come to you in the greatest of pain and suffering. I've experienced this type of pain before. It's that gut-wrenching pain that makes me feel physically sick. This hurts, God. I'm hurting for my brother, my family, and

myself, God. Where are you? Have you deserted me, God? You've always fixed things. You've always made me feel like everything was going to be alright.

How can this be all right? You've allowed my hero to be taken from me. Why, God? Why? I can't bear this one. I can't take this pain, God. I need you to show up like you always have. I need you to fix this nightmare. Help us. Please don't make me live without my brother. Please. Amen.

The Lord is close to the brokenhearted and saves those who are crushed in spirit.

—Psalm 34:18 (NIV)

Chapter Twenty-Eight

NINETEEN NINETY NINE

The first day in my townhome was scary. I hadn't been alone since I got out of treatment when I first came to Lansing. I depended on God daily during that time. However, this time I let the fact that I had been able to move into this townhome without a struggle or wondering how I was going to be able to do it, make me forget to count on God. I had gotten too cocky. Again, I felt it was "Lavinia" that made this move.

The drugs had me, but I was still on top of my game, or so I thought. I had called the methadone clinic to help me get off the heroin while still with Charles. The crack, I thought, I could control. I let my mind go to the point of making me think that what happened before I came to Lansing would never happen again. I was no longer with Felix or Charles. It was all their fault. That's why I lost control. If I hadn't been with them, all that happened wouldn't have happened. *Alone, I won't go as far. The methadone will help me*, I thought. Funny how we can convince ourselves that we don't need help, that we are not the problem; it's always someone else.

Well, I was alone now, and I was about to find out that I *was* my biggest problem. I started going to the methadone clinic about a week or two before I moved. Once on my own, I stopped blowing the heroin. I didn't need it. I had found something new to alter my mood, and I loved it! This methadone kept me good and high.

At times I would think about the young man that shot me, and fear of the unknown would rise. Even though he was sentenced to fifteen years, I thought of his friends and his family. I continued to move forward though. I kept working at the salon when I first moved, but it didn't work out. Charles wouldn't say a word to me all day, but as soon as it was time for me to go home, he would go to locking the doors. He always needed to talk. "We need to talk," he'd say. "I've been here all day. Why didn't we talk when there were no clients in the shop?" I had to get home. I had children to get dinner for, a home to run, so it didn't work out.

I had a big decision to make at this time. It hurt me dearly because I had to walk away from my own business. When I told Charles I was leaving, his comment was "Get the hell on! Nobody needs you here!" I told him, "You'll be closed in six months!" Actually, it didn't take that long. I started doing my clients hair from my townhome, which was against the rules, but my landlord was cool. People have shown me favor throughout my entire life. God has had his hand on me since the day I was born. I was the one who made my own life difficult. I rejected God's love for me at times. I would lose contact with him because of drugging.

The longer I used drugs, the deeper off into sin I stepped. I was now on methadone, and it made me nod all day. When I felt I was too down, I'd buy some crack to speed me up, and boy did it ever! It did more than speed me up. Physically, it took me to a place that was disgusting. I'd been there before, and this place never ended pretty, yet I continued to go there. "Why was I so sick that I would continue killing myself? What could be so wrong that would make me hate myself like this?" I had become addicted to the misery of drugging.

Once I started smoking the crack, I needed a downer, so I would go see Charles in the midnight hour. I used drugs daily by now. I couldn't blame it on Charles. I just didn't have to listen to somebody else tell me when and how to use. Now I used whenever I wanted to. I controlled my own using now, and I felt I was better off. Charles was all-in by now; he was outright selling. No shame in his game. He too was off and running. We would come together in the wee hours of the night and have sex, which was also led by drugs.

As time went on, Charles started to get into trouble. He was in my vehicle late one night, playing his music loud, and the police approached him. The cop said that he didn't roll his window down when she asked. When she told Charles and the other man in the vehicle to exit it, he put the vehicle in reverse and backed out of the driveway. She said that he hit her as he backed out. He drove up the street and came to a blockage that stopped him from going any further. Then he jumped out of the vehicle and ran. He left the vehicle behind. About three thirty in the morning, I got a call from the police asking where my vehicle was and who had it.

About ten minutes after that call, Charles called, "If the police call, you tell 'em you don't know where your vehicle is."

"Too late, I already told them you had it. Why? Where are you, and what's going on?"

"I had to leave it because the police was trying to get me to step out of the vehicle, and I didn't. I'm in the basement of an empty house. I can hear dogs trying to track me down."

He stayed in that basement for hours. The story was in the newspaper the next day. I had to go get the vehicle, which had been impounded, not only because it was in my name but because Charles was now a wanted man. Basically, he was on the run. He ran from the police for months, during which time he started using more and more drugs. He also sold on a small level.

The police called my house looking for him almost every week. I started getting angry with him because he was in and out of my house like he had lost his mind. I felt trapped because the drugs he supplied me kept me from putting my foot down. He had stopped doing hair. After he left the salon, he lived in an apartment that he used for drug purposes. I saw the destruction firsthand. He couldn't see it, though, and that was the problem.

I continued to go to the clinic and smoke crack at night with Charles. I was destroying myself as well. I knew I was out of order, but I had given in to darkness years ago, and I couldn't stop. I prayed regularly. Prayer was nothing new to me. God had been watching my back as I self-destruct. The police knew that Charles would eventually show up at my house. He was just in and out so much that they never could catch him until that day. It was in the evening. He stopped by to bring me drugs. He went into the bathroom, and while in there, the phone rang. It was the police officer that Charles was accused of hitting. "Is Charles there?"

She already knew that he was because the car he got out of was in the parking lot and his friend was sitting inside.

"Yes," I said.

"Would you open the door?"

I didn't answer.

"Is he beating on you?" she asked.

"No."

"We're not going away, Lavinia. Open the door."

I hung up the phone. "Charles! The police are at the door!"

"Don't open it! They can't make you open the door if they don't have a search warrant."

The knocking got so loud that it scared me. I ran down the steps to open the door. Charles pushed the cover off the attic and climbed up into it. The police had two dogs with them, and they were barking and trying to leap on me. I ran out of the door to my next-door neighbor's. As I made it next door, I heard Charles kicking in the walls in the attic. It sounded horrible! *What is he doing?* I thought. Fear was racing through me. I was praying that they didn't kill him if they caught him. I felt like I did when I skipped school that day to get some sleep and the police banged at the door when Charles, Jr. had extorted that white family. The only difference was that I was now praying that Charles wasn't killed.

Now I was drugging and living in sin so much that the only time I spent time with the Lord was in the middle of the night after the high wore off. I had just smoked my dope, and prayer was the furthest thing from my mind. Anyway, Charles went from one townhouse to the next, kicking the walls in like a madman. When the police apprehended him, he was in the townhome four doors down from my house. This was so embarrassing, not just for me but for my kids. I thank God they were not home.

When I visited Charles in jail, he told me that the only reason he came down from the attic was because the police threatened to put the dogs on him. Plus, it was so hot up there. Wouldn't you know it? I actually went up there one day looking for crack. Charles told me that he dumped what was in his pocket up there. I never found any.

Anyway, Charles was bonded out for a short time. A trial was held, and he was found guilty; he went away to prison. When he left, I continued to use drugs and take methadone. I was eventually put out of the clinic because I had been there two years and never got a clean drop. You had to leave your urine at random. I didn't even care that I couldn't get a clean drop. I was just trying to stay high.

Calvin, by now, had gone away to college. Playing football had gotten him a scholarship. I was proud of Calvin, yet I continued to shame him by demonstrating unhealthy behavior. At his high school graduation, his dad and I were asked to leave. I got upset about something Felix said to me, and I hit him. He hit me back. A lady who was one of Charles's clients from the salon witnessed it all and told the police. The officer told all of us to leave the property. Charles was ranting about what he was going to do to Felix; that's the only reason he had to leave. So now with Calvin gone and Charles, I continued to fall. I went buck wild! I had no discipline. I started using heroin again.

I was stealing from the department store in East Lansing daily. I had met a local booster, and the two of us became partners in crime. She had been to prison before and stopped using heroin, but she still smoked weed. She took mental medications. She never got busted while working with me. She too was sick in that area. Now I had opened up that can of worms again. I couldn't go to work without getting at least a blow first. I got up every morning. The mind-set of my being so sharp that my being high didn't matter, had returned.

Whenever I went to visit my husband, Charles, I would be high as a kite but sharp as a tack! I didn't care that he would complain.

He would be so embarrassed. "Beanie, you look a mess! You don't think people can tell you high?"

"I don't care what people can tell! People ain't giving me a dime—you either!"

Man, I was lunching yet again! All types of things started to go wrong during this time in my life. I got tickets for speeding and had several car accidents. One time, I had been so high off methadone and pills that a local doctor was prescribing that I nodded out while driving, ran a red light, and hit a woman in her car.

When I came out of the nod, the woman was trapped inside her car, which was tipped over on to its roof. She was upside down in the car. Her car was totaled. Mine was also wrecked pretty badly. She was hurt and taken to the hospital. I, on the other hand, walked away yet again from another serious accident without a scratch. This took place before Charles went to prison. Now with him out of the picture, I was driving while high daily. I was leaving home at two or three o'clock in the morning chasing crack.

Every type of sin you can think of, I dibbled and dabbled in. My small kids paid the price. I thought if I stole them enough clothes and bought them enough toys and games, I was a good mother. I got a call from Vanessa one day during all this madness. She told me that Mama was sick and that she was having exploratory surgery. I had gotten myself off into a heavy situation that was driving me crazy. One day, while out in the streets, I hooked up with this young chick that had turned me on to her man. He was a panhandler that sold crack. I copped from him for days. Then one night this chick decided to steal my jeep in the middle of the night because she thought I was fooling around with him. I called the police, and a cop by the name of Lloyd Taylor assisted me.

I found myself behaving in ways that I was ashamed of even then. I was going to jail often, mostly a day or two for traffic violations. I went once for walking out of a department store with a cart full of electronic devices. I had become scandalous in my boosting. I used no finesse when I was drugging now. I'd be high off a mixture of prescription pills that I got every month and street drugs. I had totally lost my mind.

One time I was on a drug run and hit a car from behind. I didn't stop. I kept right on driving. A driver in a van followed me. I saw it in my rearview mirror, but I was on a mission. When I made it to the pay phone at a corner store, I got out of the car and started to dial the dope man's phone number in on the pay telephone, and the police pulled up. I actually put a finger up to the police as if to say, "Just a minute, I have to take care of this business first."

The officer said, "Hang the phone up. Now!"

So much was going on during this time that I had no control over my life. He asked me to sit in the police car. He found out I had a warrant, so he was ready to take me to jail.

But immediately, I said, "I'm on a mission for Officer Lloyd Taylor."

"Where is Lloyd Taylor?" the cop said.

"Call him, call him!" I said.

The cop did just that.

I didn't go to jail because I had lied about Officer Lloyd, and he lied for me. Actually, I hadn't spoken with Lloyd. He was the cop that answered the phone when I called the police after my jeep was stolen. "I've been calling the police now for three days, and my jeep ain't been found yet. I know it's still in the city. I feel like the police just don't care."

"What does your vehicle look like? I'm about to hit the streets. I'll look for it," Lloyd said.

"It's a green SUV."

"What's your phone number? I'll call you if I see it."

An hour later, my phone rang. A man on the other end said, "I found your SUV."

I was so excited to hear his words. "Oh my god, thank you, thank you!"

"I'm going to have it towed," he said.

"No!" I said quickly. "I have no money to get it out. Can I just come get it now?"

"You have to hurry. I can't just stay here," he said.

"I'm on my way right now," I told him.

He told me the location of my vehicle. I hung up the phone. I asked a neighbor if she would give me a ride to get it. When I arrived at the location, I could see my SUV. The backlight was missing on the driver's side. When I got out of my neighbor's car, I was smiling cheek to cheek as I approached the officer.

"Thank you," I said.

As I began walking back to my SUV, I felt the officer staring at me. He said, "That's the least of your problems. You can't turn it off because your ignition has been stripped. Once you turn it off, it will have to be fixed before it will start again."

"I just want to get home," I said. "Then I'll worry 'bout what you're saying."

"You owe me," Officer Taylor said.

"Thank you again."

I headed home, and as I drove to the other side of town, my mind wondered what the officer meant when he said that to me. I didn't think on it very long, but that statement didn't set too well with me, so I let it go.

Well, about a week after Officer Taylor found my SUV, I was home styling a client's hair, and I received a phone call. "Hello, Lavinia. It's Lloyd, the cop that found your car. I'd like to speak with you."

"About what?"

"About what it is you owe me. I'd like to stop by to discuss it."

I was very uncomfortable with what this cop was saying to me. As a child, the police were at our house every other week. I thought the police were to be called whenever you needed help. I'd never been called by one saying that I owed them for doing his job. I thought about Mrs. Benson being in the front getting her hair done, so I decided that if I had to let him come, I'd do it while she was there. I told him I had a client and that he could stop by. When Officer Taylor arrived, he was carrying a brief case and had on regular street clothes like he did when I went to get my SUV. Mrs. Benson looked at him with a look of suspicion when I opened the door.

"Excuse me a minute," I said to her as I opened the door.

Then I led him into the living room. He was very impressed and looked around at my home and said, "Doing hair didn't get you a home like this."

"What is it you need to speak with me about?"

"I went out of my way and found your car. Oh, by the way, you have a warrant for your arrest."

I felt nervous.

"Don't worry. I'm not going to take you in. However, you are going to pay me what it is you owe me."

"And what is that?"

"Some head would be nice," he deviously stated.

I couldn't believe what I just heard! This cop had just told me he wanted me to suck his penis. Now I see why he lied for me.

"I'll take care of the warrant, but you are going to have to pay up! You know you got this computer to work from."

I caught what he was saying, but I immediately started correcting him. "I don't know what you're talking about. That computer is for my kids. I don't even use it." He was implying that I used the computer for clients as a call girl.

"And I'm not talking about *hair* clients."

He really insulted me. *What's really going on?* I thought. I'm sure my reaction would have been totally different had I not been using drugs. But I wasn't able to comprehend that. All I had to say was, "I don't owe you anything, and if I have a warrant, arrest me, or leave my home." I did what any other addict would do: I called myself buying some time. I said, "I have a client that I need to get back to. You need to get back with me." He agreed, and then he left.

When I stepped back to my station to complete Mrs. Benson's hair, she said, "Lavinia, who was that? He ain't right!" I knew he wasn't, but I couldn't tell her. As addicts and alcoholics do, I felt I had to lie to her. She wouldn't understand the truth. Eventually, she stopped letting me do her hair.

A few days went by and Officer Taylor called again. This time it was early in the morning. My kids had gone to school. I needed to get my daily drugs. By this time, I was no longer on methadone. I couldn't stop smoking crack, so the clinic started detoxing me. I went back to heroin. He called me when I was about to get dressed to hit the stores. My thinking during that time told me that *Maybe this cop could come in handy. He said he was going to get rid of the warrant. I just might like him in my life.* But in reality, I felt so belittled. I was beginning to feel like I got caught up with something too heavy. So what was I going to do about this cop? I let him come over. I didn't feel I had a choice. I had to get on with my day, and he was holding up my plans, so I thought I should take care of that business and get my day going. I knew I had to be back home by the time my kids returned from school.

When the cop got to my house, I asked him, "What about the warrant?"

"You're fine. I'll take care of it. By the way, you're going to need me . . . in the line of work you do."

"What line of work? I do hair!" Although in the back of my head, I told myself that I was also a booster, but he didn't need to know that.

This stopping by my house had gone on a few months. I was in such bad shape. I had no idea how this madness was going to end. I didn't see a way out. I was so ashamed of what I felt I had to do that I couldn't stand myself. I had to alter my mood daily so I could cope, sometimes two or three times.

> Father God,
>
> I humbly come to you, for you are Almighty God. I know if it had not been for your Son dying on the cross, this would not be possible. Thank you, God, for your grace and mercy. I am once again in such pain. I know that you are the source of my strength. I know that you are the only reason I am alive. I thank you, Lord. I thank you for saving me one more time, God. How did I get here in my life again? My life is such a mess. I don't see a way out, God. I need you yet again to help me. God,

help me to escape this nightmare. Heavenly Father, save me. Amen.

Create in me a pure heart, O God, and renew a steadfast spirit within me.

—Psalm 51:10 (NIV)

Then I acknowledged my sin to you and did not cover up my iniquity. I said, "I will confess my transgressions to the Lord." And you forgave the guilt of my sin.

—Psalm 32:5 (NIV)

Chapter Twenty-Nine

PEARLS, RUBIES, AND DIAMONDS

By this time, I was a full-blown booster. Nothing made me feel better than wearing a $600 or $700 suit. I was into making money, and I didn't have time for pettiness. I was stealing blouses that cost $200, which was a lot back in the day. My partner that I teamed up with and I sold our merchandise for half price, so we didn't have to steal much a day. Our favorite spot was a high-priced designer department store in East Lansing.

When they went out of business, my partner liked to brag that we put them out of business. I, on the other hand, knew why they ran out business: the decline in customers. Since childhood, Mama taught me that they were going to get theirs, and right or wrong, that's what I told myself to justify my criminal activity.

I had come to that point where I couldn't live with myself. I could no longer look at myself in the mirror. I actually had come to the point where I was having violent encounters with small-time drug dealers. Them young dudes come from an era where they snapped about any little thing! I was hit in the forehead with a bottle—messed me up both mentally and physically. This was by the nephew of my so-called partner in crime. Very messy family, yet these were the type of people I dealt with. While out hustling, my partner and I got into confrontations daily. She once told me that I had a heart of gold until I blew heroin, and then I became like them.

I cheated on my husband during this time. All this occurred after that cop had me feeling so degraded. I had begun to allow evil to rule my life. I felt like trash already, so continuing in garbage didn't really matter. I was losing my mind. My two young children paid the price. Even still, God was right there. In the middle of the night, when I talked to him, asking him to help me, I felt him—his comfort, his love. He put me to sleep on so many nights that I couldn't sleep. He loved me, all night long, but by morning I no longer felt the Spirit of God. Evil had returned. "GET UP," the drug habit said. "IT'S TIME TO FEED ME. IT'S TIME TO GO TO WORK FOR ME."

I got into a big fight with the young dude that Charles was working with. He started to treat me like I was a scum of the earth, unless I had some clothes for him or he needed me to help him get next to my husband's people. I didn't really know them, but they knew my husband, so he used me. During this time, Vanessa called to tell me that Mama had exploratory surgery and that the doctor found cancer inside her, that her entire insides were full of it. Vanessa had cleaned her life up, and she was a nursing assistant. She was very good at what she did. She stuck by Mama. I wanted to be there. I wanted to help Mama, but I couldn't. I was caught up.

I felt bad one day, so I went to see Mama while she was in the hospital. My kids were with me. I was so high that I was detached from all my feelings. I really couldn't even wrap my mind around the fact that my mama, the woman I loved so much, even with the sick relationship I shared with her, who at the time had me where all I wanted to do was please her, had cancer. I couldn't connect at this point. I felt nothing. Small talk, that's all we did. I said nothing to her about what Vanessa told me. Mama visited mostly with my kids. She loved Katrina. She was one of her favorite grandkids, and she had no problem showing that fact.

Anyway, I was ready to get back to the madness, so I told Mama that we had to get back home. When I returned to the car, I was breaking, but I turned what I was trying to feel—off. When I made it back home, I hurried up and called the dope man. I knew my mama was dying, yet I wouldn't allow myself to go there. No way was I about to feel that pain. So the rest of that summer, I stole, dressed, let a cop degrade me, got high, went to see Charles with the mask on, and did a few heads of hair. My clientele had fallen off, but the few people that stuck by me, I did their hair.

After I got my drugs in me, Mrs. Benson, who was an elderly lady, continued to let me do her hair. We became friends. I never told her what was really eating me alive. Being sexually degraded weekly was taking a toll on me. The rest, I felt I could deal with. I didn't see that it all had really become too much. Mama had tried chemo once or twice, but after trying it, Vanessa called me. She always informed me of what was going on. I was in so much pain from this situation that I was numb, but I had to talk to my mama. I now knew that she was leaving me.

As bad as I was on drugs, Jesus was right there once again. When I allowed myself to listen to him, he told me that I could go talk to Mama. He told me that he would be my strength. So one day, after boosting, I asked my kids to ride with me to see Mama. It was God's grace that I didn't kill myself and my kids on the highway. He was the only reason I didn't. I was so high.

That evening I was on a mission. I had to talk to Mama before she died. She was no longer in the hospital; she had been released to spend her final days at home with the help of the hospice. When I got to her house, Vanessa was not there yet, which was good because I felt I needed to speak with Mama alone. I had taken my kids to be with relatives before I came over to Mama's. I didn't want them to hear our conversation. I was high when I got to Mama's deathbed. She knew it was me. She had gotten so frail. Looking at her was like looking at the body of a child.

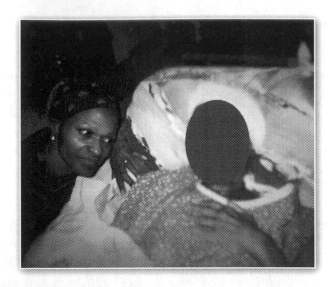

"Mama, it's me, Bean."

"It's Bean?"

"Mama, I need to talk to you. Can we talk?"

"About what, Bean?"

With tears in my eyes, I said, "Mama, did you know you were sick before the surgery?"

"Yes."

"Why, Mama, didn't you tell me that you were sick?"

"Bean, I know how you are, and there was nothing you could've done. I didn't want you to know."

As we talked, she took my hand and held my hand in hers and started rubbing her stomach up and down. I felt the cancer. Together, we cried. I laid my head on her stomach as I sat next to her bed. She was in the living room lying in a hospital bed. You could smell death in the room. I worked in a nursing home before and had learned that smell. As she talked, I asked her about Vanessa. I asked her if Vanessa was taking good care of her. She said that Vanessa was a beautiful child.

"Yeah, Mama, she is. Do you have anything you want to say to me?"

"Lavinia Lynn, you leave them drugs alone."

As I was crying, I said, "What?"

"Leave them drugs alone."

I didn't say anything back. Instead, I got very angry and thought about the time when I was scared to model and she gave me a valium. "Leave the drugs alone? That's all you have to say to me? You started me on the drugs."

As I was crying, I said, "That's all? That's all you have to say to me?"

She dozed off and went to sleep. This messed me up. Her male companion was in the bedroom. As Mama dozed in and out, I started to feel much pain. "I can't handle this." My high was wearing off. Her morphine pump caught my eye. "How can I get this morphine out of this container? How can I stop this pain?" I disconnected the pump while she slept.

When she began talking again, I conversed with her, small talk again. While I was talking, I was removing the container of morphine. Finally, I had it! It was in my hand. "Man, I gotta use the bathroom!" I went into the bathroom. I didn't know how much of the morphine I could drink. I knew that I wasn't supposed to drink morphine, but at this point, I just wanted the pain to stop. I didn't really care if I killed myself. I just wanted the pain to end.

I turned that bottle of morphine up to my mouth. It tasted so nasty, but I drank it anyway, but not all of it because I didn't want Mama to be without. I just drank enough to stop my pain. If it was stopping her pain, I felt it would stop my pain. After I drank what I felt was enough, I took the bottle back inside the living room and placed it back on the pump. Mama was asleep, so I woke her and said, "You don't have anything you wanna tell me?"

By this time, Vanessa had pulled up. I saw her car out of the picture window in Mama's living room. Mama's companion never came out of the bedroom until Vanessa came walking through the door. Vanessa looked at me and saw how high I was. She checked to see whether Mama needed anything. When she pulled back the bedsheets, she saw that I had removed Mama's dressing off her tailbone. I thought I was helping her tailbone heal by letting it get some air.

"What happened to her dressing?" Vanessa asked.

"I took it off," I said. "Let the sore breathe."

Vanessa frowned. I saw that she was getting upset with me. At this point, I didn't care. She looked at Mama's morphine, "Mama's getting low on her pain medication. I better call the hospice."

Yeah, you call them, I was thinking. "I gotta go, Vanessa."

Now I was good and high. Mama didn't want to talk to me. "She's dying, and she's just go' leave me like this? Yeah, okay. I'm cool with it!" I didn't even wake her to tell her I was leaving. I told Vanessa that I had to go get my kids. She was glad that I was leaving. All I did was make her job more difficult, but I didn't care about that either. I told Mama's man goodbye, and I left. God's angels encamped around me that day. The more I think about it, his angels have been around me all my life.

Anyway, I picked up my kids. How we got back home, I couldn't tell you. Little Charles and Katrina had fallen asleep. It was late. How I stayed awake, only God knows. Why I didn't overdose, only God knows too. I was high for four days. I was acting like a drunk. My kids must have been worried about me. Katrina kept saying, "I wanna go with my dad."

Once back home, I was awake all night. When it was time to get my kids up and dressed for school, I'm sure they could tell that I was high because I was still acting drunk. One thing for sure, I no longer longed for my mama's love—the love I've always longed for and never got. I was once again stuffed with the feeling of pain.

On the inside, I was hurting bad. My mama was about to die. I had a need for her to release me from the pain of feeling that the only time she showed me anything was when I could steal or provide something for her. I was always the one that she bragged about: "Bean's this, and Bean's that." Now because Bean was on drugs and there was no need for her, Vanessa was the "beautiful child." Wow! That's how I felt. At that time, drugs had my thoughts all screwed up.

Once back at home, the drugging continued, so did the weekly visits by that cop when my kids left for school. I used drugs to live. I didn't feel I had a choice. I couldn't be no punk. I had too many people counting on me. My husband needed me. But my habit came first before anything or anyone. My habit had taken me to hell. I was now all-in. I always had a personality that I did my best with whatever I did. I really thought I had it all together. When I fell apart, I shook it off and kept going.

I learned from Vanessa that Mama had taken a buyout from her manufacturing job, so she had no more life insurance. "What? When?" I couldn't believe she had done this. "Who had Mama take a buyout?" But right now, that wasn't important, but how she was going to be buried was.

I listened to Vanessa talk about cremation. "Mama said she wanted to be cremated."

"When did she say that, Vanessa?"

"Since she's been sick."

I wasn't feeling what Vanessa said. The mama I knew told me several times, "Bean, when I die, I want to be buried in white. I want to look like I'm sleeping. I want the white to have pearls, rubies, and diamonds on it. You took care of your daddy, Bean. I know when I die, you go' take care of me."

Those words had been implanted in my head for years. Every time I went home to see Mama, she said the same thing to me. No way was I going to allow what Vanessa was saying to take an effect on me. I already knew what my mama wanted, and even though a part of me was angry with Mama because she was going to die and not even talk to me, another part felt it was my responsibility to see to it that Mama's final wishes come true.

Surely I'd been through this before. Daddy didn't have a dime when he died either, yet a month or so before his funeral, I felt God had me fill out the application for life insurance. Even though I never paid a dollar, I was able to get the funeral home to bury him, thinking they were going to get paid. Now it was Mama that worried me more than the fact that she was really dying. What was I going to do once she was dead? This was Mama, and there was no way she was going to be cremated! Not saying there's anything wrong with cremation, if that's your choice, but I knew what my mama wanted, and she was going to have her final wishes by any means necessary.

That's the space I was in at the time. I didn't go back to see Mama anymore after the time she told me to leave the drugs alone. I did talk to her on the phone. She would be so high. "Mama, you high?" I'd say. She always said she was a legal junkie. Even though she stopped taking all her mental medication, she used as much pain medication as she needed. "I'm high as a kite," she'd say. "I'm a legal junkie." I would sort of laugh, but it really wasn't funny. Mama was dwindling away before my eyes, and there was nothing I could do to stop it. I had become an expert at shutting down all feelings, so I knew what I had to do to get through it all. To be honest, this was a bit too heavy for me to wrap my brain around. So I just didn't try. I continued to do what it was I was doing at that time.

Larry, Jr. was very angry with me. He lived up the street, and when he stopped by, he had no problem letting me know how upset he was with me. He just didn't understand. I couldn't tell my son what I was running from. The pain was too overwhelming. I couldn't face it. The madness went on for a few more months, and then I got a call from Vanessa. "Beanie, you need to come!" I didn't ask questions; I just went. In my heart, I knew.

When I arrived, Vanessa had called and had Mama transferred to the hospital. She was concerned because Mama was very agitated. When I walked into Mama's hospital room, I could not believe what was going on: Mama's entire body was lifted off the bed!

"Why is she doing that?" I said.

"I don't know," said Vanessa.

Vanessa was walking back and forth to the ice machine. She started packing Mama with ice. I helped her. The ice melted as soon as we put it on her body. "Wow!" I just stood still, and I heard the Lord say, "Let your mama go."

I looked at Vanessa. "Mama's leaving us."

"No!" Vanessa quickly said. "No, she's not!"

"Vanessa, you said that when it was time, you could let her go. Now is the time."

Vanessa looked at me confused and said, "I need to go home and bathe and change clothes."

"Yes, you go on," I said.

I could tell Vanessa was hurting. I was numb to the pain, so I was cool. When Vanessa left the room, I went back out to get more ice, but as I reentered the room, I said, "Man, it's a lot of demons on Mama!" I don't know why I said that, but I said it. I put the ice in the sink in the back room. Mama continued to lift off the bed. It looked like something from the movie *The Exorcist*. The doctor came inside the room. Vanessa had called him. He said that he could only give her something to comfort her. The doctor looked at me and saw in my eyes that I knew that was not going to help. He knew I was aware that my mama was trying to cross over to the other side, but she was being tormented all the way to the end.

I walked over to Mama and got on to my knees on the floor. Vanessa had told me that the sense of hearing was the last thing to go when a person is dying, so while on my knees, I spoke into Mama's ear and began talking to her. "It's okay, Mama. It's okay. I'm going to be fine, Mama. Go home, Mama. Go home. I love you. I've been very seldom kissed by you. I've always longed to be hugged by you, but I'm okay, Mama. Go home."

I felt I had made my peace with her. Once the doctor gave her a shot that didn't work, I looked at Mama for a few more minutes and said, "Bye, Mama," and turned and walked out of the room. The ride home was so painful. I knew I'd never see my mama again. I knew that I now stood alone. I was now solo, and that hurt bad. Regardless of what Mama did or didn't do, she was my mama. My thoughts reverted to the talks we had. "Bean, when I die," she often said to me since I was twenty years old, "I want to be buried in white. I want to look like I'm sleeping. I want to have pearls and diamonds and rubies on my gown. I want it to be beautiful, Bean." For years, that was in my head. I had to grant Mama's last wishes. I had to.

I got home. At about two o'clock, the phone rang. It was Johnny. "Hello," I said.

"Mama just took her last breath about ten minutes ago," he said.

I dropped to the floor, making a small whimper, and then I stood up. I called my son on the phone and told Little Charles. Katrina didn't know what to feel. She loved Mama. Mama was her joy.

Anyway, I hadn't been on the highway this much since Charles was home. I traveled back and forth for days, taking care of business to have Mama buried. Vanessa and other family members were still talking cremation. "Mama wanted that."

"That's not what Mama wanted! You don't tell your daughter for years how you want to be buried, and then all of a sudden, you want to be cremated!" I was not going for that. "Over my dead body!"

That first day after she died, Johnny and I had a big fallout. He had the nerve to say, "I will escort you out of here, Lavinia!"

"What—try to escort me!"

Family members had to come between me and Johnny. We both apologized to each other when we calmed down, but we were actually about to fight. Mama didn't have life insurance, so the pressure was on us. No plan was put in motion that evening. I was feeling uncomfortable. I was not leaving to come back home until my mama was at a funeral home, so I went to Vanessa's house with her. She went to bed.

I called the local funeral home, the same one that took Daddy's body. "My mother is at the hospital. I would like to know when you can get her body."

"Immediately," they said.

I told them to go get her. I had no idea how all this was going to be paid or even what next. I did know, however, that God would make a way. I did not feel God's will was for Mama to be cremated. Once Mama was at the funeral home, I waited 'til early morning, and then I called her sisters and brother. "Mama's body is at the funeral home. They will meet with us at one o'clock today. See you there."

"They're kind of expensive, aren't they?" said my aunt Mabel.

"No, goodbye," I said and hung up the phone.

Vanessa and I were at the funeral home on time. Mama's sisters and brother were also there, and so was my brother. We all put our heads together and made Mama's funeral happen. My aunt and uncle split the money that needed to be paid. Uncle Kevin went to the state's family assistance agency to get help. Vanessa did the flowers on the casket, and I was responsible for the outfit.

Once the meeting ended, we all went about the business we had committed to doing. I was feeling a lot better that my mama was going to have the funeral she deserved. She had always been a giving woman. Even if she had a motive, she gave. Sometimes I felt that was how Mama manipulated me and others—by giving. Money meant nothing to Mama. She was the one that taught me "It ain't nothing but some money—here today, gone tomorrow" and "There's more where that came from." Mama was something else. I loved my mama.

I was now on a mission. I had to find the white lingerie with pearls and diamonds. I went everywhere in Lower Michigan. I looked for days. That last day, when I was about to give up, on my way home, right in Okemos, I saw a small boutique off the side of the road. I said to my boosting partner, "I wonder if they have anything. I've looked everywhere. I may as well look in here. Just in case, you know what to do."

"Yeah," she said.

So into the boutique we went. Once I started looking, I realized that I had lucked-up on the prettiest gowns and robes I'd seen in a long time, and then there it was—it was beautiful. My partner distracted the saleswoman, and I got the gown and robe. I felt so good knowing that I was granting Mama her last wish of me, a wish she had talked about for many years. I almost felt like I had been programmed to grant her wish. I gave this mission no second thought.

Heavenly Father,

King of Kings, Lord of Lords, you are Almighty God. I don't understand why you are allowing this tremendous amount of pain, why at times I feel I can't breathe. Mama was my life. Mama was everything to me. How will I live without Mama rooting me on? I've shut down all feelings, God. I have to. I have work to do. As always, "Suck it up, Lavinia—no time for that weak stuff." God, give me the strength I need. Give me the peace that I'm not getting from these drugs. I need you, God. Jesus, Jesus, help me! Amen.

I will turn their mourning into joy, and will comfort them, and make them rejoice from their sorrow.

—Jeremiah 31:13 (KJV)

If your heart is broken, you'll find God right there; if you're kicked in the gut, he'll help you catch your breath.

—Psalm 34:18 (MSG)

When I feel hurt or brokenhearted, God binds up my wounds and cures my pain and sorrow. (Paraphrase)

—Psalm 147:3 (AMP)

Chapter Thirty

TRUE LOVE

We came together as a family. On the day of Mama's funeral, Charles, Jr. was missing. I missed him. I knew that if he wasn't in prison, there was no way Mama would be in a cardboard box, or there would be no limousine. Charles, Jr. would have made a way for Mama to be put away the way he felt she deserved by any means necessary. No one had even made the call to the prison on the day Mama died. When I arrived at Mama's house that evening, the first thing I asked was whether Charles, Jr. knew. Johnny said that he didn't, so I immediately called the prison, and they allowed him some time to call us. He never talked to Johnny.

This was too much. Mama's dead, and my two brothers still won't be brothers, not even now. Charles, Jr. had a right to be a part of this time in our life. It really bothered me that my two brothers acted like they hated each other. I was always the go-between for them. They both would talk about each other to me. I wanted to fix it, yet I couldn't. I always wanted to tell Charles, Jr. that he was wrong, but at that point, I never did. He had to be hurting as well as we were. Charles, Jr. and I were a lot alike in more ways than one.

I sometimes wondered who allowed Mama to take a buyout from the automotive plant. I wanted to dig deeper into the answer, but she was gone now, and I had missed so much of the last few years of her life. She had a man in her life, and she appeared to be doing fine. At least she wasn't flipping every other year anymore. She took her medication like she was supposed to, and I thought she was fine. I used to look at her as she took all those pills, and I actually would pray that I would never have to take medication like my mama, yet I had already started.

I wasn't just on street drugs. I had a local doctor that had no problem giving me all the pills she felt I needed. Sometimes I would be so high I couldn't even see straight, yet God allowed me to not kill myself and my kids as I continued to drive in that state of mind. I was off into my own world of misery now. I didn't know much about Mama's business. Vanessa was the one who helped Mama; and yes, I must say she did it well. I was so proud of my sister.

Sometimes I could see the pain in Vanessa's eyes, but she never expressed it, at least not to me. She had a job to do at that point, and she did it. I never thought Vanessa had it in her, but she pulled it off. When I think of Vanessa today, I think of the strength she showed when Mama was dying, not the Vanessa that couldn't handle anything when we were small kids because of the panic attacks she would have when the fighting between Mama and Daddy occurred. I'm so proud of my sister. I love her so much.

Anyway, we all met at the church, the same church that Mama had been a member of since she met and married Super Fly. We never heard from him after that ended. That was no surprise though. Mama loved her pastor, but I wasn't feeling him. Something about him did not sit right with me. He actually reminded me of the pastor before him that got put out of the church. But Mama loved him, so he did her funeral.

As I walked toward the casket, all I could think about was what Daddy always said, "You can put me in a cardboard box for all I care. I won't know. I'll be dead." Now here was Mama in a cardboard box. She had worked most of her life and didn't even have life insurance. As I looked at the body, I inspected the white gown and robe. I had already seen the gown on her the night before when I drove all the way from Lansing to put on Mama's makeup and see that the funeral home had Mama looking like she would have wanted. I was pleased, but that day I had to take one more look. *Mama*, I pleasantly thought, *I did it.* The outfit she had on cost more than the casket. I used to wonder years before we knew Mama had cancer whether she knew something and wasn't telling. She always had stomach issues. Ever since I can remember, she's always had a nervous condition too. Mama used to shake so bad.

I gotta be honest and say that I had a *big* ego when I saw her wearing the outfit I had stolen—I really did. I checked to make sure she looked the way she had described to me all those years. Johnny was at the casket looking as well. "You did this?" he asked. "Yeah, you like it?" He never answered. He didn't have to. I liked it. And I felt Mama would have liked it, and that's all that mattered. I had done what Mama wanted. I didn't let Mama down. Anyway, the funeral went well, not as sad for me as I thought it was going to be, and I wasn't even as high as I had been in the time leading up to this day.

Brenda and a young lady (a hair client) I had living in my home with me came to the funeral with me and my kids. The young lady drove my car for me that day. Both of them were a big support. I saw Crystal at the funeral. I didn't know how to respond to her. I felt she helped to destroy us as a family. She was always spitting venom on Johnny. She had it all wrong, yet I couldn't even say anything because I knew Charles, Jr. was behind how she felt.

What a mess! I always wondered how Mama felt knowing that her two sons didn't speak, that they treated each other like strangers. I drowned my feelings in drugs about my brother and everything else I had on my plate at that time. Mama and Daddy gone so soon—Mama, sixty-three, and Daddy, fifty-one. What a waste of lives is how I felt at the time. Both lived very unhappy lives to me. Both had issues that started in their childhood that they carried into their adult life that affected my life.

I never cried at the funeral. I couldn't. I felt nothing, to be honest. I had worn that mask so long that I did what I did best. I pretended that I was fine that entire day. *I can handle it. I handled everything else*, I thought. But when I got home in the middle of the night, when the drugs had worn off and the pain set in, that's when

313

I called him. "Jesus," I cried, "Jesus, help me, please. My mama, my mama, help me, God!" I couldn't breathe. I felt sick. I couldn't face another day. "God, I need you. I have no one." I sometimes wonder had I been brought up in a totally different environment, would I have been happier in life? Would I have made it to Hollywood and become that stylist or artist that dressed the rich and famous like I wanted to? I knew I had it in me.

I used to study the way the stars dressed. I learned a lot watching and listening to a talk show host that would criticize what Hollywood stars wore. She was very smart when it came to style. I'm not talking about fad, I'm talking about fashion. You have to know the difference. I learned how to act according to how I was dressed. I loved the way Jackie Kennedy and Bette Davis dressed. They had class!

Clothes worn the right way require one to carry themselves a certain way. If you want to look your best, you must know how to wear the outfit. I learned how to wear my mask well. I was so into wearing my mask that without boosting, I don't think I could have covered up the pain as well as I did. Sometimes I believe that's why I never went to prison. I believe that God will allow things to happen and not happen. He is Almighty God. He is in control. Why he allowed me to be sexually harassed by a police officer, I couldn't understand. I was trapped in a no-win situation, so I thought.

Then one day another cop that I came in contact with confronted me. "Lavinia, I know what Officer Taylor is doing to you." I was shocked! I didn't know that to say. I didn't know if I could even trust him. I did know that I was tired of what was going on. It's a horrible feeling when you feel there's no way out, when you wonder yourself how and when is this going to end. My kids were all worried. When Calvin came home from college one day, he said, "Ma, if you keep doing what you are doing, I'm calling Child Protective Services (CPS)." Of course, I didn't believe him. I wanted to stop, but I couldn't. I had a heroin habit, and I was smoking crack and popping all kinds of pills.

My habit was calling early that next morning, so was Officer Taylor. He had already made the statement when Mama had died.

"You know you got a warrant, so don't go down there and make me have to come looking for you." So I answered the phone and allowed him to come by when my kids left for school again. After he left my home, I called my boosting partner. She gave the money for my drugs. No way could I go to work sick. She always got her money back off the top. We worked well together in the stores.

However, it was after work when all hell broke loose. We couldn't get along ten minutes once I was high. I often told her to get out of my car. One time we got into it, and somebody called the police. When we were pulled over, I went to jail. While in jail the next morning, I was called out of my cell. I entered a room where a black man was waiting for me. He was the cop that said he wanted to help me. He wanted to expose Officer Lloyd Taylor.

"Sit down," he said.

I sat there looking at him. *What's up with him?* I wondered. *Is he really going to help me get out of this mess I'm in?* Well, he did. He spoke up for me in court, and I was let out of jail. When I went home, the young lady that lived with me was very upset. She moved out. My kids were also upset. My older sons were very angry with me also.

A few days later, CPS knocked on my door. It was a black man, and he told me that they received a call that I was on drugs and my kids were being abused. Immediately, I became angry with Calvin, and I told the man, "I don't need any help! You can look wherever you want!" He did just that. At the end of the visit, he said, "Miss, there's nothing I see that would call for me to file a complaint, but I want you to know that if what you say is true, that your son is just mad and he called, I want to tell you that your son must love you and his brother and sister very much. Can you even think of how he must have felt to call CPS on you?"

Anyway, I wasn't hearing this man at that point. I was raised. Don't tell me what goes on in my house. Even Katrina and Little Charles had told the man that we were fine, so no, I wasn't feeling Calvin at all. The CPS worker left my house, but things got worse. I was losing my mind. My kids were being abused. Mentally, I was no longer a mother. I felt it, but I didn't know how to be honest.

I felt I had to keep up the image that all was well. To be honest, everybody knew it wasn't well but me. That cop did help me end the nightmare of being degraded. The state police got involved then Internal Affairs. They all set Lloyd Taylor up. He was busted! They watched him come to my home. They had surveillance in my home. He was caught red-handed! I was so happy that this was over.

Now I had to call CPS back on myself. That was one of the hardest things I ever had to do. How do you call CPS on yourself? You think about the love you have for your kids first. You think about the past and where drugging took you with your older sons and you step to the plate and you do the right thing. Sure I was afraid of what would happen. I talked to God through this time in my life.

Actually, I had never stopped talking to him. There were periods in my life that I didn't feel his presence, that he didn't talk back, but this was not one of them. It seemed the more I did the right thing, the more I felt him, the more I heard his voice. We always hear voices. When we listen to the bad voices, that's when Satan is in control; but when we choose to listen to the good voices, that's God. The good voices are the easiest voices to listen to, and I have learned the hard way that they are the best voices to listen to.

Even though I was mentally unstable, I knew I had to do this. My kids deserved much better. "God, I need you. Please don't let me be making a mistake. I need you to make me know that I'm doing the right thing." I was so far gone mentally that I used to wake up and put on the best clothes I had, the ones that I hadn't sold for drugs. Yes, I was finally to the point that I was selling my clothes now. I never thought I'd get to that point. When I was younger, I never got to that crossroad because Felix had cut up all my clothes before I got that bad. Now I *was* there mentally. The heroin came first, even before the clothes that I loved so much.

I would put on the clothes and talk to myself. Satan was telling me that the police were on their way to arrest me and that they knew all about the stealing I had done. I was ready to go to jail. I felt, *If I gotta go, I'm going sharp!* Then I got real paranoid about

Katrina and Little Charles. I thought "they," whoever "they" were, were out to get my kids. I started watching for the school bus, and I would walk out looking crazy to get my kids. I know they were embarrassed by me. Katrina kept saying she wanted to go with her dad. Little Charles was not about to leave me. He felt he had to take care of me. Now you know you are sick when an eight-year-old wants to take care of you.

Anyway, I got the courage, and I called. Once I called, I knew there was no turning back. "God, help me. Please stay close. I can't do it without you, God. Please don't leave me—not now. I need your strength." Once I made the call, I let CPS back into my home. This time I told the truth. Everybody in my family was upset with me, from Charles to Katrina's dad. I had let her go to his house. His mother was there, so I let Katrina go, but in my heart, I knew he was on drugs also and she deserved better. I told CPS about how he used to beat on me and his violent past. I also told them he had a history of drugs. They immediately got us into court. Felix came thinking that he was going to speak negative about me in court, not realizing that I had told them everything. He thought he was going to get Katrina, but things didn't go the way he thought they would.

Larry, Jr. was in court. I knew he loved his sister and brother, even though he was very disappointed in me. I, however, had to do what I felt was best for my kids. I knew that this was going to hurt them, but I also knew that if I continued to live the life I did, it would only end in disaster. I'd been there before. I wouldn't and couldn't allow the past to repeat itself. Not only was I mentally unstable, but I was also sick because I needed drugs; I didn't realize that I was losing custody of Little Charles and Katrina.

Once court was over, not only had my kids been placed in foster care, but they were also wards of the state now. This was mind-blowing. "What have I done?" This didn't feel very good. "Will I ever get my kids back?" Now I was scared. I had just given my kids away. Actually, this became the biggest motivator I'd ever had. I knew at that minute I was on a mission, and there was no longer an option. I had to get my kids back home, and I had to do it quick. I cried on the way home. Katrina was swept out of the courtroom with CPS. She looked terrified. I was told that I couldn't see Little Charles; they would pick him up from school. I was told that it was best for him.

If that was the case, why didn't it feel like that's what was best? All I thought about was how Little Charles must have felt—strangers coming to his class and telling him he couldn't go home anymore and that he had to go with them. I wasn't able to say goodbye to my kids, well, not goodbye because it wasn't goodbye; it was "I'll be back to get you, I promise you that. I'll never let anybody take you!" That's all I wanted to say, but I couldn't.

That next day I was taken to treatment by CPS. The supervisor was a good woman. I must say that CPS helped me. They get such a bad rep from the public, but in my experience, I learned that they were not the enemy—the dysfunction and addiction in my life were. I needed help, so CPS helped me get the help I needed. Charles's brother as well as Katrina's family tried to get Little Charles and Katrina. But I stood by my decision. I wanted them together, and I wanted them close to me. I didn't want anyone taking my kids miles away where I couldn't see them.

For the first week, I could not talk on the phone, except the first day when I told both my kids' families that I wanted them to stay in foster care. I knew in my heart that this was temporary. That first day, while sick, I wrote my kids. I promised both of them that I would come back to get them. I told them the truth. They knew I needed help. I talked to God all day every day. Those first few days were rough. I hurt so bad that I would get in the shower and cry out to God.

One night I remember being in so much pain mentally more so than physically. I started crawling on the floor of the shower. "Jesus, Jesus, I need you! Please help me, God. Please give me the strength to do this. Build me up, God, to even face tomorrow because, right now, I can't do it. Help me, God!" I hollered as I crawled. Ain't no pain like the pain of a mother! As the water hit my back, the tears wouldn't stop coming. I stayed in that shower crying out to God 'til the water turned cold. When I stepped out, I felt much better. I felt

God's strength helping me to even stand back up. I did this every night for days. God gave me the strength I needed day after day.

I wrote my kids every other day. The supervisor promised me that she would get the letters to them as soon as she received them. When she was waiting in the lobby with me that first day, she saw the pain in my eyes. She leaned over and whispered into my ear, "I'm so proud of you." I heard her words, but at that point, I didn't feel very proud of myself. I made it through the first week though. I started eating after a few days. I was so small. I looked so bad. I didn't like myself at all. When I tried to look into the mirror, I didn't like what I saw. I hadn't been drug free in years.

All the feelings were coming at once. I thought I cried a lot when I first moved to Lansing, but this took the cake. I would cry if you looked at me too long. The pain and grief of Mama dying, I felt it. The pain and humiliation of being sexually degraded for over eleven months, I felt it. The pain of the decision to call CPS on myself and have my kids taken from me, I felt it. The pain of my brother getting life in prison, I felt it. The pain of what was left of our family being divided because of brothers turning on each other, I felt it. The pain of my only sister and I never being able to get along, I felt it. The pain of knowing that I had let my older sons down yet again, I felt it. The pain of how Charles looked at me when I visited him in prison and was so high that I embarrassed him, I felt it.

Talk about hurting—I definitely was hurting, yet I knew that I could not let this pain control me. I had to get through this pain someway, somehow. God was how I survived for this long. He was the answer. I had to trust him. He never let me down before. That being said, I began to spend so much time talking to God that, day by day, he showed me that he was right there, just like in the past when he would talk to me. I heard him. I always heard him. He actually would tell me what to do, step by step, day by day. I let go, and I let him. I felt him building me up day by day. It was amazing!

Once I was feeling better and felt that I was headed in the right direction, I was hit with a blow that shook the core of my soul. New patients came and went by the week. One day, I was in group therapy sharing about my childhood. I began sharing about my brothers. I love my brothers, and my heart had been heavy for years about how they used to be so close. Now they hadn't spoken to each other for years. Anyway, as I shared, I gave them my eldest brother's name, Charles, Jr., and then I gave my youngest brother's name, Johnny.

There was a young man named Marshall in the group who interrupted, and he yelled out, "Charles, Jr. and Johnny? Do you know who I am?"

"No," I said.

"Do you know Jason Reed?

My heart dropped. I felt sick. "No," I said. "I don't know him."

"Well, he's my brother, and I always said that if I ever saw anybody in Charles, Jr.'s family, I would do to them what he did to my brother!"

I began to feel very uncomfortable, not scared but uncomfortable. *What is going on, God?* I thought to myself. *How can this be? What is the purpose of this? How come I'm in treatment with the brother of the man that my brother is in prison for and accused of killing? Only in a million years would something like this happen. Only to Lavinia would this happen.* Wow! This is unreal! I didn't know what to say or how to respond to this young man. I could see his pain. I could see his hatred for my brothers.

The therapist immediately stopped group and got help in the room. I was taken out of the room in one direction, and Marshall was taken out in the other direction. The remaining people in group were looking at one another in shock. This was surely a mindblower for them and me too. I was taken to the administrator's office. The woman there began speaking with me about their policy and that the treatment center felt it was a conflict of interest for me and Marshall to remain in the center. I was told that since I was there first, he would be placed in another facility. They asked me how I felt. I felt I heard the Lord at the moment say to me, "Let him stay." I spoke out and said, "No, don't ask him to leave. I believe in God, and I feel that God has a reason why this is happening. I would like to find out why and what God is doing here, so let him stay."

It was not easy the first few days. At night I dwelled on what Marshall said, so I was scared to go to sleep for days. During the day, the ice was broken when I went up to him and apologized for his loss. I let him know that I too was in pain. I told him that two families had been destroyed. I shared with him that my brothers hadn't spoken to each other since that day.

Marshall and I began to talk daily. We even started to hug each other. At that point, I saw what God was doing: He was healing Marshall, and He was healing me. Whenever Marshall received visitors, I felt the stares at me. His sister, who was Jason Reed's wife, would look at me for what felt like hours. She would even have Jason's kids with her. Marshall was actually Jason Reed's brother-in-law. He was in a lot of pain because his niece and nephew no longer had a father. I was able to feel for him and his family. I was able to feel my pain. I learned over nine years ago, when I first came to Lansing, that drug addiction was a disease of the feelings.

I was able to feel at that point, and I didn't know whether I liked it. I do know that my soul needed to be healed, and God was doing just that. God even placed a woman from a Lansing church to facilitate one of the spiritual groups. She read Psalm 139. She spoke to us about how God knew us before we were born and what we would go through. She told us that he knew us better than we knew ourselves.

That spiritual group ministered to me more than any other group I was involved in the entire two weeks. It encouraged me the rest of the time I was in treatment. Marshall and I became close before I got out of treatment. On the day that I was leaving, he and I had learned a lot about each other. He asked me questions, and I asked him questions. We shared with each other a lot about our families. He hugged me and said, "I don't know why God placed you in my life, but I'm glad he did. I even find that I like you." We laughed, and I told him that if he ever came to Lansing, to look me up.

During that time in treatment, I had learned so much about my feelings. I even felt resentful toward the cop that had a lot to do with me going as far as I did on drugs. I had destroyed not just my life but my kids' lives. As I left the treatment center, I was on a mission, and that mission was to get my kids home and see to it that this cop paid for what he had done to me.

> Father,
> I love you. You have been my strength since I was a little girl. Whenever I turned to you, you have always been right there. Even when I don't seek you, you protect me. You are wonderful! You are my rock. I need to know that you will comfort and protect my kids, God. I love them, Lord, but I know that you love them more. God, make me know that I have done the right thing. I don't feel I've ever had to make a decision harder than this one. I know it's the best one, yet it feels like the worst. Make me know it's going to be okay. Thank you, God. Amen.

I will be glad and rejoice in your unfailing love, for you have seen my troubles, and you care about the anguish of my soul.

—Psalm 31:7 (NLT)

I am strong and courageous. I am not afraid or discouraged, because the Lord my God is with me to help me fight my battles. (Paraphrase)

—2 Chronicles 32:7–8 (KJV)

My faith does not rest in the wisdom of men, but in the power of God. (Paraphrase)

—2 Corinthians 2:5 (KJV)

Chapter Thirty-One

LCOGIC

As soon as I got home, I felt like I was kicking again. I learned that I kicked the street drugs the first four days, except for the pills. I didn't even start to feel the effects of them leaving my system until almost twelve days later, so again, I felt horrible. I went to community mental health and started seeing a therapist the next day. I went to meetings and did everything I was told to do for my kids. I walked and took the bus every place I went because I didn't have a car. I had wrecked it a week or so before I went to treatment—another accident that I walked away from without a scratch.

Mrs. Benson's husband had died, so I started riding the bus to her house. She needed help, and I needed money. I began talking to her about my personal life. I told her about my kids, and I also shared with her about the cop.

"I told you I didn't trust him," she said. "He didn't look like he was up to nothing good. What are you going to do?"

"I don't know," I told her.

While in treatment, I felt the Lord had placed on my heart to file a lawsuit, but I wasn't so sure. That day I called to schedule a visit with my kids. I couldn't wait to see them! Little Charles looked like he was unhappy. Katrina was also very sad. They wanted to come home. I didn't like that their hair was not cut and relaxed. I also saw that they had on dirty socks. I told them both that I was doing all I could to get them home. I prayed and asked God to bring my kids home before the next school year began. I remember asking the supervisor if I did everything the courts asked of me, could they come home on August 15. She said that it wasn't her decision to make.

Anyway, I asked God to bring them home by that date. I visited them every week. I was allowed to do Katrina's hair while visiting them. Larry, Jr. came to cut Little Charles's hair whenever it needed cutting. I missed my kids so bad. I couldn't let it get me down though. I had to keep doing what was necessary to get them home. It wasn't easy, but I couldn't give up.

One day I went to the mailbox and grabbed the mail. When I got inside the house, I saw that I had received a letter from the police department, Internal Affairs. I immediately opened it. "Your complaint has been found substantiated," it read. I gave thought of what to do now. I was not told what action had been taken against the cop, but I learned that he got three days off with pay. That angered me. "What? Oh no, that can't be! My life has been turned upside down, and he gets three days off with pay? We'll see about that!"

I remember, when I first moved to Lansing, I would listen to this pastor on the radio on Sundays. I also remember him being in the news for helping the less fortunate who had been wronged by the police. He organized marches and rallies. I called him and shared with him what had happened to me. He treated me like I had told him that I had a disease that he was about to catch. He was very cold. "I don't know what to tell you, miss, I'm sorry." But that didn't stop me. I called several other pastors in Lansing. They all wanted nothing to do with me or what I had been through. I still didn't let that stop me. I called the first pastor back and said, "I thought you helped people. Why don't you want to help me?"

He gave me the name of another man that worked at the city hall. I called this man and explained to him what happened to me and that Internal Affairs had substantiated my complaint. He told me to call that pastor back and tell him that he said to get me an attorney. When I called the pastor back, surprisingly, he said, "Oh yeah?" Afterward, he started treating me a lot different from how he did in the beginning. He told me to call an attorney that he felt could help me, and I did. The attorney took my case. However, in my opinion, he didn't have my best interests in mind. He was campaigning to be a city official. I was no fool. When he suggested that I take an offer of $40,000 because "there was baggage," as he put it, "in my past," I went to Detroit for attorneys.

It's funny how the pastor that recommended that attorney invited me to visit his church when he learned that I had a lawsuit, but I declined. I had been through too much not to be able to see right through people. I continued to spend time talking to the Lord daily. He told me what to do and when to do it. He gave me the strength to stay focused on the missions at hand: my kids and making sure that cop didn't get away for the hell he put me through. "My children are in foster care, I lost my mind, and he gets three days off with pay? No way!"

At this time, I was clean and had a continuous contact with God, but the only problem was that I didn't have a church home. I didn't have other godly people in my life. I didn't think I needed anyone else. I did fine standing solo for a while, but Satan was in my ear daily. I had ignored him because the task at hand was more important than listening to the devil. I prayed all day every day. Even with prayer, there were days that I chipped. I would get high when I felt nobody knew.

Then after the drugs were gone, I felt like killing myself because I knew what I had done, and I could not believe that after all I had been through and taken my kids through, I actually had the urge to use drugs. "What is my problem? What is missing in my life that I keep going back to drugs over and over, knowing the pain that the drugs bring? I keep going back. Why, God?" Then my thinking tells me, *Charles could make me happy. I'd stop if he were out. We'd stay clean together.*

As I jumped through all the hoops the court asked me to do, I started going to this church that my daughter, Katrina, told me her foster mom attended. Sundays, my kids went with her. She told me the name of the church, Lansing Church of God in Christ

(LCOGIC), on Wise Road; Samuel L. Duncan, Jr., was the pastor. I started thanking God that he placed my kids in a Christian home. I started talking to the foster mom when she brought my kids to see me. I liked her. I didn't feel that she was one of those evil foster parents that were in it just for the money and were dogging my kids. They would have told me if that was the case.

It wasn't long before Katrina started to rebel. Little Charles also started acting out. He would have temper tantrums. The foster mom and the caseworker from the courts planned to get therapy for both of them. I didn't agree that they needed therapy. I felt they just needed to come home. I wasn't thinking of the damage that had been done mentally to my kids. The more I realized how much being taken from their home had hurt them, the more I wanted revenge. The more I wanted the city to pay for allowing a cop like this to work in public safety. I was no longer hurt, I was angry, yet I was afraid. I felt my kids were in the best place for them though. I felt they were safe.

I didn't really know how this cop was going to respond to the lawsuit. Through my therapist's recommendation, I started seeing a rape therapist. Soon afterward, I was placed on antidepressants. One night, around three o'clock in the morning, I was sleeping and heard this loud bang downstairs. It was so loud that it woke me up from a deep sleep. I sat up in bed and jumped to my feet. I ran to the window in my daughter's room. I saw a red pickup truck pulling away with two white men in it. I ran downstairs.

After turning on the lights in my home, my heart was pounding. I could not believe what I saw. My front door had been kicked off the hinges. I called the police. When they arrived at my home, the police woman asked me who I thought would do something like this. I showed her the letter I received from Internal Affairs. She said, "No police officer would do this." I asked her and her partner to please leave my home.

Once they were gone, I said to the Lord, "You've protected me all these years. I know this today. Please protect me now. Please let me go back to sleep. If they are going to kill me, God, let me be asleep when it's done." I went back upstairs, leaving my door propped up against the frame, and I went to sleep. I thought about my kids before I fell asleep and said, "Thank you, God, that they are not home. Continue to protect them, God. If I don't wake up, please tell my kids, all of them, that I'm so sorry and I love them."

I did wake up, and when I did, it was daylight. I had slept the rest of that night by the grace of God. I called maintenance early that morning, and they came and fixed my door. That made me feel good, but I knew in my heart that the door wasn't really any protection. The true protection came from God. That is why I slept like a baby the rest of that night. But getting the door fixed was needed for appearance. After that incident, I started to feel like, with God, I could take on the mission at hand! And you know what? God really did take away the fear and gave me the strength and more, as I needed it. I just stayed close to him.

My new attorneys were already representing a white woman who had a lawsuit against the same cop. Believe it or not, I met her through my rape counselor. One day she said to me during our session, "I have another patient that I'm sure is a victim of the same police officer. Would you be willing to meet her?" I told her that I would give it some thought. After a week or so, I told my rape therapist that I would. When I met her, I got angry all over again. When I told her about my front door being kicked in that morning, she told me that Officer Lloyd Taylor had a red truck. That was no surprise to me. I hired the same attorneys she had.

When the police officer that helped me end the nightmare found out I was suing the police, he didn't sound too happy. I tried to understand his attitude, since he was a cop at the same precinct. I don't think he thought I had enough sense to do what I was doing and to do it alone. All I can say is never judge a book by its cover, especially when God is involved. I wanted to tell him not to take it personally. I really did.

Well, my prayers for my children were answered a few months later. I walked into the courtroom on August 12. I had done all that was asked of me and more. I also had done what I'm learning about now, what was most important: I had been praying. I was so happy when I walked out of that court! The judge actually spoke personally to me. I will always hold her words in my heart. She said to me, "Ms. Reynolds, I want to commend you. You have done outstanding work. No child has ever come through the system this fast."

I said, "Thank you, Your Honor, but you didn't have my kids. I would have crawled to get my kids back home if you'd told me that's what I needed to do."

"The children will be placed in the custody of the natural mother on or before August 14," she said.

I started crying. August 15 was the day that I asked God to let them be back home so they could go back to their schools in September. "Thank you, God! Thank you, God!"

Once my kids were back at home, I continued to go to church. I enjoyed hearing Pastor Duncan preach. His message from the Bible gave me hope as well as comforted my soul. Little Charles and Katrina felt like this was now their church. God put the foster mother, Pat, in my path to lead me to Pastor Duncan's church. I swear I never would have set foot into this church. I had always been told by Mama that "Them sanctified people are too far out . . . They live weird lives." What she meant was that they teach on holiness. Pastor Duncan used to say, "I don't just preach and teach the word of God. I live it!"

I had attended so many churches in my life—churches that I liked but even more churches that I didn't like. I couldn't feel the presence of God in so many churches. I also had resentment toward a lot of local churches because the way they treated me was not of God. If you didn't have the right job or a certain status in life, some of the churches treated you like you were a "nobody." Some would even turn their nose up at you. However, this Pastor Duncan was different. He treated me like I was one of God's children. His wife, the first day I walked through the front door, gave me the biggest hug. That shocked me. I said to myself, "Who was that lady that just hugged me?" She just didn't know how important that hug was to me. I was hurting, and I hadn't been shown love in years—if ever.

I liked Pastor Duncan's church so much that I went to the altar to join. Then I got baptized again. I was so grateful to God for his grace in my life that I wanted to live right. I swear I did. But I had so much baggage that I didn't know how to let go of it. Once I was baptized, I went to the altar almost every week for prayer. I remember a bad experience I had one Sunday at the altar. A man prayed for me, and he started to speak about when he used to like me. I opened my eyes and thought, *What did he just say? This is inappropriate!* My kids were with me at the altar. From that point on, I never went to the altar and let just anybody pray for me. I was very particular about who I let pray over me.

There was one particular lady who would pray for me named Sister Jackson. Whenever she prayed for me, I felt the presence of the Lord. Her prayers and Pastor Duncan's prayers were so powerful! This Pastor Duncan was anointed, and you felt it! He was the real deal. I had experienced so many fake preachers in my lifetime. I remember when the pastor that baptized me as a teenager was exposed for cheating on his wife. It hurt me because I didn't realize he too was just a man. So many people look at the pastor as God. Pastor Duncan used to say, "I can't get you into heaven. Keep your mind on Jesus. I'm just the messenger." I liked how humble he was, never once putting himself on a pedestal.

Anyway, things were back to normal at home with Little Charles and Katrina being back. School had begun, and I was starting to feel good about myself. My husband, Charles, was getting out of prison soon. I felt this time it would be different because he'd been in prison, and I knew that now he wanted to live right. When he got out, he moved in with me. The courts felt he needed to be a part of the family help program. We were both clean, so I knew this time we'd make it. I had been telling my kids that Charles was getting out and coming to live with us.

His first day out, we started out setting ourselves up for failure. We shared some wine, thinking it wasn't the same as using drugs, so we were doing good. That day was nice. I enjoyed being with him. That feeling didn't last long at all. I saw that he was going to be a problem with the court officer. He told her, "You won't tell me how to raise my son!" So he started rebelling and talking nasty to the court caseworker. He wouldn't drop, so she took him to court, and he got thirty days back in jail that quick. After that, he really started to resent the court worker. We told her that Charles moved out and lived up the street. He started associating with the same dude he hustled with before he went to prison. This concerned me. He went right back to selling and using drugs.

I dropped dirty one day, so I had to do a weekend in jail. I remember getting out of jail feeling like I had a habit again, so I went straight to the dope house. I had an addictive behavior. Actually, I had several. I was addicted to drugs, Charles, the lifestyle I lived, chaos, sex, clothes, even failure, and so much more. I was sick, and I knew it. I had no self-control. I had no discipline whatsoever. I always tried to hang on to the little control I thought I had.

Charles, however, had different plans. He got out of prison knowing that he was going back to the street life. I was the one in denial. I shared with Charles what was going on in my life with the lawsuit. I told him his so-called partner was not for him— one minute, he called me mom, and the next minute, he tried to hit on me. He even put his hands on me, treating me like he treated everybody else that used his product. I was just another dope fiend to him. His partner made the mistake of forgetting who was buying the drugs he sold. When you treat your customers bad, you end up in prison. People turn on you quick. I thought Charles didn't believe me. "How can you partner up with someone that really isn't for you? He will cross you at the drop of a dime."

Charles started spending all this money. He made me think he was making this money. He started wearing $800 shoes and $800 suits. He was buying new furniture, appliances, and more. Everything in my home was brand new. This did not make me happy though. I wanted a husband. I knew Charles was headed for trouble.

"How do you think you can break the law right in the police's face while I'm suing them? If they can't get me, who do you think they're going to get?" So I felt Charles was just like me—addicted to failure.

We went to church on Sundays during this time, so we could wear the clothes that Charles was buying. He loved showing off his expensive shoes, diamonds, and money. Church was where we did that. I remember Pastor Duncan approaching Charles one Sunday with the word. Charles told Pastor Duncan right in front of me that he wasn't ready. Pastor Duncan said, "So you're going to make me work hard, leading you to serve the Lord?" Charles said, "You don't have to work hard. I said I wasn't ready." I was so disappointed. I had hoped that going to church would change us. However, we only went on Sunday. And once we returned home, we didn't live what the word said. We were just perpetrating.

As much as I turned to God, I turned on him when I felt I could control things. Charles would take me to see the attorneys down in Detroit with his $800 shoes and his diamonds and things on. The attorneys thought he had it all together, but he was just as messy as he could be. I was right in the mix of the mess with him. This behavior went on for a year. I promised my kids that we would never go through anything like that again, and already, I was back doing what I was familiar with doing.

I didn't see much of my husband, except late at night, and then we got high. He was in the streets most days, and I was home, thinking I was being a good mother. I once again sneaked and did heroin throughout the day. I remember one day I had my drugs in my jewelry box as I cleaned up. Charles had just come to take Little Charles to football practice. When he left, I went upstairs and blew my dope. I started to relax after a nice bath. Charles came back in the door. He went to the bathroom in our bedroom. I went downstairs to see the big-screen television that he had just purchased. I couldn't stand being in the bedroom knowing he was in the bathroom getting high. It was okay when I did it or we did it, but I had a problem with him coming back to my house to use drugs and not share with me, especially when my daughter was right in her bedroom. Even though we all closed our doors, I just felt the kids knew what was going on.

While sitting on the floor watching TV, the door flew open. I screamed as the armed police walked in a line toward me. They had on full armor. The officer in charge said to me, "Up against the wall!" I saw Katrina coming down the steps. She was also told to stand against the wall. We both were handcuffed as the remaining police went up the stairs.

"Who's upstairs?" they asked.

"My husband," I said.

As they were going up the stairs, they called out to Charles, but he didn't answer. They stopped for a minute. They called again. He never answered. All of a sudden, I heard a lot of movement, like fighting. Scared the daylight out of me—I'm thinking that they were hurting Charles because he was resisting.

I asked the officer that stayed downstairs, "Can I move to the wall so I can be near my daughter?"

The officer said, "Yes."

I asked Katrina if she was all right, and she said, "Yes."

I thought about Charles, Jr. I'm so glad he wasn't home.

The officer in charge asked me, "Does this house belong to you?"

"I'm here, ain't I?"

"Shut up!" he said.

At this point, I was getting upset, so I acted like I didn't hear him. "This ain't no dope house! This is my home. Why would you come into my home?"

I thought about the drugs I just blew. I'm so glad that I didn't wait until later like I was first going to do—I would have went off to jail with a case. God protected me again. For Charles, on the other hand, that wasn't the case. The police didn't find any drugs in my home, thank God. I had told Charles never to keep any drugs in our home. Our kids lived here, and this was no dope house. We didn't allow people to just hang out at our house. I never let people come to my house like some drug addict's did. My kids were never exposed to that type of living. Ever. This was a mindblower to have my house raided. This had never happened, not even in the past. I thought to myself, *How could this be happening? What is Charles out in the streets doing?*

As the police came downstairs with Charles in handcuffs, I didn't look directly at him. I was too busy telling the police, "I told you, you wouldn't find no drugs in my house. You need to be raiding a *real* dope house, not my home." I was told that lots of drugs were found in the trunk of Charles's car. The search warrant was for the cars at my house also. I could not understand why Charles had drugs in his clipper bag in the trunk. He was slipping. He had just taken Little Charles to football practice in that car. Wow!

When the police were gone with Charles, the phone rang. I thought of Little Charles. I told the police that I had to answer my phone. "It's my son. The coach is waiting for Charles to pick up Little Charles." The officer in charge let me answer. I asked the coach if he could bring Little Charles home. When Little Charles got home, the address was missing from the door. It fell off when the cops kicked in the door.

"What happened?" Little Charles asked.

"Your dad's in jail. The police raided our house. Your dad had drugs in his trunk."

Little Charles was no fool. None of my kids were. They knew what was going on. I never fooled anyone but myself. Once the police were gone, my bedroom was a wreck! The bed was broken down. Clothes were all over the floor. The attic door was lifted. The officer in charge told me why my husband had been arrested. The car he had was towed away.

After all that chaos, I put my home back together. I spoke to the landlady, and she seemed to be okay with what happened. A month later, that manager was replaced with another manager that once worked at the office but moved to another city. She was now back in Lansing. She stuck to the rules. Not only did she evict me, but she also informed the government that my house had been involved in a drug raid. The past manager was cool. She was even one of my customers that I sold clothes to when I was boosting. Now Charles was in jail, and I had to move out.

Father God,

O God, why do I continue to let you down? Why can't I stay off drugs? Why can't I change? I need your help again, God. Help me and my kids. Help my husband. What a mess! I'm lost. I don't know how I'm going to make it, God. I have to move. I have no place to go. I have no money. I just got my kids home. Now I have no home. Make a way, God. You've never let me down. Please don't stop now. Thank you for protecting my kids. Now help us find a place to live.

Praise be to the God and Father of our Lord Jesus Christ, the Father of compassion and the God of all comfort, who comforts us in all our troubles, so that we can comfort those in any trouble with the comfort we ourselves receive from God.

—2Corinthians 1:3–4 (NIV)

I have told you these things, so that in me you may have peace. In this world you will have trouble. But take heart! I have overcome the world.

—John 16:33 (NIV)

Have I not commanded you? Be strong and courageous. Do not be afraid; do not be discouraged, for the Lord your God will be with you wherever you go.

—Joshua 1:9 (NIV)

Chapter Thirty-Two

EAST LANSING

Fear had me frantic. I didn't know what to do. I prayed, and then I took matters into my own hands. First, I told the manager a piece of my mind. She was only doing her job, and I didn't like her for that. Then as always, my brain started to click: I remembered that Charles had an insurance claim for a car that he bought. On our way home one Sunday, going seventy miles per hour on I-75, the hood just flew up, crushing the roof of the car. None of us were hurt, by the grace of God. It was one more of the many incidents in my life that God showed me and my family his protection. Charles managed to slow the car down and pull it off the road. He had always been a very good driver—good at working the insurance companies too.

I knew in my heart that my husband was not getting out this time. He was into so much criminal activity that God told me months before it happened that he was going back to prison. I even told him that he was setting himself up if he continued to do wrong. We were so involved with the street life that it was all we knew; it was our comfort zone.

Well, that insurance check came in the mail for Charles. I was his wife, which, in my opinion, gave me the right to cash it. Before Charles went to prison, he wanted to live in East Lansing. I really didn't, but I was willing to move because he wanted it. We found a house to lease with an option to buy. The house was filthy. When

I first saw it, I thought, *I'm not moving my kids into this dump!* But on the other hand, I saw the potential it had; and Charles said he would do what it took to make it livable. He paid the deposit, and we signed the lease. But when he was arrested, I wanted out of the lease. I wanted to stay where I was familiar.

I called the leasing company and told them that I had changed my mind. I would not be moving into the house. They told me that I wouldn't get my money back if I didn't move in, but they would let me out of the lease. I didn't care about the money. I've never been a person that was in love with money. I've always felt there was more where that came from, even if it came from a life of criminal activity. Patty taught me that when I was a little girl. I was scared to move alone way out in East Lansing. But now I had no choice.

The plan was to use this money to clean up this house and paint it, but I needed somebody to do the work. My thoughts went to the elderly man that was a runner for Charles and his partner. He was on drugs, but I saw more than his drug habit. I could tell that he wasn't scandalous. He actually had some morals and values. He was different from the other addicts, just like I was. I felt like he had a caring heart. When he brought me the drugs I had ordered that day, I asked him, "If I pay you, would you be interested in a job painting a house and moving me and my kids in?" He said he would take a look at the house and we could go from there.

The next day I met him at the house. He had a friend of his with him that would be helping him. After looking at the job, he agreed to do the work. I told him I'd pay him $800 to paint the entire house, basement included. I supplied all the paint and other materials. He was responsible for paying his help, although I kept them both high, which meant the work always ended when we got high. I had been working high all my life, so I didn't have a problem with the job. I just got tired of having to keep them high.

I was grateful that the house was shaping up. I did keep money in Charles's account, seeing that it was his money. He knew, however, that I had to use the money to relocate our children. I felt I wouldn't be moving if it weren't for him, so I really didn't care if he had a problem with what I was doing. It took about three weeks to get all the painting and cleaning done, but once done, my kids and I moved in right before Christmas 2003. I was very scared. To be honest, this was the biggest move I'd ever made.

It's funny, but I put my trust in God. I talked to him day and night. Don't ever let anyone tell you that God don't hear the sinner. God hears who he wants to hear. He heard me, and I know he heard me. He gave me the strength to keep going. He gave me the courage to live in a neighborhood where the white people treated me so unkind and unfriendly. Sure I was still doing wrong, but I had a heart for Christ.

I had so much going on in my life. I had the feds intimidating me about my husband. I had the city attorneys doing all they could to stop my lawsuit. I had a drug habit that I was hiding. I had two kids that I had put in an unhealthy environment again. Now I had to hold myself together for their sake. But I couldn't without the help of Almighty God. I was not just afraid of living in East Lansing, I was afraid of what was yet to come. My husband had lost his mind. He was not only in jail, but he was also making demands on me that I was trying to fulfill. On the other hand, God was also trying to talk to me.

I straddled the fence for years. I used, and did it "Lavinia's way" by day and sought God by night. I stayed in battle. The devil had a stronghold on me that I couldn't let go of. So nightly, I talked to God. "I can't do it alone, God. I've tried, and I keep going back. Drugs, street life—that's all I know, God. Help me change."

After Christmas, the money was gone. I didn't know that all I had to do was put all my faith in God and trust him; I always felt I had to help God out. I first thought about how I needed a job, a job that paid cash. No taxes coming out. That way, I didn't have to report the job to anyone. I needed all the money I could get, not any of what I was getting to be taken. So I called Mrs. Benson. She told me to come over so we could talk. I had to tell her the truth, that Charles was in jail and that he had been busted selling drugs. She showed me compassion and gave me a job to help her early in the morning. She was setting pretty since Mr. Benson died. He left her in good shape. All she did was sit in that kitchen and call the shots. She was so unhappy though. Ever since her husband died, she would say that she wanted to be with him.

She looked forward to seeing me come over. I made her feel alive again, even if I was bringing the messy life I was living. She met the elderly man that had become my friend one day when he came to bring my drugs, but I lied and told her he was bringing me some cigarettes. (He did that too.) I told her so many lies. When she met him, she was attracted to him. I believe she was desperate. She came up with a job for him to do, the outside work.

The problem was that she already had a yard worker, but that was her way of having Mr. Terry around. He not only did all the work that Mrs. Benson paid him to do in her yard, but she also began to express to me that she had not felt the touch of a man in years and she desired to spend time in the presence of a man. So I spoke to Mr. Terry. I asked him if he would spend time with Mrs. Benson alone. He agreed to but not unless his drugs were taken care of for the night.

I pulled some strings to make that happen. I always told her some outright lie to get the money in the beginning. I didn't have a problem doing that because I always got my high off the top. In my sick mind, I was regulating not just him and what he got from her, but I was regulating her too. She was no dummy. She knew that had I not been in in the picture watching over things, Mr. Terry would have taken advantage of her in more ways than one.

I loved Mrs. Benson. I felt it was my responsibility to protect her, but she started to do things that I wasn't okay with. She started taking Mr. Terry to a well-known high-priced men's clothing store in Downtown Lansing and dressing him. She said that he had to look appropriate to be seen with her. She had "pull" at the hotel she went to on a regular basis, and she didn't want to take him anyplace with her, unless he was well groomed. And I mean, she set him out!

I started to feel like I was losing ground. She was paying me well, of course. But I felt she was starting to give Mr. Terry way too much money. She started to talk to me in a way that I hadn't been talked to by any woman. She felt, because I worked for her, I was going to do it her way. I felt, *She's got her people mixed up. If it weren't for me, you couldn't control this situation.* I believe she knew that, but the evilness in her always had to show me who had the money. We got into arguments almost daily. A good friendship was falling apart. We both needed each other, but we started treating each other very nastily. She would have me help clean her up after she had an accident. She basically needed my help for all her basic needs.

She started to act ungrateful for my help. I started to resent her. I told her how I felt about her actions, and all she said was "Lavinia. You get all the perks." I felt, *She's not hearing me.* I started stealing from her. She would talk to me like I meant nothing. Then she would give me the code to get into her safe and ask me to get money out for her. *I'll show her*, I thought. Then when I got home, it would eat my insides up, what I had done. It got worse once I started stealing from her. I stole just about everything.

Then I felt a need to hear God's word. I would go into the Christian store and steal the gospel CDs and play them every morning on the way to her house, crying and asking God to help me. Then when I got to Mrs. Benson's house, I flipped like night and day. I went from worshipping God to plotting how to get Mrs. Benson and my dope for the day. Total madness! I threatened to stop working for her practically every other day.

I was on drugs, and I had become just as ungrateful for all she did for me. Yet in a sick way, we loved each other. I talked to her about every situation I was facing in my life. My dad taught me the importance of talking to an older person. There is wisdom that a mature person can share with you that you can't get from anyone else. Yet I didn't feel Mrs. Benson's wisdom was godly at times. She had a streak of evil in her—she's one of them people that would give you advice about life but all along had a motive, never doing anything out of the kindness of her heart, always to manipulate you.

She was into buying people. She tried so hard to buy me, but what she didn't know was that I couldn't be bought. She was insulting me whenever she bought things for me, my home, or my kids. She felt she could call the shots because she paid for my food, etc. Mrs. Benson pretended to be a Christian, I thought. But she was no Christian. She would have her pastor over to eat lunch that I helped prepare and serve. Then he'd talk about how he needed her money. She used her money to manipulate everybody that crossed her path. I hated her for that.

I made a comment that when my lawsuit paid off, I was going to pay her back for everything she bought me, like the time my kids' computer crashed. She hurried up and bought them a new one. "Mrs. Benson, I promise you. I'll give you back every dime." She didn't believe me. I saw that—how she treated me.

I went to church from time to time during this time. I even went to Mrs. Benson's church with her every now and then. I wasn't feeling her church. She was a member at the same church denomination where Daddy was a deacon when I was a child—one of them churches that if you ain't living right and been partying all night Saturday, you fell asleep quick.

I loved going to LCOGIC. There was this woman named Linda Gordon who worshipped there. When I went there, other than listening to Pastor Duncan preach the word, her voice comforted my soul every time I heard her sing. She had a real strong voice. I loved it! I loved the strength in her voice. It gave me strength. Pastor Duncan never failed to speak a word from God that made me feel that I could continue in this cruel world among all these vultures. I never stayed in church long enough to meet anyone. When Pastor Duncan was done with the word, and Sis. Linda Gordon was done singing, I got up and walked out. My kids had learned the routine. They would look at me, and when I said, "Let's go," we left. I went back to the life I lived, the world that I always found a way to maneuver through so well until now.

The time had come for my deposition in court about the rape. After many trips to Detroit, long nights of prayer, being hit with painful accusations that my husband was a drug dealer and that I was a drug addict, never once did anyone consider, mention, or care about the fact that I only called the police because my car had been stolen, or the fact that my children had been placed in foster care during this madness, or the fact that my door had been kicked off its hinges. None of this mattered to anybody. The only thing that mattered was them stopping me from getting the money due me.

At that point, I no longer cared about the money. I felt that I had been mentally whipped. Pastor Duncan would speak with me whenever I asked for an appointment with him and First Lady Duncan. He may not know it, but his words helped me stay sane. Through my struggle dealing with the lawsuit, I've always valued what he said to me. His wisdom, his godly words have helped me for years. He never knew the details of my problems. He never asked. His only concern was to minister to my soul with the word of God and to pray for me.

I can remember when I got the letter in the mail stating the date of the deposition. I started to cry, not because I knew that this was it, the time had finally come that justice would be done; I cried because I wasn't ready for this money. I was afraid that I would kill myself. I was already using drugs to avoid the pain I was in. I was also buying methadone off the streets. I was so miserable and depressed. I never just totally gave up though. I had kids, and that gave me the strength to keep fighting, to survive. I thank God for my kids. But right on Mrs. Benson's back porch, I told God, "Not now, I'm not ready. This is not what you said it would be when I was in the treatment center and you told me to file the lawsuit. Everything has gone wrong. This is not how it's supposed to be." I cried until I was interrupted by Mrs. Benson.

The day of the deposition, I was ashamed because I had to drive my car. Months before, I had been hit by an old lady that ran a red light. She slammed into my car and destroyed the back end. Katrina was sitting in the back, and she was hurt, but we never went to the hospital. I had no insurance or money, so after I was hit, I continued to drive this ugly car. I was barely making it in East Lansing. I was robbing Peter to pay Paul daily, not just to pay bills and eat but to keep my drugs.

Anyway, I got dressed and went downtown. I got to the court first, so I waited in the car. About ten minutes later, my attorneys pulled up. Wow! I thought my attorney was so sharp. I loved her suit—yellow with yellow shoes! Once in the attorney's office that would be conducting the deposition, I was asked to leave the room, along with the other woman that was also suing this policeman and his employer. It seemed like we waited for days. Our attorney had a young man wait with us. Then about seven hours later, I saw both of my attorneys exiting the building. They both needed to speak with me.

First, I had the biggest case because Internal Affairs had substantiated my complaint. I saw on their faces that this wasn't going to be good. But like I said, I had a mind-set of "whatever." I was tired of fighting. I felt so alone. I missed my husband, Charles. *We were supposed to be in this together*, I thought. Now here again, I stood alone. So at this point, all I wanted was for this to end. My attorney said that she fought hard for me. She said that she made sure that I walked away with enough money to buy a house for me and my kids. She said they made an offer of $240,000. "I feel we should take it," she said. She also said that the issue of my husband being indicted by the feds was one of their issues; otherwise, I probably could had gotten what I sued for—$2 million to $4 million.

My character had been ripped apart so many times in this situation. Sometimes I felt like all of this with lawyers and feds and lies by cops was causing me to stay high. It was too much, so I took their offer of $250,000. I felt I had no choice. I was hurt. My life had been changed forever. The wounds that would never go away were only worth $250,000. Then when the attorneys got their share, I walked away with $140,000.

The husband that I turned to for everything said to me, "That ain't no money."

I'll show him, I thought, *since it ain't no money*.

I didn't feel it was what I deserved either. It wasn't enough to do what I had planned to do, but at that point, I didn't know what I had planned. The drugs were taking a toll on me. Believe it or not, I got high, and while high on drugs, I spent so much time with God. I heard him speaking to me even then. "God," I'd say,

"I'm hurting. Help me, God. I don't feel like I can go any further. I can't do this another day." I remember calling Pastor Duncan at his home. I was hurting so bad one day.

"Pastor Duncan," I said, "did you read the paper today?"

"Yes," he said.

"I feel like I've been had, Pastor Duncan."

"Don't feel like that," he said. "'Vengeance is mine,' said the Lord."

I was not feeling Pastor Duncan at that moment: "Yeah, well, Pastor Duncan, thank you for even taking my call. I gotta go."

I hung the phone up and went straight to the dope house. When I got high, I was even more afraid. "God, please don't let this money kill me. Help me to not die. Help me to do right by you with this money," I prayed. When I got the check, I got five $10,000 cashier's checks: three to give to my grown sons, one to give to my landlord as a deposit to buy my home, and one to give to God, his church. The shame I felt from riding in a beat-up car caused me to walk into a car dealership and pay $32,000 cash for a brand new car. I bought the first one in this series. It was a 2005 model that I had purchased in 2004.

Even still, after all that I bought and gave, I was still unhappy. I kept using drugs. Today I know that it was God's grace that kept me. Sometimes I would be so high that I would be out in the streets at 4:00 a.m. looking for drugs. It's a wonder nobody ever carjacked me or robbed me. Actually, the sellers were quite nice to me. I was so sick. God kept me.

I remember when I got up one Sunday morning. It was not my plan to go to church. I was in the bathroom looking in the mirror. "Oh my god! I look a mess!" God started talking to me as I looked at myself. "Go get dressed for church. Wake up your kids and go today and give that check now." I started to think about how I was jacking off a lot of money. I knew that if I didn't do anything else, I needed to do what God told me. He had stuck by me all my life. I had to give God his share because I already knew that he would be here for me, even when all the money is gone.

So I got dressed and went to church. Pastor and First Lady Duncan were not in service that Sunday. I had the check in my purse. When it was time to give tithes and offering, I started shaking. I began to second-guess if it was really God I had heard. As I got up and walked to the front, shaking, I dropped the check in the offering basket. In my heart, I knew I'd done the right thing. I knew that nothing I'd done or given with that money meant more than this one act. I always knew God had my back. Plus, I was scared to *not* do what I heard God tell me to do. I was spending the money quick and using drugs heavy. I needed God to keep me from overdosing and have my back when I no longer had the money.

As I walked back to my seat, checking the time on the clock, I thought, *Man, I could have bought a lot of drugs with that money.* And then I prayed, "I'm tired of doing this, God. I can't stop. I need you." No sooner than I was done praying, I walked out of the church and headed straight to my drug partner, Mr. Terry. I continued to get him high as he bought the drugs for both of us. I couldn't stand how Mr. Terry allowed them drug dealers to treat him. As much money as I was spending, I had a problem with them making him wait too long.

"Oh no! They got their people mixed up. Let me speak to him. Let me speak to him," I said.

As Mr. Terry called the dealer for what seemed like the tenth time, he handed me the phone.

After saying hello, I told the dope man, "All that money Mr. Terry has been spending with you (which I'm sure he already knew), is my money, and for the type of money you are getting, you will not leave me waiting like this. You are not the only candy store in town!"

I asked him if he understood.

"I'll be right there," he said. And he was.

Mrs. Benson, by this time, knew what time it was. She knew that I was getting high. She had started dibbling and dabbling with liquor. She thought I was a fool. "You'll be broke before summer," she said one day. "Why you giving that church all that money?

"What would you give?" I asked her.

She said, "I'd give $500."

I looked at her and said, "You know what, Mrs. Benson? You've never had to depend on God like I have all my life. You don't know him like I do. So yeah, that's all you probably would give him. I bet all that money Mr. Benson left you, you ain't gave your church $500 yet. Oh, then again, you may have given them money, but I bet you had a motive. I see how you say 'jump' and they all say 'how high.' You regulate your pastor and the elders with your money, and that is not of God."

I had no problem telling her the truth. I had paid her back every dime she spent on me and my kids. She didn't want to take it. "Oh, you go' take this money. You can't control me. I'm no puppet," I said.

We had been making plans in between our fights to do some traveling. She had been to several places and wanted me to travel with her since she couldn't go alone. It all sounded good, but in reality, I knew it would never happen. My drug habit was too out of control. I needed to stay close to the dope man, but we were enjoying our time together now.

I'll never forget the morning I woke up and called her to wake up and get dressed. The night worker was with her. We had made plans to go to breakfast after I dropped my kids off at school. "Mrs. Benson, wake up," I said to her. "I'll be there as soon as I let Little Charles and Katrina out at school." I went straight to get her. I knocked on the door, and she never came to answer it. I looked at the bathroom window because it was open. I thought that was strange because Mrs. Benson does not usually leave it open. The night worker's car was gone, so I thought she went to eat with him. I thought nothing more. I got back in the car and went home, back to bed. My telephone kept ringing, but I didn't answer. I knew it was Mrs. Benson. *I'm sleeping now*, I thought. *I'll be back as soon as I wake up.*

When I did wake up, the phone continued ringing. I finally answered. It was the night worker, "Lavinia, Mrs. Benson is at emergency. Can you come?"

"Yes," I said. But I took my time. She was always at emergency. This time, she'll have to wait for me.

An hour and a half went by and the worker called back, "Lavinia, I thought you were coming?"

"I am," I said.

"Well, that won't be necessary now," he said. "Mrs. Benson is dead."

"You lying!" I said.

"No, why would I lie about something like this?" he said.

My heart dropped to the bottom of my feet. I was crushed. I started to cry. I didn't even cry like this when my own mama died, but Mrs. Benson? I was devastated! *She was my only friend*, I thought. Now I had no one in my corner. "God, why do you keep doing this to me? Why is it that everybody is taken from me? I have no one now. Why God? Why?"

Mrs. Benson had a heart attack while sitting on the toilet. She was so overweight that the paramedics had trouble getting her out of the bathroom. By the time they got her into the ambulance, it was too late. I never even let my mind think that something was wrong. *Mrs. Benson being Mrs. Benson*, I thought, *she ain't fixing to work my nerve today*. I couldn't believe that she was gone.

Even though she had a lot of health problems and had started living very unhealthily, I had just told her that I didn't think she should be drinking and hanging out like she was, but she wanted to hang with me and my people. She never listened to me. I was a "nobody" in her opinion. I didn't tell *her* what to do, she told *me*. Now she was gone, and I was in a lot of pain once again.

I went to her house, and I waited. No one was there, so I went to the funeral home which was up the street from her house. Her only son was already there. He allowed me to stay while he made final arrangements. The thing was, Mrs. Benson had told me that she made her funeral arrangements when she buried Mr. Benson, so I was not okay with her son attempting to change her final wishes. I looked at his wife with this look of concern and said, "Don't let him change the casket she picked. Please tell him to let Mrs.

Benson have what she wants. She wouldn't have prearranged what she wanted, unless she knew what she wanted."

"Honey," she said to him, "I think we should give your mom what she's already picked out." He agreed. So Mrs. Benson had it her way, and that made me happy. I loved that woman, and already, I missed her.

"What am I going to do now? I have nobody, God. Why Mrs. Benson? You act like you just want me to hurt all my life. What am I even here for?"

Mrs. Benson had all that money, and at the blink of an eye, she was gone, and none of it went with her. She did nothing, in my opinion, to truly help people that she couldn't manipulate, yet I felt she was all I had. Now I had no one.

> Father God,
>   I swear I'm not feeling you. This hurts. The drugs ain't working. I'm angry, God. I need you to tell me what life is even about—to suffer? Why? I feel right about now that Mrs. Benson was the lucky one. She don't have to feel this type of pain no more.
>   At times I wish I was her. Then at other times I'm glad I'm not her. What gives me the drive to want to keep fighting this fight called life? Fill me, God. Fill me with your love. Let me know that you are here. Let me know that I'm not alone. I need to feel your presence. Amen.

But God said to him, "You fool! This very night your life will be demanded from you. Then who will get what you have prepared for yourself?" This is how it will be with whoever stores up things for themselves but is not rich toward God."

—Luke 12:20–21 (NIV)

Chapter Thirty-Three

....

PRESSURE WILL
BURST ANY PIPE

....

I was also hurting for my husband, Charles. He continued to give the courts a hard time. In giving them a hard time, unnecessarily, pressure was constantly put on me. When I first got the lawsuit money, Charles had already told me that he was going to go with the attorney that his partner had hired, an attorney that also had issues with drug addiction, an attorney that couldn't take on a federal case. In my opinion, the attorney didn't have the knowledge to take on a case of this magnitude.

Nevertheless, that's what Charles chose to do. Even after I offered help, I felt that he put more trust in his partner than in his wife. Then when he realized that not only his partner snitched on him, several of his runners had snitched also. In my own I was trying to help him by not lying when asked questions by the feds. But he wasn't willing to be honest. Charles had lost his mind and wanted me to do and say things that I felt a husband had no right to ask of his wife. Yet I wanted to help him.

The feds kept coming at me, this time to tell me that my husband had chosen to go to trial. This was more than a year after the raid on my house. They had uncovered a phone call that was placed to my phone from the Michigan Department of Corrections. They weren't playing fair now. I was told that if I did not testify against my husband, I would be charged with aiding in an illegal drug operation. They did whatever they had to do to assure themselves that Charles would not win in court—even came at his own wife.

I personally always thought that a man's wife could not be forced to testify against him. Not so in this case. The feds told me that they had a recorded conversation between me and Charles's partner. When Charles called my home from prison, I placed another call and let Charles speak with the man that he had set in place to continue running his business. How stupid was that? I had no idea that it would get this messy or that I was actually hanging myself. I had called a drug dealer for him and let them talk business from my line. If I didn't testify against my husband, I would be charged with helping an illegal drug operation continue to operate.

I started to lose it. I felt I was just put in a predicament that was unreal. "How, in God's name, am I going to do this? How can I testify against the man I love? What is he doing? How can he do this to not just me, but his own son? What about our son? What are you thinking?" As I slipped mentally, I thought of this lady that prayed for me in church. Every week she had given me her phone number. I called her one night about 3:30 a.m. or 4:00 a.m. I woke up and just picked up the phone. I said some things to her that I, to this day, can't explain.

I told her, "This is Jesus. He wants you to know that he loves you."

She said, "Lavinia, you called my house this time of morning talking like this? God is not a God of confusion."

"I ain't confused," I said.

"You need prayer. You need to come at 6:00 a.m. for prayer."

I bet she thought I didn't hear her. When she got to the church a few hours later, I was waiting for her. I could tell that I had frightened her. She let me come inside the church with her. She was looking at me with this strange look. Pastor Duncan came in the church right after us. As she opened the doors to the sanctuary, I asked her if I could speak to Pastor Duncan.

She said, "Sure."

"Alone," I said.

"Sure." Then she went back by the doors of the sanctuary.

Pastor Duncan sat in a seat that was in the lobby in the church. I sat down also. I told him that I felt like I was going crazy. I told him what my husband was doing. I'll never forget what Pastor Duncan said to me, "You're not going crazy, Sister Lavinia. You are not going crazy. You're just under a lot of stress, but you are not crazy. If you'd have lied, like your husband wanted you to do, what would happen to your kids?" He told me that I needed to think of my kids.

I looked at Pastor Duncan and said, "Can you tell her I can't do this now."

"Sure," he said.

As I walked toward the door, I looked over at Evangelist Jackson. She was looking at me with this puzzled look. I thought, *Wow, I scared her. I didn't mean to scare her,* and I walked out of the door. I went home and got my kids and took them to school. Then I went to get my friend, Mr. Terry. But when I got to his sister's house, I flipped on her. "Come get this cat," I hollered.

Her cat frightened me like cats did when I was a little girl. So I hurried out of her house and got on the highway going to the jail in Charlotte. I was so confused. I couldn't remember how to get to Charlotte. I was trying to go see Charles, but I couldn't remember the way. Then all of a sudden, I couldn't even remember where I was going. Everything was leaving my mind. If it had not been for God, I know I would not have made it to the jail.

When I was able to mentally grasp for a moment where I was, I was pulling up at the jail, wondering, *How did I get here?* I got out of my car and went inside the jail. When Charles came out to visit me and sat down, I said to him, "God is going to release you and Charles, Jr. The attorney for one of the men who also had the same case as Charles, which so happened to be the attorney that Charles, Jr. paid to represent him on the murder case, that I heard call my brother stupid, was going down. God was coming at him." I then got up, didn't say goodbye, and I walked out leaving my husband, Charles, sitting there. I had lost it! So how God got me back to Lansing, I don't know. I went home for a while, and I called Crystal. I told her that Charles, Jr. was coming home.

After being home a while, I realized it was time to get my son, Little Charles, from school. After getting him, I drove to the church. I told him I had to go in the church for a minute and to come with me. I had been talking out of character for some days now, so I'm sure Little Charles was scared. He went inside with me. The first person I saw as I walked in the office was Sister Henderson. She was behind the desk. I called her Jenny. She looked like Jenny to me, but she wasn't. I had lost it!

I remember seeing Brother Gordon also. I told him that he was kin to me. I said that, thinking of Daddy's people. His mother was a Gordon. I remember speaking to Pastor Duncan. I was telling him that I had talked to Pat Johnson, my kid's foster mama. I don't know what Pastor Duncan and I talked about. I just know that Pat showed up. Pastor Duncan asked Little Charles how long I had been acting this way. He told him two days. Pastor Duncan asked Little Charles for Larry, Jr.'s phone number. Then Pastor Duncan told Sister Henderson to call 911.

I don't remember everything I said, but I do remember First Lady Duncan coming to the church at the same time Larry pulled up. By this time, I had made my way outside. Brother Gordon came up and asked me if I would like some water. I knocked the water out of his hand and said, "Don't nobody want no water!" I remember being on the ground. How I got there, I don't recall, but I do remember saying, "First Lady Duncan, I'm go' pull his pants down," speaking of Bishop Duncan.

She said, "Oh no, don't do that."

As the ambulance pulled up, Larry, Jr. was saying, "Mama, let me help you get in the ambulance."

As I was getting in, I remember First Lady Duncan saying, "It's spiritual warfare."

I had never heard this term in my life, but I felt if she knew why I was being put in this ambulance, she needed to be going too.

I remember saying, "First Lady Duncan, you coming?"

She said, "Oh no, baby, your family will go with you."

As the doors to the ambulance shut, they drove off and took me to the emergency room. I was in the hospital for several days, mostly for rest, rest that was needed. I was beyond praying for myself. While in the hospital, I wanted out after a day of sleep. I had to get some drugs. That's all I needed. "If I get high, I'll be fine." Wow!

Anyway, I got out, and I kept on using drugs. Then one day, I was at a red light after taking my kids to school. My kids went to school in East Lansing the first year, but they didn't like going there. I saw how the teacher in the elementary school was doing all she could to hold Little Charles back. She called every week to say that he was talking too much. Never once did she say that he was one of the smart kids in her class.

I stopped at the corner store and bought a newspaper. I sat the paper on the front seat next to me. While sitting at the light, I looked down and saw a picture of a white man on the front page. I looked. "Oh my god! It's him! That cop!" The title read: POLICE OFFICER FIRED STEALING OXYCONTIN. I hadn't been happier since the time I got my own hair salon.

I called Pastor Duncan. I was so excited! "Pastor Duncan, Pastor Duncan, did you read the paper today?"

"Yes, Lavinia."

"You said it, Pastor Duncan. You said it. You said vengeance was the Lord's. You were right. Thanks, Pastor Duncan!"

After that, I got tired of using drugs again. I had the money to pay for treatment this time, so I went to a day methadone clinic. (I didn't have to pay before because of my income limitations.) Things got a little better, but then again, they got worse. Katrina was cutting up. I did so much wrong with all my kids. You cannot use drugs and think that your kids won't rebel. Katrina always had a mouth on her and said whatever she felt; she didn't bite her tongue at all. I always called her out of her name when I got mad until one day when we were arguing and I called her out of her name and she called me out of mine. I could've fell out! *What did she just say?* I thought. "Don't you ever call me that!" I said.

That was the end of me calling my daughter out of her name. She ran away and didn't come home for days. She started seeing this boy that I really didn't like.

Another day, I hit Katrina, and she pulled a kitchen knife on me. Then she called the police on me. Since I lived in East Lansing, I knew they would take me to jail quick, so I told myself to calm down. When the police knocked at the door, I opened it. I was so calm that I couldn't believe myself how I had gone from a rage to "May I help you, Officer?"

Katrina went to hollering, "My mom hit me, and she threatened me!"

I said, "Officer, she's lying. She pulled a knife on me and threatened to kill me. I just defended myself. See, the knife is still on the kitchen floor."

When they saw the knife, they said to Katrina, "Turn around. You're under arrest."

They handcuffed her. She was looking at me like, "Mama, save me." I didn't say a word. I was tired of her. She was giving me a very hard time. Four sons and it's my daughter that's pushing me to my limit. Once she was in the police car, the officers came back to the door and said, "You know we can't keep her."

I said, "Yeah, but keep her as long as you can."

I didn't go get her from the precinct either until I had to.

She got inside my car and said, "I'm sorry, Mama."

"No, you're not, Katrina. You're sorry that you went to jail, not for what you did."

It didn't take her two days and she was back at it again. Girlfriend was no joke—she would flip at the drop of a dime. I wasn't the best mother I could have been, but in my sick mind, none of my kids ever went hungry, raggedy, or homeless. I was the Mama. I begged, borrowed, and stole for my kids. "How dare you disrespect me!" That was when I was angry. When I wasn't angry, I felt extremely guilty for all I did wrong and didn't do right. It was a cycle, a cycle that I got relief from by drugging. Since I wasn't on heroin, I started back smoking crack with the methadone.

My husband, Charles, called one day to tell me that he was going to take the plea bargain from the feds. He told me that if he took the case to trial and lost, that they would probably lock him up for life. I was glad to hear this, but by the time he had made this decision, I had been coerced into signing an agreement that I would testify for the prosecution. This tore at my heart, but I had no choice. I couldn't leave my kids. I couldn't do what he was asking me to do. I felt so sorry for my husband. When he called me back and told me that he was sentenced to fifteen years, I said, "What?" He hadn't killed anyone. He was a husband and a father. He did some things to break the law but nothing that called for a sentence like this. I, once again, was devastated. He had convinced me that it was my fault. "If you hadn't been fooling with cops, I wouldn't be in prison," he would say.

Anyway, I started going back to LCOGIC. Evangelist Jackson would pray for me every time I'd go to the altar. She was a makeup representative and asked me if I would be interested in selling cosmetics. At that point, I was willing to grab on to anything or anybody, so I invested into selling cosmetics, even though, in my heart, I knew it wasn't for me. I just wanted to be in Evangelist Jackson's life. I did try for a short while to sell it, but I gave away more than I sold.

One time there was an alcoholic walking down the street as I waited in the car while Mr. Terry was in the dope house. I asked him, "If I give you something, will you promise to buy something for yourself and not drink it up."

At first, he thought I was joking with him. Then as he looked at me, he realized I was serious.

He said, "Yeah, I'll buy something for myself."

I handed him two $100 bills.

About three months later, I saw him in a liquor store. He was excited. "That's that lady! That's that lady that gave me that money! I bought a TV, I bought myself a TV!"

"Good!" I said as I looked at him.

"Okay, I bought a drink too," he said.

We laughed as I said, "But you bought yourself something you needed first. I'm glad."

It did my heart good when I could help somebody that was in misery. Surely I knew the feeling. I'd been in misery all my life. The money from the lawsuit was running out, so I turned in what was left of the cosmetics I'd purchased to sell and got my money back. I took a loss, but one more loss didn't matter. That too was something I was used too.

After that, I was hit with an eviction notice from my landlord. After two years of trying to befriend the church pastor's wife next door to my house, who owned the house, I found out by doing things like shoveling their snow, they finally decided to throw me out. I was disappointed because I had sent the board members of the church several letters, never receiving a response, expressing my interest in owning the house. In good faith, I paid them $10,000 under the impression that I would be able to buy the house. However, I was told by the leasing company that the owner of the house decided to change it into a place where they would conduct Sunday school. Once again, I was devastated. Two years of hard work flashed before my eyes, two years of pain and tears, two years of using drugs in the closet, and I fooled myself thinking nobody knew.

Calvin and his wife came by often. Calvin and I argued about my drugging. I wasn't on heroin, and I didn't want my kids to know that it was methadone that had me so high. I was told that I was in recovery. *Nice way to be in recovery*, I thought. This methadone had me just as high as, or higher than, heroin. Calvin went to breaking vases and throwing things. One day he stopped by and I was high. I always felt the fact that he needed more money, and me telling him I didn't have anymore contributed to his anger. I called the police on him that day. Little Charles looked so hurt to see the destruction in our family. By the time the police got to the house, Calvin had gone, so I was unable to file a complaint which was probably best.

As I gave thought to the memories in East Lansing, the tough times I'd come through, the church and how cold they had treated me for two years, I often got high and looked out of my window. I remember the New Year's Eve that I was high and looked outside my window. I saw the people next door with white robes on. I woke up Little Charles and told him, "Get dressed! Them church people next door are a racist cult. If they start burning a cross in the yard, we're outta here!"

I put way too much on Little Charles. He always felt like he had to take care of me instead of me taking care of him. So many days he came home and saw me out of my mind on crack. One time he found me outside in the middle of the street as he came home from football practice.

"Mama, ain't nobody in the house."

"Yes, it is. The police are in the basement," I said.

"I'll show you, Mama, ain't nobody."

When he showed me that the police weren't there, I went back inside. Wow! Too much to put on a young boy, but I did.

You know, somehow, I managed to actually plant flowers in the summertime in East Lansing. I even asked the neighborhood committee if I could help when I saw them planting flowers. They wanted no part of me. They told me they didn't need any help. So now it seemed like everybody in East Lansing was against me. I never felt I belonged in East Lansing, anyway, yet I felt I was being thrown out. And I was. God always made a way for me, even though I went through my usual depression, worry, and fear.

Anyway, I found a townhome in Lansing, off Martin Luther King Boulevard, that had been remodeled and available to rent. It was close to the school Little Charles attended. It also was right in the middle of a lot of drug activity. I didn't know that fact when I applied to move in. After being accepted, I didn't start packing until the last minute. I spent a lot of time with God as I always did. God had been my strength all my life. He never walked away from me. It was always me who walked away from him. But when I was faced with fear, fear of the unknown, I never failed to seek him.

As God spoke to me, I started to accept that it was time to move on once again. I called Mr. Terry to help. I wasn't able to pay him like I did the first time, but nevertheless, I did pay him. I heard God as he told me that he was not pleased with his church. He told me to move on. He told me that, in due time, he would bless me with everything I'd lost in life. Call me crazy if you like, but I believed him! I've always believed God.

Anyway, I was able to take that next step and move on. I moved into the very last townhome in the complex. It was at the back, near lots of old trees. It was a little spooky at night. This is when I learned quick that I was among the drug addicts and petty dope sellers. One drug addict recognized another. I saw, on my row alone, three other people that used drugs. I watched them leave out to go cop. Before long, I asked them to cop for me. Crack, that is. I was on such a high dose of methadone that if I sat for more than five minutes, I would nod out. I burned up everything when I nodded—the bed, the floor. My chest was spotted with burns. I'd nod then smoke crack to come down while my kids were in school or asleep.

Once I started smoking the crack, I was off to the races, chasing after that high I got from the very first hit, which I never got again. But I did whatever to get the money I needed to smoke. All my jewelry and Charles's were gone by now for little or nothing to the pawnshops. One hit was never enough. I gave the dope man that I met in the neighborhood rides for a twenty rock. Mr. Terry was my drug partner for years. I never was the type of person that trusted anybody, but if I did befriend you, I treated you like I wanted to be treated. I thank God that even when I was strung out on drugs, I was able to stay loyal to a person, not to say I got the same treatment in return.

Anyway, my daughter continued to rebel. She hurt my heart daily. I had no control in her life anymore. She fought over this one boy weekly. Once, I went to get her from school, and when I pulled up, I saw a fight. It was my daughter. I got out of my car to stop the fight. I knew not to be high on drugs when it was time to get my kids from school because anything might jump off with my daughter. Once I got her inside my car, her window was down, and the girl she was fighting with leaped through the window on my daughter. I could not believe it. I hollered at her, and she got off my daughter.

I pulled off, and my daughter started saying, "Let me out! Let me out!"

I said, "No, you need to go home!"

Anyway, I had stopped at a red light on MLK. All of a sudden, my daughter jumped out of the car into the middle of the street. "Katrina," I hollered, "you get back in this car!"

She took off. I made it home and called the police. When the police got to my house, after taking the police report, the female officer said, "Lavinia, I'm going to have to take you in because you have a warrant for an unpaid ticket."

"What? So I'm arrested?" Dealing with Katrina, I didn't know I had a warrant. I wouldn't have called had I known.

Anyway, I went to jail. My son, Larry, and his girlfriend bonded me out. The police officer brought me back home. When I turned on to my street, who did I see walking up the street? Katrina. Like nothing had happened. I had four sons and not one of them took me though the hell my daughter did. It hurt me when she lashed out at me because I felt her father had poisoned her mind. I knew he spoke negative about me to her at times. He was the reason my daughter would say "I hate you." Wow! Those were strong words that would cut me to my core.

I got high during the year on Vincent Court to escape the pain I was in. I was daily thinking about and praying that God would release my husband, Charles, somehow, someway. "God, he don't deserve that much time." Both my husband and my brother had been snatched out of my life. That's how I felt. So many losses. So much pain. Talk about being miserable. I can honestly say that I had become addicted to pain. By now, it was all I knew. I functioned off pain.

Little Charles was getting older. He was my joy. He was my sunshine. I wouldn't have made it if it weren't for Little Charles. He was one of the reasons I continued to try. He needed me. I had jacked off so much money. I remember when Christmas came and I had no money. I had to humble myself and set an appointment to see Pastor Duncan. I didn't want to ask him to help me. He never asked me any questions about why I had no money. He treated me, once again, like the true man of God he was. I remember him saying, "One of our members just asked today who they could bless this Christmas." It was Brother and Sister Gordon. She was always such a nice and pleasant lady. She came to my home and brought me a card with money in it.

As much as I had messed up money, I never used the money that I felt God gave me from his house, his church, for anything but what I said I needed it for. I feared the Lord. I didn't believe in hustling God's house. I was so grateful for that help. I never wanted to involve Pastor Duncan or his members in the messy lifestyle that I kept dipping off into. I respected Pastor Duncan. He earned my respect. He was a true man of God. I never felt anything phony or fake about him. He would say, "You need to come back to church." I'd tell him, "I know, Pastor Duncan."

He never judged me. I never sensed that he was perping. I always felt that Pastor Duncan cared. It's so true. People don't care what you know 'til they know you care. He is truly a caring pastor. My life has always been full of chaos. I stopped looking for anything different. When there was no chaos, I didn't know how to react. I was now on methadone, crack, and pills. After abusing the prescription drugs that my doctor freely gave me, I would drop eight to nine sleeping pills a day. I stayed comatose.

One time I got high all night. When it was time to take my kids to school that next morning, Katrina asked to drive. I said no, but when I got outside, she was sitting in the driver's seat. "Please Mama," she said. She had been learning how to drive, but her driving wasn't the problem; it was her listening.

I told her, "Only to Little Charles's school."

I got in the backseat and left Little Charles in the front. Would I have made a better choice if I wasn't still feeling the valiums? Yes, but I was cool, although I wasn't making very good decisions.

Katrina started out driving too fast. "Katrina, slow down, you are going too fast!"

"I know what I'm doing."

Again, I said, "Katrina, you are going too fast." I told myself that, "As soon as she gets to this school, I'm taking over."

She made it to the school. She made a turn and then lost control of the car and hit a tree. I mean, she hit hard! She was speeding. *Oh my god*, I thought. *I let my insurance expire*. I started hollering, "I hate you!" I got out of the car. When I looked at my car, I cried. It was a mess.

When the police arrived at the accident scene, they said, "Why are you crying? You and your children aren't hurt."

"I have no insurance."

The officer said, "Oh yeah, I'd be crying too."

What a loss in a matter of seconds. My car was gone. I ended up selling it as is and bought another car. That day, I called Mr. Terry. I used so many drugs that I couldn't see straight. That car was all I had for the pain I felt from being humiliated by the cop a few years prior. Life on Vincent Court was awful. I had put in an application for subsidized housing. I couldn't afford anything better at this point. I had been stripped of everything. I was behind on my rent. My car had been destroyed. I was hanging on by a thread, a very thin thread.

Heavenly Father,

I stand before you. I ask you to forgive me for my sins. God, I need you to save me from the power of guilt. The guilty feelings have a strong hold on me. I ask that you, in Jesus's name, lift the pressure. I can't take the pressure, God. It has driven me out my mind. I need you, Lord. I need you to help me now. In Jesus's name, I pray. I thank you, Lord. Thank you for never leaving me. Thank you for your love. Amen.

Like a city whose walls are broken through is a person who lacks self-control.

—Proverbs 25:28 (NIV)

I was upright before Him and blameless with Him, ever [on guard] to keep myself free from my sin and guilt.

—Psalm 18:23 (AMP)

Chapter Thirty-Four

THE BATTLE IN MY MIND

When I got the call from the subsidized housing office that I needed to come in to finish my paperwork, instead of being happy that my kids and I wouldn't be homeless, I fell deeper into depression. The lady in the office gave me a form that I had to take to the police station and get a history of their records on file of my history. I froze, knowing that my home had been raided three years prior. I was told even before I put in the application that if there was anything to do with drugs on your police report, you would be denied.

I started praying and asking God to not let the report show the raid. When the officer handed me the report, I looked at it, and I swear the raid on my home was not on the report. After my police report was accepted, I was taken to look at a duplex, a duplex that looked clean at first sight, but as I looked at the stove and refrigerator, I began to get sick. Both were filthy. The floors were shining, but as I looked deeper, I saw the dirt had been covered with wax.

As a little girl, my daddy always said that we would never end up in the projects. He didn't think he was better than anyone that was less fortunate than him, but he always said that if a person worked hard and wasn't lazy, they didn't have to live in the projects. My dad, I felt, would be very disappointed in me. I was disappointed in myself. "Look what I've done to myself." Better yet,

I felt, "Look what Charles has done to me and our kids. How could he do this us?" My daddy would say that he wasn't a man. No man would put his family in jeopardy like Charles did.

Anyway, I called on Mr. Terry again. This would be the third time moving within three years. I'd never moved this much in my life. I was one of those people that lived in the same home for years. All the moving alone had me depressed. I felt so unstable. I felt I was going backward in life instead of forward. To be in my late forties and end up in the projects was killing me.

Once I moved in, things got worse. Not only did I hate my home, but I also ended up losing the car I bought with the money I got from selling the wrecked car. My daughter continued to self-destruct. She quit school. Young Charles (Little Charles) continued to do what was right, but I felt that he was setting himself up for the same way of coping that I had used: act as if nothing was wrong and keep it moving. He had experienced so many disappointments in life at such a young age.

I worried about Young Charles daily. I worried about the damage I had done to all my five kids. I don't know if you can comprehend how I straddled the fence my entire life. On one hand, I prayed to God and tried to get my life together, and then on the other hand, I drowned my pain by staying high. I started walking to the methadone clinic at five thirty every morning.

Once I lost my driving privileges due to tickets, I had to walk to get to where I needed to go. While I walked, I formed a deeper relationship with God. I would be the only person out at that time in the morning. I found myself talking to God about everything like I did when I was a little girl. I heard him when he spoke back to me, yet the other voices in my head would take over. This went on for years. I'd call Evangelist Jackson to take me to morning prayer at the church, and she never failed to pick me up. I know she had to be getting frustrated with me, but she never showed it.

My doctor had turned me into a human guinea pig. She placed me on mental medication that I would always stop taking. As I went to morning prayer, the sisters at the church prayed for me constantly. I still ended up in the mental ward of the hospital though, not once but several times. Every time I lost my mind, I'd go to the church to see Pastor Duncan. I remember calling him once, asking to see him. He said to me, "If there was time." When the van picked me up that day, I made it to the church right before Pastor Duncan was about to deliver his sermon. I was then told by his son-in-law that Pastor Duncan wasn't available. I said, "Fine, I'll see him in service." He quickly said, "Just a moment." I was then taken to the conference room where Pastor and First Lady Duncan came in.

I wasn't very stable mentally. A few days before I asked to meet with him, I was spending time with God. As I looked out of my kitchen window, I saw a large pole in the backyard of a neighbor's house that was backlit by a nearby streetlight at the end of the dirt road. As I prayed and meditated, I thought I was losing my mind, yet I felt more peace than I'd ever felt before in my life. The pole started to look like a cross. Then I saw the image of the back of a man in a white robe. He was walking away from the cross as he said to me, "I AM THE LIGHT OF THE WORLD, FOLLOW ME."

In the meeting, I began sharing with Pastor Duncan that God said, "Because he was a true man of God, that treated his daughter with love, he will be blessed dearly." Pastor Duncan and First Lady Duncan thought I was losing my mind. I would hear God's voice one minute, and then the next, I would hear, "Now you really gone crazy. God ain't said nothing to you." This battle went on for years.

I remember, before I stopped driving, I used my friend, Charlotte, for a ride to the methadone clinic. I started talking to her about my life as a child. She asked me, "What kind of life did you live? You need to write a book! I ain't never heard nothing like this in my life!" We laughed, and I thought nothing more about it. Then one day as I walked at five thirty in the morning, spending time with God, I started to cry as I asked God, "Why am I alive? Why me? Daddy's dead. Mama's dead. Mrs. Benson is dead. All my friends are dead, God. Why am I alive?" I clearly heard God say, "It's the life you lived. Now use the many testimonies you have to win souls."

I was crying like a baby that day as I walked and watched the night turn to day—such a peaceful time. I didn't feel I really had anyone. My kids were all living their lives, and I didn't feel I was wanted in their lives. I felt Young Charles was ashamed of me. I felt Calvin had a wife, and he didn't care for me to be a part of their life other than to babysit when they were desperate. Larry was doing well also. He had a girlfriend, and they never really included me in their life either. David had left Lansing. Katrina said she hated me. My husband, Charles, would call and feed me false hope every month as well.

My mind was being tormented daily. The time I spent with God walking at five thirty in the morning was the only time I felt a peace of mind. I stayed comatose. The rest of the day I was on a mission to kill the voices. I did have a neighbor, Marilyn, that I started talking to. She would always ask me to sit on the porch with her. But I wasn't feeling her; I stayed to myself. I had no desire for company—for people period. All I wanted to do was nod. I didn't want to face the pain in my life. I was slowly dying inside, yet I didn't know how to grab on to the love God was trying to offer me.

I continued to straddle the fence. I tried to do what Evangelist Jackson told me I needed to do. I called her from time to time and asked her if I could go to early morning prayer. She still never said no. She has always picked me up, and most of the time she had other members of the church with her. These women would pray for me. As they did, I cried, and I cried. I wanted to change so bad. I remember once saying to First Lady Duncan, "God told me that I should write a book and share how he saved my life over and over."

Pastor Duncan always told me, "If God said it, it will come to pass." He would also say that as much as I talked about Evangelist Jackson loving the Lord, that I would too one day. I felt I did love God, but she showed how much she loved him to everybody. I told Pastor Duncan I wanted to be like her, but I couldn't stay in the church long enough. I stopped coming again.

After that, I experienced my first real nervous breakdown. Marilyn, who used to live next door, had moved out. For about four months, the duplex was empty. Then this man moved into the duplex with his little daughter and son. On the day I totally flipped, he was not home. His son, however, heard me banging on the wall that was between the two duplexes. I was hitting the wall next to each of my children's pictures that I had hanging on the wall. I was saying all kinds of crazy things to myself as I beat that wall. My neighbor, Mr. Joe, knocked on my door when he got home. His son had told him what I'd been doing. His son told him that I sounded like I was tearing up my house.

"Are you okay?" he asked.

When I opened the door, I told him, "Come on in. Felix and Charles are waiting in the basement to kill you."

Mr. Joe said, "I'm not coming in there!"

"Why? You scared, ain't you?"

Mr. Joe walked away and went and called the police. About the time the police pulled up, Young Charles had come home. He had to have been so embarrassed. I said a lot of off-the-wall nonsense to him as well. Young Charles hurried up and left. He was walking up the street when the police came inside my place. It was a female cop.

She began talking to me as if she knew me. "Lavinia, we want to take you to be checked out. You're not acting your usual self. Something is wrong."

"The only thing wrong is that man next door! I know he called. Take him—he the one need to be checked out!"

The officer spoke so calmly and nice to me. I told her I would go, but she had to wait 'til my son was gone. I didn't want to embarrass him. She said, "Sure." Once Young Charles had disappeared, I went to the police car. She asked me if she could put the handcuffs on me for my protection. I said, "Do I have a choice?" I was taken to the community mental health center for examination. I was admitted for about four or five days. I told the doctors that my family doctor had tried so many different pills on me and that I was tired of taking the psych medication she prescribed, so I stopped taking it.

"The medication is what's driving me crazy!" I told them. "I was very upset because I was watching President Obama being sworn in and I was checking out Michelle. I had heard so much about the way she dressed. She was being compared to Jackie Kennedy, and I wanted to see if she had style like Jackie O. I know clothes. When I was young, my friends called me Jackie O. Jackie O was a dresser. Nothing was ever out of place. I used to study her. Michelle Obama was sharp, I'll give her that, but she couldn't hold a candle to Jackie."

Talk about being obsessed with clothes—the doctors were staring at me and decided I needed further evaluation. I never wanted to end up like Mama, yet I was on so many different pills, along with the methadone. My kids never knew I was on methadone. I had so many secrets. I was a full-blown pill head.

When I was released from the mental hospital, I went home. I didn't like my neighbor because I thought he was out to get me. When Young Charles wasn't home, I'd pour bleach in the cracks of the floor in my basement to stop the poisonous gas I thought he was pumping into my duplex to kill me. I was in and out of the hospital for over two years. I fought hard to keep a grip on life. During this time, I was losing. I walked the streets talking to myself. At one point, I was on so much medication and methadone that I actually nodded out while walking. I stood in front of a lady's house, asleep for over thirty minutes. She called the police. When they arrived, I had started back walking, but I was so out of it. The officer told me that a concerned woman called because she thought I needed help. I told them I had been walking all morning and I was just tired. I was asked my name and address, even my birthdate. When I said what was on my state identification, I was released.

When I arrived back home, I realized that five hours had passed. I had been standing asleep more than half of those hours. I managed to get to the church for prayer in between the hospital visits. I remember asking First Lady Duncan, Evangelist Jackson, and another woman of God to come to my house and pray, to bless my home, because I felt Mr. Joe was trying to kill me. I felt my home was full of evil. My life had fallen apart.

First Lady Duncan had to go to work, but she came to my house anyway. I'll never forget. She read Ecclesiastes 3 ("A Time for Everything"). As soon as she walked through the door, she looked toward the floor. She said she felt some discomfort at my door. I looked down at the two black wild cat statues I had at my door. I picked them up and walked to the back door and sat them down to be thrown out. I was in such turmoil that I would have thrown out everything at that point. She started to read from the Bible after telling me that they were there to pray for me, and I didn't have to throw my belongings away. I heard her, but I felt something in my home was tormenting me.

As she read, Evangelist Jackson and the other woman with her started to pray. First Lady Duncan stopped and looked at a plaque of a black face on my wall. She didn't say a word. She didn't have to; I saw how she looked at it. I immediately snatched the plaque off the wall, and this time I threw everything out the back door. I know Mr. Joe was thinking, *Oh my god! What is she doing now?* But I'm sure he could tell these were Christians in my home.

First Lady Duncan prayed for me. Then she told me she had to leave to get to work, but Evangelist Jackson and the other women would continue to pray. Once they were done, Evangelist Jackson said to me, "God is in control." I could barely hear her because the voices in my head were telling me, "You know you ain't no Christian. You ain't even crying. If you were receiving the prayer, you would be crying." The two women had just walked out of the door, and I hollered out, "Shut up! You don't know what I am! I've been crying for days. You shut up!"

I felt I had really flipped. Now I was talking back to and answering these voices. I had been diagnosed as being everything—from manic depression to bipolar, to schizophrenic, to having multiple personalities—with a prescription of psych medication to go with each diagnosis. I saw a repeat of Mama. I wasn't okay with what was happening to me, yet I saw no way out. I started back going to church, but my mind wasn't right. I was so paranoid that I thought the members of the church were following me. I didn't trust any of them, except Pastor Duncan and Evangelist Jackson.

Brother Allen used to be the van driver, and one time I forgot that I rode on the van to church. When service was over, I was in the conference room speaking to Pastor Duncan and First Lady Duncan again, and Brother Allen came to get me because the van needed to leave. I took offense to him and said, "You could have just left, if you got a attitude. You didn't have to wait for me." I was so rushed that I left my purse in the conference room. I didn't retrieve it for at least two or three weeks. That's how sick I was. I couldn't remember where I had left my purse. I felt like I was in a trance.

So again, I quit taking the medication, even the methadone this time. I ended up in the emergency room. This time I was placed in a straightjacket because I kept getting out of the bed. I saw a young man in the hall that I was calling Larry. I told the nursing staff that my son would make them let me go. I remember security telling me that he wasn't my son. Then I started fighting the nurses because I thought it was the end of the world and I heard the loud sound of a trumpet. In my mind, the room was shaking. I told the nurses, "This is it! We all go' die." Wow! I was medicated to stop the confusion in my mind. I woke up in my own room with a twenty-four-hour guard. I tried to stop taking all the pills, methadone, and psych medication several times only to end up in the hospital. I felt I was in a no-win situation. If I took all the medication, I felt crazy; and if I didn't, I went crazy. I just felt crazy.

I got out of the hospital again on more medication. I was stable. I started back to walking to community mental health for my methadone, walking and talking to God. I enjoyed talking to God. He was the only friend I felt I had. I was still going through hell with Katrina. By now, she was pregnant and determined to have a baby. Young Charles never said much, but in my heart, I worried about him. He was very withdrawn. He had to be worried about me, about his future, which I'm sure felt so uncertain. He never knew what was next with me.

As I talked to God, I asked again why I was still alive and everybody else dead. One day, through the tears, I said, "God, you said I would have money, that I'd be rich. What's up with that?"

I heard God say to me, "You *are* rich."

I said, "I know, God, rich with your love and presence. I know that."

God said to me, "It's in the life you've lived."

I asked myself for at least three days what did God mean. "It's in the life I've lived?"

Then the lightbulb came on. "Oh my god! It's the life I lived! Write books! Share with others! Give God glory for all that he's done for me!"

Just like Charlotte said, "Write a book."

So I started tape-recording the story of my life. I would call Charlotte and ask her to listen to what I had taped. She told me that she could barely understand me because of how much I was crying. "I know," I said. "This is just a rough copy." I had a total of ten tapes that I had recorded. Then I started having anxiety attacks. This stopped me from taping any more of my life's story. I began to think of my husband, Charles, and blame him for me and my kids ending up in subsidized housing and struggling like we were.

One day, as I spent time with God in between the anxiety attacks, I went into my closet and got all the expensive shoes that Charles had and put them in a big green bag—$8,000–$10,000 worth of shoes, eight pairs. They had only been worn once or twice. I donated them. In my mind, I started to realize that I didn't want to poison Young Charles, thinking that by keeping the shoes, I was condoning drug selling. I had already kept Charles's belongings in my closet for at least seven years now, right in my closet like he was coming home any day. I was angry with Charles. He had actually stopped writing and calling for a while. I guess I was too crazy for him or maybe on too much methadone.

Anyway, Mr. Joe and his wife never stopped looking out for me. She worked in a hospital, and she helped me on many days. She was the first to tell me I was having anxiety attacks. She told me to relax, to try to calm down. "Where is Young Charles?" I asked as I came out of my house with just a slip on one time. Mr. Joe could tell that I was flipping again when he looked at me. "Young Charles is okay," he said. "He's probably up the street at that event at the church. He's all right. Here, sit down." At that point, I looked down at myself and realized I only had on a slip. "I can't sit out here with no clothes on," I said. And I shot back inside the house.

I tripped for hours, going to the hospital for the third or fourth time. When the paramedics arrived with the police, I had on Katrina's winter boots and a long tee shirt. I was talking out my head. "Whatcha come here for?" I said to them. They were talking to me as though they knew me.

One of the officers said his name and said he knew my son, Calvin. "I went to college with your son."

I guess he thought that would win me over, but it did just the opposite. "You did? Well, you probably working with him to lock me up!"

Needless to say, I ended up in the hospital again, only this time I would only go if I could take my daddy's Bible with me. I'd had this Bible since Daddy died. He got it the year I was born, 1957. He had written in it all about his family, when he got married, all his children's names, when we got married, and so on. I was on my way to the hospital, talking about my daddy, my brother, and my sons. I was telling the paramedics that there was a conspiracy to kill the black man.

I started telling them about the Bible speaking about the man being the head of the family but that the government had been on a mission to stagnate the growth of the black family since the slaves were freed. I told them how the prison system is the new form of slavery. I talked to them about things that I'm sure they thought I was crazy for saying. But was I crazy, or did I see something in my craziness that really wasn't as crazy as they thought? Once in the hospital this time, I would not take the medication that was prescribed. I constantly tried to read my daddy's Bible. I even struggled with a nursing tech who tried to take it. I had some pictures inside that Bible that got lost, unfortunately.

Evangelist Jackson and one of the other members of the church came to visit me. I saw how Evangelist Jackson never gave up on me. She continued to pray for me. I know at times she had to think, *God, are you hearing my prayers for Sister Lavinia?* But she never gave up. I asked Evangelist Jackson if she would take Daddy's Bible home with her. She said, "Yes."

After she left, I went into my room and wouldn't come out other than to eat. The administrator of the hospital actually came in my room to ask me what I expected from my hospital stay. I told him that I wanted to rest and that I wanted his nursing staff to me leave alone. I told him I felt that his hospital thought all black people were stupid.

"That's not true," he said.

"Then tell 'em to stop trying to stop me from worshipping and depending on God."

"Lavinia, enjoy your weekend and rest," he told me as he left the room.

He was really telling me that on Monday, I was getting out of his hospital, ready or not. I was cool with that. I didn't trust them anyway. When I got out this time, I tried hard to go to church again. Pastor Duncan even told me that I needed to be in church and stay in church. I heard him, yet I couldn't get it together long enough to stay. I continued with the in-and-out pattern I had formed. Yet I really did want to be "right" with God. I prayed and cried to God daily, "Help me, Jesus. Help me."

> Father God, Almighty,
>
> In Jesus's name, I come before you, and I repent for any sin that I have committed. Lord, I need you to help me once again. Your word says that if I fear not, I shall not be ashamed; neither will I be confounded and depressed. I shall not be put to shame (Isaiah 54:4). You are not a God that you should lie, so therefore, I trust you, God. I know that someday you will bring me out from such a sick mind. For I know that you are able. So I say thank you, God, thank you in advance, for it's already done. Amen.

And the peace of God, which passeth all understanding, shall keep your hearts and minds through Christ Jesus.

—Philippians 4:7 (KJV)

Therefore, with minds that are alert and fully sober, set your hope on the grace to be brought to you when Jesus Christ is revealed at his coming.

—1 Peter 1:13 (KJV)

Chapter Thirty-Five

GIVING UP

I continued to watch the television ministries, but I hadn't been to my own church in a while. I started to struggle, mentally again, to the point that I had taken everything I could from my bedroom and put it all on my living room table. My home had never looked like it did now. Nothing was neat and in order like I kept it all my life. I had sat up in my home and become afraid of the world and everybody in it. I was going to my family doctor, and she was giving me whatever came to her mind to prescribe, and I took it.

Johnny was talking to Young Charles and spending time with him on a regular basis. One day Johnny showed up at my house to talk to me. He felt I had lost it and needed to get some help again. I don't know how it happened, but Johnny and Calvin arranged for Young Charles to move to New York. Even though I agreed that I couldn't do for my son at that time, I was lost without him. I got worse. All my life, it was my children that made me press on even when I felt I couldn't make it. Now my son was way in New York. I was so scared for him. I always thought something was going to happen to him.

I called Evangelist Jackson and started going to morning prayer again. I prayed for the return of my son. He called one day and said, "Mama, I'm coming home." I shared with him that I wasn't myself and that I couldn't do the things for him that a mother should for her teenaged son. I had only been to one of his football games since he was a kid. I had let my son down. He told me that he was sixteen now and he didn't need me to do for him. He said that he would do for himself. After many days of prayer, Young Charles did, in fact, come home. I was so glad he did. I needed my son. He gave me a reason to want to live.

I wasn't mentally healthy, I told my son. I had just gotten out of the mental hospital for the last time, and I was very unsure of myself. I was not well at all. I went to the corner store daily. Whenever I had the money, I'd pay for what I needed, if I wanted to, and if I didn't, I stole what I needed. I had gone from stealing from designer stores in East Lansing, Novi, and Bloomfield Hills, to stealing from the corner store. My world had become so small. I had lost everything both mentally and physically. I thought I had hit my bottom. Even though I felt bad for a moment when I stole from the corner store, I continued to do it until the day I was caught stealing some cheese by the owner's wife.

Not only was I caught, but I was also with Larry's girlfriend, and I was so embarrassed when the owner's wife said to me, "Can I have my cheese back?"

I saw her when she went to check her stock behind me, but because I was not thinking very clearly, that went right over my head.

I said to her as I opened my purse, "If everything in here wasn't so high, I wouldn't have to take it!"

She said, "Don't even go there."

I handed her the cheese and walked out with my son's girlfriend. I was concerned more about what my son's girlfriend thought of me than getting caught stealing. But when I got home, for the first time, I started to feel like I was wrong. When I was a kid, I was scared that I would get caught, but I never felt I was wrong. Mama had convinced me that the stores I stole from had insurance and they wouldn't miss a little outfit, that they were overpricing their merchandise. But this was different. I didn't feel the way I used to feel. Maybe it was because the owner never called the police on me or told me not to come back in their store. *That lady must be a godly lady*, I thought. I went back to that store because I didn't have a car to drive to another store. I felt so much shame and guilt when I went inside there after being caught with that cheese.

Even though the owners never treated me any differently than how they treated their other customers, the guilt ate at me so much that I took $100 to the store and handed it to the owner one day. He reached for it, and then he looked at me and said, "No, I can't take that. You get you some help. You go and get some help." I started crying. I've never stolen again in my life. Never. A life of stealing, and just like that, I stopped. I did go to community mental health for help, thinking that I was going to change. I started to withdraw from Evangelist Jackson and going to church after Young Charles returned home. I was still drinking enough methadone to knock a bull out. I nodded all day and all night while I smoked cigarettes and burned up my chest with them.

One day, after all I had been through, I woke up and couldn't straighten up. I was bent over at my waist. I thought it was temporary and I would straighten up as the day went on, but I didn't. After a few days, I began to worry. "What's going on?" I no longer could walk early in the mornings. This white lady at the clinic asked me if I needed a ride. She asked me what was wrong with my back. I told her I didn't know. We both said, "It'll straighten up." But it didn't for months, eleven to be exact.

During this time, I began to give up. I had been told by my family doctor, Dr. Cramer, on the last day of the last mental stay in the hospital that I had to have one of my kidneys removed. I didn't believe her, so I chose to block out what she said. *How could that be?* I thought. *I've been in and out of the hospitals for over two years. Nobody ever said anything was wrong with my kidneys.* So I didn't believe her.

I had started losing confidence in Dr. Cramer. She wasn't a good doctor anymore; she was only about the money. I saw that, and I didn't trust her, so I didn't go to the specialist whom she referred. Now I not only walked like I was eighty years old, but I also was starting to feel sick from the kidney not working. I had experienced a lot in my life, but I'd never been sick like this. I was afraid. I walked around in denial at least five or six months after being told about the kidney failure. Then one day, I ended up back at the doctor's office due to pain. This time I knew I had to have one of my kidneys removed. I thought of Daddy and what he went through when his kidneys failed him. I had gone from mental illness like Mama to kidney failure like Daddy. Plus, I was walking like an old lady.

Talk about depression. I don't think I could have gotten any more depressed. Depression will cause you to withdraw from life totally. I had the surgery to remove my kidney. It was a difficult time because I was still bent over, so I had to sleep sitting up for a while after the surgery. I had no family support. My older sons never helped me. My daughter was destroying herself, and there was nothing I could do to help her. My youngest son had to helplessly watch me slowly die, which is what I was doing. I was dying inside and on the outside. And I no longer cared.

I no longer fought to overcome my situation. I gave in to it. I heard the voices all the time telling me that it was over now, I had lost, and I may as well just give up. And that is what I did. I stopped all contact with anybody positive, anybody that could put a good word in my soul, except my new friend, Pam. She was very nice to me, but I didn't share a lot with her at first. I stopped talking to God because I felt he had deserted me. I felt God had given up on me. After all these years of God helping me, I felt I had made him angry by the abuse I had done to my body with drugs. I stopped listening to his word. I became so withdrawn.

My sister, Vanessa, called me one day, and I shared the truth with her. All my life Vanessa has always come to see about me. She has always had a love for me that was so unhealthy, yet we knew we loved each other. Vanessa came over eighty miles every other day to help me. She tried to lift my spirits. She did my hair. She bathed me. She did everything she could to help me. To be honest, she did more for me than I was willing to do for myself. She took me to a specialist that told me if I came to physical therapy twice weekly, my back could be straightened back out. Vanessa was there for every appointment. I hated going because I didn't see any progress.

All the therapist was doing was giving me false hope. He would say, "You're getting better," but I couldn't see it.

One day, when I got on the therapy bed, I said to the therapist, "I don't feel good, and I need to go."

"How do you expect me to help you if you don't want my help?"

I guess he could tell that I had no hope of ever straightening my back up. I felt God was punishing me for all I had done wrong all my life.

I said, "I don't know," and I got off the bed and walked out of the room.

Vanessa would always smile at me to make me feel better. I was so proud of my sister. She had helped Mama. Now she was helping me. I loved my sister for how far she had come. I remember she was struggling with some issues. Our family has always had issues.

"What's wrong?" she asked me.

"Nothing, I just don't feel like doing this today. I wanna go home."

"Okay," she said, and she took me home.

I never went back again. Then Vanessa got into a car accident and was unable to come back. After that, the only person I saw was Pam. She picked me up in the morning to go to the clinic, and she took me to get food. I started chipping on heroin on and off. I was miserable. I wanted to die. I started praying, asking God to take me in my sleep, the little I got. He never did. I became angry with God for waking me up. I was smoking two packs of cigarettes a day. I didn't eat. I had lost so much weight. I looked frail, like I had been smoking crack all day.

After Vanessa couldn't come anymore, I stopped taking baths. I had not taken a bath in over three months. My hair had not been combed in over three months. It was so matted that I couldn't get a comb through it any longer. My toenails had grown so long that I wore my daughter's shoes, a size 9.5. I couldn't wear my size 8 because my toenails were too long. I had never worn tennis shoes in my life, yet I was walking around in a pair that was a size and a half too big. My feet looked horrible. I was home most of the time, but whenever I had to leave out and go public, people looked at me like I was some sort of freak. My neighbors called me that old black lady. I was fifty-three years old, but to my neighbors, I looked eighty.

I hated myself. I didn't want to be alive. My home was filthy. I could no longer keep it clean. I didn't want to. I never washed my dishes. Young Charles started trying to keep them washed. I only bought frozen food for him to eat. I no longer cooked. I no longer did anything. I was afraid of everything and everybody. I got scared to go outside, especially if it was snowing. I was scared of the snow. I didn't want it to fall. I didn't feel secure or stable enough to be outside in the snow. Whenever I saw people that I knew out in public, they stared at me. No one ever asked me how I was doing or if I needed help. They would only stare.

Young Charles had to be worried about me. One day he asked me what I did while he was at school. He didn't really know what to say to me at this point. Vanessa would call to check on me. She too was worried about me. One day she said, "You don't even talk no more, Lavinia. You act like Mama did before she died. She stopped talking too." Well, I had died too. I was just waiting for the natural death to happen. I had totally given up on life. The voices had me thinking that I was all washed up, done; it was all over for me.

One day I took out all the tapes that I had been saving to resume taping my story. I shredded the tapes into pieces. I destroyed them all. The voices told me, "Nobody wants to hear that mess. What were you thinking?" After I destroyed the tapes, I was all-in, smoking and slowly killing myself. Then one day I got out of bed after sleeping for a few hours in the same position and not being able to move. I struggled to get up every morning, but this morning I didn't really pay attention to the fact that I didn't struggle. I was so used to walking bent over.

For eleven months, I had walked bent over. I didn't even look in the mirror at myself anymore. I just got up and went to the bathroom. When I was coming out of the bathroom, Young Charles was at the computer. He looked up at me. "Mama! Your back ain't bent over no more!" I looked down at myself, and oh my god, I was standing straight! I graciously smiled and said, "Sho' ain't." I could not believe what I saw. I walked back to my bedroom and stood in the mirror to see if I really saw my back straightened or if my eyes were tricking me. "Yes, I was straight!" I didn't know whether to thank God or what!

Although my back was straightened, I had abused my lungs so much by now that I felt I was dying anyway. I hadn't bathed in so long, my hair was still matted, and my toenails and feet were hideous. Instead of thanking God that I had straightened up overnight, I continued to look at what was still wrong with me. "What was wrong with me?" Obviously, I was sick.

After I knew for sure that I stood tall and my back was going to stay straight, I started back to praying. Even though I didn't walk bent over any longer, I was still afraid to take a bath. I was scared I might fall and had no one that would know I had fallen in the tub. Besides, I was in a lot of pain. When I was bent over, I saw that I was starting to have problems. My muscles began to reshape themselves. Now that I was straight, I had a lump that stuck out in my lower back. This lump caused me pain whenever I tried to do any type of work or lifting. Even though I was straight up and down, I was still no good. I couldn't even lift my grandkids. Katrina had two children now, and I was not a part of their life like I would have wanted to be.

I was still depressed daily. Pam and I started to talk more. She told me about the women's center that helped ladies like me. When my back first went out, my sister was being paid to come and care for me. When she could no longer come, my caseworker called one day and gave me information about a health care company. I was not going to call at first because I didn't want any strangers in my home, but I was desperate. I needed the help. I was extremely ill mentally and physically.

When the worker, Sheila, came to my house, she was so pleasant. I liked her. Not only was she a Christian, but she was also a black woman that I felt comfortable being around. She and her brother-in-law had their own health care service. She also knew

First Lady Duncan, so that made me feel more at ease letting them come to my home. I shared with her what my family doctor had done to me. She also knew about Dr. Cramer and told me that she had also taken her sister to that doctor.

I started to cry as I thought of my kidney. Sheila said, "I'm sorry. Let's not focus on that. Let's focus on getting you well." Sheila was so pleasant. I couldn't help but love her. Her brother-in-law was also very kind. I was very satisfied with their company, so I told my health care worker that I would continue with their services. Even though I had the help, I didn't allow the worker to help me with any of my personal needs. I couldn't. I was only fifty-three and I thought, *What I look like letting somebody bathe me or help me get dressed?* I couldn't do it, so I continued to not take baths or do my hair for a few more months. You would think that I stunk, but I never smelled an odor.

The weather had started to get nicer. It was time for Young Charles to graduate from high school, and I didn't think I was going to be able to go because of how I had let myself go. I began to talk to my husband's mother on the phone on a regular basis. I actually liked talking to her. One day, as she began to speak of Young Charles getting out of school, I made the comment, "Wouldn't it be sad if I didn't make it to my own son's graduation?"

She said, "You are going to make it. You have to. Young Charles has made a big accomplishment finishing high school. He's a good kid. You have to be there."

I knew she was right. I just didn't feel like I was able to do the necessary preparation. I shared my thoughts of fear with Pam and Vanessa. Vanessa said she would help me by doing what she could. I had had enough experience by now that I knew the only way I was going to be at my son's graduation was with the help of God.

The next day, after Young Charles left for school, I got out of bed and went into the bathroom. I removed the scarf from my head. I looked at my hair. Then I looked straight into the mirror and said, "Father God, I need you. I need you to get me to my son's graduation. Help me, Jesus. Help me comb out my hair." I got a big wide-toothed comb and began combing a small section in the back of my head. It hurt so bad as I tried to comb through the hair that had tangled and matted up. Not even having the strength to lift my arm, I kept asking God to help me. As I combed, I had more hair fall out than was on my head, but I kept going, asking God for assistance as I combed.

After two hours, I was halfway done, still feeling I couldn't finish. I kept talking to God, arms tired. A few more hours and I had completed combing my hair out! I looked down on the floor behind me, and there was enough hair on the floor to make a wig. My head was very sore. I had pulled out as much as I had combed out. I gathered the hair from the floor and balled it up. I had what looked like a big basketball of hair. I couldn't figure out how I still had hair left on my head. I was tired now, but I had completed the first step in grooming myself to be ready to go to my son's graduation. I was getting excited about it! I knew his father's family was coming, and I kept what his grandma said to me as my motivation: "You have to be there." She was ninety years old. Surely if she could make, so could I.

The next day I decided to clip my toenails. I was afraid that I couldn't do them; they looked horrible. They had gotten so long and thick. When I worked in the nursing home, I had seen the elderly patient's nails, and they looked like mine now. One of them had even closed up, some type of fungus. I talked to God while I looked in the mirror once again. With the help of God, I managed to clip them, small pieces at a time. Each time I completed one toe, I said, "Thank you, Jesus." This process took another four hours, and the words of my mother-in-law kept ringing in my ear: "You have to."

When the job was complete, I looked at my feet. I actually smiled. I felt stronger. "Thanks," I said. "Thank you, Jesus." I had to clean up my mess before Young Charles got home from school. When he did get home, I was in the kitchen. He always came straight to the refrigerator when he got home. I had on some slippers that had open toes. I saw my son looking at my feet as he saw that I had clipped my toenails. He never said a word about it. My toenails had gotten so long that my toes looked deformed.

Young Charles watched me wear his sister's tennis shoes, knowing that I never wore tennis shoes. He didn't comment, but he started to talk to me with a smile on his face. He was finally seeing me try to come back to life. He saw the fight in me return, that willpower to get back up. God was showing me that through him, I could do anything.

I was starting to see that without God, I couldn't even breathe. I had taken God for granted all my life, like a child takes his parents for granted. What an awakening I experienced during this time! The next day, when Young Charles left, I got up and prayed. Then I went into the bathroom again. This time, I started to run some bathwater. I was afraid, but I had to take this bath. It had been months since I had bathed—at least four months. It was so long since that the skin on my feet was turning darker and peeling. I knew I was dirty and that it was going to take several baths to clean myself.

I looked at myself in the mirror as I had done the previous days and asked God to help me again. I took my time as I slowly got into the tub, shaking for fear that something would go wrong. I grabbed the bar of soap after soaking in the water for a little while and lathered it on me to soften up the dead skin that had been sitting for months. I'd never been in the tub so long in my life, not even when I was raped and tried to wash the filth off day after day. I scraped and scrubbed my feet with the washcloth. I scraped and scrubbed my skin. The water was so black and dirty. I couldn't tell if the dead skin made the water black or the dirt.

As I stood to get out of the tub, feeling good that I had bathed, I looked at the dirty water before I let it out. As the water went down the drain, I felt like the heaviness of the past three to four years was also going down the drain. I started to feel lighter. I felt clean, not just my body but my soul.

I made it to my son's graduation. I was very proud of him! He had beaten the odds, even with all the drama and unhealthy behaviors he faced daily. God had also allowed my daughter to get her general education diploma (GED) during this time, and I was proud of her too.

Father God,

I humble myself as I approach your throne. I know you are the Almighty God of the universe. You have all power, and you are in love with me! You are not angry with me. You love me! You love me so much that you gave your only Son on the cross that I could live. For this, Lord, I say thank you. Thank you for saving my life. Thank you for my good health. You didn't have to do it, but you did. Your word says that I am healed by the stripes Jesus suffered on the cross. Thank you for healing my body and my mind! Thank you, God. Amen.

Consider it pure joy, my brothers and sisters, whenever you face trials of many kinds, because you know that the testing of your faith produces perseverance. Let perseverance finish its work so that you may be mature and complete, not lacking anything.

—James 1:2–4 (NIV)

Dear friends, do not be surprised at the fiery ordeal that has come on you to test you, as though something strange were happening to you. But rejoice inasmuch as you participate in the sufferings of Christ, so that you may be overjoyed when his glory is revealed.

—1 Peter 1:12–13 (NIV)

Chapter Thirty-Six

THE PROCESS

At that point, I made a commitment to not give up ever again. God was giving me strength to be motivated to try. I called the Women's Center of Greater Lansing after calling other mental health facilities and learning that they all believed in medication and I needed to pay a copay that I couldn't pay. Pam had told me good things about this women's center, so I stepped out on faith and scheduled an appointment.

I'll never forget the first time I went there. There was a woman by the name of Patsy King that I instantly liked. Something about her told me that she was a woman of God. The first session I had with my therapist, I'll never forget. I was withdrawn and unsure of what I had done, but she was so nice and pleasant that I softened to her. I small-talked with her that day, and I left knowing that I would be back.

I went back every week for months. I became very fond of the staff at the women's center, especially Patsy. I started to enjoy going there. I also started going to church with my friend, Marsha, Mr. Terry's sister. She had become a very good friend to me. Her daughter picked me up every Saturday evening for church service. I remember when I first started riding with them. They would be laughing and having fun, and I would say to myself, "What is so funny? I'll be glad when they get me home." I've never been phony, so I just didn't respond to their fun. I was so quiet around

Marsha during that time, yet she continued to have her daughter pick me up.

One day I called the food bank because I was low on food and knew it would be days before I had any money. The lady on the phone told me to go to the Lansing Church of God in Christ. I said, "You don't have another church I can go to?" She said, "Not at this time. You said you would be able to go." I decided to take the appointment. When I got to the church, feelings that I tried hard to fight resumed. The first person I saw was Brother Allen. I spoke to him and asked if he remembered me. He said that he didn't at first.

"You used to pick me up in the van," I said.

He looked, and then he said, "On Southbrook?"

"Yes, Southbrook."

He asked me how I was doing. I then spoke to another member that I didn't know, but when he helped me place the food in the car, I told him, "I used to go to this church."

He hugged me and said, "Come on back!"

The hug was needed, just like First Lady Duncan's hug was over ten years before when I first walked into that church to see my kids in foster care. *I was hurting then, and I'm still hurting*, I thought.

When I got into the car and he walked away, I started to cry. I heard the Lord say to me, "You come back. You come back home. This is where your blessing started. You come home."

I couldn't stop crying. The lady that gave me the ride asked, "You all right?"

I said, "Yeah, I just realized that I miss my church, and shame was one of the reasons I wasn't back here."

I thought about the time Pastor Duncan said to me, "You need to come back to church, Sister LaVinia." I thought to myself, *I ain't coming back here after the way I clowned*. I felt like Pastor Duncan read my mind when he then said, "Nobody was here. Nobody knows what happened." I thought to myself, *You knew, that's enough!*

But now God was tugging at my heart and telling me that I was going back. I called and scheduled an appointment with Pastor Duncan, now Bishop Duncan. I thought about when I received an invitation in the mail when he had become a bishop. I felt that if any pastor deserved to be a bishop, it was Pastor Duncan. I thought about how he welcomed me into his church, even knowing that I had suffered from mental illness and my life was very messy. Yet I was now too embarrassed to go back. God has a way of making us know that our plans and thoughts are not his. Wow!

At this meeting, I told Bishop Duncan that I had been going to another church in Lansing with a friend. I told him that one reason I liked that church was because I could go as I pleased and didn't have to be worried about what I wore. Then I asked Bishop Duncan if he had a problem with what I wore. He told me that he didn't. Then I said, "I'll be back on Sunday."

I've been going to LCOGIC ever since. I thought about what Johnny used to say to me, "LaVinia, you need to go to church, any church, just go." For years, he said this to me. He was right. I now had a life, a life that at times I felt uncomfortable in but I knew there was no option. I was not turning back. I never want to go where I had been. I was changing, and I reached for the future every day of my life. I had been broken over and over and over again. I had asked God all my life to change me, and he was doing just that. I let him. I did what he told me. I didn't have a choice.

My therapist told me that she was leaving soon and I would be placed under a new therapist. This didn't set right with me. I was not a woman that dealt with change very well. God had taken so many of the things I did and had been doing all my life. He first started taking all the strongholds off me and out of my life; addiction to drugs was removed but not overnight. I believe that each time I struggled to stop and went back, God was doing it. The process was long and hard, but that day came when I no longer craved drugs or pills. The day came when I walked away from methadone after weaning myself down from 140 milligrams to 40 milligrams.

I'd walked away from methadone before, sure, but I always went back to it. I had been enslaved to altering my mood with something since I was thirteen years old. But when God stopped me, I never went back. God started slowly transforming me by renewing my mind (Romans 12:2). I was ready to do whatever was necessary to change. I was learning that the same willpower I put into my drug habits, all those years, I had to put the same willpower into my walk with God. I go to the word daily. I fast (a sacrifice of food). I have a relationship with God. I hear him when he speaks to me. If he tells me to do something or not to do something, I am obedient, and I do it.

I have found that prayer is the key. Evangelist Jackson was not only my prayer partner who I went to prayer with every Tuesday and Thursday morning, but she was also my mentor. She has taught me so much about prayer and the Christian walk. I also learned what God is saying and has said through studying the Bible, which I have learned to do every day. Bishop Duncan will never know how pleased God is with him for being a true man of God and never turning his back on me.

Marsha will always be dear to me. She has become that friend that I never had, a friend that shows me the God in her: no motives, no expectations, just true friendship. I learned how to laugh through Marsha. She took me with her to her sister-in-law's house every Wednesday in the beginning. I learned a lot about what God was saying through the apostle Paul in the New Testament. I enjoyed the small Bible class and how she had time to break down each chapter and we could ask questions.

> Heavenly Father,
>   Lord of Lords, King of Kings, I say thank you. Thank you for saving my life. Thank you for loving me when I didn't love myself. I love you, Jesus. I love you because you loved me first. You have protected me my entire life. You have carried me my entire life, and for this, I say thank you. You have been so good to me. Thank you,

Jesus, for dying on the cross for me, personally. Thank you, God. Amen.

But as for you, be strong and do not give up, for your work will be rewarded.

—2 Chronicles 15:7 (NIV)

Let us not become weary in doing good, for at the proper time we will reap a harvest if we do not give up.

—Galatians 6:9 (NIV)

But for this very purpose have I let you live, that I might show you My power, and that My name may be declared throughout all the earth.

—Exodus 9:16 (AMP)

THE PROCESS: STAGE ONE

There is power in the name of Jesus! I remember when I stopped cussing, after cussing like a sailor all my life. I even slipped a few times and cussed in church. One day I hadn't cussed all day. God has a way of bringing it to your mind when he is changing you. I said, "Man, I ain't cussed all day." Then the next day, before I knew it, I hadn't cussed in a week. After that week, I said, "Thank you, Jesus! Thank you for stopping me from cussing."

It was so ugly for a woman to be cussing like I did. Daddy was right. God took one vice at a time from me. Smoking cigarettes was next. I smoked two packs a day. I was a chain smoker for years. Nothing went better with a dope high than a cigarette first. He slowed me up. I went from two packs to one, and then I went to buying one cigarette for 50¢ from the corner store. It's amazing what goes on in the hood. One day I heard God say, "No more smoking." I haven't had a cigarette since. He's a good God! Yet all this was just the beginning.

Fortunately, I was able to choose my new therapist at the women's center. I chose her because she did not believe in medication. She believed that if a person talked honestly about their issues, no matter how deep, they could be healed. I was feeling her. I feel God will place in our life everybody and everything needed to heal us from our past. I feel that so many Christians think that because God has saved them, that's all it takes. Being saved is only the beginning. If you truly want to experience the joy of the Lord, you have to be willing to do the necessary work. Sure God can do all things. He can heal you overnight if he chooses to, but just know that he is God Almighty and he is also the author of therapists.

After I started seeing my new therapist, God continued to change me. I worked hard at renewing my mind. There were times when I would leave my therapist and I felt butt-naked. I had opened up my heart and shared some painful things with her that I used to use drugs to cover up for. The lady that worked for the health care company would say, "I think you're getting worse when you come here. You're always crying when you come out of there." She didn't realize that I was doing what it took to heal. I was shedding the tears that I never shed.

I remember the day I had been to Katrina's house and she told me I couldn't see my grandkids again. I started to cry as I walked to the bus stop. I couldn't understand why I was crying so hard. Katrina always said things like that to me. Sure it hurt, but I had gotten to know my daughter. The next day she'd forgotten she even said it. But this day I couldn't stop crying. I cried all the way to the grocery story while riding the bus. People were looking at me. Then when I got to the grocery store, I was trying so hard to stop crying that I started to make loud sniffling sounds right in front of the door of the store. People kept looking at me like I was crazy. But I wasn't. I was being healed.

Anyway, I walked into the grocery store and went to the bathroom. I called the church. I don't know why. I do know that the Lansing Church of God in Christ has been there whenever I needed them to be. I do know that God directed me to call them, just like he placed my kids there so I would come and just like he led me to the church the first time I lost my mind. Sis. Robin Duke answered the phone when I called. I couldn't even talk without sniffling and crying. I managed to tell her what had happened with my daughter. She asked me if I was someplace where there was chair. I told her that I was in the bathroom at the grocery store.

She said, "Sit on the toilet."

What? I thought, but I did what she said.

"Now breathe, breathe. Try to calm down. Relax, relax," she said.

I did what she requested. After at least an hour of nonstop crying, I finally stopped. I was so grateful for Sister Duke. I had no idea of what had happened, but I do know that when I got to church that Sunday, I looked for Sister Duke. "Thank you. Thank you," I said. "How did you know what to say to me?"

She replied, "I've been through some things myself. Just "cause I don't talk about my past doesn't mean I don't have one."

Sister Duke has been a huge support in my life. I thank God for her. When I got to therapy the following Monday, I shared with my therapist what had happened. She said, "Your feelings have been restored. You were able to do some crying that you didn't do through the years because you covered up your feelings with drugs and clothes—a wall that no one could come past."

She was right. That was the break in the ice. After that day, I started to grow stronger quickly. I will never ever forget the day I was washing dishes, spending time with Christ as I do every day. I always look out of the window because I'm drawn to remember that day when I was in the spirit realm and saw the image of the back of a man in a white robe. Anyway, while I was washing dishes, I heard God say to me, "It's over." That's all he said. That's all he needed to say. I knew what he was saying to me. I dropped the dishcloth, and I started to move through my home praising and worshipping him like never before. "Oh my god! It's over! Thank you, God! Hallelujah! Hallelujah!"

I knew then I'd never use drugs again. I knew that I'd never need another man, woman, or human being to try to do for me something that only God could do. I knew that I no longer would hurt from the pain of my past. I knew that I no longer would have resentment toward Mama or Daddy. I knew that God was telling me that I had made it through the nightmare and it was all over. Thank you, Jesus!

> Father God,
> I love you. Thank you for loving me my entire life. I realize today that you were right there through it all. You knew that in the end you would get the glory. I thank you for the pain. I thank you for the dark times. I thank you that I was blessed to hear your voice all my life, and when I didn't, it was because I blocked you out. But even then, I thank you for not walking away from me. Thank you for making me the strong woman I am today. I see that everything I went through, you used to develop my character. I am sold out, God! You have

made a believer of me because of my experience. I trust you with all my heart, God. Use my life to bless your kingdom. Amen.

Your heart's been in the right place all along. You've been in the right place all along. You've got what it takes to finish it, so go to it. (Paraphrase)

—2 Corinthians 8:11 (MSG)

Whether you turn to the right or to the left, your ears will hear a voice behind you, saying, "This is the way; walk in it."

—Isaiah 30:21 (MSG)

THE PROCESS: STAGE TWO

Once God told me that my past was over, he then spoke to me and told me that he had a purpose for my life. He saved and delivered us not so we can sit down. The work of the kingdom is why he delivered us. God told me that people today don't believe that he is doing the same miracles that he did over two thousand years ago. He told me that I was a living witness, that I couldn't keep what I know he has done in my life to myself. God told me that I was his trophy and that I was to write a book, the story of my life. "But, God, I shredded all the tapes," I said. God said, "That's okay. Now *write* the story."

God had done so much for me that I had to be obedient. I owed the Lord *big* time. I said, "Yes, yes, to you, Lord." I've never written a book in my life, but I trusted God. I knew that if he told me to write it, he would help me do it. Like Bishop Duncan used to say, "If God said it, it will come to pass."

One day Evangelist Jackson said to me, "He's completing his work." And yes he is. God places ideas and people in your life. First, he placed the Action of Greater Lansing in my life. I started going to Action because I was very upset with Dr. Cramer. I felt she was to blame for me having to lose one of my kidneys. Not only did she prescribe all those pills to me that caused kidney problems, but she also never told me that something was wrong until the hospital intervened. It was too late then. I had to have my kidney removed.

Dr. Cramer was in the local newspaper and on the news every other month for her wrongdoing. I felt Action of Greater Lansing would be a good organization to be a part of to do something about Dr. Cramer. I was also able to meet Christians and attend a leadership training program through Gamaliel Fire of Faith, a faith-based community organization, where I met so many people. I learned that Bishop Duncan had been one of the copresidents of Action. I enjoyed being a part of an organization that wanted to bring justice to the people of Lansing.

For the first time in my life, I was part of the solution and not the problem. I voted for the president of the United States for the first time in my life. After I started writing this book, God stopped me from watching television so much. I used to watch a female-owned network television reality show that had a lady on it who was supposed to fix everybody's problems, so I decided to submit my story. I was so excited when the producers contacted me through the Internet. I sent in everything that they asked me to send. I shared with my therapist that they had contacted me. She said to me that she didn't feel my family was ready to be on national television, behind cameras. She said that the network was only after ratings, and the damage this could do to my children was not their concern. Now I was confused.

One day God asked me, "Why are you trying to give them my glory? No television show can fix your life. No one can fix your family but me." Not only did I have to stop trying to get on that show, but I also had to totally stop watching television. It was causing me to lose focus, so I asked my son when he came home from college to delete everything on my computer that had to do with that particular network. God told me to stick with Christians. Whenever God tells me to do something, I do it. I know that the only way I will continue to receive his blessing is to be obedient.

As I came back to life, I began talking to my brother, Charles, Jr., in prison again. He has always been one of my biggest fans. He always wanted to see the best for me, which is why when he realized that I was finally struggling, he told me to get a clientele, and he would pay for me to start my hair salon again. Charles, Jr. had picked up on a hustle in prison, so he knew how to make some money. I wasn't surprised at my response when I said, "Thank you, Charles, Jr., but no, thank you. Doing hair is my past. God has a new job for me. I am to be a servant of God. My job today is to win souls. It's not about the money. God will take care of all my needs. I believe that with all my heart. God has made a believer out of me in every area. I trust him."

Charles, Jr. said, "That's crazy."

But the longer I talked to my brother, the more I could see that he didn't feel the way I felt. But today he respects how I feel. I even got a card in the mail from Charles, Jr. with a verse from the Bible on it. I love my brothers, and I thank God that I have learned how to love because God is love.

> Heavenly Father, Almighty God, King of everything and everyone,
>
> I love you. I give you my worship. I give you all of me. With everything I have, I give you my mind, my soul, and my heart. You are the reason I breathe. You are my everything! I am in love with you. You brought me a mighty long way, and I say thank you. I want to repay you, God, to the best of my ability. Order my steps, God. Tell me what to do today. I want to follow you, Jesus, as your disciple, every day of my life. Amen.

Being confident of this very thing, that he which hath begun a good work in you will perform it until the day of Jesus Christ.

—Philippians 1:6 (KJV)

The Spirit of the Lord is upon me, because the Lord has anointed me to bring good news to the suffering and afflicted. He has sent me to comfort the brokenhearted, to announce liberty to captives, and to open the eyes of the blind.

—Isaiah 61:1 (TLB)

THE PROCESS: STAGE THREE

As the process continued, I allowed God to lead me in the direction that he wanted me to go. As he spoke to me in prayer one day, I heard him say, "All that you have done for the devil, stick with me and I'll take you places you never could imagine." As I praised and worshipped him, I was walking in my bedroom and a classic Billy Graham crusade was on. I stopped in my tracks. I was drawn to the message Billy Graham was preaching. I started to reminisce about the late eighties when I used to watch him at the house of Felix's mother, high as a kite or coming down off a high, waiting for him to get money from her so we could get high. She loved watching Billy Graham.

Anyway, as I watched the program, she came to mind. I thought about how much she loved the Lord and how much hope she used to give me. God led me to my computer, and I found myself filling out an application for funding to attend a spiritual retreat at his training center, The Cove. It was a beautiful Christian resort located in North Carolina. Before I knew it, I was standing on the deck of it, looking out at the sunrise over the mountains. Talk about feeling the presence of God. It was a time with my Father that I will cherish the rest of my life. I met Christians from a totally different walk of life than I was from.

One morning while I was there, I thought about the day when God said to me, "Stick with me, and I will take you places you could never imagine." This was one of those places. I told the Lord while tears were rolling down my eyes, "My God, My God, I'm just a drug addict from the ghetto. I've never seen nothing this breathtaking in my life. Thank you, Jesus." I saw God working the entire time I spent at The Cove.

Anyway, I wanted to go to the chapel at The Cove for prayer, but I didn't want to walk. I had on high-heeled shoes, so I got on the bus. I rode the bus, doing the work of the Lord, witnessing to the lost souls and inviting them to church. I knew that if anyone could speak to the lost, I could because I could relate. I told God that he could use me, and I meant it! It's funny how when I was stripped of my driving privileges and my car. I was so embarrassed to be seen on the bus. Now God was using me to do his work on the bus!

The mountains looked so peaceful, but like I said, I'm from the hood. I saw people hiking at the resort, but I wasn't feeling them trails. I didn't know nothing 'bout no hiking. I wasn't ready for that yet. As the bus driver took me to the chapel, he asked me my name and said, "So tell me what you know about prayer." I said, "I know it works." Then I began sharing why I said what I said. I told him a little about myself and my testimony. He asked me if I would give my testimony at his church the next day. I agreed. I'd never done anything like this, but anything for the Lord. The next morning, when he picked me up, he shared with me that his church was where Billy and Ruth Graham were married. He showed me Billy Graham's home before he moved up on the mountains.

After I gave my testimony (which went well, I thought), I went home with the bus driver and his wife. Their home was beautiful. When I entered it, his wife said, "LaVinia, the powder room is to your right. I need to go upstairs for a minute."

Powder room? I thought. *I used to hear women say that on TV back in the day. Let me check it out. I always wondered what the powder room looked like. Oh, it's the bathroom.*

As I stared in the mirror, my mind went back to when I used to do house cleaning. I told the Lord, "You said you'd take me places I never could imagine. I'm here as their guest with nothing on my mind but you, God. Thank you, Jesus." I saw then that not only was God transforming my mind, but he also was in the process of transforming my life. After all the places I've been chasing drugs, all that I did chasing a high, I finally felt a feeling that I've never experienced. I had to come all the way to the mountains of North Carolina, in the midst of Billy Graham's hometown, to feel the peace of God that drugs never gave me. This feeling was the best high I'd ever had.

Precious, Gracious, Awesome God,

There's nobody like you. I've looked all over, and I've never met another like you. Thank you, God. Thank you, Lord. Thank you for you favor. Thank you for predestining my life. I love you, Jesus. I give you glory. Glory to your name! Thank you for bringing me out of it all. Thank you for your mercy. Thank you for your grace. Thank you for your love. Amen.

I consider that our present sufferings are not worth comparing with the glory that will be revealed in us.

—Romans 8:18 (NIV)

Dear friends, do not be surprised at the fiery ordeal that has come on you to test you, as though something strange were happening to you. But rejoice inasmuch as you participate in the sufferings of Christ, so that you may be overjoyed when his glory is revealed.

—1 Peter 4:12–13 (NIV)

Chapter Thirty-Seven

I'VE BEEN SET FREE!

Upon my return to Lansing, I had a newfound appreciation for my home that I'd never had. I was so grateful for my subsidized home. I was grateful for my life. I was grateful for all that I had been through. I was in love with Jesus! I continued to grow spiritually. As I wrote this memoir, I shared my writing with my therapist. I continued to change. I've never been happier in my life! I'm alone, but I'm not lonely. I am a Christian. My entire lifestyle has changed.

One day, while at my daughter's house, she spoke up and said to her dad, "Dad, I'm not going to let you talk about my mama. My mama has changed."

God did it. God has changed everything about me. He has shown me that when I stay about his business and allow him to use me, I experience his blessings. He told me that I am to stay humble. I wake up seeking God! I thank him for his love every day, three to four times a day. I'm not going to say that I won't have problems, but I am going to say that with God by my side, I can weather all the storms that come at me, if I don't stop doing the work he has for me to do. He will never let anything overtake me.

God has placed in my life the clothing ministry at our church. It's so amazing how he has taken my love for clothes and turned around the lifestyle of a booster into a free clothes ministry. That's who I am today. I still hustle. But today I hustle souls. I am being transformed by renewing my mind. I think of Mama and Daddy. I think about how sad it was to have lived life and never experienced the true love of God, the peace of God, never knowing what true happiness feels like.

I've never been this temporarily financially handicapped, if you will, in my life; yet I've never been so "at peace" in my life. I know today what it is to truly experience the fruits of the Spirit that is talked about in the book of Galatians, which are love, joy, peace, longsuffering, gentleness, goodness, faith, meekness, and temperance. I understand today that I must be a part of the body of Christ. I need the support of fellow Christians. I need the leadership and teachings of Bishop Duncan. I've watched God do his miracle work, not through that reality show but right at the Lansing Church of God in Christ.

I became a partner of Billy Graham's *My Hope* program, a program based on helping your loved ones become saved through prayer. I created a prayer list of friends and loved ones who needed to know Jesus Christ, and I prayed daily for them. I stayed in prayer for my loved ones to be saved. It was my heart's desire that they be saved. I have watched all my four sons give their life to Christ. I have been that light in the lives of my children. Don't tell me that God doesn't answer prayers! I don't worry about them anymore like I used to. I pray for them, and I trust and believe God for his word. Although my daughter, Katrina, has accepted Jesus Christ as her Savior, she still has setbacks like I did before I truly handed my life over to God.

In 2013, I had the privilege of going to see my grandkids in New York, a trip paid for by my son and his wife. God blessed me to go to church as a family with my son Calvin and his wife and kids. God also blessed me to be at the Christmas Day service at Lansing Church of God in Christ with not just two of my grandkids but also with my sons, David and Young Charles. I was also blessed to have been in service with my eldest son, Larry, Jr. and his son.

Look at God! He's mending all my relationships one at a time. I struggled for years with what Dr. Cramer did to me, but today, after reading in the newspaper that she pled guilty to some charges in a federal court, I actually felt sorry for her. She was once a good doctor, but she allowed the love of money to destroy her. My prayer for her is that God will comfort her with his peace during her time of difficulty.

I refuse to let the enemy take my joy! I will not hate, envy, or show any type of bitterness toward anyone. I will love all with the love of Jesus. I know, by faith, the chains have been broken off, not just off me but off every member of my family through the blood of Jesus Christ. I believe this with all my heart. I trust God. He's never let me down before. If God can change a woman like me for his glory, he can change anyone.

God was more concerned with my development in him than my comfort. It took what it took to get me to the point that I gave all of me to him. I have been in pursuit of my sanity over half my life, yet it was not until God delivered me and set me free that I realized that he has been pursuing *me* with his grace and his love.

Once I surrendered to his love and grace, my pursuit was over. For in him, I have found the peace that only he can give. Sure I've got some scars, many scars. The scars are what make me who I am. I'm no ordinary woman. I am exceptionally blessed. I give God the glory!

> You have searched me, Lord, and you know me.
> You know when I sit and when I rise;
> You perceive my thoughts from afar.
> You discern my going out and my lying down;
> You are familiar with all my ways.
> For you created my inmost being;
> You knit me together in my mother's womb.
> I praise you because I am fearfully and wonderfully made;
> Your works are wonderful, I know that full well.
> —Psalm 139:1–3, 13–14 (NIV)

Epilogue

By Bishop Samuel L. Duncan, Jr., Lansing Church of God and Christ
By now, you should certainly understand and believe that God can turn you into a new person or a new creation if you let him. The Bible tells us in 2 Corinthians 5,

> *Therefore if any man be in Christ, he is a new creature: old things are passed away; behold, all things are become new. And all things are of God, who hath reconciled us to himself by Jesus Christ, and hath given to us the ministry of reconciliation; To wit, that God was in Christ, reconciling the world unto himself, not imputing their trespasses unto them; and hath committed unto us the word of reconciliation. Now then we are ambassadors for Christ, as though God did beseech you by us: we pray you in Christ's stead, be ye reconciled to God. For he hath made him to be sin for us, who knew no sin; that we might be made the righteousness of God in him.*

LaVinia has confessed God's presence over her life for many years, even when she wasn't living and walking in the will of God. By the power and leading of God, she has been very transparent and opened herself up to public opinion. Through her experiences, she has shared with us the love, the forgiveness, the mercy, and the power of God. Slowly, she has revealed how God has transformed and delivered her from the devil's stronghold. Satan tried to keep her down, but she held on by faith. She has shown us that when you truly believe in God and expect a change in your circumstances, he will be there to pull you through.

As Christians, sometimes we cannot relate to someone who has a drug habit, has been in bad relationships, has a dysfunctional family, has had abortions, suffers from mental illness, has been raped, or has had their children taken away. Although some of us may have experienced these things, when our lives change for the better and we become Christians, we tend to forget what God has delivered us from. LaVinia has not only opened the eyes and hearts of those who have never experienced this kind of life, but she has also brought revelation to those who have and has shown them that there is a brighter day.

Although there was a lot of misfortune in her life, time after time, she gave her struggles and problems to the Lord (only to take them back a short time later). With each failure came a lesson, and that lesson was that she couldn't do it alone. However, with each portion of her life that she truly gave to God, he picked it up and made it something worthwhile. While it may seem like it took a lifetime for her struggles to end, God has demonstrated to her that he can guide her life better than she can.

LaVinia was led to our Lansing Church of God in Christ through a situation concerning her children. She did not realize at the time that it was God's divine purpose for her to show up. She simply thought she was coming to the church to visit and see her children. Her children were placed in a foster home, and the foster parent worshipped here. Once there, God began to go to work in her life and draw her into a different way of life.

Little by little, God began to deal with her through the preached word of God. She continued to come, and the Lord continued to change her from the inside out. In spite of setbacks, God remained faithful, drew her back to the church once again in an unusual way, and provided opportunity for her to be witnessed to and return to the ministry.

Some Christians describe the lifestyle of Christianity as tepid and only have a lukewarm enthusiasm for Christ. They may not fully understand who they are in Christ and that they are strong in him. Some feel God hasn't come through for them, and therefore, they are discouraged and disappointed. They sink into a place of misery that's difficult to escape. They often look for a solution to their problems and search for deliverance in all the wrong places, people, and things. Of course, this method does not work. Out of desperation, they try to control God by making something happen or taking matters into their own hands, which only makes things toxic: their marriages become toxic; their families become toxic; their health becomes toxic; and their bodies and minds become toxic. It's not until they become desperate and have exhausted all resources that they begin to look unto the Lord for help.

The Bible talks about a woman who was diseased with an issue of blood for twelve years (Matthew 9). She had spent all she had on the fine physicians and was none the better. However, when she heard about Jesus, she was determined by faith to be healed and made whole. She became so desperate that she broke all ceremonial law and got in the press. Her very thought was "If I may but touch his garment, I shall be whole." She wasn't concerned about who was watching or what people may have been saying, her main focus was getting to Jesus for her healing. Finally, she pressed through the crowd and touched the hem of Jesus's garment. The Bible tells us that within that hour, she was healed and made whole because of her faith.

LaVinia's prayer is that your faith in Jesus Christ and the price he paid for you by dying on the cross will give you confidence that there's nothing too hard for God. She prays that you will be inspired to hold on and keep pressing and believing that God will change and deliver you out of your situation. The favor of God brings blessings to our lives. It will promote you, keep you, and heal you. Your faith enables God to turn impossibilities into possibilities! Certainly, there is hope for a troubled soul—and that hope is in our Lord and Savior Jesus Christ. God will surely restore you and make you whole.

There is another story in the Old Testament, in the book of Daniel, about an earthly king by the name of Nebuchadnezzar. This king built an image of gold and called for all the rulers of the land to come and bow down with him and worship this golden image. He also called for all the nations and people of the land to bow down to the image. Nebuchadnezzar sent an order stating that whoever did not bow down would be thrown into the fiery furnace.

Three men named Shadrach, Meshach, and Abednego refused this order and were brought before King Nebuchadnezzar. They told the king that they would not worship false idols and that if they were thrown into the fiery furnace, that their God was able to deliver them.

As a result, Nebuchadnezzar had his mightiest men bind Shadrach, Meshach, and Abednego and throw them into the burning hot flames. Not only that, but he also had turned the heat up seven times hotter. The fire was so hot that as these mighty men threw Shadrach, Meshach, and Abednego into the furnace, they, themselves, were instantly killed by the fire. Shadrach, Meshach, and Abednego fell down into the flames.

Nebuchadnezzar was astonished by what he saw when he looked down into the furnace. Although he had three men thrown into the flames, he saw *four* men loose and walking about. Their bodies were completely intact, not even the hair on their head had burned. God had proven himself to be a deliverer!

As a result, Nebuchadnezzar made a decree to punish anyone who spoke against God and said, "Because there is no other God that can deliver after this sort." His faith was changed, and he began to believe in our God. Just like those three men, LaVinia kept her faith in God, and he has delivered her out of the fiery furnace—from the flames of stealing, smoking crack, hustling, mental illness, and past guilt and shame.

If you haven't let go of your addictions, or your past life is holding you captive, or your mind is wondering whether there is a way out, I am here to tell you that your struggle is over. God has brought us out of darkness and into his marvelous light! We no longer have to fight with the devil. We have won! We have victory in Jesus Christ! God has shown us through LaVinia that he is still performing miracles in our lives today. When you turn your life over to God, it will be eternally changed for good. God will be glorified because you will have put your trust in him to bring about change!

More importantly, John 3:16 tells us, "For God so loved the world, that he gave his only begotten Son, that whosoever believeth in him should not perish, but have everlasting life." Our God is a healer and a deliverer. He has set us free. His divine favor and blessing is upon our lives, but first, we must accept his sacrifice of dying on the cross for our sins by confessing our belief as Romans 10:9 says, "That if thou shalt confess with thy mouth the Lord Jesus, and shalt believe in thine heart that God hath raised him from the dead, thou shalt be saved."

If you have not received this free gift of salvation, this is the day, time, and year for you to accept Jesus Christ and have God's divine favor over your life and be flooded with his blessings! If you are not willing to let go and let God *be* God in your life, you will never experience this great love, this great peace, and true satisfaction—the satisfaction of being a Christian. By accepting him, you will no longer have to pursue sanity because the Lord will keep your mind in perfect peace.

For those of you who do believe and have already accepted Jesus Christ, my hope is that you will not judge a person by their past life, their habits, their living environment, their clothes, their way of speaking, or their mannerisms; but that you will begin to understand that God loves all of us and wants us to *have* and *show* compassion toward those who have gone through the fiery furnace and may have gotten burned but not completely consumed. If they are still in the furnace, I hope that you will intercede and pray in their behalf that their yoke of bondage be broken. Help them believe that our God is powerful and that he can deliver them from self-destruction.

Finally, God wants us to have patience and show kindness toward one another. The love that he has for us *has been shared*, and the love that he put in us *is to be shared*. His love is in us. His love is for all of us. His love never ends.

A Prayer in Behalf of the Life of LaVinia

Composed and Prayed by Evangelist Joyce Jackson

Father God, I come to you in the name of Jesus, whom I love and serve. I thank you and praise you for the gift of life. I praise you, Lord, for loving me so very much, even when I didn't know how to love myself. Thank you, Father, for your protection over me every day of my life. Your love was over me as I went in and as I came out. Thank you, Lord, for now I fully understand that you allowed me to leave a legacy for my future generations.

Father, I thank you for you mercy and your grace. So many times throughout my entire life, it was your hand upon me. Father, thank you for your grace given unto me. I have a lot to praise and worship you for. It was you, Father God, who preserved my life so many times. Thank you for still putting everything in place for me. You have always been right here for me. I praise you for opening my eyes and heart, and I ask you to forever order my steps with your word.

Thank you, Jesus, for bringing me up out of a miry pit and bringing me from darkness into light. Thank you for bringing me out of a desolate place of guilt and shame and letting me experience you as the remedy for all my pains. You truly are a healer. You have healed my spirit, soul, and body. And now I can truly say that this is my season, and this is my new day! Through many tests and trials you have been there for me. I praise you, Lord, for letting my test become my testimony to energize me as well as others.

Thank you, Lord, for the power of forgiveness and not allowing the devil to hold me hostage to my past. I have the victory because of your love for me and your blood shed at Calvary. Yes, I have been down, but you are the one who brought me up. Even during times of suffering and great loss, you were there for me. Thank you, Jesus, that I knew how to call on your name, for you are my very present help in my time of trouble. Your mercies are renewed in my life. Your compassion has always been there to prevail over every generational curse, every abuse, and every misuse. Whether drugs, or criminal acts of violence, and/or all the rest, you have never forsaken me nor left me.

And, Father, I am so grateful for your loving kindness towards me. You are great, and you are greatly to be praised! You even cause me to remain strong through the damage. Thank you, Jesus, for making me a victorious woman of God! Thank you for always giving me a heart to cry out to you. Even in my sin, my heart longed for you, and I could hear you calling my name. You have kept me and blessed me, and for these things, I thank you. Thank you for the many blessings that you have given me. I know it was because of your love for me. Not that I deserved it or merited the blessings, but because of your great grace, you have been here for me.

I now know that I am your workmanship, created in Christ Jesus unto good works. As I have talked to you down through the years and sought after your love, I know that my inheritance is with those who are sanctified. Father, I trust you to complete the work that you have begun in me as you perfect all things concerning me. I pray thy will be done on earth as it is in heaven and that thy kingdom truly comes in all you assign me to do. For it is to You I give the glory. In Jesus's name, I pray. Amen.

Overcoming (A Family Prayer)

Composed by DeMetrice French Carroll

Hallelujah!

Father God, I give you a high praise because you are worthy! I give you praise because you allow me to come to your throne of grace and have instructed me by your word how to come. You said I should come boldly to the throne of grace in the time of need and to pray for all men (mankind). (Hebrews 4:16)

You said that anything I desired, when I prayed and believed that I received them, that I should have them; and so in this prayer, I tell you the desire for my family. I tell you I believe, and I thank you for it *now*. (Mark 11:24)

I come on behalf of my family, knowing that the enemy came to kill us, steal from us, and destroy us. I thank you that you sent your son, Jesus, *and* he came (Hallelujah!) to give us life and that life more abundantly. (John 10:10)

Lord, your word tells us there are six things that you hate: a proud look, a lying tongue, hands that shed innocent blood, a heart that devises wicked imagination, feet that are swift to run to mischief, a false witness that speaks lies, and that the seventh is an abomination to you: he that sows discord among the brethren (Proverbs 6:16). Today, these are known as the seven deadly sins.

Father God, I know that all sin stems from the root of these. I ask that you forgive me and all my family from doing these sins and heal us from the damaging effects they caused. I denounce all sin that has plagued us as a result of our ignorance to your word.

I rebuke abandonment, disappointment, rejection, mistreatment, self-pity, self-rejection, and emotional hurt.

I rebuke arrogance, haughtiness, disobedience, pride, and rebellion.

I rebuke doubt, fear, unbelief, and ungodly thoughts.

I rebuke lust, perversion, fornication, adultery, homosexuality, and other sexually immoral relationships.

I rebuke hatred, revenge, retaliation, resentment, anger, bitterness, and unforgiveness.

I rebuke addictions to alcohol, legal and illegal drugs, and any mind-altering substance that would divert our attention from righteousness.

I rebuke mental illness, witchcraft, and the occult.

Lord, your word says when I make my prayer to you, you hear; and if I decree a thing, then it shall be established (Job 22:27–28), so with every denunciation, I also confess

> No weapon formed against us shall prosper, and every tong that rises against us in judgment, we will condemn. (Isaiah 54:17)

> We are established in righteousness, we have no fear; terror and oppression are far from us. (Isaiah 54:14)

> We are redeemed from the curse of the law. We are redeemed from poverty and we are redeemed from spiritual death. (Galatians 3:13)

> We are delivered from the power of darkness and translated into the kingdom of God's dear son, Jesus Christ. (Colossians 1:13)

> We are blessed with all spiritual blessings: (salvation, hope of living, the power to do God's will) in heavenly places. (Ephesians 1:3)

We are humbled, called by your name; we pray, we seek your face, and turn from our twisted thinking and doing, so that you, Lord, will hear from heaven, forgive our sin and heal our land. (2 Chronicles 7:14)

We take heed to our ways so that we do not sin with our tongues. We are like wisdom, speaking excellent things. We speak truth when we open our mouths. (Psalm 39:1 and Proverbs 8:7)

Lord, I now ask that you make yourself known to us in a greater dimension. Let us know you as the great I AM. Let us know you as *He* that is able to do exceedingly, abundantly, above all that we ask or think. In your son Jesus's name, I pray. Amen.

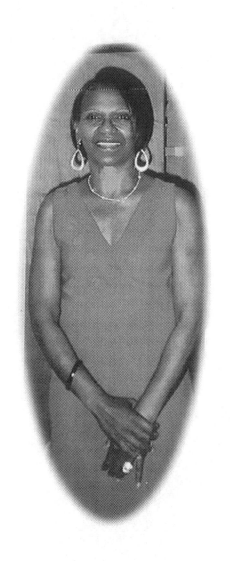